Orff and Kodaly Adapted for the Elementary School

Orff and Kodaly Adapted for the Elementary School

Lawrence Wheeler

Music Specialist, Camp Avenue School, North Merrick, New York
Faculty, Manhattan School of Music, New York City
Orff-Kodaly Consultant to Schools and Universities

Lois Raebeck

Music Consultant, New York City
Chairman, Orff-Kodaly Program, Shumiatcher School of Music
Larchmont, New York

Wm. C. Brown Company Publishers, Dubuque, Iowa

Consulting Editor
Frederick W. Westphal
Sacramento State College

Copyright © 1972 by Wm. C. Brown Company Publishers

Library of Congress Catalog Card Number: 78-190194

ISBN 0-697-03462-3

Third Printing, 1973

Printed in the United States of America

DEDICATED
to
Julie and Sandy
David and Jonathan
and all children everywhere

Contents

PART I

Speech and Rhythm

CHAPTER 1 *Tempo-Dynamic and Echo Clapping, Patschen, Stamping, and Finger-Snapping* 5

CHAPTER 2 *Experiencing Melodic and Rhythmic Ostinati* 18

CHAPTER 3 *Experiencing Meters* 34

CHAPTER 4 *Using Bodily Movement* 63

CHAPTER 5 *Creating Rhythmic Dramatizations* 78

CHAPTER 6 *Cultivating Rhythmic Improvisation* 95

CHAPTER 7 *Experiencing Rhythmic Canon*   112

PART II

Melody: Singing and Playing

CHAPTER 8 *Primary Grades*   129

CHAPTER 9 *Intermediate Grades* 183

PART III

The Recorder

Preface

Every now and then there appears on the educational scene a personality whose ideas make a profound and lasting impression on educators about the world.

Carl Orff and Zoltan Kodaly are *two* such personalities, and the nature of their impact demands exploration.

Focusing on rhythm, melody, movement, improvisation, and instrumental experiences in a way that is both unique and educationally rewarding, the innovations of these men have aroused the interest of countless educators concerned with giving children meaningful musical experiences.

Making use of the ideas of Orff and Kodaly is, however, not always easy. Special knowledge and skill are required. Then too, because both men developed their approach to music education in other countries (Orff in Germany and Austria and Kodaly in Hungary), their materials and methods are not always relevant to schools in the United States.

This book is an attempt to make the adaptations necessary to make Orff and Kodaly relevant to this country, and to set these ideas down in such a way that educators can understand and use them.

Since this is a supplementary text which can be used in conjunction with *New Approaches to Music in the Elementary School* or any other elementary music methods text, other areas of elementary music education and the philosophy underlying them, explored fully in *New Approaches* and most other texts, will not be treated here.

Further, because this book will approach Orff and Kodaly in a very concrete way, the authors would like to give a word of warning: *It is not their intent to have the very explicit experiences suggested herein be treated as strict formulae for teaching.* Rather, it is to be hoped that teachers will read and explore the ideas for experiences suggested, and will then adapt them to meet their own classroom situations in the most creative way.

It should be emphasized, too, that all activities—speech, melodic, rhythmic, and so on—overlap and interweave. Although for purposes of clarity they are treated separately in this book, in the classroom they are best experienced concurrently and in relation with one another.

The authors are aware that there are many other valid views on the proper implementation of the ideas of Orff and Kodaly. This book should be considered as only one possible approach.

In summary, this book is an attempt to: (1) suggest the educational bases upon which the concepts of Orff and Kodaly are founded, (2) clarify the types of activities which implement their ideas, and (3) suggest concrete experiences for children in the elementary schools of this country using these activities.

The book has been organized as follows:

Introduction: The Orff and Kodaly Approaches

SPEECH AND RHYTHM

Chapter 1—Tempo-Dynamic and Echo Clapping, Patschen, Stamping, and Finger-Snapping
Chapter 2—Experiencing Melodic and Rhythmic Ostinati
Chapter 3—Experiencing Meters
Chapter 4—Using Bodily Movement
Chapter 5—Creating Rhythmic Dramatizations
Chapter 6—Cultivating Rhythmic Improvisation
Chapter 7—Experiencing Rhythmic Canon

MELODY: SINGING AND PLAYING

Chapter 8—Primary Grades
Chapter 9—Intermediate Grades
Chapter 10—Upper Grades

THE RECORDER

Chapter 11—Playing the Recorder
Appendices

Acknowledgments

The authors feel deeply indebted to the many friends, colleagues, and teachers who have contributed to the formation of the ideas set forth in this book. To make a definitive list would be difficult indeed, but to those who have given most directly of their time and wisdom we offer our gratitude and thanks: Katinka Daniel; Arpad Darazs; Doreen Hall and the staff at the University of Toronto; Daniel Helldén; Polyxene Mathéy; Margaret Murray and the staff at the Orff Institute in Salzburg, Austria; Jos Wuytack, Leuven, Belgium; Harriet Spink; Joseph and Clara Sugar; Allan H. Toffler; and John Manos.

To Elizabeth Wheeler, who gave so generously of her expert secretarial and editorial talents, we give special thanks and appreciation.

Introduction:
The Orff and Kodaly Approaches

WHAT IS THE ORFF APPROACH?

Carl Orff's approach to music education for the child begins with the premise that *feeling* precedes intellectual understanding.

Thus, the infant *feels* the sensations of touch, taste, picking up, throwing, crawling, walking, and so on long before these are shaped into ideas and verbalized. Once verbalized, considerable time elapses before he learns to read and write about them.

During this period, he experiences these pleasurable activities in a multitude of ways. They become associated with people, things, and with growth and understanding. Slowly, they take on inward meaning for him. When the inward experiences become crystallized, the child begins to talk about them. And when he has verbalized them adequately, he is ready and eager to begin to read and write about them.

So it is with music. Feeling precedes understanding. And it is with this in mind that Carl Orff has evolved an approach to music education which starts with the basic element of music that is most natural to the child—that element which he has experienced and felt since birth in all his life activities, and in speech and movement particularly. That element, of course, is RHYTHM. And it is through the rhythm of the child's speech and movement that we can best encourage him to explore music.

Starting with this basic concept, Orff's approach includes specific objectives and contains many devices unique to music education in this country.

Basic Objectives

1. To use the speech and movement natural to the child as the springboard for musical experiences.
2. To give an immediacy of enjoyment and meaning to the child through active participation in all experiences.
3. To encourage the feeling that speech, movement, play, and song are one.
4. To give a completely physical, nonintellectual background in rhythm and melody, thus laying the foundation of *experience* so necessary to a later *understanding* of music and musical notation.
5. To give experience in the component parts of the basic elements of music: in rhythmic experiences, by beginning with the rhythmic pattern of a word, then two words, gradually building in

complexity into the phrase and period; in melodic experiences, by beginning with the natural chant of childhood (the falling minor third), gradually adding other tones of the pentatonic scale, tones of other modes, and finally the major and minor scales.

6. To cultivate the musical imagination—both rhythmic and melodic—and thus to develop the ability to improvise.

7. To cultivate individual creativity as well as a feeling for, and the ability to participate in, ensemble activities.

Unique Devices

1. Use of speech patterns, proverbs, and children's rhymes and jingles as the basis for developing a feeling for basic note values, meter, phrase, and clarification of rhythmic problems, as well as to develop the ability to use the voice over a wide range of pitch and dynamics (and thus help children find their singing voices).

2. Use of the rhythmic and melodic ostinati—from the very simple to the extremely complex—as an accompaniment to moving, singing, and playing.

3. Use of the natural chant of childhood as the basis for developing melodic feeling and understanding (starting with the falling minor third—sol-mi or 5-3—and gradually adding other notes of the pentatonic scale).

4. Use of unique Orff-designed instruments, along with rhythm instruments and recorders, to provide children with another immediate way of making music while cultivating a deeper response to rhythm and melody.

5. Use of the pentatonic scale (especially in beginning experiences) for song material and accompaniments with the resultant minimum of complications for children.[1]

WHAT IS THE KODALY APPROACH?

Zoltan Kodaly offers to the musical education of the child precisely what Orff has not emphasized—a sequential system of sight singing which leads into the understanding of musical notation. Kodaly's basic aim is to teach children to read and write music through singing.

Like Orff, Kodaly begins the child's singing experiences with the falling minor third. The remaining notes of the pentatonic scale are then introduced, gradually, in a sequential manner. Notes which create major, minor, and other modes are introduced later.

Rhythmically, Kodaly first develops the feeling for the basic beat through clapping and stepping the beat, gradually leading children to a feeling for word rhythms and their musical symbols.

A carefully structured sequence of activities, involving both rhythmic and melodic understandings, is adhered to. For example, children in grade one learn to sing and notate the quarter note and quarter rest, eighth notes in pairs, and the pentatonic tones sol, mi, la, and do. (Songs using other tones are sung, but are related to rhythmic rather than melodic understandings.)

Although Orff and Kodaly agree on many of the aspects of the rhythmic and melodic development of the child, Kodaly suggests specific music reading skills to be developed in the elementary grades, whereas Orff does not concern himself with music reading.

In view of the fact that the Kodaly concepts are as yet not fully developed or standardized for use in the elementary schools in this country, only Kodaly's approach to rhythmic counting and his use of hand signals to help develop inner hearing and feeling will be explored in this book.

---

1. Dissonances seldom occur when using the pentatonic scale.

Rhythmic Counting

When the child has had adequate experience in responding to rhythm, he is ready to *see what he has experienced*, to *count it rhythmically*, and to *notate it*.

Needless to say, his first experiences with notation are with the most basic and easily understood element of his speech—the word—and progress slowly to speech patterns, measures, phrases, and the period. Similarly, he moves from notation using only one kind of note value to that using two kinds, and so on, gradually adding in length and complexity to his learning. All experiences are related to speech, and all are preceded and accompanied by clapping, bodily movement, and singing.

There are many ways of counting note values. Kodaly uses the word "Tah" to represent the quarter note and the words "Tee tee" to represent two eighth notes. However, the authors have found the following to be effective. (It should be emphasized that whatever system is adopted should be used consistently throughout.)

Chart of Rhythmic Counting and Clapping

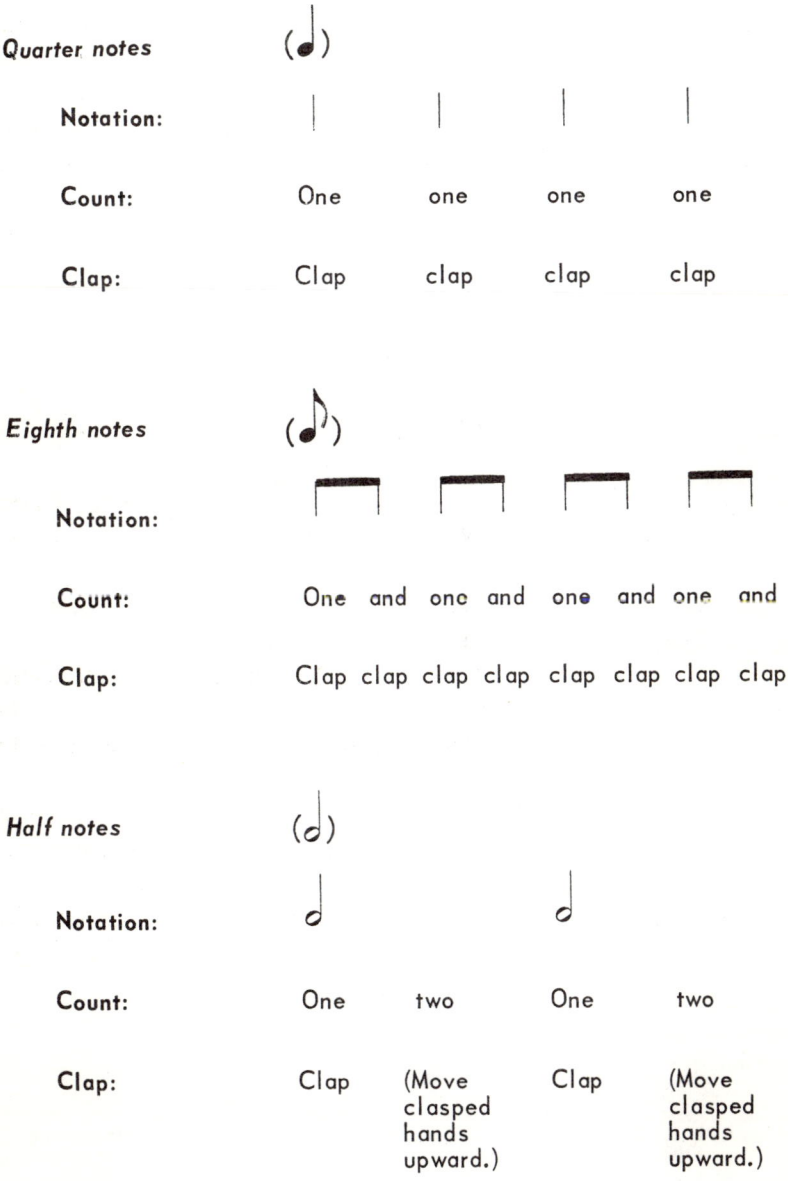

Quarter notes (♩)

Notation:								
Count:	One		one		one		one	
Clap:	Clap		clap		clap		clap	

Eighth notes (♪)

Notation:								
Count:	One	and	one	and	one	and	one	and
Clap:	Clap	clap	clap	clap	clap	clap	clap	clap

Half notes (𝅗𝅥)

Notation:			
Count:	One	two	One	two
Clap:	Clap	(Move clasped hands upward.)	Clap	(Move clasped hands upward.)

Dotted half notes (𝅗𝅥 ·)

Notation:	𝅗𝅥·			𝅗𝅥·			
Count:	One	two	three (or dot)	one	two	three (or dot)	
Clap:	Clap	(Move clasped hands upward.)	(Move clasped hands upward.)	Clap	(Move clasped hands upward.)	(Move clasped hands upward.)	

Whole notes (𝅝)

Notation:	𝅝			
Count:	One	two	three	four
Clap:	Clap	(Move clasped hands upward.)	(Move clasped hands upward.)	(Move clasped hands upward.)

Triplets

Notation:													
Count:	Tri	- p²-	let	tri	- p -	let	tri	- p -	let	tri	- p -	let	
Clap:	Clap	clap	clap	clap	clap	clap	clap	clap	clap	clap	clap	clap	

Rests (𝄽 or 𝄾 or 𝄿)

Notation:	𝄽 (or one of above)
Count:	Rest (spoken)
Clap:	No clapping. Move hands forward, palms up, or tap fingers of left hand on left shoulder and simultaneously, fingers of right hand on right shoulder.

---

2. For musical purposes, the word *triplet* has been changed to a three-syllable word (tri-p-let), the middle syllable to be pronounced *puh*, with a slight emphasis on the first syllable.

Sixteenth notes

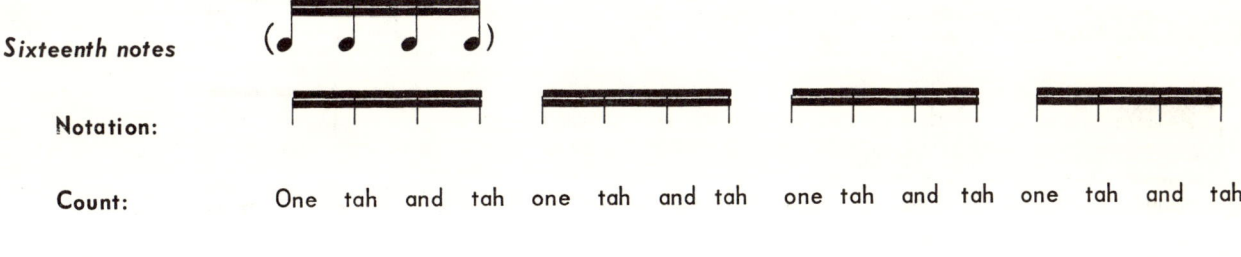

Notation:				
Count:	One tah and tah	one tah and tah	one tah and tah	one tah and tah
Clap:	Cl cl cl cl	cl cl cl cl	cl cl cl cl	cl cl cl cl

Combinations of eighth and sixteenth notes

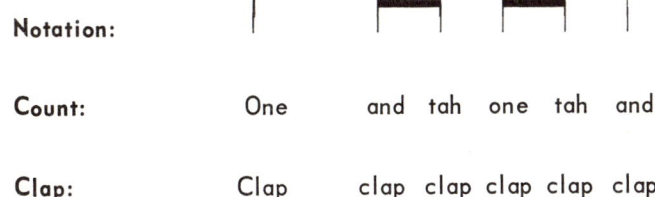

Notation:			
Count:	One	and tah	one tah and
Clap:	Clap	clap clap	clap clap clap

Ties

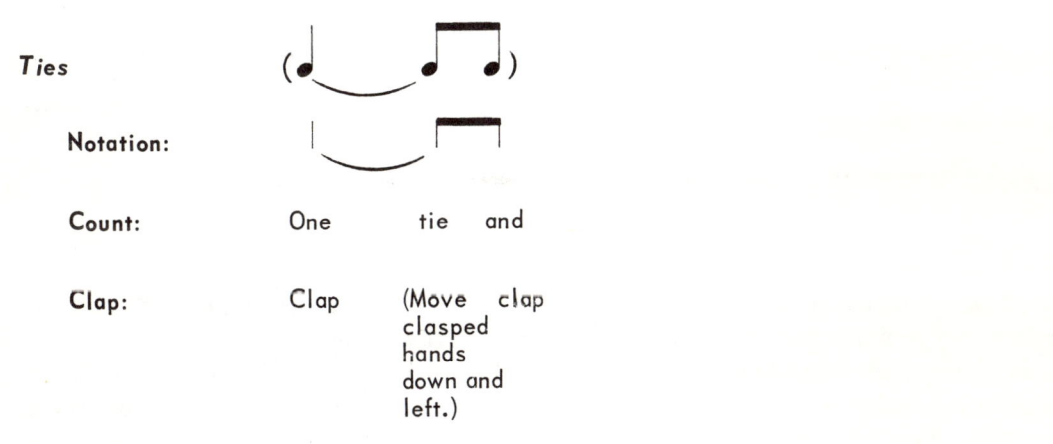

Notation:

Count:	One	tie	and
Clap:	Clap	(Move clasped hands down and left.)	clap

Dotted quarter and eighth note

Notation:

Count:	One	dot	and
Clap:	Clap	(Move clasped hands down and left.)	clap

Dotted eighth and sixteenth note

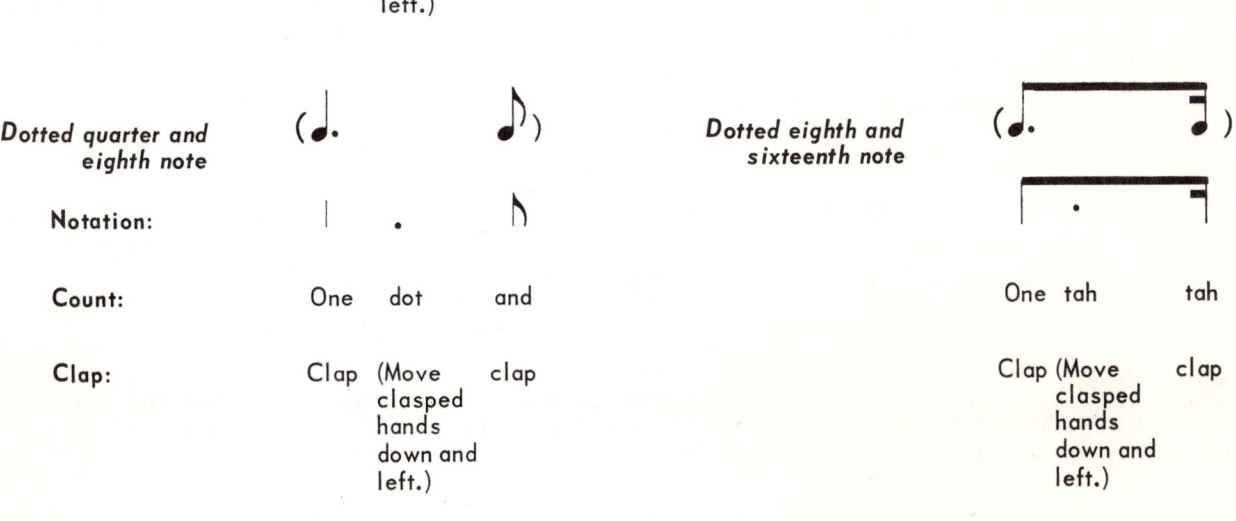

Count:	One tah		tah
Clap:	Clap	(Move clasped hands down and left.)	clap

Syncopation   a.

Notation:				
Count:	Syn -	co or	-	pah
	One	and		and
Clap:	Clap	clap (On second half of note, move clasped hands down and left.)		clap

	Syn - co -	pah	
	One tah	tah	
	Clap clap	clap	
		(On second half of note, move clasped hands down and left.)	

b.

Notation:			
Count:	Syn -	co or	- (Think pah)
	One	and	(Think and)
Clap:	Clap	clap	(Move clasped hands down and left.)

	Syn -	co or	- (Think pah)
	One	tah	(Think tah)
	Clap	clap	(Move clasped hands down and left.)

Hand Signals

Kodaly's system of hand signals offers a vital ingredient to the task of learning to sight read—it gives the child another way of experiencing what he hears—through the visual image.

Using the basic system of hand signals developed by the Englishman John Curwen in 1870, Kodaly has developed a method which enables children to *see* the general height or depth of the sound they *hear*. That is, they learn to move their hands up or down in a degree relative to the produced sounds. Moreover, the signal for each tone is related to the function of this tone in the scale to which it belongs. Thus, do, mi, and sol, which give a relative feeling of rest, are accompanied by hand signals which do the same. Re, fa, la, and ti,[3] which seem to move, are accompanied by signals which suggest motion.

When hand signals are introduced individually, along with the introduction of each new tone in the scale[4] as an integrated part of the total experience, children learn them quickly, enjoy their use, and benefit enormously through increased ability to feel and hear tonal relationships.

---

3. There has been much controversy over the question of whether to use numbers rather than syllables. The authors feel that either is feasible, but use of one or the other should be consistent.
4. See Part II, Melody—Singing and Playing.

Chart of Hand Signals

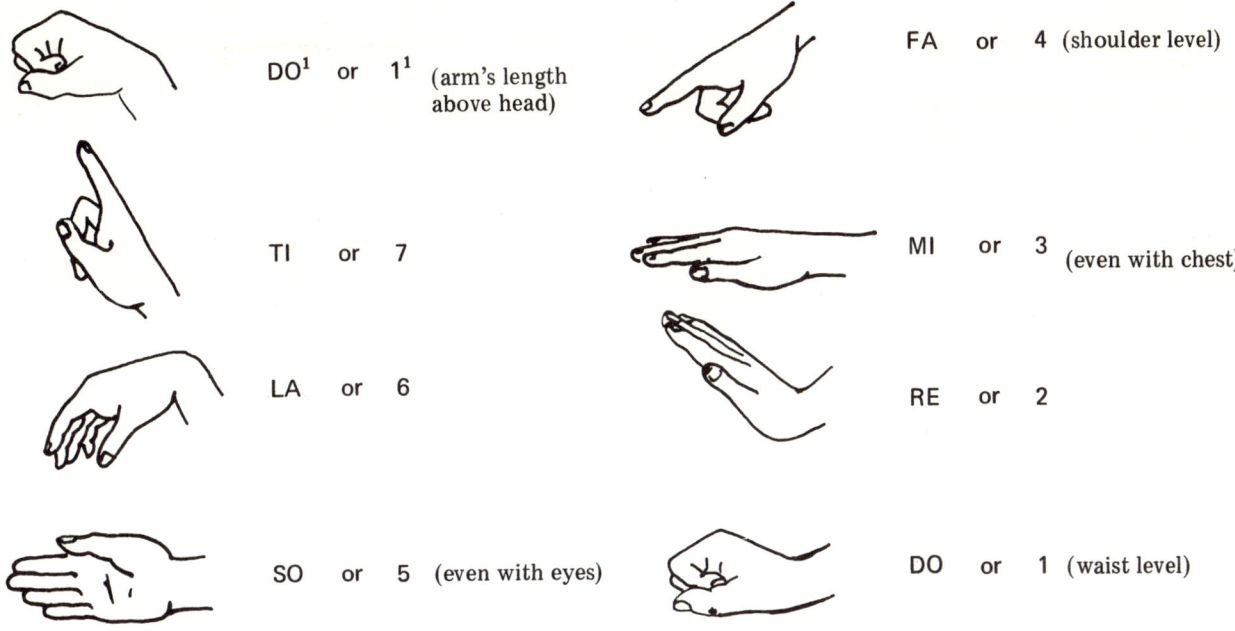

From *New Approaches to Music in the Elementary School,* 2nd ed., by Lois Raebeck and Lawrence Wheeler (Wm. C. Brown Company Publishers, ©1969).

Note: In any scale the first seven tones are noted with syllables only. Tones from high Do and up are indicated with a "1" above each syllable; tones below low Do are indicated with a "1" below the syllable, to indicate the lower octave.

WHY COMBINE AND ADAPT ORFF AND KODALY?

To some, the question may arise: "Why Orff and Kodaly? Why not pure Orff? Or pure Kodaly?" These are valid questions, and some music educators would argue that one or the other, used in its pure form, offers the best music education for children in the United States.

It is the authors' contention, however, that there are insurmountable problems to using pure Orff or pure Kodaly.

(1) Song material, in both cases, is foreign to the temperament and background of the American child, is inadequate, and, in the case of the many volumes of song material provided in the Kodaly method, not relevant to current practices in elementary school music in the United States. Although some of the material from the Orff books may be used, these books are meant to serve simply as models for the Orff approach. (Orff himself advises using folk material of the native country as song material.) In addition, only the melodic aspect is treated sequentially; instrumental accompaniments are not treated in sequence of difficulty. They are meant to suggest the multitude of ways in which a song may be accompanied.

(2) The demands of the music curriculum now in use in the schools of the United States necessitate an adaptation. Attention *must* be paid to the current philosophy, practices, and materials of music education, the need to keep these relevant to our culture, and the song series currently in use through which they are reflected. Further, other important aspects of the music curriculum must not be minimized: music listening, glee clubs, bands, choruses, and many other creative activities.

(3) Music educators in this country are not adequately prepared to teach pure Orff or pure Kodaly. Generally they have not been adequately trained in either approach.

Finally, the authors feel that the musical concepts and activities developed by Orff and Kodaly, when combined, most definitely complement each other.

Orff, for example, stresses the development of a musical vocabulary—nonintellectual experiences in rhythm and melody (speaking, moving, singing, and playing of instruments) with the teaching of music reading being dealt with primarily through instruction on the recorder.

Kodaly, on the other hand, is more concerned with a systematic method leading to sight singing. Although Kodaly too gives preparatory experiences to develop inner feeling and hearing, his main concern is with teaching children to sight read.

Thus, it is the author's opinion that by combining Orff and Kodaly, while retaining the best features of our current practices in the elementary schools, the child can receive a thorough musical education.

In this volume, the early experiences—beginning in the kindergarten and extending on to first grade—will be basically Orff in approach: speaking, singing, moving, and playing of instruments. Kodaly will be introduced in the first grade and will be developed progressively and paralleled with the more advanced Orff activities throughout the elementary grades.

It is hoped that the Orff approach, while it retains its spontaneity and fluidity, will thus become entwined with the systematic Kodaly structure.

SEQUENCE OF ACTIVITIES USING ORFF AND KODALY

Basic activities using the Orff and Kodaly concepts are not numerous or complex. They begin in a simple, elemental fashion, and as the child grows throughout his school years, these activities take on a spiral development, evolving into ever more complex responses and understandings.

While the basic activities to be experienced will be treated in great detail in later chapters, a general outline of activities in the Orff and Kodaly approach include:

Speech (patterns, rhymes, proverbs)
      chanted in varying pitch, quality or color, and dynamic levels.
      accompanied with rhythmic and melodic ostinati.
      related to notation.
      accompanied with bodily movement.
      developed into pentatonic songs.

Singing
      two-tone songs, evolving to notes composing the pentatonic scale, major, minor, and the modes.
      accompanied with rhythmic and melodic ostinati and bodily movement.
      by ear, and in conjunction with rhythmic and melodic notation.

Playing instruments (Orff instruments, percussion instruments, and recorder)
      to accompany speech, singing, and movement.
      with and without musical notation.
      to develop ability to improvise.

Bodily movement (clapping, stamping, patting, snapping fingers, moving entire body)
      to develop a response to rhythm.
      to accompany speech, singing, and playing.
      in conjunction with rhythmic notation.
      in response to musical form (rondo, canon, etc.)
      to develop ability to improvise.

GENERAL TEACHING SUGGESTIONS

The teacher beginning to use Orff and Kodaly techniques will be met with a unique kind of problem—one that stems from the great variety of activities which provide almost an overabundance of potential experiences.

So *many* kinds of activities present themselves that there is a temptation to do too many things at once. And the longer the ingenious teacher works with Orff and Kodaly concepts, the wider grows the horizon! New ideas present themselves. One is tempted to rush on, to skip over important preliminary steps—to try too much too soon.

It is for this reason that the following list of teaching suggestions is offered—with the hope that it will help avoid the difficulties that often arise in using Orff and Kodaly concepts.

1. Be prepared. Know exactly what your aims and objectives are, and how you are going to proceed.
2. Break down each experience into the smallest unit. Build from there.
3. Go slowly. Do one thing at a time.
4. Proceed to new step only after first step has been fully developed.
5. After developing a second step, combine steps one and two (sequential development).
6. Prepare children for each activity, and especially for playing orchestrations.
7. Have variety in activities.
8. When difficulty develops in any one step, simplify, approach in a different way or come back to it another day. *Don't* use endless drill.
9. In creating orchestrations, *don't* clutter. Keep orchestrations simple and transparent, until children are secure and stable, both rhythmically and melodically.
10. When using original Orff-Schulwerk books, remember that they are not sequential.
11. Feel free to make your own adaptations of ideas suggested in this book.
12. Be aware of the value of using song materials from earlier grades for developing musical understandings in later grades.
13. Be consistent.

COMBINING ORFF AND KODALY WITH OTHER APPROACHES TO MUSIC EDUCATION

How does the utilization of the Orff and Kodaly approach affect the methods of teaching music already in practice?

If, as the authors suggest, the ideas of these men are adapted to meet the needs of this country, use of Orff and Kodaly can only enhance what is already being done.

There is surely no reason to discard any idea—in singing, listening, bodily movement, or instrumental experiences—which has validity for musical growth. Rather, it is hoped that techniques presently successful will be retained, as ideas of Orff and Kodaly are integrated into the music curriculum.

For those looking for a more concrete way of developing musical growth (helping children move in musical understanding from the ear to the eye in singing, for example) use of the Orff and Kodaly approach may be extremely helpful, since the natural sequence suggested therein makes for a logical development in this direction. But all other meaningful experiences in singing have their place, and should be retained. There is no reason why very young children, for example, cannot sing songs in the major and minor, using a non-Orff approach, while they are limited to songs in the pentatonic at times when the teacher wants to follow the Orff-Kodaly approach which leads them toward music reading.

Further, many Orff and Kodaly techniques may be used to enhance other areas of music. A music listening experience using a non-Orff technique may be enriched by encouraging children to play the themes on a xylophone. Bodily movement in the non-Orff tradition may be made more interesting through the addition of an accompaniment (rhythmic or melodic) straight from Orff.

Thus, it is the authors' view that Orff and Kodaly may be used not only to meet the goals of their own purposes, but also to enhance the goals and purposes of the elementary school music methods already in use.

SUGGESTIONS FOR CLASS DISCUSSIONS OR REPORTS

1. Discuss the concept that rhythm, rather than melody, is the proper springboard for experiencing music.
2. Discuss speech as a means of experiencing rhythm, the pros and cons of using speech, as well as all the different types of speech experiences available for use.
3. Discuss ways in which speech might be combined with bodily movement for meaningful rhythmic experiences.
4. Discuss the concept that children should be encouraged to have the feeling that speech, movement, play, and song are one. Discuss the meaning of such a statement as well as the means through which such a feeling might be developed in the classroom.
5. Discuss the idea that Orff's approach is physical rather than intellectual.
6. Give examples of ways in which children might be encouraged in Orff experiences to explore the component parts of the basic elements of music.
7. Discuss the implications, for later musicianship, in learning how to improvise.
8. Discuss the gains, both musical and social, which might come from ensemble experience.
9. Discuss the idea of using the pentatonic scale in beginning musical experiences with children.
10. Discuss the musical growth that might take place through learning to play the Orff instruments—xylophone, metallophone, glockenspiel, as well as percussion instruments and the recorder.
11. Discuss Kodaly's system of rhythmic counting—what it is, how it differs from standard musical counting, and the advantages (and/or disadvantages) gained from its use.
12. Discuss Kodaly's use of hand signals: what they are, and what musical value children gain from using them.
13. Discuss the pros and cons of combining the ideas of Orff and Kodaly in elementary school music.

PART I

Speech and Rhythm

Humpty Dumpty sat on a wall,
Humpty Dumpty had a great fall,
All the King's horses and all the King's men,
Cannot set Humpty up again!

Listen to a child chanting a nursery rhyme. Observe the natural lilt of his voice as he instinctively groups words into strong and weak beats of varying lengths. Watch for the tendency to respond rhythmically with his body, and to turn the rhyme into a chant, with strong pitch differences that create a simple song.

It is this natural affinity with rhythm—which is present in all living organisms and is felt not only in breathing, eating, walking, and playing, but also in virtually all life experiences—that expresses itself so superbly in speech—and thus makes speech the logical cornerstone for all further rhythmic experiences.

BASIC OBJECTIVES

Starting with the natural rhythms of speech—as expressed in the chants, jingles, nursery rhymes, and games of childhood—experiences with speech and rhythm can, with proper guidance, develop in children a feeling for, and understanding of the more complex world of rhythm as it relates to music. Further, it can encourage the ability to perform these rhythms through bodily movement, singing, and playing instruments.

In order to accomplish this, our specific aims and objectives must be:

1. To develop relaxation and freedom in responding to rhythms.
2. To develop a feeling of pulse—strong and weak beats—and the resultant patterns in meter.
3. To develop rhythmic stability (tempo control) and ensemble.
4. To develop rhythmic independence in saying, clapping, and playing rhythm patterns (the ability to reproduce one rhythm pattern or patterns accurately while hearing contrasting patterns).
5. To develop a feeling for the time—space length of speech rhythms and their counterpart in note values.
6. To develop a feeling for the phrase.

1

7. To develop a rhythmic memory (the ability to remember and reproduce accurately longer and more difficult phrases in rhythm).
8. To develop the ability to use the voice in varying dynamics, pitch levels, and tone colors.

RESPONSES TO SPEECH AND RHYTHM

What specific responses to speech and rhythm can help us attain these aims and objectives?

Chanting, the most obvious link between speech and rhythm, suggests itself immediately as a most natural response. For the child it is as instinctive as it is delightful. For him it is part of play, a source of interesting images and sounds. Whether he chants nursery rhymes passed on from generation to generation, or rhymes he helps create about people and things with which he is intimate—games rhymes, or rhymes enjoyed in themselves—he enters into this activity naturally and joyfully.

With guidance, his chanting can open the door to all rhythmic and melodic experiences. Words can begin to take on color; the quality of speech begins to reflect the meanings he is trying to portray. High and lows—both in pitch and dynamics—can develop. And, throughout, a feeling for the various kinds of meter is acquired.

Clapping occurs spontaneously as children begin to feel the rhythm of speech. Because it is the simplest form of rhythmic response using bodily movement, it gives children the most immediate way of expressing bodily their responses to the basic rhythmic arrangements of their speech.

When it is used imaginatively—with emphasis on a variety of tempi (fasts and slows), dynamics (louds and softs), and rhythm patterns—it not only produces rapid rhythmic development, it is, in addition, a sure way of capturing and keeping the attention of all children.

Bodily movement, using hands, fingers, arms, legs, and the entire body, is a natural outgrowth of clapping, and adds immeasurably to the child's ability to feel and express strong and weak beats, and metrical arrangements of words, as well as to the feeling for tempo and dynamics he has experienced in his speech. In addition, bodily movement, when it encourages the child to use his body in creative interpretations of speech and rhythm, offers the child a dynamic way of expressing his own individual responses.

Playing instruments (Orff-designed and percussion instruments) as an adjunct to speech experiences has infinite value: it gives a feeling of rhythmic stability, underlines the basic pulse, gives contrasting rhythm patterns and color, gives experience in independent parts as well as ensemble experience, and bridges the gap between rhythm and melody.

Although most teachers will quite naturally make adequate use of the Orff-designed instruments, it should be noted that the imaginative use of percussion instruments can not only provide a simple background of texture, it can create and maintain changes in mood and atmosphere as well. In all experiences which suggest use of percussion instruments, the teacher will want to encourage children to explore to the fullest the many variations in background and texture, as well as the dramatic and atmospheric effects made possible through the creative use of percussion instruments.

SEQUENCE OF ACTIVITIES

All of these responses to speech and rhythm may be explored and developed through the following sequence of activities:

1. Tempo-dynamic clapping
2. Tempo-dynamic patschen[1], stamping, clapping, and finger-snapping
3. Echo clapping
4. Echo patschen, stamping, clapping, and snapping
5. Experience with melodic and rhythmic ostinati

---

1. Patschen is meant to direct children to pat left hand on left knee, while simultaneously patting right hand on right knee. In all experiences following, this is the intention when the word patschen is used.

6. Activities in speech, meter, and movement
7. Cultivating phrase building through question-and-answer clapping (improvisation)
8. Experience with the rhythmic rondo
9. Experience with the rhythmic canon

On the following pages will be found suggested experiences for the sequence of activities listed above—the first of many suggested experiences to be found throughout this book. It is important to note that all advanced experiences necessitate much preparation in order that children have the proper background for successful participation. Children who have not had this background will find many of these advanced experiences beyond their ability, and therefore frustrating.

Further, these experiences are not meant to be rigid formulae for teaching. Rather, they are meant to be suggestions only—experiences which have worked with children, and which may help the teacher find a way of exploring successfully her own ideas. Through critical reading of these experiences, it is hoped that the teacher may find ways of utilizing the ideas contained herein to develop her own ideas for initiating successful experiences in the Orff-Kodaly approach.

It should be noted, too, that although the main emphasis in each experience follows the sequential listing of experiences, there will be overlapping of all activities throughout the book, in accord with the Orff-Kodaly concepts.

CHAPTER 1

Tempo-Dynamic and Echo Clapping, Patschen, Stamping, and Finger-Snapping

Tempo-dynamic clapping (or clapping, patschen, stamping and finger-snapping) is the performance of these movements by the teacher, in different tempi and dynamics, and, as simultaneously as possible, by the group.

Echo clapping, on the other hand, (or echo clapping, patschen, stamping, and finger-snapping) implies the execution of rhythm patterns using these movements, performed first by the teacher, then by the class.

Both activities, when engaged in with freedom and spontaneity, have the enormous value of giving children the opportunity to experience rhythm in a meaningful way—through the body—as they build a rhythmic vocabulary upon which future musical experiences can be cultivated.

Tempo-Dynamic Clapping to Develop a Feeling for Changes in Tempo and Dynamics—For Primary Grades

Note: This activity should be used frequently throughout the elementary grades to precede other experiences.

1. Tell children to clap *with* you, doing exactly as you do.[1] Clap quarter notes, beginning with a steady tempo and gradually varying the tempo and dynamics. Adapt your movements to the dynamics—large, broad movements for forte passages—smaller, lighter movements for piano passages. The following is one possible sequence:

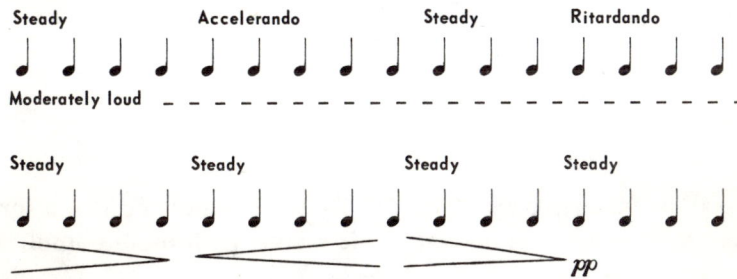

1. The teacher will want to make certain that children clap in the most effective manner: the left hand extended at waist level, fingers of right hand clapping into palm of left hand with a free wrist movement.

2. When children can clap the above easily, select one child to play the tambourine instead of clapping. Repeat, with variations, as child plays tambourine.

3. Select other children to play percussion instruments while class claps—one to play tone block, one to play drum. Repeat; as children play instruments, class claps.

Tempo-Dynamic Patschen, Stamping, Clapping, and Finger-Snapping
(Duple and Triple Meter)—For Primary or Intermediate Grades

1. Tell children that today they are going to pat knees (patschen), stamp, clap, and snap fingers in rhythm. Tell them to do exactly as you do; then do the following, with varying tempo and dynamics, repeating each pattern as many times as necessary until children can follow easily.

Note: The teacher should be aware of, and distinguish between, experiences in echo clapping and movement and tempo-dynamic clapping and movement. The emphasis in tempo-dynamic experiences is the numerous repetition of a pattern by teacher and children simultaneously.

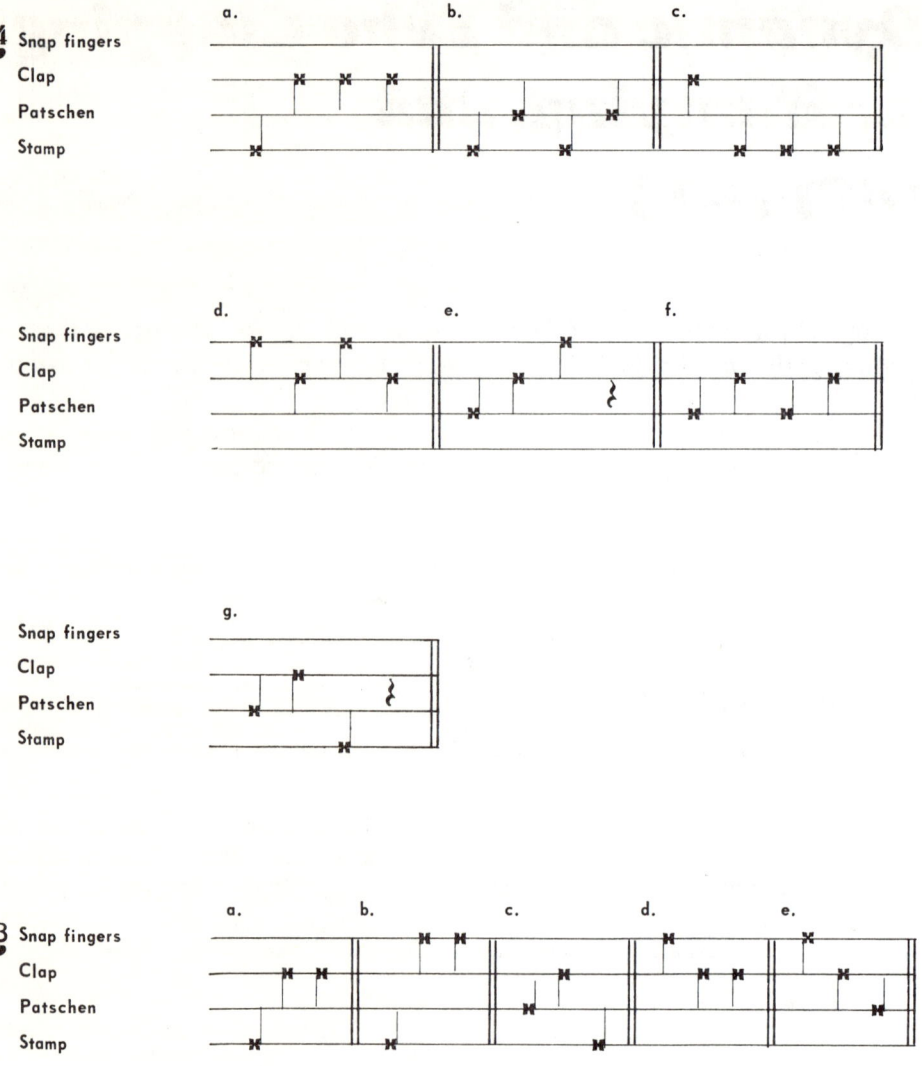

2. As children become able to do the above patterns with facility, give them experiences of a similar nature, using patterns of two measures length in triple and duple meter, with more complicated rhythms.

Tempo-Dynamic Patschen, Stamping, Clapping, and Finger-Snapping
(Duple and Triple Meter)—For Intermediate or Upper Grades

1. Tell children that today they are going to stamp, clap, snap fingers and patschen (pat knees) in rhythm. Tell them to do exactly as you do; then do the following with varying tempo and dynamics, repeating each pattern as many times as necessary until children can follow easily.

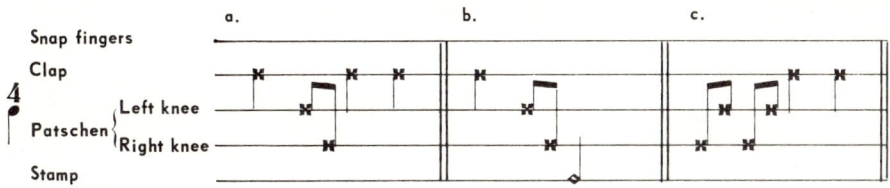

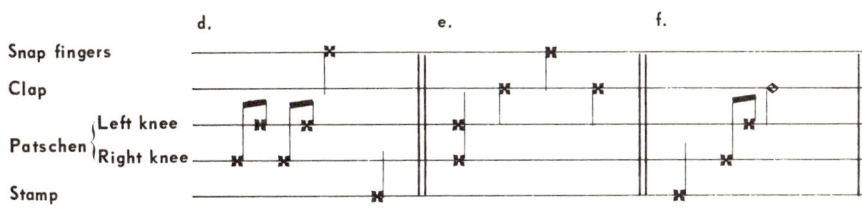

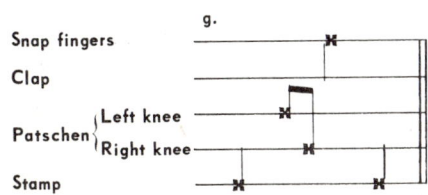

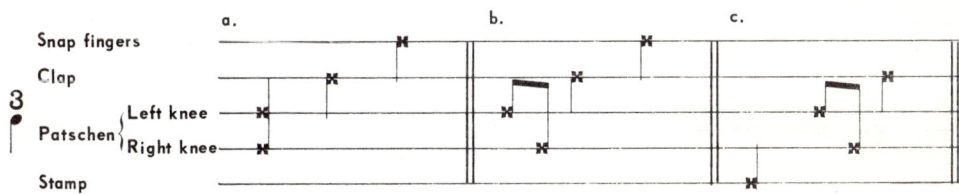

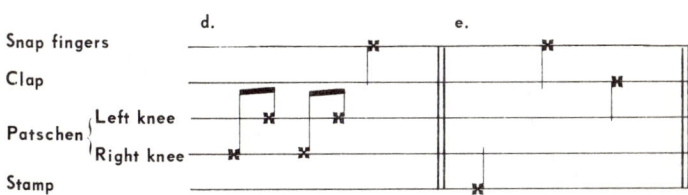

2. As children become able to do the above with facility, give them similar experiences, using longer, more complicated patterns in duple and triple meter, with wider variations in tempo and dynamics.
3. When children have had many experiences with this type of bodily movement, let individual children assume the role of the teacher in tempo-dynamic movement.

Tempo-Dynamic Patschen, Stamping, Clapping, and Finger-Snapping
(Irregular Meter—5s)—For Upper Grades

1. Tell children that today they are going to stamp, clap, snap fingers, and patschen (pat knees) in rhythm. Tell them to do exactly as you do; then do the following, in a slow tempo, with varying tempo and dynamics, repeating each pattern as many times as necessary until children can follow easily.

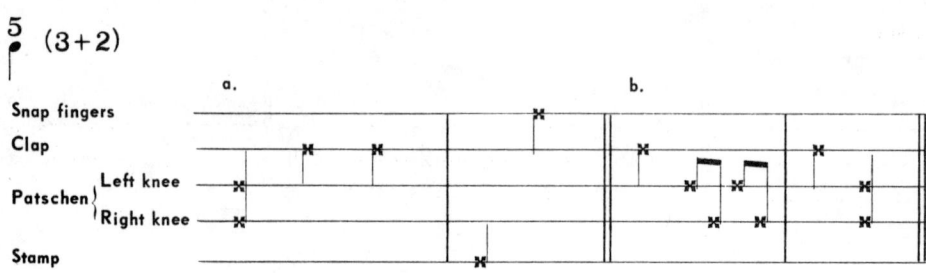

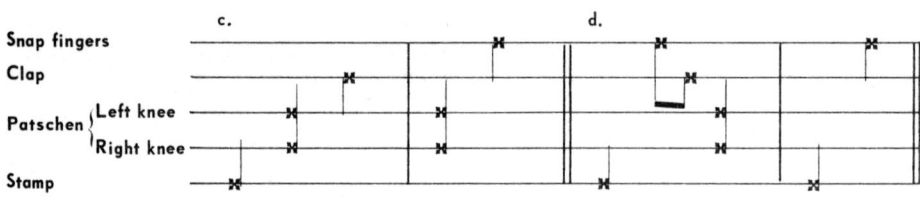

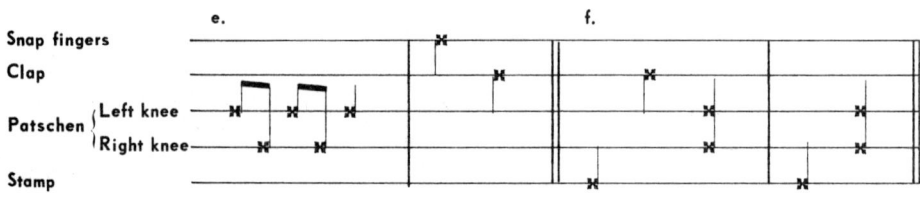

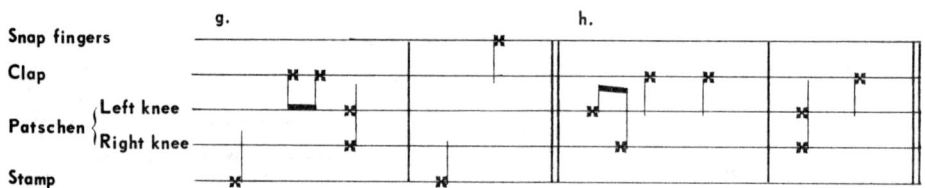

2. As children become able to do the above with facility, give them similar experiences, using longer and more complicated patterns in irregular meter, with wider variations in tempo and dynamics.

**Tempo-Dynamic Patschen, Stamping, Clapping, and
Finger-Snapping—For Upper Grades**

1. Tell children to stand and to do exactly as you do. Do the following, beginning in a slow tempo, then varying tempo and dynamics as children gain facility. Repeat each pattern as many times as necessary until children can follow easily.

Note: Since each of the patterns involves coordination of hands and feet, in *most* cases the teacher will want to begin movement of either the hands or feet *alone* before combining movement of hands and feet together.

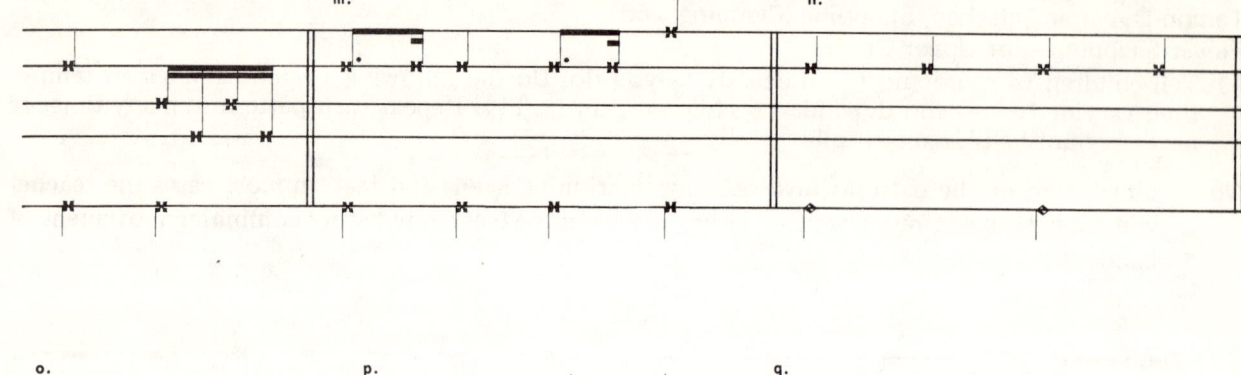

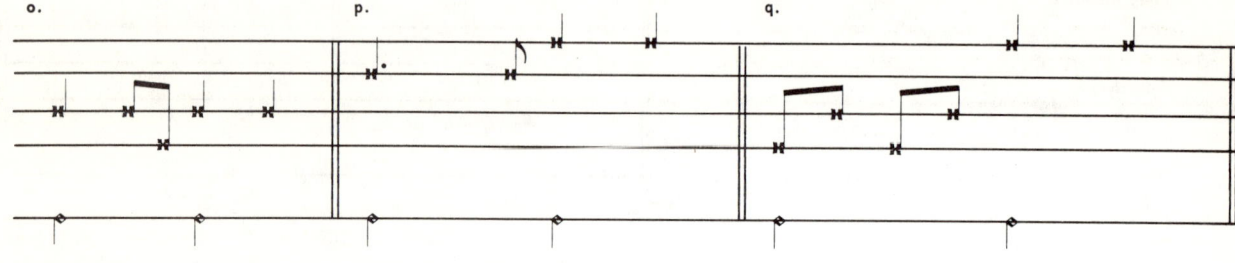

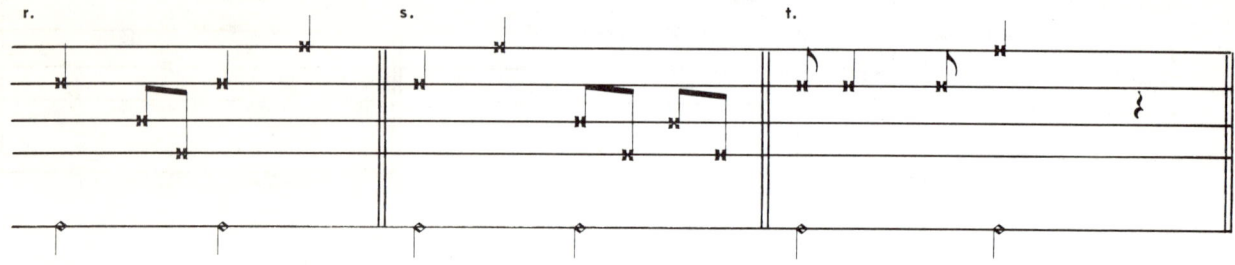

2. For enrichment of this type of experience, give similar experiences using patterns in 3, 5, and 7 meters.

Echo Clapping (Duple Meter)—For Primary Grades[2]

1. Tell children to listen to you clap, then to clap exactly what they hear (echo). Clap the following sequence, beginning in a slow, steady tempo, then gradually varying the tempo and dynamics as children begin to echo easily. If children have difficulty echoing any one pattern, repeat, chanting a word pattern that fits the rhythm exactly. For example, the following rhythm patterns fit the words beneath them:

---

2. Experiences with echo clapping contain various aspects of which the teacher should be aware: (1) Children must be given a signal so that they know when to begin to echo. Any of the following can be used: nodding head; signaling with the hands; saying, "Now," on the last beat. Any signal used should preserve the steady flow of the rhythm. (2) When children do not echo accurately, proceed with as many of the following steps as necessary to correct rhythmic errors: (a) Repeat pattern (without comment to children); (b) Clap pattern more slowly; (c) Break pattern into smaller units, clapping each unit as many times as necessary, then combining units; (d) Add speech pattern to emphasize correct rhythm. (3) Since echo clapping generally precedes and serves as a preparation for other activities, the teacher may find it of great value to base the patterns to be echo-clapped on a song or rhythmic pattern to be used later, thus avoiding potential rhythmic problems.

On Mon - day morn - ing

Will you clap with me

One! Two! Three!

Teacher:

Students:

2. On following days, gradually increase the length and complexity of the pattern to be echoed, using dotted quarters and eighths, dotted eighths and sixteenth notes, etc.
3. When children have had many experiences with echo clapping, let individual children assume the role of teacher and lead the class in further experiences.

Echo Clapping (Duple Meter)—For Intermediate Grades

1. Tell children to listen to you clap, then to clap exactly what they hear (echo). Clap the following patterns, beginning in a slow, steady tempo, then gradually varying the tempo and dynamics as children begin to echo easily. If children have difficulty echoing any one pattern, repeat, chanting a word pattern that fits the rhythm exactly. For example, the following rhythm patterns fit the words beneath them:

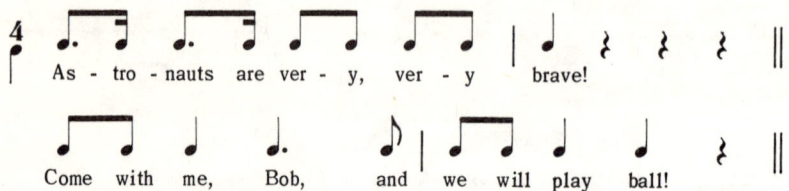

Note: In this, and in all succeeding experiences with echo clapping, the teacher's part only will be given.

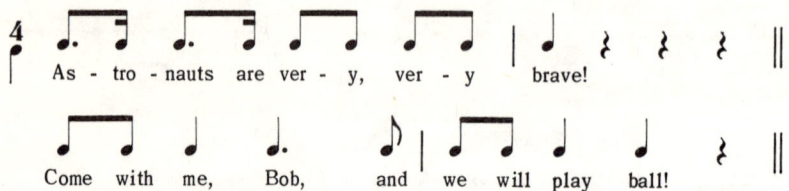

2. On following days, gradually increase the complexity of the pattern to be echoed.[3]

---

3. Since echo clapping generally precedes and serves as a preparation for other activities, the teacher may find it of great value to base the echo-clapping patterns on a song or rhythmic pattern to be taught later, thus avoiding potential rhythmic problems.

Echo Clapping (Triple Meter)—For Primary Grades
(Children should have had experience echo clapping in duple meter preceding this experience.)

1. Tell children to listen to you clap, then to clap (echo) exactly what they hear. Clap the following sequence, beginning in a slow, steady tempo, then gradually varying the tempo and dynamics, as children begin to echo easily. If children have difficulty echoing any one pattern, repeat, chanting a word pattern that fits the rhythm exactly. For example, the following rhythm patterns fit the words beneath them:

2. On following days, gradually increase the length and complexity of the patterns to be echoed.

Echo Clapping (Triple Meter)—For Intermediate Grades

1. Tell children to listen to you clap, then to clap (echo) exactly what they hear. Clap the following sequence, beginning in a slow, steady tempo, then gradually varying the tempo and dynamics, as children begin to echo easily. If children have difficulty echoing any one pattern, repeat, chanting a word pattern that fits the pattern exactly. For example, the following rhythm patterns fit the words beneath them:

2. On following days, gradually increase the complexity of the pattern to be echoed.

Echo Clapping (Irregular Meter—5s)—For Upper Grades

1. Tell children to listen to you clap, then to clap (echo) exactly what they hear. Clap the sequence below, beginning in a slow, steady tempo, then gradually varying the tempo and dynamics, as children begin to echo easily. If children have difficulty echoing any one pattern, repeat the pattern chanting a word pattern that fits the rhythm exactly. For example, the following patterns in rhythm fit the words beneath them:

2. On following days, gradually increase the length and complexity of the patterns to be echoed, using dotted quarters and eights, etc.

Echo Patschen, Stamping, Clapping, and Finger-Snapping
(Duple and Triple Meter)—For Intermediate Grades

1. Tell children to watch you, then to echo exactly what you do. Do the following, in a moderate tempo. If children have difficulty with any one pattern, repeat. If the difficulty persists, add words to the pattern. For example, the following rhythm patterns fit the words beneath them:[4]

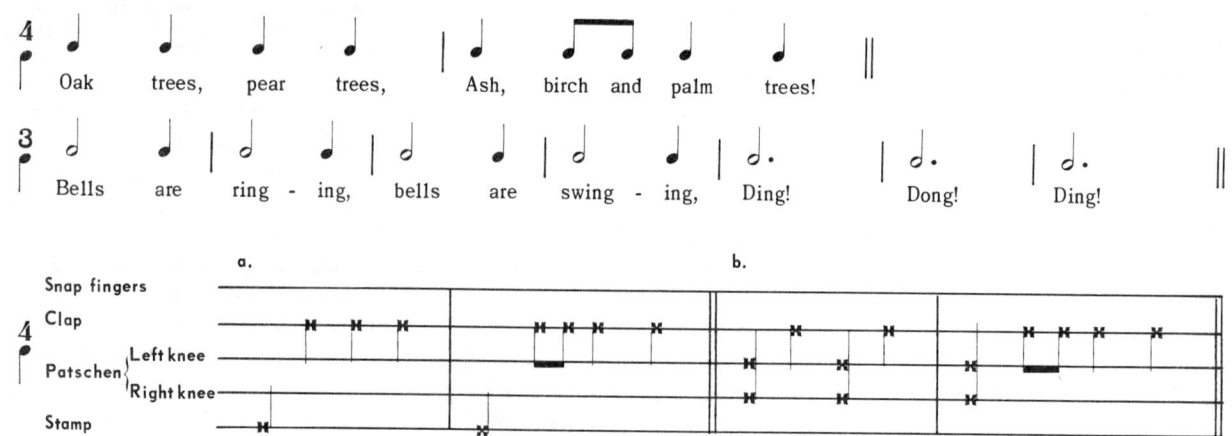

---

4. Since this type of rhythmic activity has great value when used as a rhythmic ostinato for a speech pattern or a song, the teacher may want to include, in similar echo experiences, patterns which will later be used as a rhythmic ostinato.

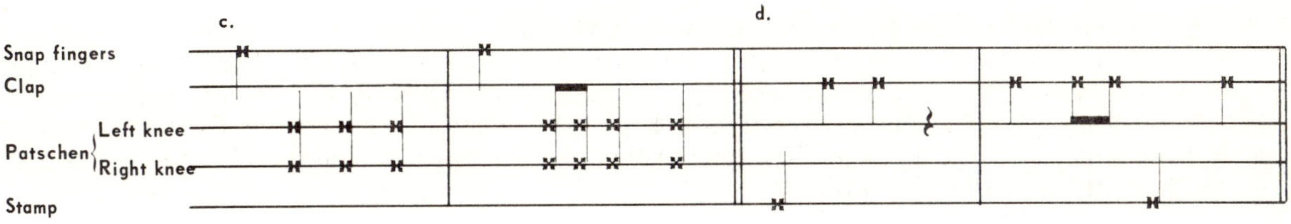

[Rhythmic notation staves labeled: Snap fingers, Clap, Patschen (Left knee / Right knee), Stamp — examples c., d., e., f., g., h., and in 3 meter a., b., c., d.]

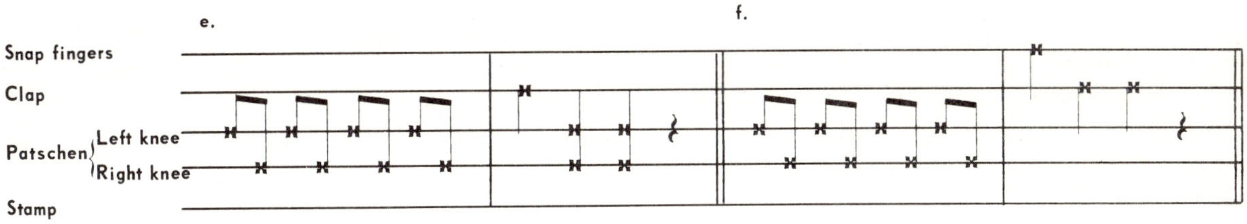

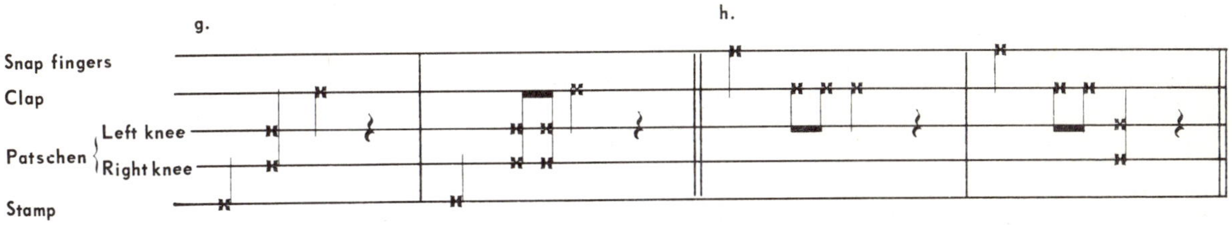

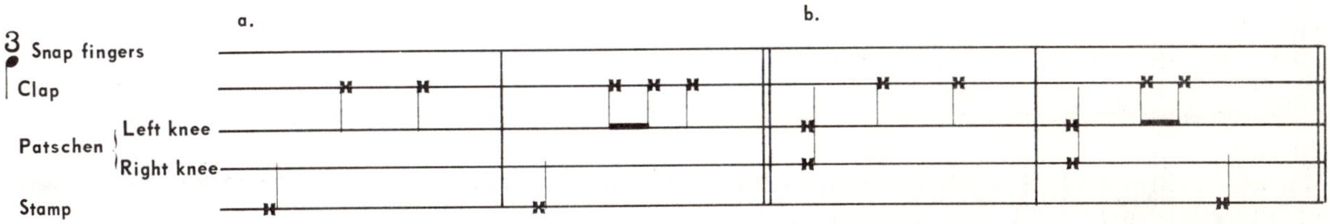

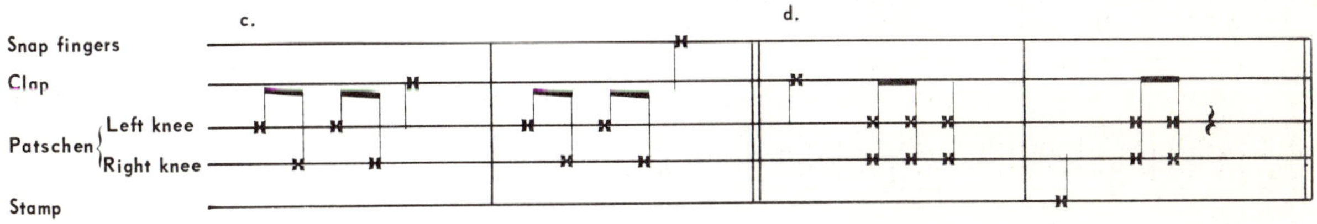

2. On other days, give children similar experiences using more complicated patterns of longer length. Children will also enjoy and benefit from selecting a suitable pattern from the above to be used as the basis for a rhythmic ostinato for speech or a song.

Echo Patschen, Stamping, Clapping, and Finger-Snapping—For Upper Grades

1. Tell children to watch you, then to echo exactly what you do. Do the following in a moderate tempo. If children have difficulty with any one pattern, repeat. If the difficulty persists, shorten pattern to one measure. When this becomes easy, teach the second measure, then combine the two. If the rhythmic problem still persists, add words to clarify. For example, for the first pattern, the following words might be used:

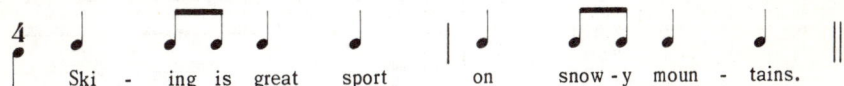

Ski - ing is great sport on snow-y moun - tains.

For the fourth pattern, the following words could be used:

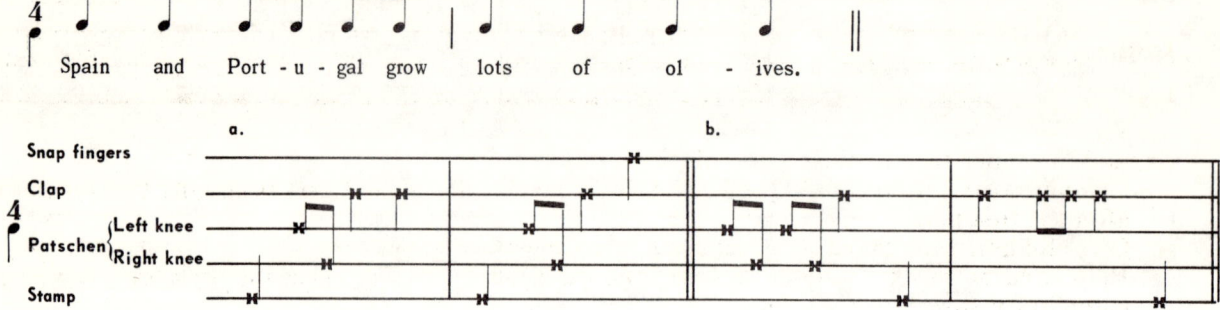

Spain and Port - u - gal grow lots of ol - ives.

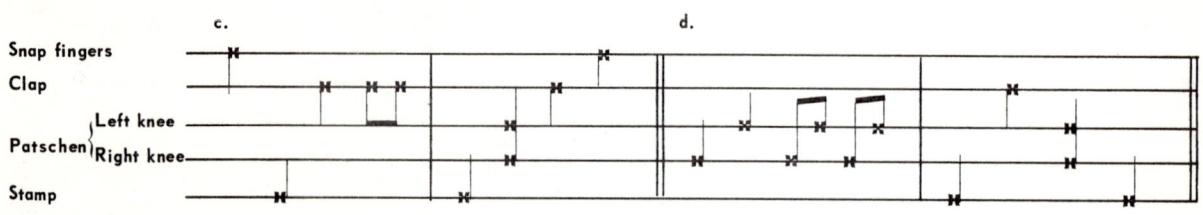

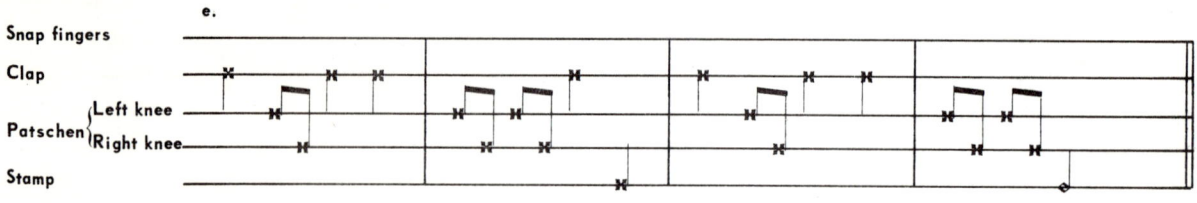

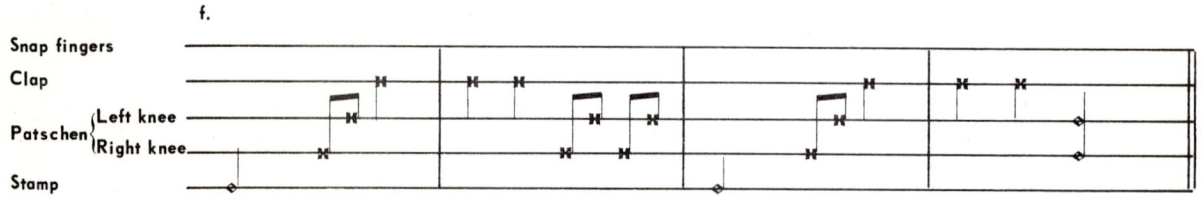

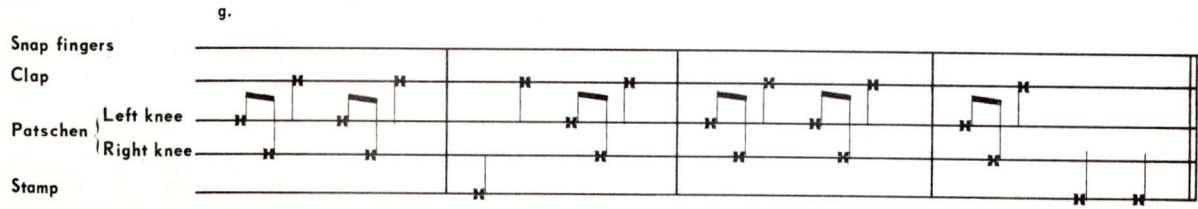

2. Expand the experience in one of the following ways:
    a. Combine two patterns and create a rhythmic canon, the second part beginning two measures after the first part.
    b. Give children a similar experience, using more complicated patterns.
    c. Help children select a suitable pattern from the sequence to be used as the basis for a rhythmic ostinato for speech or for a song.

CHAPTER 2

Experiencing Melodic and Rhythmic Ostinati

Melodic and rhythmic ostinato are musical figures repeated to form the accompaniment to a chant or song. Children revel in the opportunity to make music in this relatively effortless way, and benefit musically in numerous ways: they develop increased rhythmic stability; acquire a feeling for the basic pulse; gain the ability to hear contrasting rhythm patterns, interval relationships and color, and the ability to play an independent part in an ensemble.

Using Melodic and Rhythmic Ostinati to Accompany the Rhyme _Hot Cross Buns_—For Primary Grades

1. Give children a period of echo clapping.
2. Tell class to join you as you do the following:

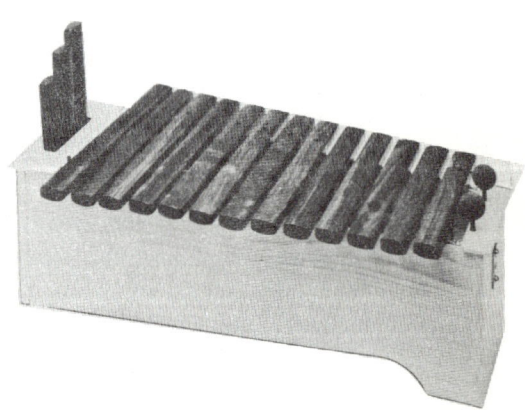

Photo courtesy of C. Bruno & Son, Inc., Melville, New York 11746.

Note: This type of experience (i.e., class mirroring teacher's hand movements) prepares children for the exact movements their hands will make in playing a specific ostinato on an instrument, as in 3 (following page). Children should be prepared in a similar fashion before playing each new ostinato. In order to decide which hand movements should be used to properly prepare children for playing any given ostinato, the teacher should stand _behind_ the instrument to be played, as though facing the child, who is in _front_ of the instrument prepared to play it, with lowest notes to teacher's right. She should then move her arms as though playing the instrument, putting her hands on her knees or thighs, instead of on the notes. Thus, she will be making motions which, when mirrored by the class, will be exactly those needed to play the ostinato.

3. Select a child who shows ability to move his hands properly in 2 (page 18) to play the following accompaniment:[1]

Alto Xylophone
(To facilitate playing, remove the A, F, E, and D bars.)

4. Tell class to join you and do the following:

5. Tell class you would like them to echo you as you chant a rhyme. Have them begin the rhythmic accompaniment in 4 (above) with you. When they are rhythmically stable, bring in the alto xylophone.[2] When the alto xylophone and rhythmic accompaniment are coordinated, have children continue and, without stopping, you begin chant, as below. Have alto xylophone and rhythmic accompaniment continue for two measures after end of chant.

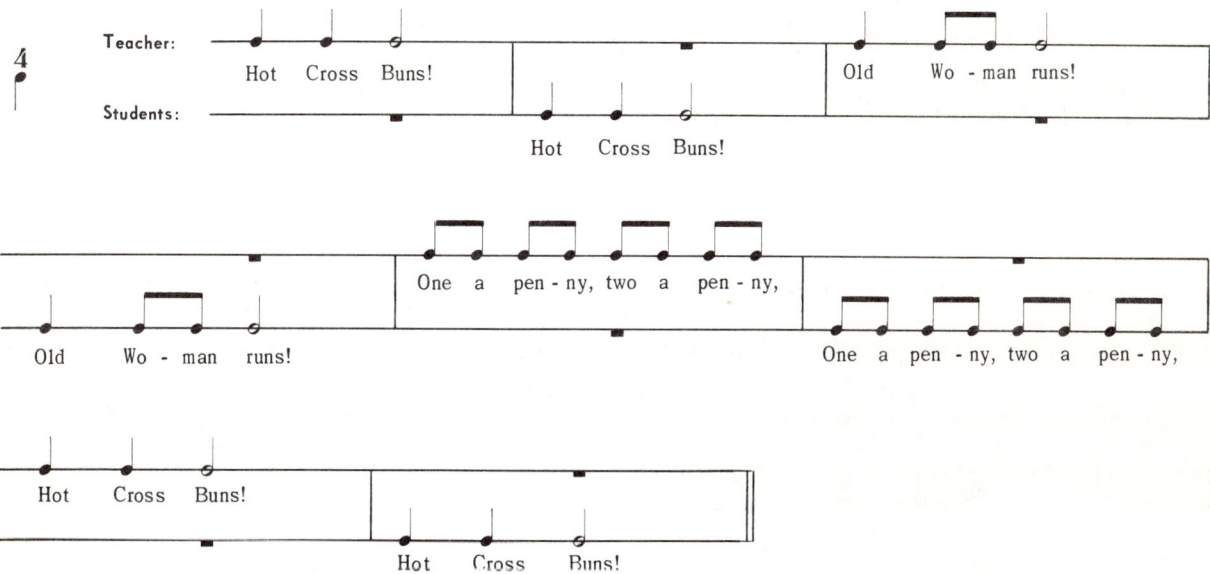

6. Tell children you would like to see if they can do the rhyme all the way through without echoing. Have them begin rhythmic accompaniment. When they are secure, bring in the alto xylophone. Several measures later, have class begin chant with you.

7. As an enrichment, help children to do one of the following:
   a. Learn the following instrumental accompaniments:

Note: In the preparation for playing instrumental accompaniments throughout the book, the hand movements for the teacher are given. Children will mirror, doing just the opposite.

Preparation for Playing Timpani:

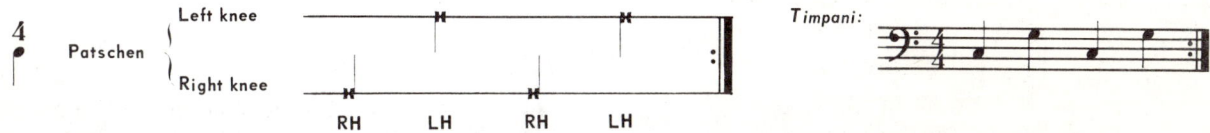

Note: In all experiences throughout this book, RH will indicate *right hand*; LH, *left hand*.

1. This is an ostinato which should be played throughout the song.
2. In this, as in all experiences playing an instrumental accompaniment, it is vitally important that the child playing an instrument also sing or chant the song or rhyme he is accompanying.

Preparation for Playing Soprano Xylophone:

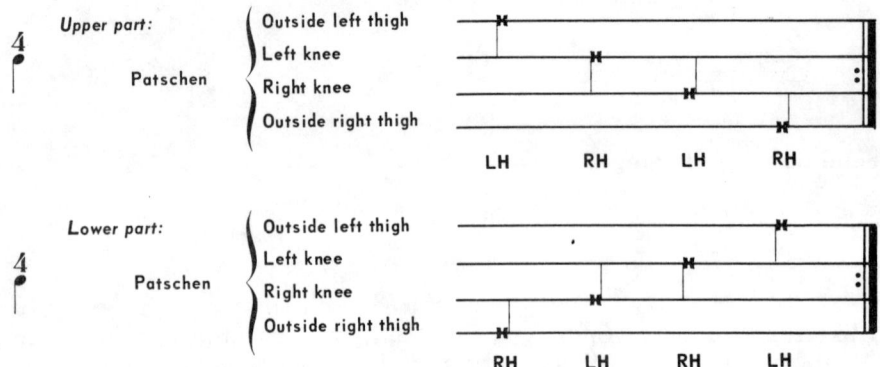

Soprano xylophone: (Two children, each using two alternating mallets.) (Remove B and F bars.)

Note: It is of vital importance for a child to use two mallets in all instrumental accompaniments of this kind in order to develop correct mallet technique.

Preparation for Playing Alto Glockenspiel:

Note: When playing half notes on an instrument, the second beat should be pulsed by crossing mallets silently in the air .

Alto glockenspiel: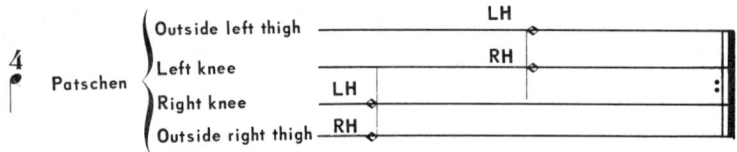

Preparation for Playing Alto Metallophone:

Alto metallophone:

b. Walk the beat (quarter notes) as they chant the rhyme, using a variety of dynamics as they chant.
c. Chant the rhyme, using heavy—then light—voices, as they walk the correspondingly heavy or light steps.
d. Chant the rhyme slowly as they walk slowly; quickly, as they walk quickly.
e. Chant the rhyme using different pitch levels. (For example, children may want to start with low voices and gradually move higher and higher, chant the entire rhyme in high voices, or chant the rhyme in very low voices.)

**Using Melodic and Rhythmic Ostinati to Accompany the
Rhyme** *Doctor Foster*—**For Primary Grades**

1. Give class a period of tempo-dynamic clapping.
2. Give class a period of echo clapping.
3. Tell children to do as you do; then do the following (preparation for playing alto xylophone):

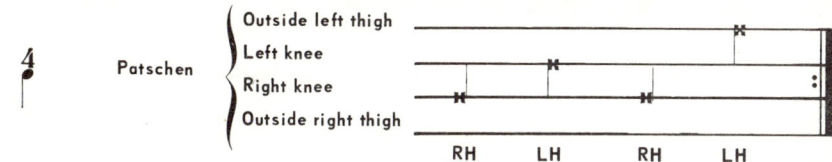

4. When class is doing the above easily, tell them to continue as they listen, then to echo you. Do the following:

5. Show a child how to play the ostinato for alto xylophone:

6. Tell class to do as you do, then do the following (preparation for playing timpani or bass xylophone):

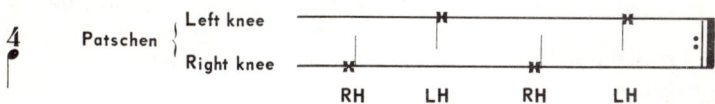

7. When class is doing movement in 6 (page 21) easily, continue movement and signal alto xylophone to begin. After two measures of alto xylophone, begin chant again, using a different pitch and dynamic level, indicating that children should echo in the same manner.

8. Show someone how to play the timpani or bass xylophone:

9. Tell class to do as you do and do the following (preparation for playing soprano xylophone):

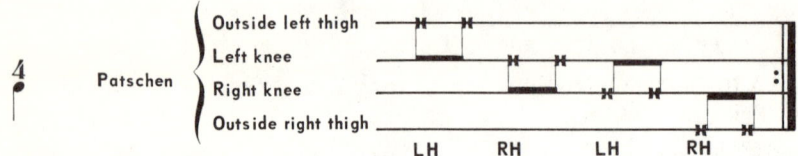

10. When class is doing above easily, signal alto xylophone to begin; two measures later, signal timpani or bass xylophone to begin. Then do chant, using different pitch and dynamic levels as class echoes you.

11. Show someone how to play the soprano xylophone:

12. Teach a child to play the alto metallophone:

13. Tell class you would like to see if they can do the chant all the way through with you (no echo). Tell them to do the following with you:

14. When they are doing the above easily, have them continue as you signal the accompanying instruments to begin, entering at two-measure intervals in the order listed below. Signal class to begin chant two measures after the entrance of the alto metallophone.

Alto xylophone
Timpani or bass xylophone
Soprano xylophone
Alto metallophone
Chant

15. To enrich the experience, help class do one of the following:
    a. Create a rhythmic interpretation of the chant, showing Dr. Foster walking to Glo'ster, then leaving hurriedly in disgust.
    b. Add sound effects to the chant to indicate Dr. Foster's walking, stepping in a puddle, and so on.
    c. Turn the experience into a pentatonic song, singing it with the ostinati and rhythmic accompaniments. The following is one possible arrangement:

Doc - tor Fos - ter went to Glo' - ster, In a show - er of rain; He

stepped in a pud - dle; right up to his mid - dle and nev - er went there a - gain.

Using Melodic and Rhythmic Ostinati to Accompany the
Rhyme *To Market, To Market*—For Primary Grades

1. Give class a period of tempo-dynamic clapping.
2. Give class a period of echo clapping in duple meter.
3. Begin the following rhythmic accompaniment in a moderate tempo, indicating that children should follow you:

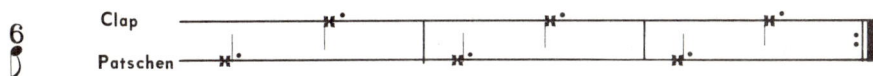

4. Continuing the above, begin chanting the speech ostinato indicated below, encouraging children to join you.

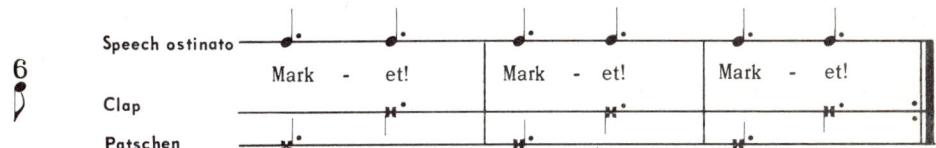

5. When children are able to do speech ostinato and accompaniment with security, tell them to continue exactly what they are doing, as you do something different. Continuing to clap and patschen with children, chant the nursery rhyme, as below. Have children continue speech ostinato and accompaniment for two measures after end of rhyme.

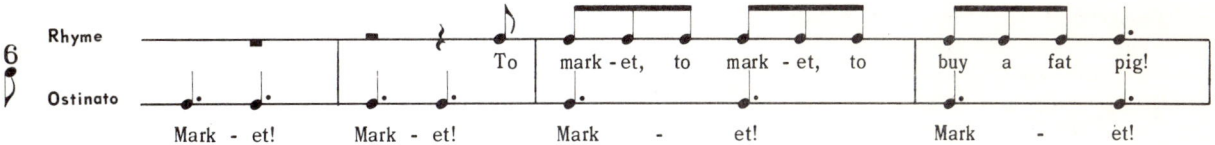

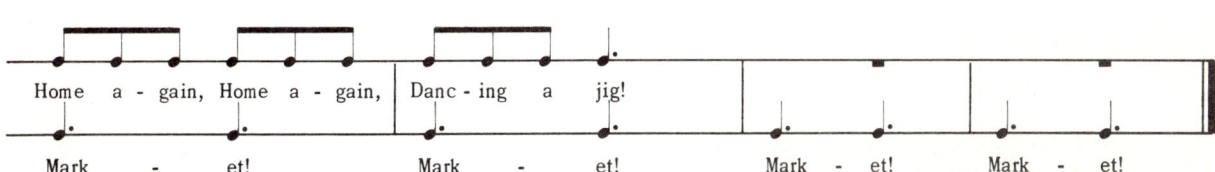

6. Select a small group to chant the ostinato, "Market! Market!" as the rest of the class chants the nursery rhyme with you. Have entire class begin doing the rhythmic accompaniment (patschen-clap). When they are secure, have the small group begin chanting the ostinato. When they are stable, have rest of class begin chanting the nursery rhyme with you.

7. Select a child to accompany the ostinato. Remove the bars adjacent to the notes to be played (see below), and teach him to play the following:

8. Let the small group chosen to chant, "Market! Market!" Practice with the alto xylophone player until all are secure.
9. Have entire class begin rhythmic accompaniment (patschen-clap). When they are rhythmically stable, have small group chanting ostinato begin. After two measures, bring in the alto xylophone, followed two measures later by the entire class chanting the rhyme.
10. Teach a child to play the following on the alto metallophone:

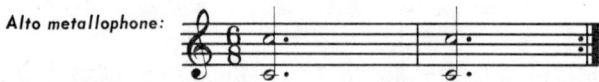

11. Have entire class begin rhythmic accompaniment. After two measures, have the small group which is chanting ostinato begin. Allowing two-measure interludes between each new entrance, bring in the alto xylophone, the alto metallophone, and the remainder of the class chanting the rhyme.
12. To expand the experience further, do one or more of the following:
   a. Teach the following ostinati:

Preparation for Playing Soprano Xylophone or Glockenspiel:

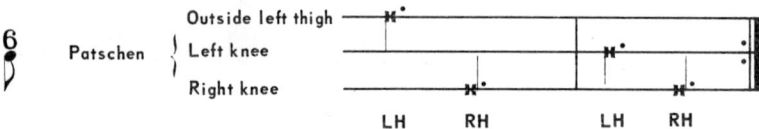

Preparation for Playing Timpani:

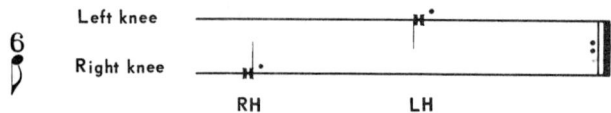

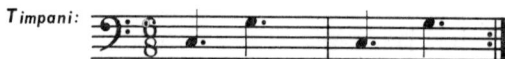

   b. Add the following rhythm instruments:
      (1) Maracas playing the rhythm of the alto xylophone.
      (2) Triangle playing the rhythm of the alto metallophone.
      (3) Tone block playing the following:

c. Let one child gallop off "to market" and back as class chants, does patschen, claps, and plays instruments.

d. Encourage class to turn chant into a song, as follows:

To mark-et, to mark-et, to buy a fat pig! Home a-gain, Home a-gain, Danc-ing a jig!
To mark-et, to mark-et, to buy a fat hog! Home a-gain, Home a-gain, Jig-get-y jog!

Using Melodic and Rhythmic Ostinati to Accompany the Rhyme
Deedle Deedle Dumpling—For Second and Third Grades

1. Discuss with the class the hand signals they know for each of the tones in the pentatonic scale, having them sing each tone with you, using syllables and hand signals.[3]
2. Explain that you are going to sing short phrases, using syllables, but no hand signals, and that you would like to see if they can echo you, but *using* hand signals. Sing one measure phrases in the pentatonic scale, accompanying yourself, if desired, on the autoharp, guitar, or ukelele. If children have difficulty with the hand signals for any pattern, repeat, helping them by making the hand signals with them.
3. Begin the following rhythmic accompaniment in a moderate tempo, indicating that children should participate with you.

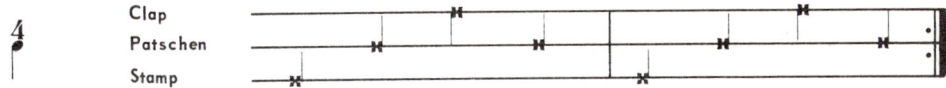

4. Continuing the above, begin chanting the speech ostinato below, encouraging children to join you.

5. When children are able to do speech ostinato and accompaniment with security, tell them to continue exactly as they are doing, as you chant a rhyme. Continuing to clap, do patschen, and to stamp with children, chant the nursery rhyme as below.

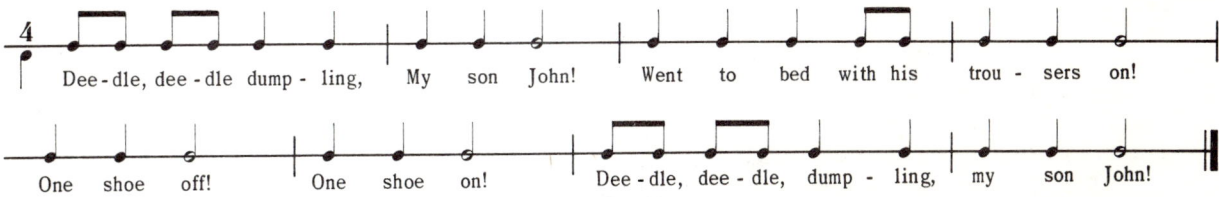

Dee-dle, dee-dle dump-ling, My son John! Went to bed with his trou-sers on!
One shoe off! One shoe on! Dee-dle, dee-dle, dump-ling, my son John!

6. Select a small group to chant ostinato as the rest of the class chants the nursery rhyme with you. Have entire class begin the rhythmic accompaniment (stamp, patschen, clap). When they are stable rhythmically, have the small group begin chanting the ostinato "Deedle, deedle." When they are secure, have rest of class begin chanting nursery rhyme with you.

---

3. Hand signals, which are discussed in the Introduction will have been presented before this experience.

7. To prepare for the first instrumental ostinato, tell them to do as you do. Place left hand on left knee and leave stationary as you do the following:

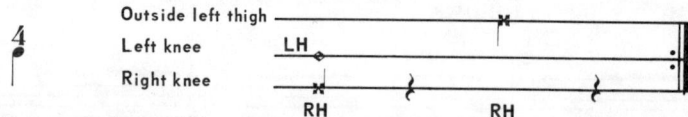

Note: Class will mirror your actions, doing just the opposite. This rhythmic movement is the first step in preparing to play the ostinato for alto xylophone. By breaking down the more complicated pattern, children are able to master the complete movement more quickly.

When children have facility doing the above, do the following, asking them to imitate you.

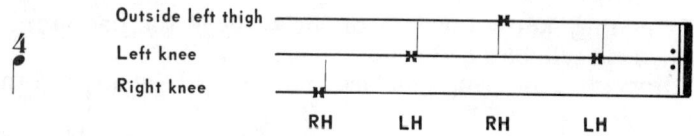

8. Select a child to accompany the ostinato. Remove the bars adjacent to the notes to be played and show him how to play the following, using two mallets:

9. Have entire class begin rhythmic accompaniment (stamp, patschen, clap, patschen). When they are rhythmically stable, have small group begin chanting ostinato. After two measures, bring in the alto xylophone, and, two measures later, the rest of the class chanting the rhyme.
10. To prepare for the next step tell children to do as you do; then do the following many times:

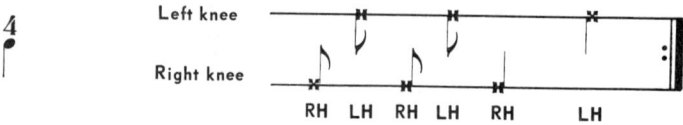

11. Select a child to play the following ostinato. Remove bars adjacent to notes to be played. Show him how to play the ostinato using two mallets.

12. Have entire class begin doing the rhythmic accompaniment. Bring in speech ostinato, alto xylophone, soprano xylophone, and finally the rest of the class chanting the rhyme, at two-measure intervals.
13. Expand the experience further by doing one or all of the following:
    a. Teach the following ostinati:

b. Add a triangle, playing the rhythm of the ostinato for the metallophone; a maracas playing the rhythm of the soprano xylophone; a tone block playing the rhythm of the alto xylophone or an independent rhythm as below:

c. Encourage individual children to experiment with a rhythmic dramatization to the rhyme, as class chants, accompanied rhythmically and instrumentally.
d. Encourage class to turn chant into a song, as follows:

Dee - dle, dee - dle, dump - ling,   My   son   John,   Went   to   bed   with his   trou - sers   on!

One   shoe   off!   One   shoe   on!   Dee - dle, dee - dle, dump - ling,   My   son   John!

Using Melodic and Rhythmic Ostinati to Accompany the Song
Camptown Races—**For Intermediate or Upper Grades**

1. Give class a period of echo "sing-backs." (Sing short phrases from the pentatonic scale, using syllables, as class echoes you, using hand signals.)
2. Begin the following rhythmic accompaniment in a moderate tempo, indicating that children should follow you:

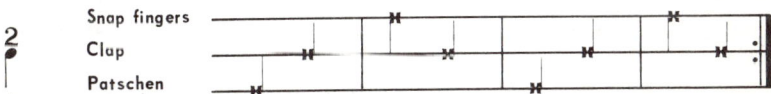

3. Continuing the above, begin chanting the speech ostinato below, encouraging children to join you.

4. When children are able to do the ostinato above with security, tell them to continue exactly as they are doing; as you sing. Continue to pat, clap, and snap with children as you sing *Camptown Races.*

Camptown Races

De Camp-town lad-ies sing dis song, Doo-dah! Doo-dah! De

Camp-town race-track five miles long, Oh! doo-dah day! I

come down deh wid my hat caved in, Doo-dah! Doo-dah! I

go back home wid my pock-et full of tin, Oh! doo-dah day!

REFRAIN

Gwine to run all night! Gwine to run all day! I'll ___

bet my mon-ey on de bob-tail nag, Some-bod-y bet on the bay!

5. Select a small group to sing *Camptown Races* with you as the rest of the class chants the ostinato. Have entire class begin doing rhythmic accompaniment (patschen, clapping, snapping). When they are rhythmically stable, have rest of class begin chanting the ostinato. When they are secure, have small group begin singing *Camptown Races*.
6. Add a few more children to those singing, and repeat above. Continue in this manner until a good balance exists between the song and the ostinato.
7. To prepare for the first ostinato accompaniment, tell children to do as you do, then do the following:

8. Select a child to play the ostinato. Remove bars adjacent to the notes to be played and show him how to play the following:

9. Let group selected to chant "Oh! doo-dah-day!" practice chanting with the alto xylophone part until both are secure.
10. Have entire class begin rhythmic accompaniment. Allowing two-measure interludes between each new entry, bring in group chanting rhythmic ostinato, alto xylophone, and finally the rest of the class singing *Camptown Races*.
11. To prepare for the second ostinato, tell children to do as you do, then do the following:

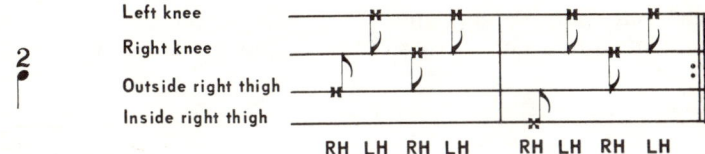

12. Select a child to play the soprano xylophone. Remove the bars adjacent to the notes to be played and show him how to play the following, using two mallets.

13. Have entire class begin rhythmic accompaniment. Bring in speech ostinato, alto xylophone, soprano xylophone, and finally the rest of the class singing *Camptown Races*.
14. To expand the experience, do one or all of the following:
    a. Teach the following ostinati:

    b. Add the following rhythm instruments:
        (1) Triangle playing the rhythm of the alto metallophone.
        (2) Maracas playing the rhythm of the soprano xylophone.
        (3) Tone block playing the rhythm of the alto xylophone or an independent part, as follows:

    c. Encourage children to experiment with bodily movement which interprets and reflects the rhythmic quality (light, fast) of the song or the speech ostinato.

Patschen, Stamping, Clapping and Finger-Snapping as an Ostinato to the Proverb *As He Has Sown*—For Intermediate Grades

1. Give children an experience in tempo-dynamic patschen, stamping, clapping, and finger-snapping.
2. Give children an experience in echo patschen, stamping, clapping, and finger-snapping.
3. Tell children to do the following rhythm pattern with you:

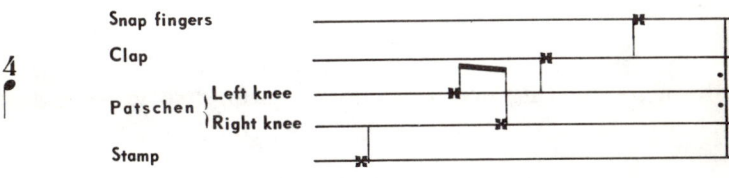

4. When children can do the above easily, tell them to continue doing this pattern with you, and, simultaneously, to listen, then echo anything you chant. Chant the following, using a variety of dynamics and pitch levels:

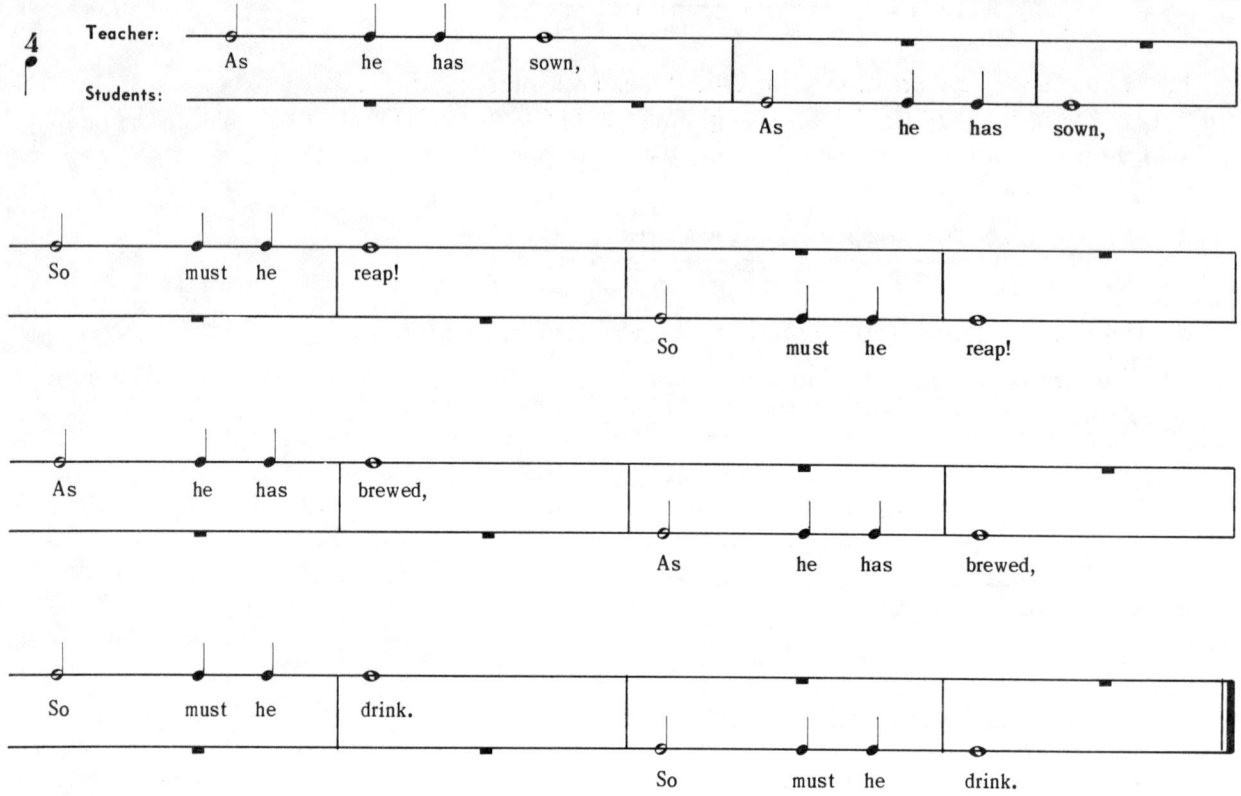

5. Tell class that you would like to see if they can do this as a canon. Remind them that a canon is a type of composition similar to a round, that is, one group begins first, the second group begins later—both continuing until the end, the second group ending last. Divide the class into two groups. Have entire class begin the rhythmic accompaniment. After two measures, give group one a cue to begin. After group one has finished the first measure, give group two a signal to start. The following should result:

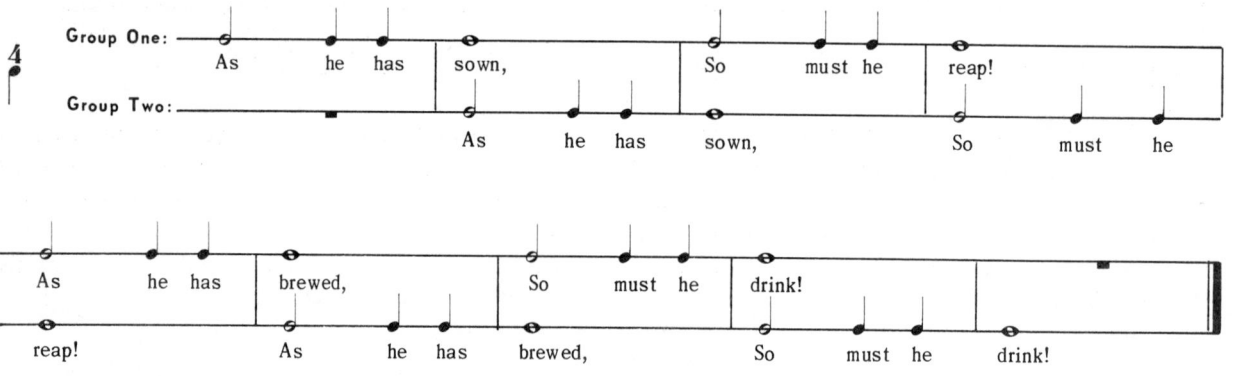

6. To expand the experience, do one of the following:
   a. Help children turn proverb into a song, using notes of the pentatonic scale. One possible melody could be the following:

1. As he has sown,   so   must he reap.
2. As he has brewed,   so   must he drink!

   b. Guide class in the creation of an ostinati accompaniment, using Orff instruments.

   c. Help class do proverb in a 5/4 rhythm. One possibility is the following:

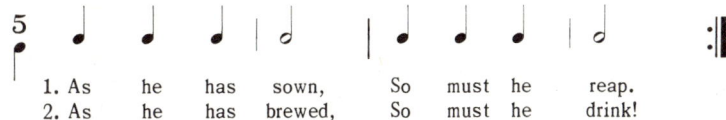

1. As   he   has   sown,   So   must   he   reap.
2. As   he   has   brewed,   So   must   he   drink!

   d. Help children develop a rhythmic accompaniment to the rhyme in 5/4. Two possibilities might be:

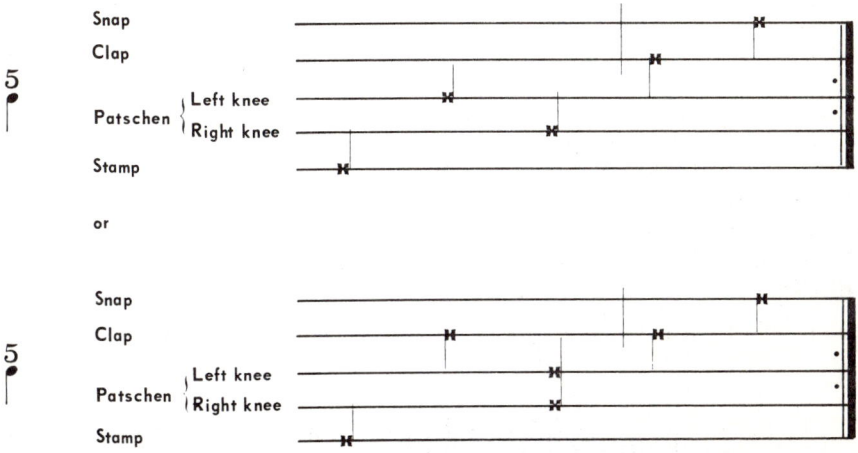

Patschen, Stamping, Clapping, and Finger-Snapping as an Ostinato to the Song *Skip to My Lou*—For Intermediate Grades

1. Give children an experience in tempo-dynamic patschen, stamping, clapping, and finger-snapping.
2. Tell children to do exactly as you do (echo you); then do the following patterns, with varying tempo and dynamics, repeating each pattern as many times as necessary until children echo easily.

3. Tell class you would like to make the last two measures of the last echoed pattern (pattern c) the basis for a rhythmic ostinato—that is, a rhythmic background for a song. Have them do this pattern with you. When they are rhythmically secure, tell them to continue, as you sing the song *Skip to My Lou*.

Skip to My Lou

1. Lost my girl, Now what'll I do?
   Lost my girl, Now what'll I do?
   Lost my girl, Now what'll I do?
   Skip to my Lou, my darling.
2. I'll get another, a better one too (3 times)
   Skip to my Lou, my darling!
3. Cat's in the buttermilk, skip to my Lou . . .
4. Flies in the sugarbowl, shoo, fly, shoo . . .
5. Little red wagon, painted blue . . .
6. Needle in the haystack, two by two . . .

4. Invite the class to sing *Skip to My Lou* with you as they do the rhythmic ostinato.
5. When class can sing refrain and do the rhythmic ostinato easily, sing the verses, encouraging them to join you.
6. Expand the experience by teaching the following accompaniments, which should be placed on the blackboard or a large cardboard:[4]

4. Children must be prepared with hand movements which simulate the movements their hands will make when playing the instruments. For detailed instructions as to how to prepare children, see the experience "Using Melodic and Rhythmic Ostinato to Accompany the Rhyme *Hot Cross Buns*" earlier in this chapter.

Alto metallophone:

Soprano xylophone:

CHAPTER 3

Experiencing Meters

Rhythm is felt in twos and threes, as well as in a combination of these (fours, sixes, fives, sevens, and so on). Children learn to feel (and later to understand and notate) these differences in pulse by experiencing them freely and happily in the forms most natural to them—the rhymes and movements of childhood.

Using Names of Children to Develop a Feeling for
Accent and Meter—For Primary Grades

1. To get children "warmed up," give them a short period of tempo-dynamic clapping.
2. Tell class that this time they are to *listen* to you clap, then to clap exactly what you clapped (echo clap). Clap one measure patterns in 4s, using combinations of quarter and eighth notes and quarter rests. Following is one possible sequence of patterns.

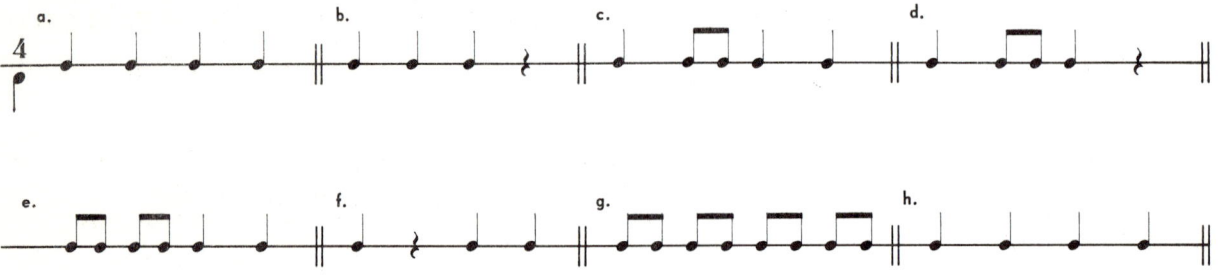

3. Tell class that this time you are going to clap their *names*. Tell them to listen, then to do exactly as you do. Go around the class, clapping and chanting names of children in a manner that reflects the contrasting tone colors represented by the names, letting class echo you each time. Some examples of what might occur follow:

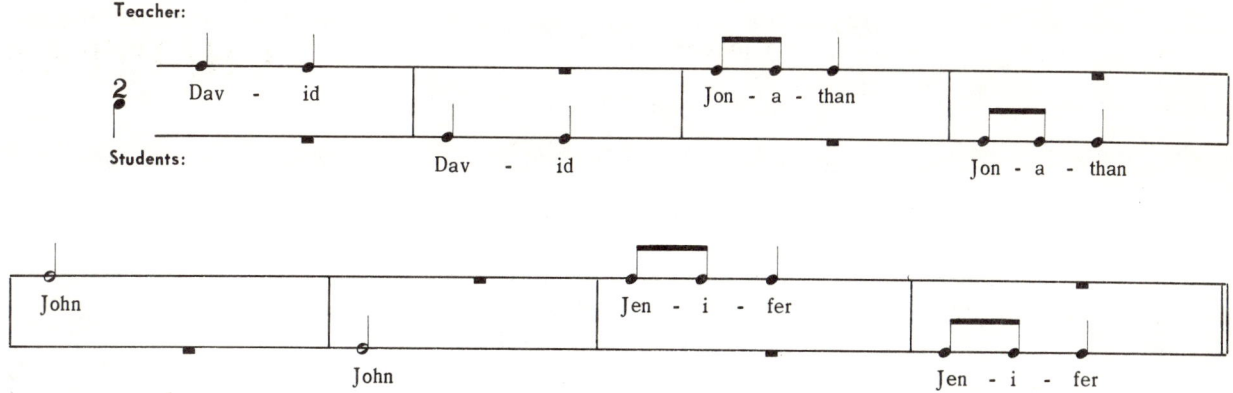

4. If children are seated in a way that they can easily pass an instrument from one to another, give the child whose name will be clapped first a percussion instrument (tone block or tambourine, perhaps). Tell him to play the instrument when his name is chanted, as the class claps and chants. Then tell him to pass the instrument on to the next person, who will play and chant *his* name as the class claps and chants. Go around the room, chanting and clapping names, as each child whose name is being chanted plays the instrument in rhythm clapped.

5. Gradually extend the length of the phrase to be clapped to include several names, as:

6. Create short phrases using names, for example:

to be used as rhythmic ostinati for chants or songs.

Creating Rhymes Using Names of Children to Develop a Feeling for Meter—For Primary Grades

(Children should have had previous rhyming experience.)[1]

1. Give class a period of tempo-dynamic clapping, then echo clapping, ending with echo clapping and chanting the names of some children in the class. (See previous experience.)
2. Ask children to think of a rhyme for their name or nickname. Discuss the rhymes they think of, letting them help each other and giving your own suggestions, if necessary. Some examples are:

Joan—bone, cone
Bob—cob
Jim—limb, him, rim
Jeany—teany
Jean—bean, lean
Jill—hill
Dave—wave
Peg—leg
Paul—fall
Chip—skip

---

1. In this, and all experiences involving speech, encourage children to get the maximum differences in qualities of sounds and high and low inflections. Thus, "Jean! Jean! Found a bean!" suggests a much brighter and higher quality than "Paul! Paul! Had a fall."

3. Tell class that you know a rhyme that uses a boy's name. Tell them to listen as you clap and chant it. Clap and chant the following or a similar rhyme:

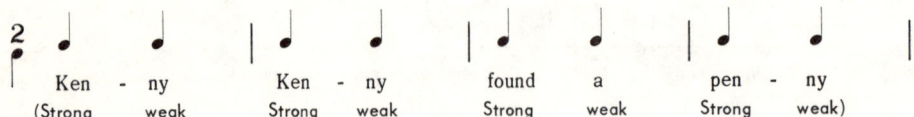

4. Tell class to clap and chant the rhyme with you. Clap and chant with the class, emphasizing the strong beats.
5. Ask class if they can think of rhymes using their names. Be aware and encourage rhymes which are created in all metrical arrangements—2s, 4s, and 3s. As children make suggestions, accept all without censorship, having class chant and clap each with you, even when rhyme is imperfect or the rhythm undefined. With practice and positive comments on especially good rhymes, all children will improve in their ability to rhyme. Some rhymes which might occur follow:

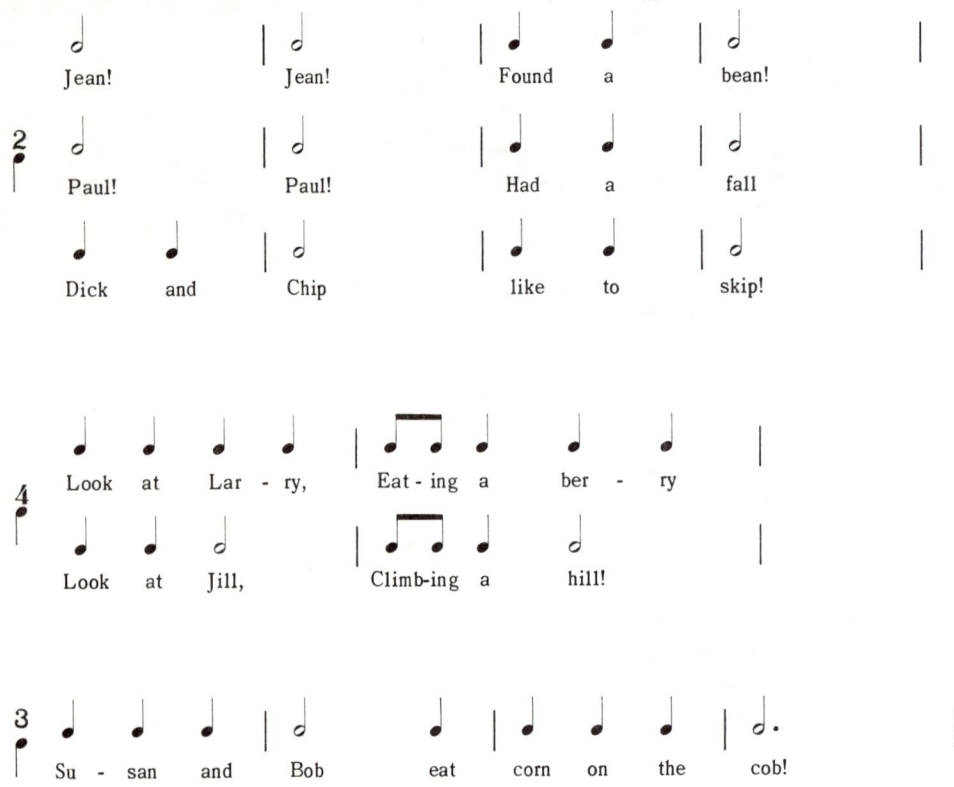

6. This experience may expand in a variety of ways, depending on the instruments available, the physical nature of the classroom situation, and the children. Some possibilities are:

   a. Letting each child play the rhythm of his rhyme on a rhythm instrument as the entire class claps and chants it with him.
   b. Letting each child step the exact rhythm of his rhyme as all clap and chant the rhyme.
   c. Letting children improvise free dramatizations of rhymes that suggest action.
   d. Combining several rhymes and having children play accompaniments to their chanting. One possible accompaniment might be:

e. Combining several rhymes and having children develop a rhythmic ostinato to accompany them. An example is:

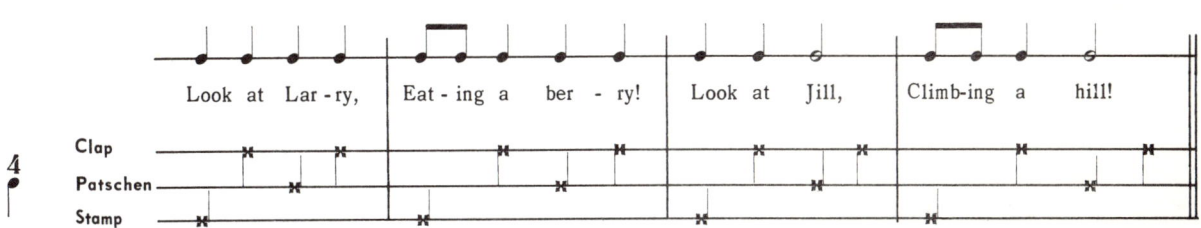

Experiencing Duple Meter Using the Jump-Rope Chant *Chickeree, Chickeree, My Little Pup*—**For Primary Grades**

1. Begin a steady accompaniment as follows, indicating that the class should do the same:

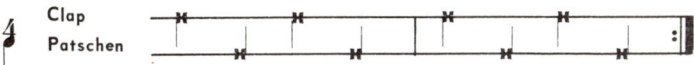

2. Tell class to continue to clap and do patschen with you as they listen to you chant, then to echo what they hear. Chant the following, using a voice that reflects the sound quality of the words.

3. Continuing with the clapping and patschen accompaniment, chant the entire rhyme as children accompany only, then have them echo—chanting, clapping, and doing patschen.

4. To check the ability of children to remember the word rhythm patterns, have them clap entire rhyme *without* chanting the words. If there are errors, have children rechant rhyme as they clap, then have them try clapping the rhyme once again without chanting words. Children may clap alone, or if desired, teacher may clap along with them to serve as a stabilizing force.

5. Expand on the experience in one or all of the following ways:

    a. Have children stamp pattern of words with feet, without chanting.
    b. Have children step quarter notes with feet, clapping and chanting the rhyme.
    c. Have children join you in the clapping and patschen (the accompaniment above), as they say *only* the first and last words aloud but *think* the remainder of the rhyme.
    d. Let children accompany chant with the following ostinato:

Alto xylophone:

    e. Let children accompany rhyme with the following speech ostinato:

Chick - er - ee   Chick - er - ee

6. On still another day, help children make this chant into a two-tone song, accompanied by the preceding bordun, played on the alto xylophone.

S S M S S M   S M M S   S M M S M   S S M S
Chick-er - ee, chick-er - ee, my lit - tle pup,   fell down the stairs and could-n't get up.

S S M S S M   S M M S   S M S M   S M S
Chick-er - ee, chick-er - ee, my lit - tle cat,   ate so much that he got fat!

Experiencing Duple Meter Using the Nursery Rhyme
Pease-Pudding Hot—For Primary Grades

1. Give children a period of tempo-dynamic clapping to "warm-up."
2. Give children the following sequence of echo clapping:

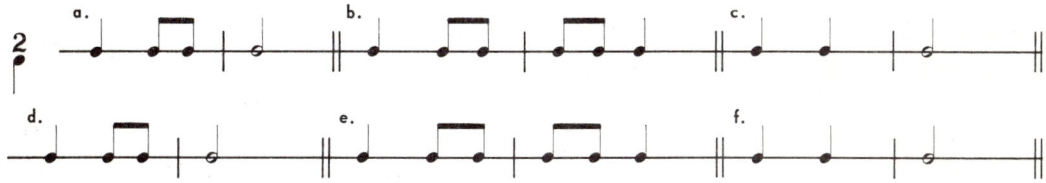

3. Tell class to do as you do; then begin the following sequence:

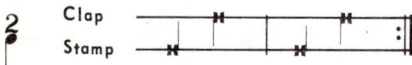

Clap
Stamp

4. When children are well established stamping and clapping with you, begin chanting the nursery rhyme, encouraging them to follow:

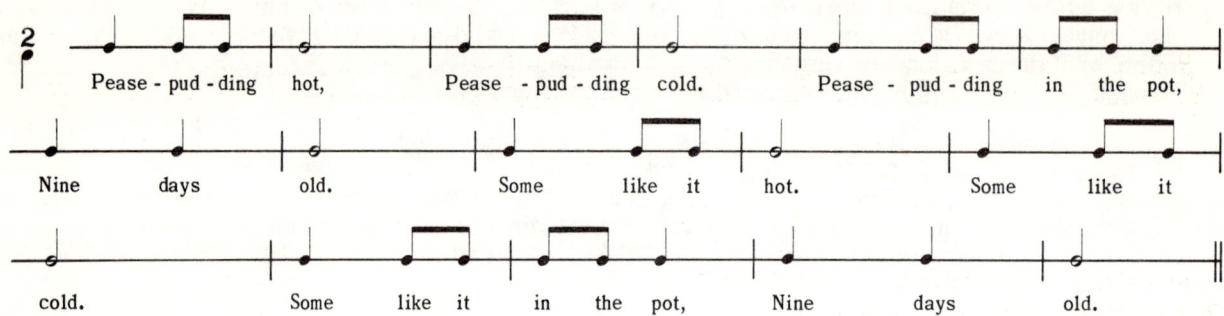

5. When children can chant, stamp, and clap the above simultaneously (perhaps on another day), begin the following speech ostinato, encouraging them to join you:

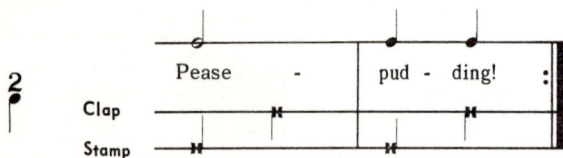

6. Divide the class into two groups: one to stamp, clap, and chant the rhyme; the other to stamp, clap, and chant the ostinato. Have all children begin to stamp and clap. When they are rhythmically stable, have group chanting ostinato begin. When this group is secure, have the group chanting rhyme join in.

7. When children have mastered the above, probably on another day, the experience may be expanded through one of the following:

 a. Encouraging individual children to improvise free movement (using arms, legs, entire body) as class chants, stamps, and claps.
 b. Teaching individual children to play the following instrumental accompaniments:

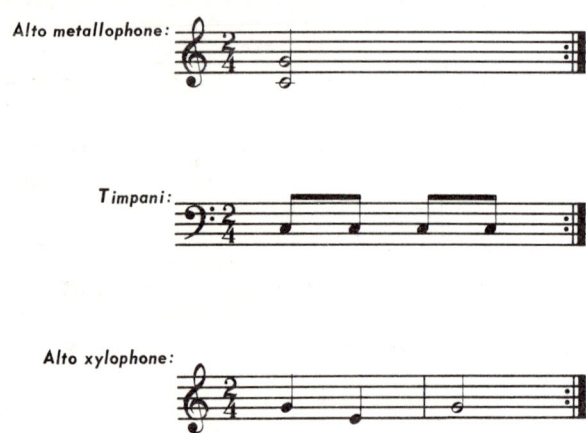

 c. Help children turn the chant into a song by singing the following. They will follow you.

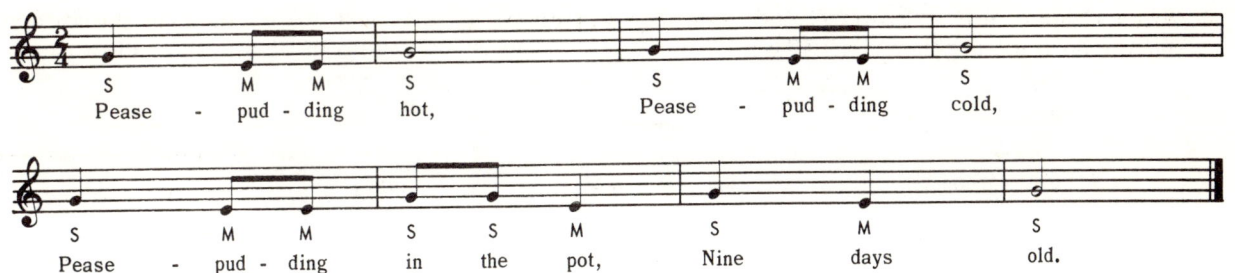

S   M   M   S   S   M   M   S
Pease - pud - ding hot,   Pease - pud - ding cold,

S   M   M   S   S   M   S   M   S
Pease - pud - ding in the pot,   Nine days   old.

Experiencing Duple Meter Using the Proverb *All's Well That Ends Well*—For Intermediate Grades

1. Using tones from the pentatonic scale with which the class has had much singing experience (singing syllables with hand signals), ask children to echo you as you sing one measure phrases using hand signals.

2. Using the following patterns, give children an experience in echo clapping, repeating each pattern as many times as necessary until children echo easily.

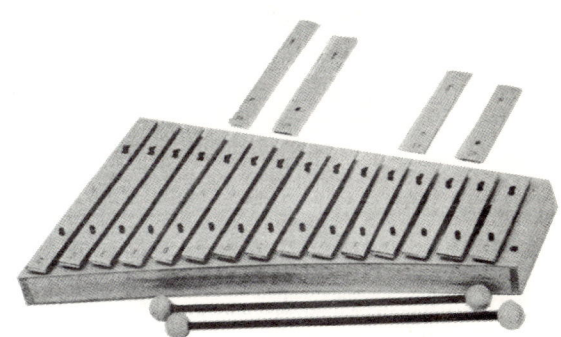

Photo courtesy of C. Bruno & Son, Inc., Melville, New York 11746.

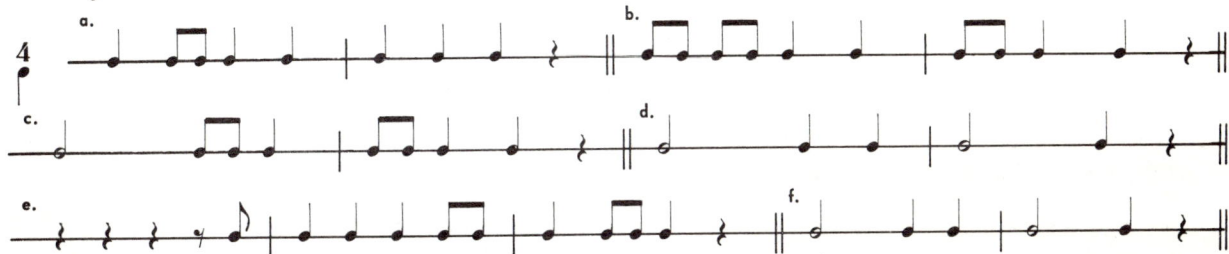

3. Tell class to do as you do, and begin the following rhythmic accompaniment:

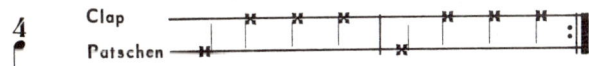

4. Tell class to continue the accompaniment above with you as they echo your speech pattern. Do the following:

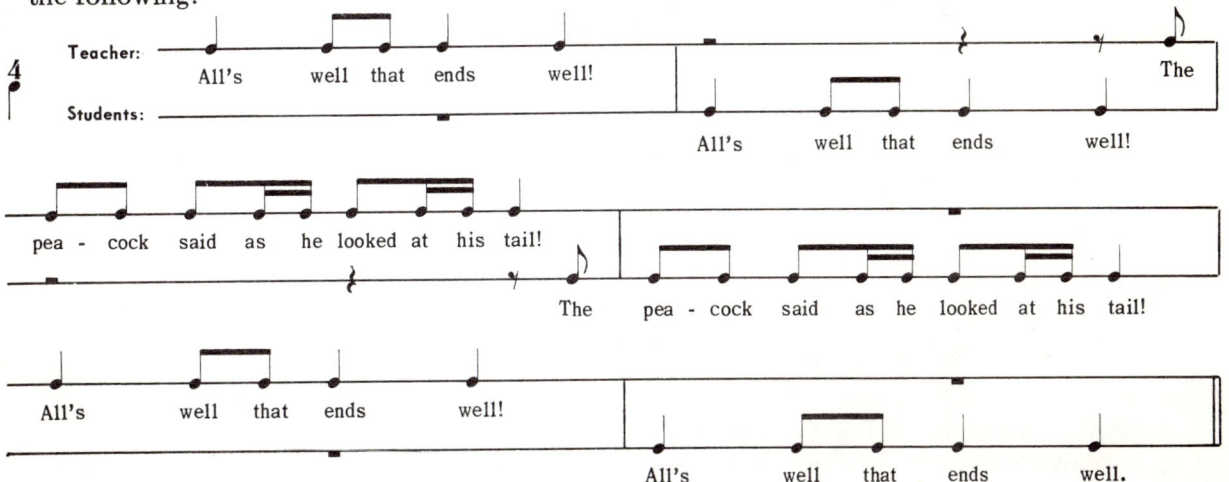

Teacher:
All's well that ends well!   The

Students:
                   All's well that ends well!

pea - cock said as he looked at his tail!

                   The pea - cock said as he looked at his tail!

All's well that ends well!

                   All's well that ends well.

5. To prepare children for playing the ostinato for alto xylophone (below) tell them to move their hands as you move yours (mirror); then do the following several times until children follow easily.

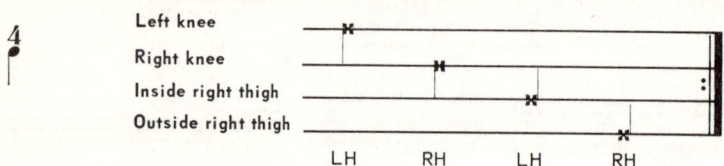

6. Select a child to play the ostinato. Remove the bars adjacent to the notes to be played, and remind child that his hands will move in the same direction as just practiced. Show child how to play ostinato, using two mallets, on the alto xylophone.

7. Select a small group to chant, "All's well! All's well!," in rhythm with the alto xylophone, and let them practice together.

8. Have the class begin doing the rhythmic accompaniment learned previously (clap, patschen). When they are rhythmically stable, have child playing the alto xylophone and the group chanting, "All's well!" begin. When all are secure, have remainder of class begin chanting the rhyme, as follows:

9. On other days, expand the experience by doing one or all of the following:

    a. Adding the following ostinati:

    b. Adding maracas to play the rhythm of the ostinato suggested for soprano glockenspiel, and the triangle to play the following:

    c. Encouraging individual children to improvise free movement, to chant as rest of class chants, plays, and does rhythmic accompaniment.

d. Encouraging children to turn chant into song using only sol, mi, and la, as:

All's well that ends well, The pea - cock said as he looked at his tail!

e. Encouraging children to turn the speech pattern into a speech round (canon).

Experiencing Triple Meter Using the Rhyme
Hickory Dickory Dock—For Primary Grades

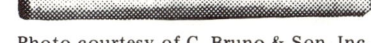

Photo courtesy of C. Bruno & Son, Inc., Melville, New York 11746.

1. Give children a period of tempo-dynamic clapping.
2. Tell children to listen, then echo your clapping. Echo clap the following sequence:

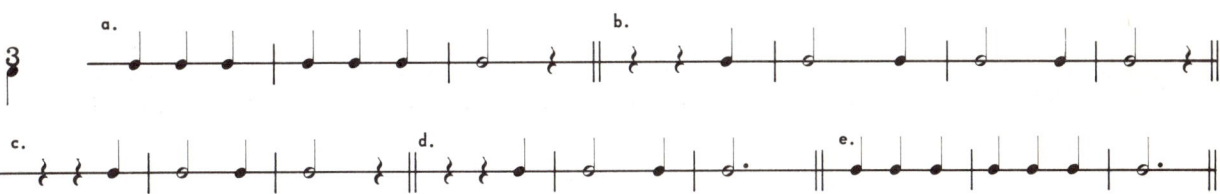

3. Tell class to do as you do; then begin the following:

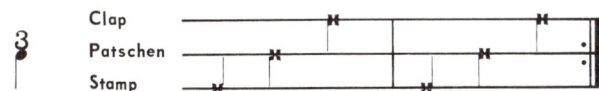

4. When children can do the above successfully, begin chanting the nursery rhyme while continuing to stamp, clap, and do patschen. Encourage them to follow you.

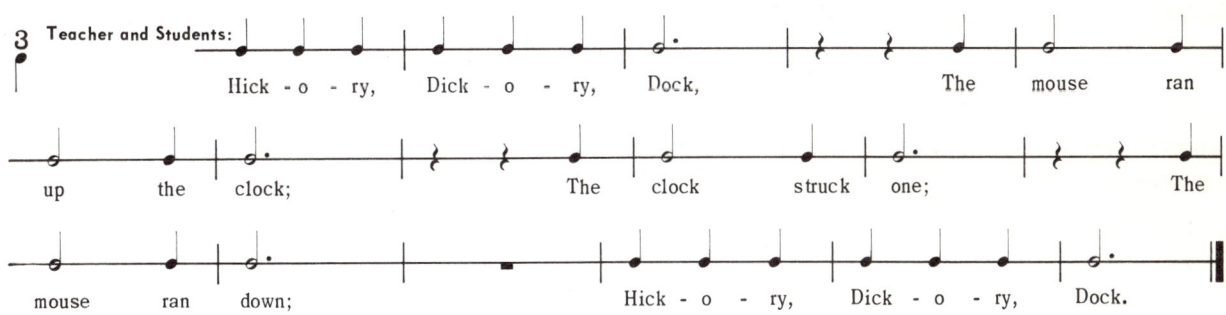

Hick - o - ry, Dick - o - ry, Dock, The mouse ran

up the clock; The clock struck one; The

mouse ran down; Hick - o - ry, Dick - o - ry, Dock.

5. When children can chant the nursery rhyme as they stamp, clap, and do patschen, select one child to play a tone block on every beat. To give him opportunity to practice, have entire class begin stamping, clapping, and doing patschen, then cue him in, playing on every beat. When he and class are rhythmically stable, have class begin chanting nursery rhyme.
6. Ask children which instrument might make the sound of the mouse running up, then down, the clock. Demonstrate a few to show how they might sound. (An ascending and descending glissando on a glockenspiel works very well.)
7. When class has decided which instrument they want to use, select one child to play the instrument, and decide where he will play each part. (The ascending glissando might well be played on the word "clock"; the descending, on "down.") Let him practice.

8. Have entire class begin stamping, clapping, and doing patschen. When they are well established, cue in child playing tone block, then the class chanting the nursery rhyme. Signal the child playing the part of the mouse running up and down the clock to play at proper times.

9. Ask class what other part of the nursery rhyme might be played by an instrument. (The clock striking "one.") Ask them which instrument might best play the clock striking "one." (A triangle, or a note on one of the xylophones or metallophones would do.) Select child to play the instrument on "one" in the nursery rhyme.

10. Have entire class begin stamping, clapping, and doing patschen. When they are rhythmically stable, have child playing tone block begin. Next have the class begin chanting the rhyme. Bring in sound effects of mouse and clock at proper times.

11. To deepen children's understanding of meter, on another day, have them do the rhyme in 6/8 meter (duple compound). To simulate a clock ticking, use two differently pitched tone blocks, as below:

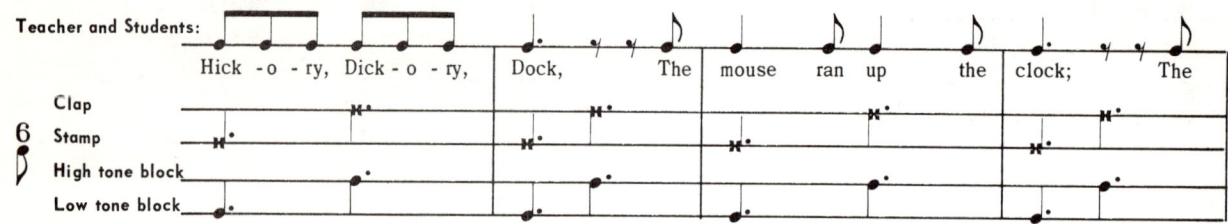

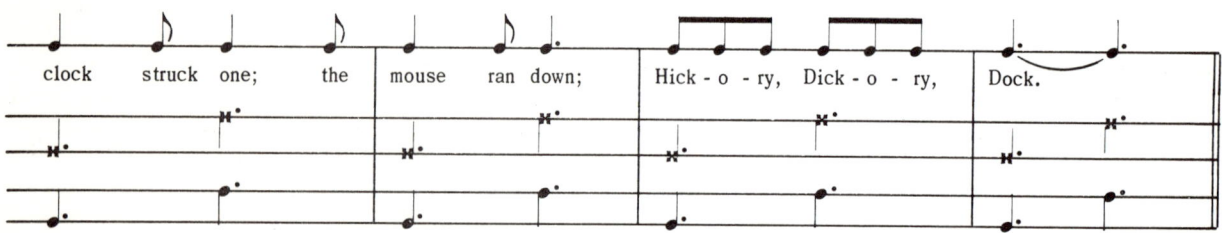

Experiencing Triple Meter Using Names of Children in a Rhyme—For Intermediate Grades

1. Give children an experience in "sing backs." (Sing one-measure phrases from the pentatonic scale, using syllables and hand signals, as children echo you.)

2. Tell children to do the following with you:

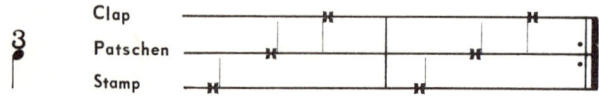

3. Tell children to continue the rhythmic accompaniment above as they listen, then echo your chant. Chant the following, reflecting in your voice the contrasting tone colors suggested by each phrase.

4. Tell children you would like to see if they can do the rhyme through without stopping and without missing a beat as they do the rhythmic accompaniment. Have them begin rhythmic accompaniment (stamp, patschen, clap). After two measures give them cue to begin chant. Have them continue rhythmic accompaniment two measures after end of chant.

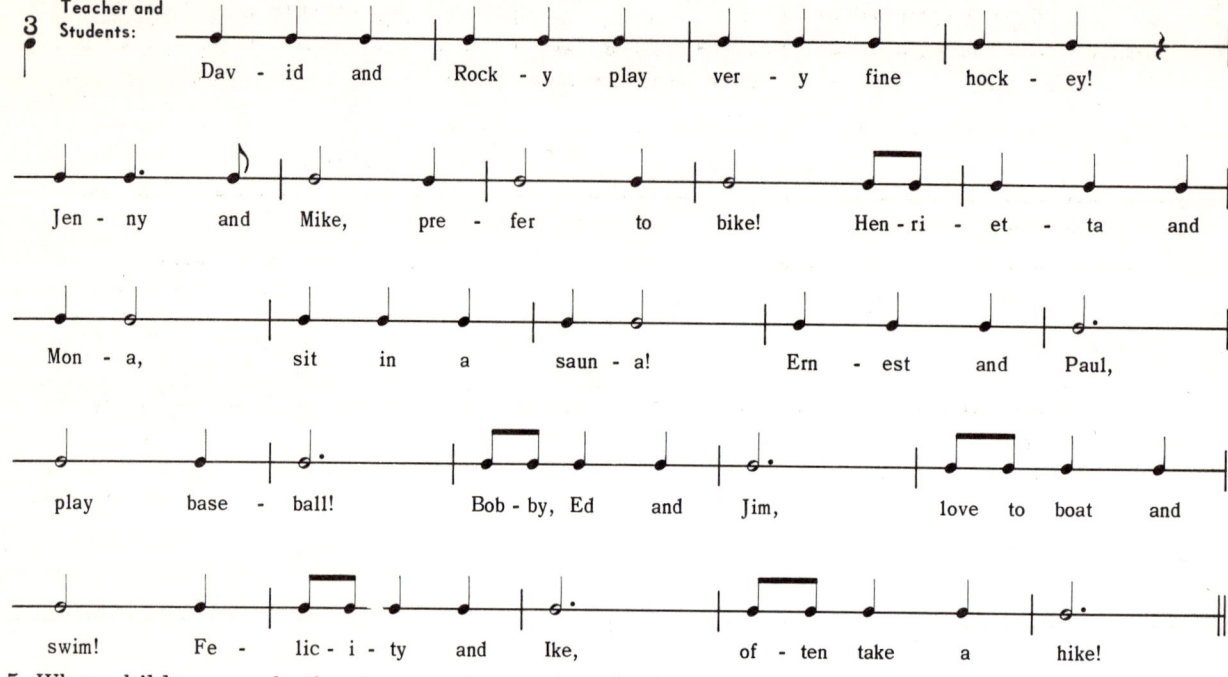

5. When children can do the above easily, teach a child to play the following on timpani:

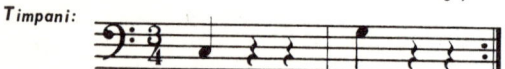

6. Have children chant the rhyme and accompany it rhythmically (stamp, patschen, and clap), as the child playing the timpani plays his part.

7. Expand on the experience in one or all of the following ways:

    a. Help children create a speech canon, dividing class into two groups, group two beginning one measure after group one.
    b. Help children create the following orchestration:

    c. Help children turn chant into a song using only the tones of the pentatonic scale.
    d. Have children create dramatizations, dance steps, or movement patterns to accompany the rhyme.

Experiencing Irregular Meter (5s) Using Names in Rhymes—For Upper Grades

1. Begin a steady accompaniment, as follows, indicating that the class should follow you:

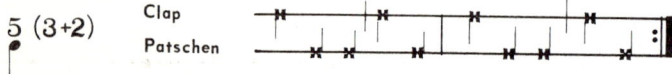

2. Tell class to continue to clap and to do patschen with you in the pattern above as they listen to you chant, then echo what they hear. Do the following:

3. Continuing the same clapping and patschen accompaniment, tell children to chant all four rhymes through, allowing two measures of the rhythmic accompaniment to precede and follow the rhyme.

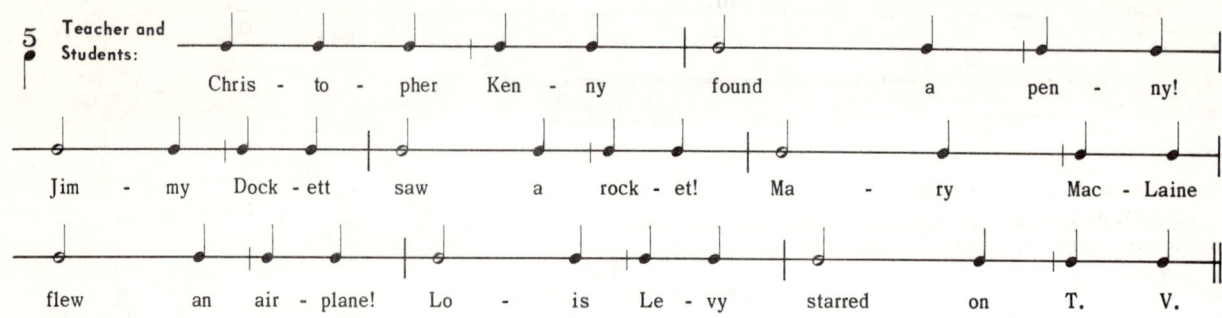

4. Have children chant rhyme with rhythmic accompaniment alone—no help from you unless absolutely necessary.
5. To check the ability of children to remember the rhyme patterns, have them say only the first and last words of the rhyme ("Christopher" and "T.V."), *thinking* all the other words as they do the rhythmic accompaniment for the entire rhyme.
6. Expand on the experience in one or all of the following ways:

   a. Have children step pattern of words without chanting.
   b. Help children learn to accompany chant with the following ostinato:

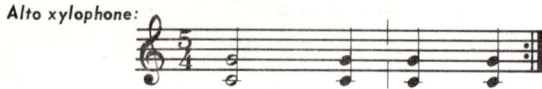

   c. Have children chant rhyme as they do one of the following rhythmic ostinati:

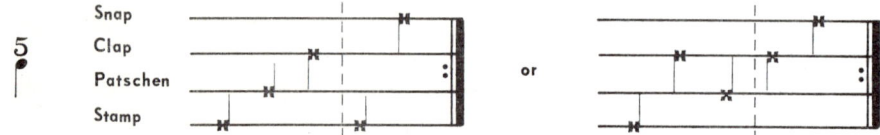

   d. Help children turn chant into a song, as:

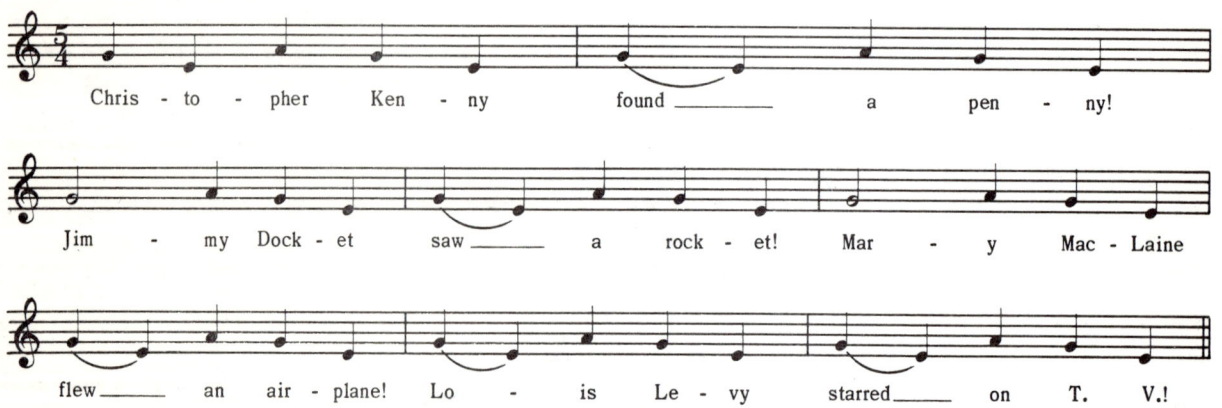

   e. Help children turn rhyme into a speech canon (second part beginning on fourth best, as first part says, "Kenny").

Experiencing Irregular Meter (7s) Using Names of People and Places—For Upper Grades

1. Begin a steady accompaniment, as follows, indicating that the class should follow you:

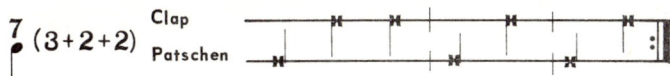

New Era Instruments, made in England by Premier Drum Company, LTD., exclusively distributed in the U.S. by Selmer, Elkhart, Indiana.

2. Tell class to continue to clap and to do patschen in pattern above as they listen to you chant, then to echo what they hear. Do the following:

Teacher: John and Jim Brown,
Students: John and Jim Brown,

Drove to York - town!
Drove to York - town!

Jen - ni - fer, Jean and Roy,
Jen - ni - fer, Jean and Roy,

Flew out to Ill - i - nois!
Flew out to Ill - i - nois!

Paul - ine Bel - mont,
Paul - ine Bel - mont,

Skied up in Maine and Ver - mont!
Skied up in Maine and Ver - mont!

Dave, John and Joe,
Dave, John and Joe,

Jet - planed to Id - a - ho!
Jet - planed to Id - a - ho!

I - rene, E - laine and Han - nah,
I - rene, E - laine and Han - nah,

Walked to In - di - a - na!
Walked to In - di - a - na!

3. Tell class that this time you would like to see if they can do the rhyme through with you, without stopping, using the same rhythmic accompaniment. Have class join you in doing the clap-patschen

accompaniment used above. When they are rhythmically stable, begin the chant, encouraging them to join you. Continue rhythmic accompaniment for two measures after end of chant.

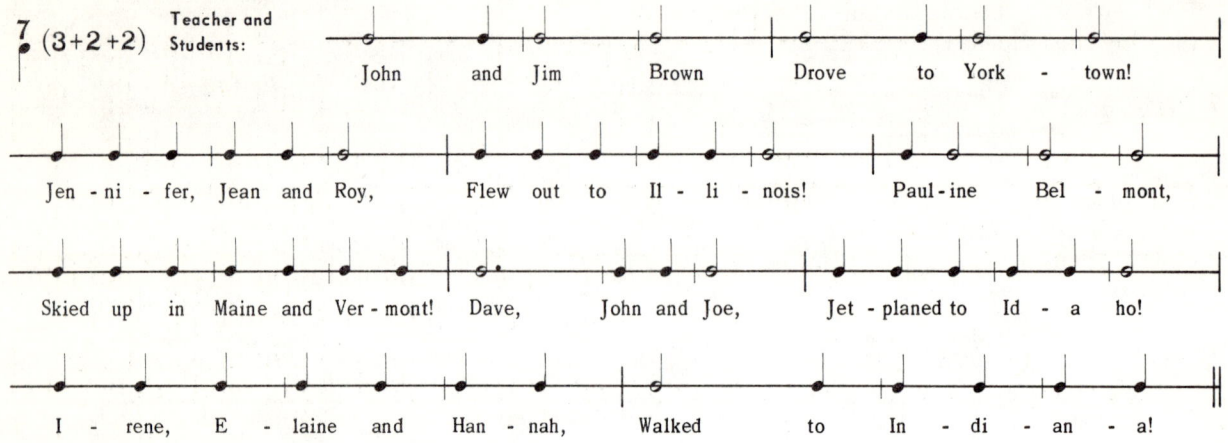

4. On other days, expand the experience in one or all of the following ways:

   a. Help children do this in canon form—that is, divide the class into two groups. Have entire class begin rhythmic accompaniment. When they are stable rhythmically, have group one begin chanting. As group one begins second measure, have group two begin at beginning.
   b. Help children create melody for the words using only notes in the pentatonic scale.
   c. Help children learn to accompany rhyme using one or more of the following ostinati:

   d. Have children orchestrate with rhythm instruments:

   e. Have children accompany rhyme with one of the following rhythm accompaniments:

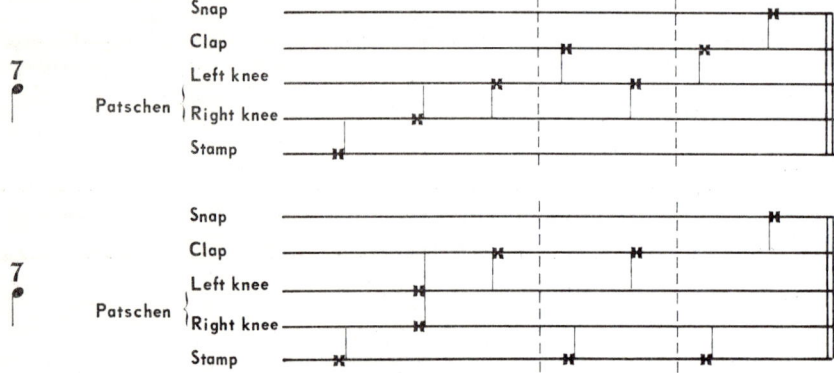

Experiencing Contrasting Meters Using the Chant *Two Little Astronauts*—For Intermediate and Upper Grades

1. Give class the following experience in echo clapping:

2. Have entire class begin doing the rhythmic pattern below. When they are stable rhythmically, tell them to listen, then echo your chant while continuing the rhythmic accompaniment.[2]

2. The teacher may find this speech pattern too long for intermediate grades. In this case, it may be treated as an ABA form by adapting as follows: "Two little astronauts, nibbling on a prune, Decided to visit the man in the moon. 'I'll get the rocket,' said one of the pair! 'Good,' said the other, 'And I'll comb my hair!' Two little astronauts, nibbling on a prune, Decided to visit the man in the moon."

3. Divide the class into two groups. Tell group one to chant, clap, and do patschen on the phrases in duple meter (4s); group two to chant, clap, and do patschen on the phrases in triple meter (3s).

Have group one begin, and help, if necessary. Bring in group two at the proper time, and help whenever necessary. The following should result:

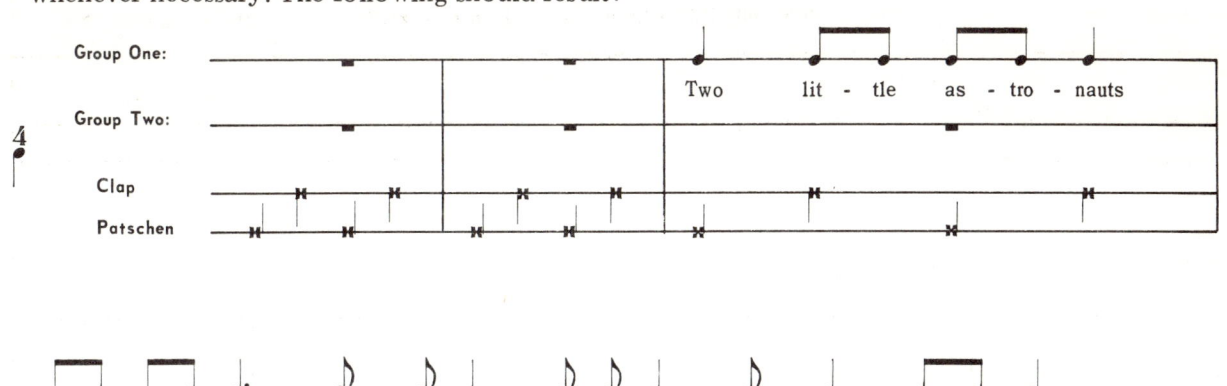

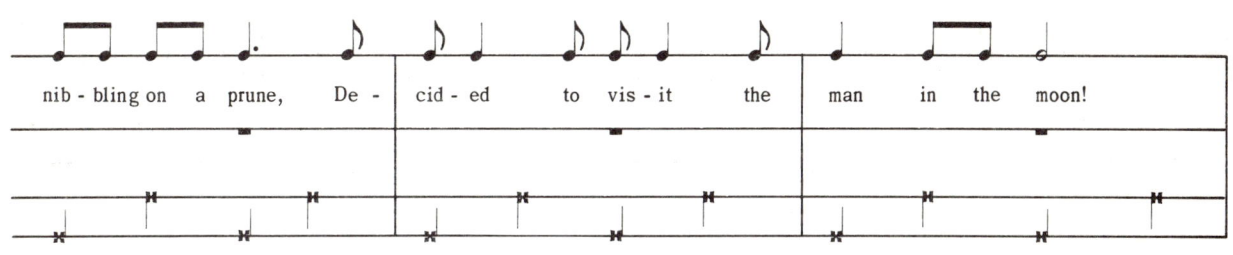

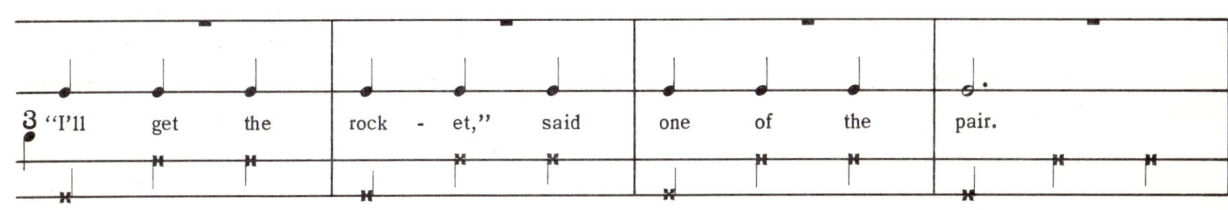

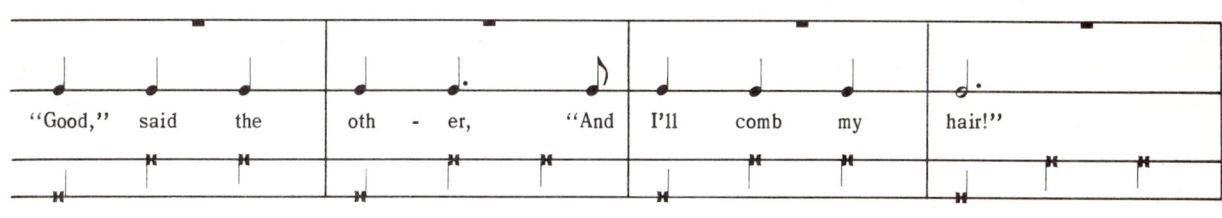

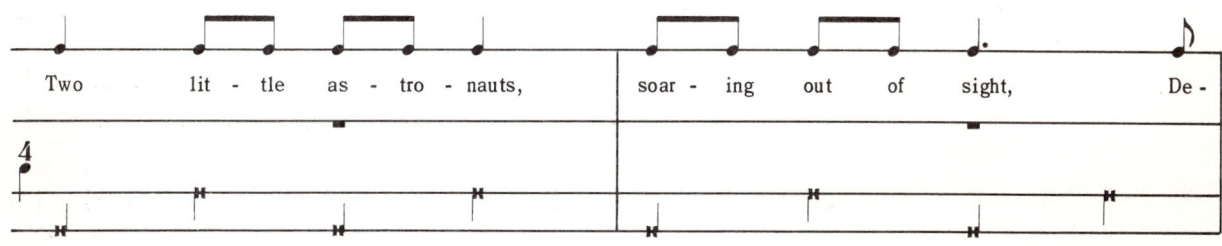

4. Repeat above, switching groups—group one becoming group two and group two becoming group one.

5. Expand the experience by using one or all of the following:
   a. Have class chant the entire rhyme as they do the rhythmic accompaniment.
   b. Teach class one or more of the following accompaniments:

Timpani: (playing on sections in duple meter)

Percussion: (playing on sections in triple meter)

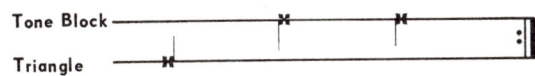

Alto xylophone: (playing on sections in duple meter)

Soprano xylophone: (playing on sections in duple meter)

Alto metallophone: (playing on sections in triple meter)

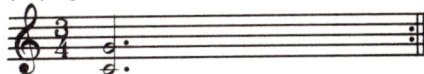

Alto glockenspiel: (playing on sections in triple meter)

Rhythmic accompaniment: (for sections in duple meter)

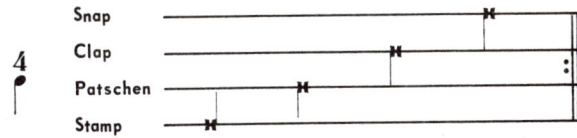

Rhythmic accompaniment: (for sections in triple meter)

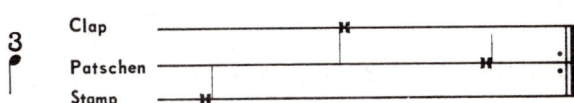

Experiencing Contrasting Meters Using the Proverb
All That Glitters Is Not Gold—**For Upper Grades**

1. Give the following experience in echo clapping:

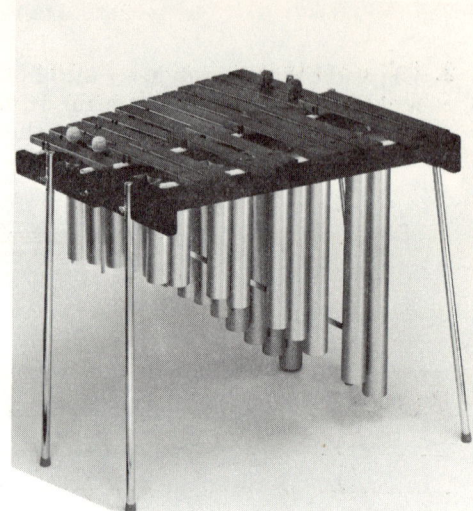

Photo furnished through the courtesy of the Kitching
Division of Ludwig Industries.

2. Tell class that you are going to see how quickly they can switch meters. Tell them to do exactly as you do; then do the following many times, changing the sequence each time.

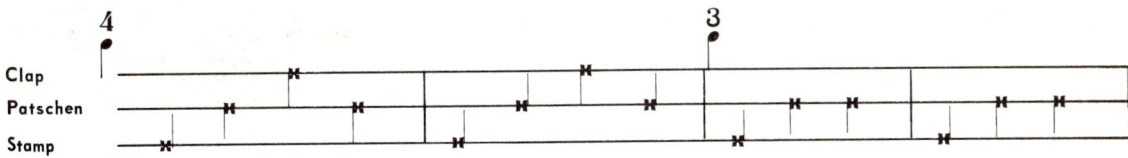

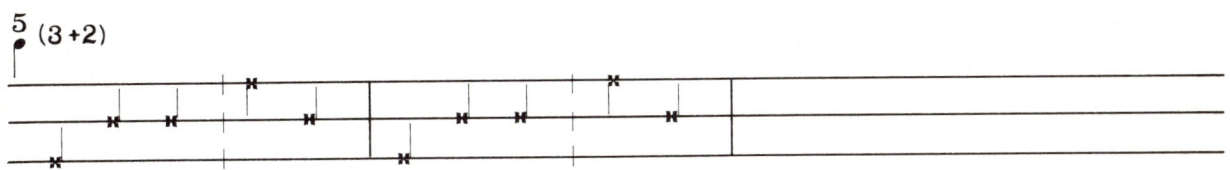

3. When class can do the above easily, tell them you would like to challenge them still further. Tell them to follow your rhythmic movements, as above, and at the same time to listen to, then echo, your chant. The following should result:

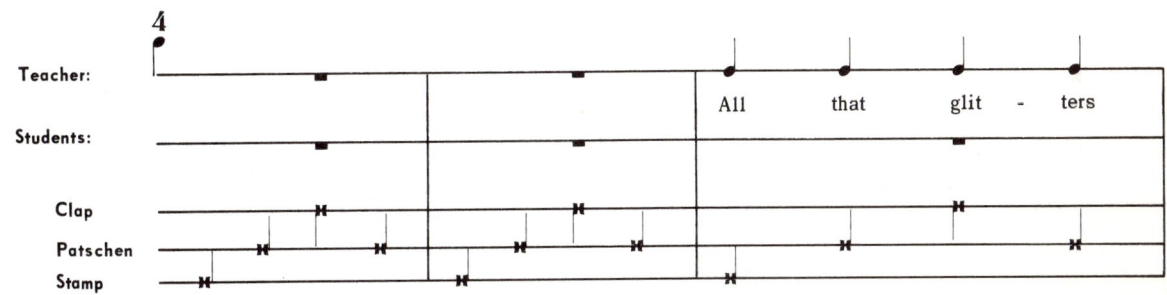

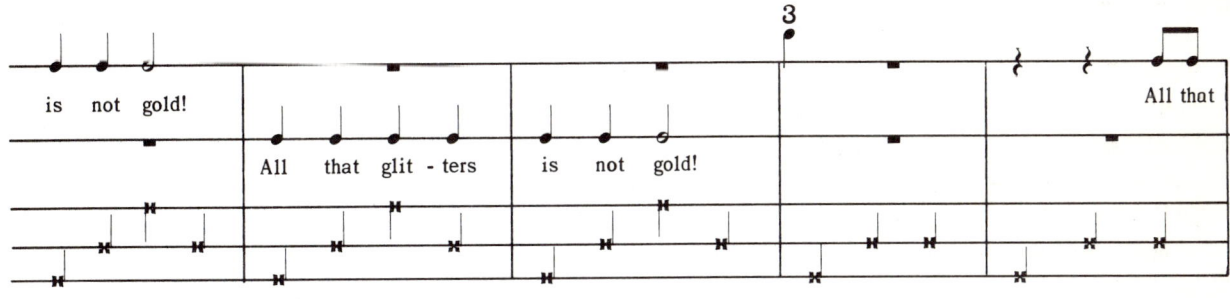

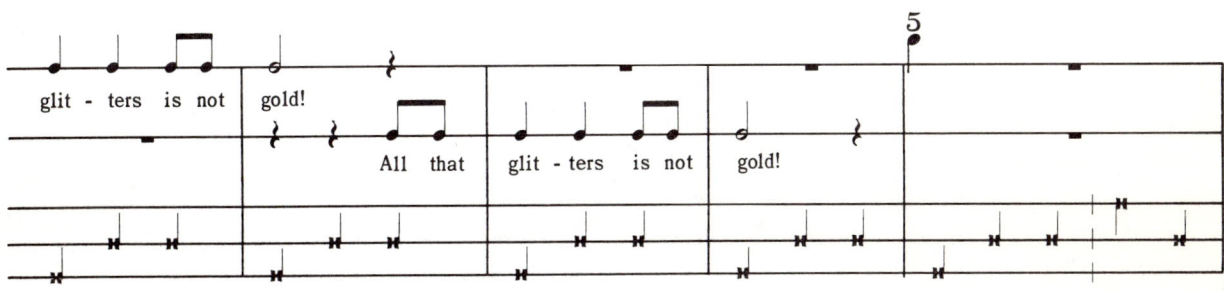

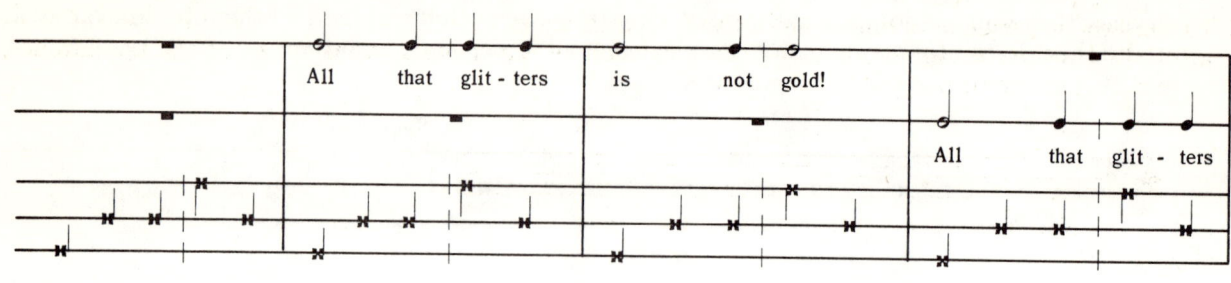

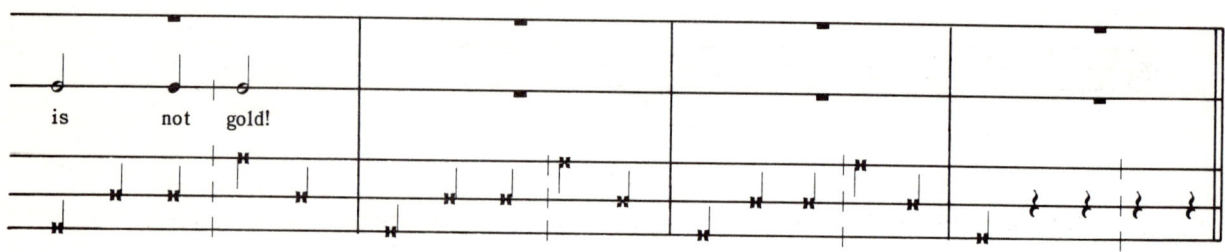

4. Tell children you would like to see if they can do the chant in all three meters, one immediately following the other, as below:

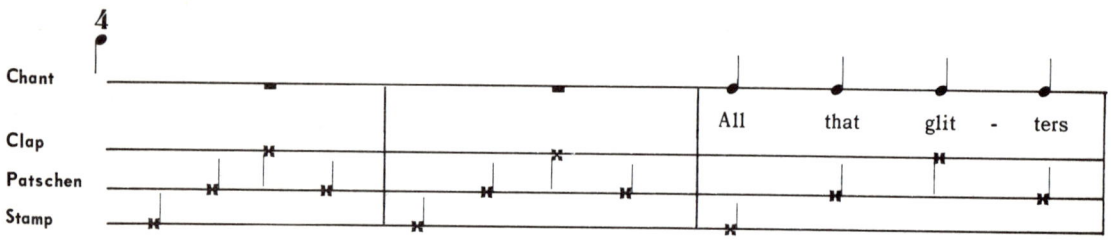

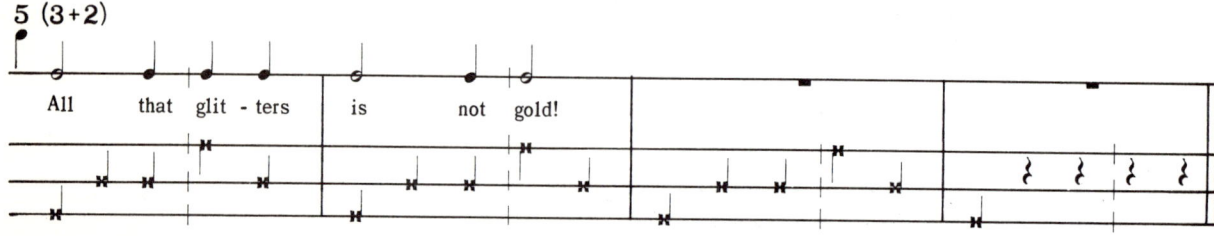

5. Expand the experience in one or all of the following ways:
   a. Help children create original melodies in each of the meters, using notes of the pentatonic scale. A group of possibilities follows:

   b. Help children learn to play ostinati for each meter. Following are possible examples:

Soprano xylophone:

Alto xylophone:

Alto glockenspiel:

Soprano glockenspiel:

Bass xylophone:

Alto glockenspiel:

c. Help children learn the following rhythmic accompaniments;

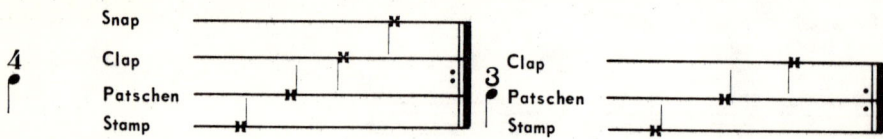

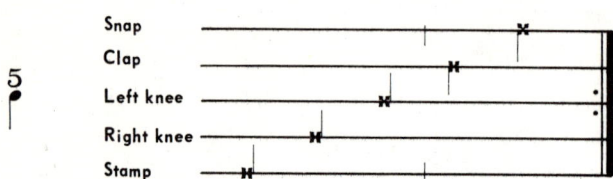

CHAPTER 4

Using Bodily Movement

The joy of childhood is perhaps best seen in the free, uninhibited movement of children at play. Children love to move.

The development of an inner feeling for rhythm—so dependent on abundant joyful experience with bodily movement—can thus utilize activities and experiences which children thoroughly enjoy. Party games, simple dances, floor designs, circles, squares, one line of children moving rhythmically against another—all are part of the rhythmic experience. Children walk, run, skip, sway, and bend using any movement and rhythm suggested by the word, the rhyme, the song, or the story. Responses can reflect either a specific relationship to each word (a movement for each syllable) or a general rhythmic response to the pulse.

All help internalize the meter, the pulse, the rhythm pattern, the phrase. All help prepare the child for later participation in more sophisticated musical experiences.

Stepping the Rhythms of Names of Children—For Primary or Intermediate Grades

1. Give children an experience in "echo sing-backs" using tones and hand signals they know from the pentatonic scale.
2. Give children a period of echo clapping.
3. Tell class to echo you as you clap and chant. Do the following, letting your voice reflect the weight (heavy or light) and pitch (high or low) suggested by each name.[1]

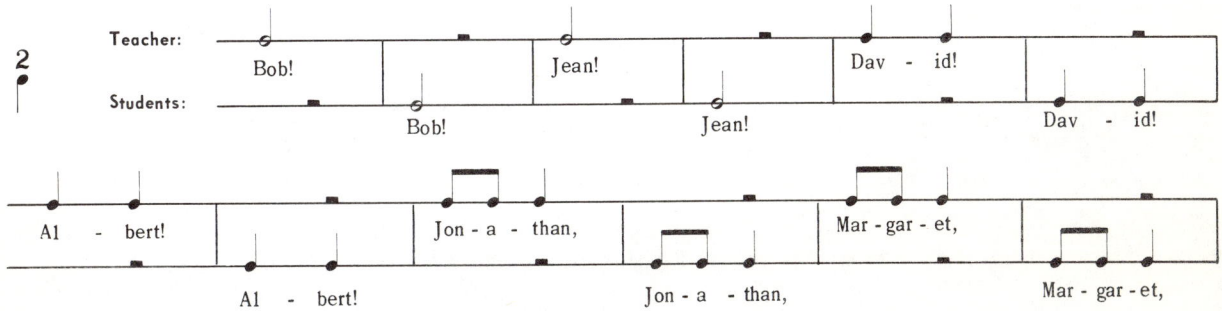

_____
1. The names of children in the class may be substituted for the names used here.

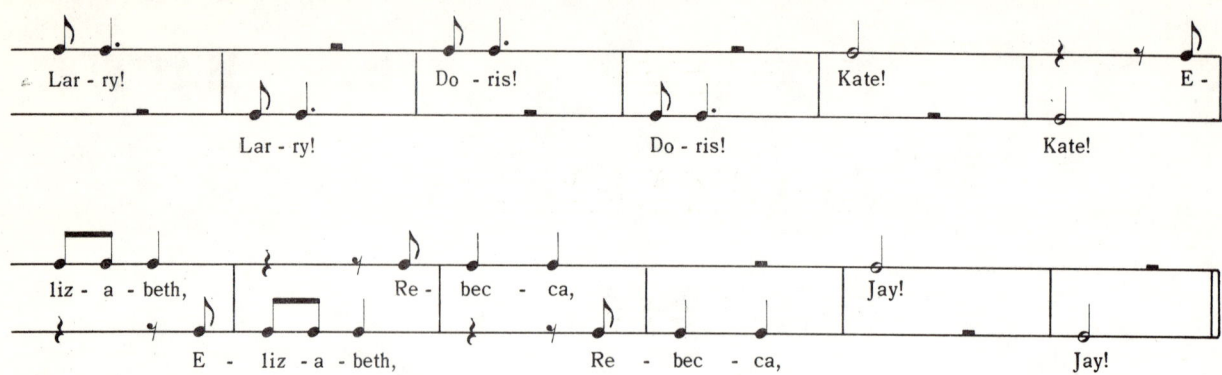

4. When children can successfully echo chant and clap the above, tell them you would like to see if they can recognize names from the rhythm only. Clap individual names, without chanting. After each name, ask children to identify the name clapped. As each name is identified, ask the child who identified it to *step* the name, making his feet do exactly what your hands did.
5. Expand the experience in one or all of the following ways:
   a. Select a few favorite names and help children create a rhyme from them. For example:

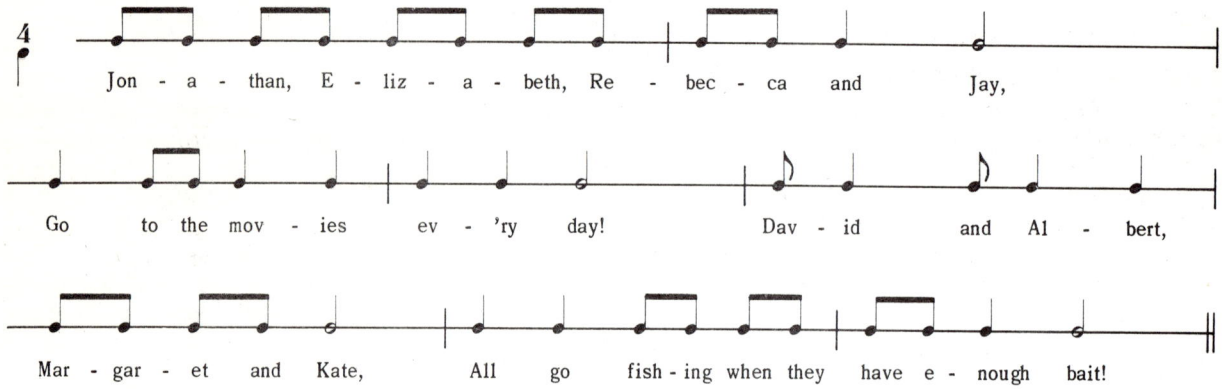

   b. Have some children step the rhyme or create a rhythmic improvisation to it as the rest of the class chants and claps it.
   c. Help children create a speech canon: Divide class into two groups; first group beginning, second group starting two measures later.
   d. Help children create a song using notes of the pentatonic scale. One possibility is:

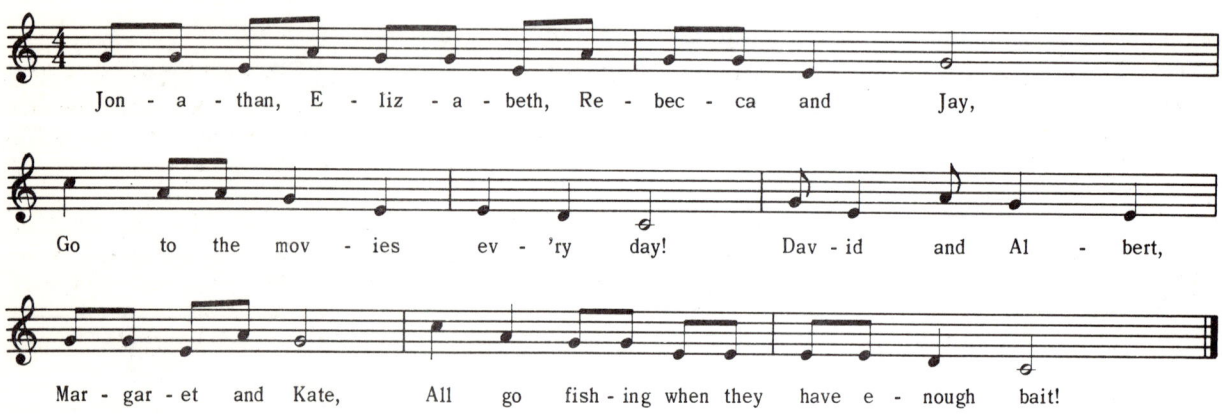

   e. Help children create an orchestration for the song. Some possibilities are:

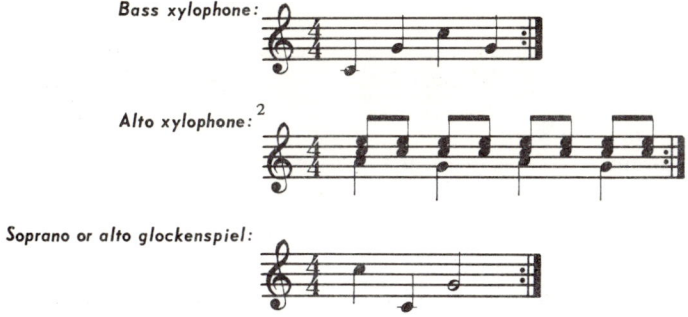

Bass xylophone:

Alto xylophone:²

Soprano or alto glockenspiel:

f. Give children the experience immediately following in which they create a circle game out of the rhythms created with their names.
g. Give children a similar experience using names of animals or cities.

Creating a Circle Game Out of Rhythms Suggested by Names—For Primary or Intermediate Grades

(Children should have had previous experience stepping their own names.)

1. Give class a period of tempo-dynamic clapping.
2. Give class a period of echo clapping.
3. Remind children of their past experience stepping names. Tell them that today you would like to make a game out of stepping names, but that first you would like to be certain that they remember how to step their own names.
4. Tell class that first you will all clap and chant the name of each child in the class. Go about the room clapping and chanting the name of each child, encouraging entire class to participate.
5. Tell class that now you would like to see if each person can step his own name. Go about the room letting each child step and chant his name, as the class maintains a steady rhythmic accompaniment.
6. Explain that the game begins with everyone doing the following:

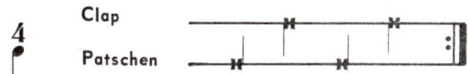

Clap

Patschen

7. Have class do the above many times until they are rhythmically stable.
8. Explain the game, as follows:
   All children form a circle. One child is secretly given a button (or other tiny object). The entire class does the rhythmic accompaniment above. One child is "it" and upon signal begins stepping his name, as practiced, across the circle to a position behind some other person, who then begins stepping *his* name across the circle to a position behind another person. The game continues until someone steps his name to a position behind the person with the button. The person who does so is the winner.
9. Have class form circle. Have them close eyes and give the button to a child who has a pocket in which to put it. Have class open eyes. Select a child to be "it"—the first to step his name. Have entire class begin the rhythmic accompaniment. Signal the child to begin stepping his name and help class chant his name as it continues accompaniment. When it is time for each new child to begin stepping, signal him to do so, and begin chanting his name, continuing until he reaches the next person, while continuing the rhythmic accompaniment.

---

2. In orchestrations which call for more than two notes to be played simultaneously, the teacher may either use two children (in this case, one to play the eighth notes and one to play the quarter notes) or use the experience to encourage the development of two-mallet technique. That is, she may help children learn to hold two mallets in one hand, the second mallet resting between the index and middle fingers, both stems beneath the palm.

Using Bodily Movement to Accompany the Rhyme
*Baa, Baa, Black Sheep—*For Primary Grades

(This experience should take place in a room so arranged that children can move freely in a circle.)

1. Give children a period of tempo-dynamic clapping.
2. Give children the following experience in echo clapping and chanting:

3. Tell children you would like to see if they can clap and chant the entire rhyme, as below:

4. If space is available, have entire class form a circle. (If necessary, let a small group form circle, the rest of class remaining seated.) Tell children to step as you clap the following:

(A drum may be used instead of clapping.)

5. When children are moving easily in the exact beat you are playing or clapping, tell them to chant and clap *Baa, Baa, Black Sheep* with you. The following should result:

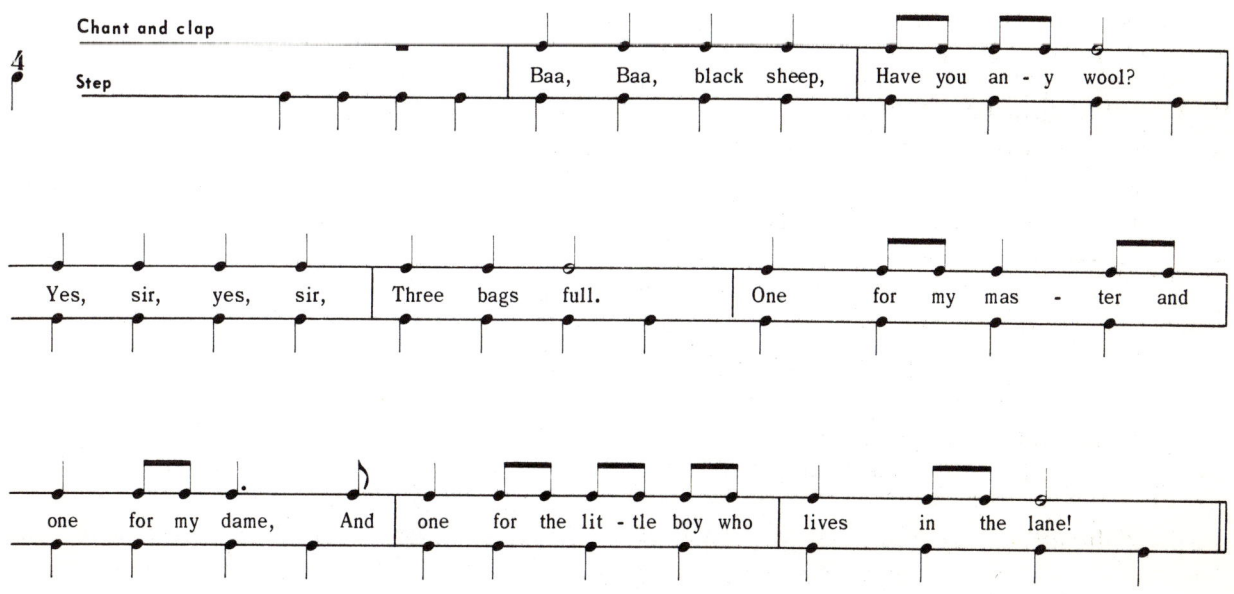

6. When children can step the basic beat, and can clap and chant the rhyme, tell them to continue to step as they clap and *sing* the song with you. The following should result:

Clap and sing:

Baa, baa, black sheep, Have you an - y wool _____

Step:

Yes, sir, yes, sir, Three bags __ full _____ One for my mas - ter and

one for my dame, And one for the lit - tle boy who lives in the lane! ____

7. Expand the experience by helping children learn one or all of the following accompaniments:

Alto xylophone:

Bass xylophone:

Soprano glockenspiel:

Soprano or alto metallophone:

Timpani:

Using Bodily Movement to Accompany the Rhyme
Jack and Jill—For Second or Third Grade

(This experience should take place in a room so arranged that children can move freely in a circle.)

1. Give children a period of tempo-dynamic clapping.
2. Give children a period of echo clapping.
3. Have children form a circle. Tell them to step in rhythm with your drum.

Play:  as chil-

Photo courtesy of C. Bruno & Son, Inc., Melville, New York 11746.

dren step. (Clapping may be substituted for the drum.)

4. When children can follow the beat above, tell them to continue to step in that rhythm as you clap a different rhythm. Clap the following rhythmic ostinato:

5. Tell children to clap the rhythmic ostinato with you, making certain they continue to step as above.
6. When children can step the basic meter and clap the rhythmic ostinato without becoming confused, begin chanting the following:

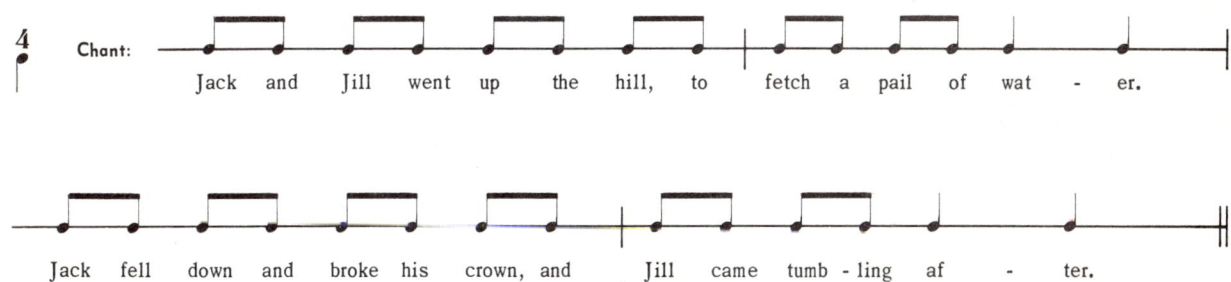

7. When children can step the basic beat and clap the rhythmic ostinato as you chant the rhyme, encourage them to join you in chanting the rhyme.
8. When children can chant the first verse of the rhyme, clap the ostinato, and step the basic beat, help them chant the second verse as they clap and step.

Verse 2

9. Help children to turn this into a song using tones from the pentatonic scale. One possible melody might be:

Jack and Jill went up the hill, to fetch a pail of wat - er;

Jack fell down and broke his crown, and Jill came tumb-ling af - ter. Then up Jack got and home did trot, As

fast as he could cap - er, And went to bed to mend his head, With vin - e - gar and brown pap - er.

10. Expand the experience in one or all of the following ways:

   a. Teach a child to play the stepping rhythm on a drum:

   b. Teach a child to play the clapping pattern on the tone block or hand drum:

   c. Teach individual children to play the following accompaniments:[3]

Experiencing ABA Form Through Bodily Movement, Using the Rhyme
Follow Me, Honey—For Intermediate Grades

1. Tell class you are going to do a chant which has motions. Tell them to listen, chant, and do the motions with you, as soon as possible. Do the following as many times as necessary until class follows easily:

---

3. In this and in all experiences using instruments, when the accompaniment is too complex or too difficult, do not hesitate to simplify.

Follow Me, Honey!

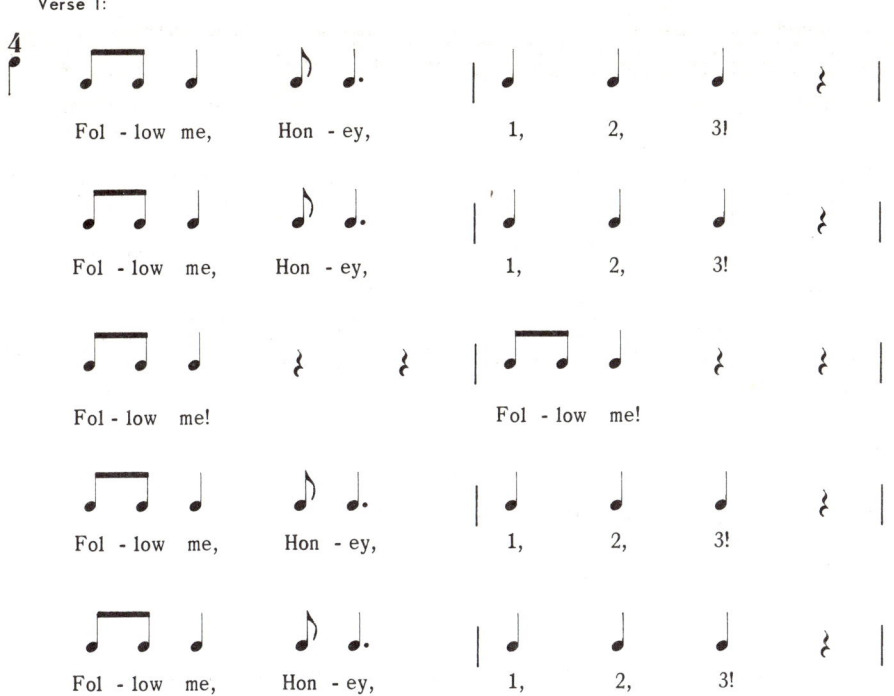

Verse 2: Tap your knees, Honey, 1, 2, 3!

Verse 3: Sway a little, Honey, 1, 2, 3!

Motions: *Verse 1:*
On the word *follow*, tap both hands on head.
On the word *me*, tap both hands on shoulders.
On first syllable of word, *Honey*, stamp foot.
On each of the words 1, 2, and 3, clap hands.

Verse 2:
On each of the words, *tap*, *your*, and *knees*, tap
both hands on knees.
On the word *Honey*, stamp foot.
On each of the words 1, 2, and 3, clap hands.

Verse 3:
On the words *Sway a little*, sway.
On the word *Honey*, stamp foot.
On each of the words *one*, *two*, and *three*, clap hands.

2. Ask children which of these lines is different from the others. (The third line of each verse.)
3. Ask them what they could call the third line if the first two lines were called "A." ("B.")
4. Explain that this chant is in a form we call "ABA": the beginning and end are alike and are therefore called "A," and the middle part is different and called "B." Print ABA on the board to help them remember it.

5. Tell class you would like to see if they can do the chant with the motions only, keeping the exact rhythm throughout. Help them by doing it with them.
6. Tell class you would like to see if they can turn it into a song. Tell everyone to sing the first line. Ask for volunteers to sing it alone. Let class decide which they like best. Write it on the board. Have everyone sing it. (If possible, select a tune which falls in the pentatonic scale.)
7. Help class work out rest of song in the following manner: Let volunteers sing a second line alone, preceded each time by class singing first line. Have class select second line. Write second line on board. Have class sing first two lines, followed by volunteers singing a third line, and so forth.
8. One class created the following:

9. Teach class to play the following ostinati accompaniments:

Soprano and alto xylophone:

Timpani:

Using Bodily Movement to Accompany the Song *Oh, Susanna*—**For Upper Grades**
1. Give class a period of "echo sing-backs."
2. Give class a period of echo patschen, stamping, clapping, and snapping fingers.
3. Tell class that you would like to see if they can clap the words and step the meter of a familiar song, *Oh, Susanna*. Tell them you will give them the signal to begin stepping the meter, then to clap and sing the words. Signal class to begin stepping meter (remaining seated), then to begin singing and clapping words, as below:

4. When class can do the above, seated, have them stand and do the same—stepping meter with their feet, clapping, and singing the words.
5. When class can successfully step the meter and clap and sing the words, tell them you would like to see if they can *step* the words. They may either stand or sit down, but in either case, they should alternate feet in stepping the word patterns.
6. When children can easily step the word patterns with their feet, tell them you would like to give them a really difficult rhythmic task—you would like them to step the words and clap the meter.
7. Taking a very slow tempo, have class begin clapping the meter. When they are rhythmically stable, signal them to begin singing and stepping the words. If there is difficulty (and there will be), tell them to *think* the words instead of singing them, and break the song down, phrase by phrase. If difficulty persists, let part of group clap meter as the others step words, everyone chanting or singing. Then reverse groups.
8. On other days, let class try one of the following:

   a. Stepping the words and clapping the meter of other familiar songs.
   b. Stepping the meter as they say first and last words only, hearing the remainder in their heads.
   c. Creating different movements for alternate phrases (stepping beat of words on one phrase, clapping beat of words on next phrase, and so forth.)

Creating Melodic and Rhythmic Improvisations Using the Rhythm of the Polka—For Upper Grades

1. Put the rhythm of the polka on the chalkboard, omitting the words for rhythmic counting.

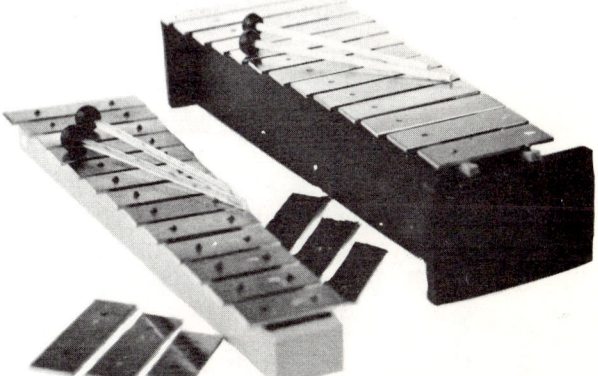

Photo courtesy of Lyons Band Company, Elmhurst, Illinois.

2. Explain that this is the rhythm of the polka. Ask for a volunteer to clap it. Have entire class clap it, saying the words for rhythmic counting. Repeat until they can do it easily at a moderate tempo.
3. Explain that you would like them to clap this rhythm as you sing a melody, and that after you finish you would like them to sing the melody with you.
4. Have class begin clapping rhythm at a moderate tempo. After four measures, begin singing a melody in the polka rhythm, ending in a way that makes the phrase a kind of "question." For convenience, let us assume you sing the following using a neutral syllable or syllables—la, loo, lee, lay, and so forth.

5. Immediately after you sing the last note, indicate that the class should sing the phrase with you. Have them sing it several times, without stopping, until they know it.
6. Explain that the phrase they sang was really the first part of a longer phrase—the part that seems to pose a "question." Explain that now you would like them to sing this phrase again, and then immediately to sing an "answering" phrase.
7. Select a child to play the rhythm of the polka on the tone block. Have him begin playing. Have class begin singing the "question" phrase on the upbeat of the fifth measure, indicating that each should go on and sing his "answer" immediately after the conclusion of the "question" phrase.
8. Make a positive comment on their efforts at singing the answering phrase, and ask for volunteers to sing their answers alone. Select several children. Explain that the class will sing the "question," and that immediately afterward you will point to a volunteer who will begin to sing his answer immediately, without missing a beat. At the conclusion of his answer, the class will sing the "question" again, followed by an answer from another volunteer, and so on until all volunteers have sung an answer alone.
9. Have child playing polka rhythm begin. On the upbeat of the fifth measure, have class begin singing. Just before the end of the "question" phrase, point to a volunteer and have him sing his "answer" without missing a beat. (Help, by indicating in an unobtrusive way, the rhythm and length of the phrase.) After he finishes, bring in class again, without missing a beat, singing the "question." Proceed in this way until all volunteers have had an opportunity to sing their "answers" to the class' question.
10. Make positive comments on the efforts of the children singing the "answers." Ask class which "answer" they prefer. Get a consensus of the favorite "answer" and have that child sing it again, helping him, if necessary, to remember what he did by having class sing the "question" again, followed by his "answer."
11. Put the answer on the chalkboard, below the question. Let us assume the total melody is now as follows:

12. Have class sing entire song as you point to the notes.
13. Ask if anyone knows the dance steps for the polka. If so, let a child demonstrate it; if not, demonstrate it yourself:

14. Ask child playing polka rhythm on tone block to play as children experiment dancing the polka. Let as many children experiment with the dance as there is time and space. When ample experimentation has taken place, select several children to dance the polka in couples and let them practice together with tone block until they can do the dance easily.

15. Explain that you would like the tone block to provide an introduction as before, and the class to sing the complete melody as the children dance the polka. Have child playing tone block begin. On the upbeat of the fifth measure, have class begin singing and children begin dancing.

16. At the conclusion, explain that what was just heard and seen was Section A of a rondo. Explain that for Section B, C, and D, you would like individual children to improvise a dance, using the polka step as the basis for their movement, but feeling free to move in any way they like to show differences in range (high and low), weight (heavy and light), and so on. Select volunteers to dance B, C, and D. Remind child playing tone block to continue playing throughout.

17. Have tone block begin. Bring in class singing and couples dancing on upbeat of fifth measure. At conclusion of Section A, have child selected for Section B begin dancing, helping him by indicating rhythm for the full eight measures of his section, and having class begin singing and dancers dancing immediately after he finishes, without missing a beat. Bring in Sections C, A, D, A in the same manner, always without missing a beat.

18. Make positive comments on the improvisations for B, C, and D.

19. Help children create an orchestration for the rondo. With the creation of each ostinato, select a new set of children to improvise Sections B, C, and D, and have class do entire rondo through again. One possible orchestration follows below:

Section A:

Sections B, C, D:

20. On other days, help children use other dance steps to develop a rondo. Some possibilities are:

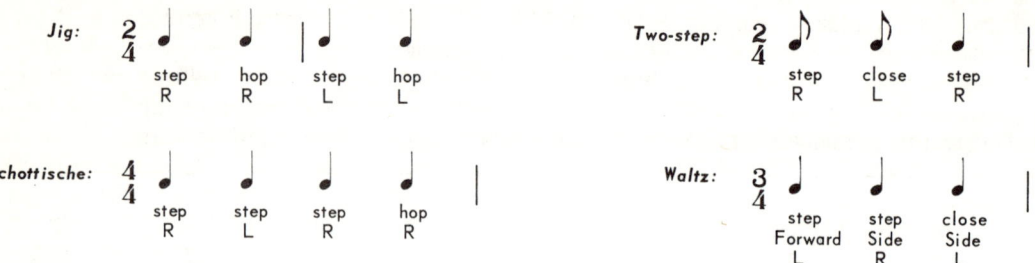

Improvising Bodily Movement to the Proverb *Speech Is Silver*—For Upper Grades

1. Give class a period of tempo-dynamic patschen, stamping, clapping, and snapping fingers.
2. Give class a period of echo patschen, stamping, clapping, and snapping fingers.
3. Tell class to do what you do and do the following, repeating many times until class is rhythmically stable.

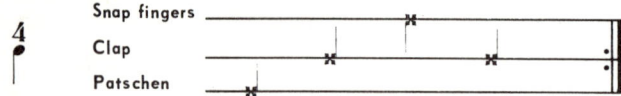

4. Continuing the above, tell class to listen, then echo whatever you chant. The following should result:

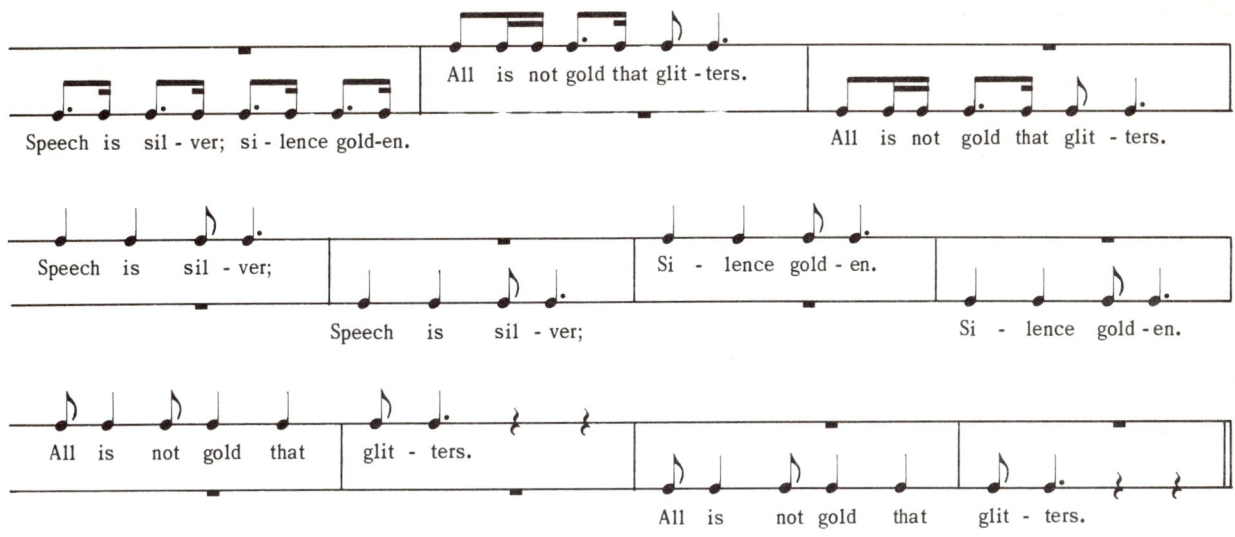

5. When class can echo you easily, tell them you would like to see if they can do the entire chant through, as follows:

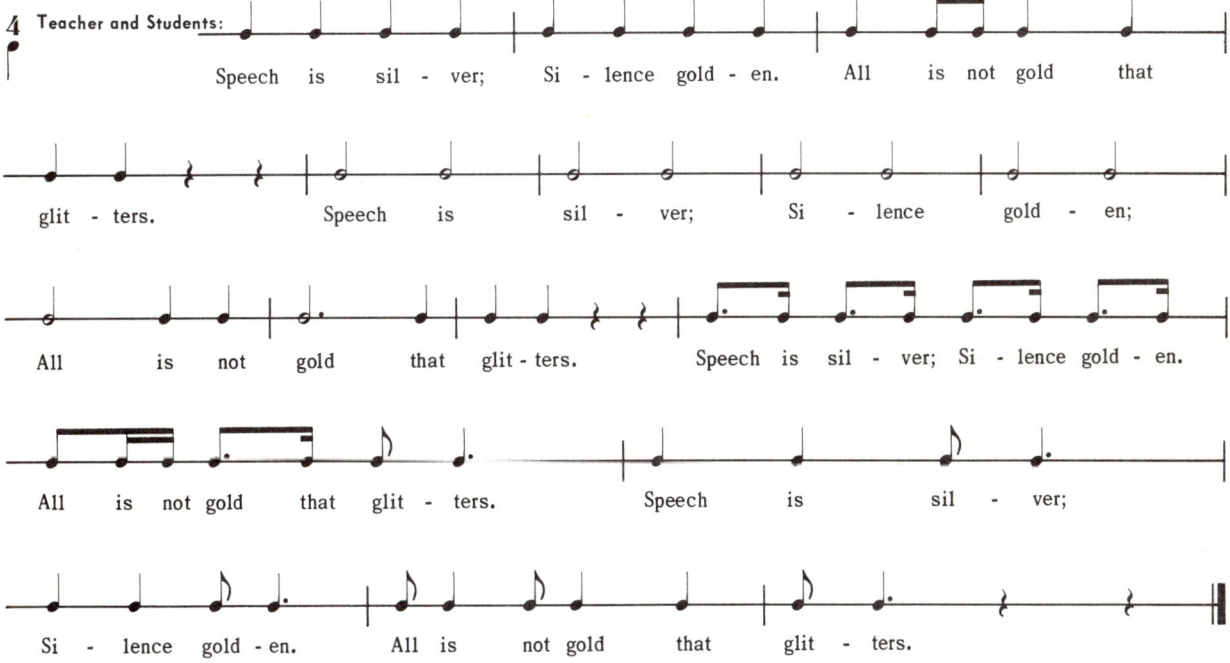

6. Discuss with class all the possible movements their bodies can make—legs, arms, hands, torso. Emphasize large and small movements, long and short movements, curved and pointed movements, heavy and light movements.

7. Discuss possible movements for each of the variations on the proverbs just chanted.

8. Ask for volunteers (only enough to fill available space without overcrowding) to experiment with movements that would fit the various rhythms. Remind those selected that they may move about in any way they wish, the only rules being to try to make movements that express the rhythms being interpreted without touching anyone.

9. Have the class begin the rhythmic accompaniment and chant as in 5 (above) going through all variations, as children selected experiment with their movements.

10. Make positive comments, where possible, on movements created. Select other children to take their places. Repeat, until all children have had the opportunity to participate.

CHAPTER 5

Creating Rhythmic Dramatizations

Rhythmic dramatizations of songs, poems, chants, and stories add a dynamic dimension to experiences in rhythm, giving children the opportunity to express not only their rhythmic responses, but their inner feelings and attitudes as well.

Children delight in the opportunities for self-expression inherent in this new form, and enter eagerly into experiences with rhythmic dramatizations.

Creating a Rhythmic Dramatization to the Song
Little Miss Muffet—For Primary Grades

1. Give children a period of tempo-dynamic clapping.
2. Give children a period of echo clapping.
3. Tell class you would like to teach them a song which they will later dramatize. Using a rhythmic accompaniment similar to that suggested below, teach the song, phrase by phrase, with you singing and accompanying rhythmically, and the class echoing.

2. Mister Spider sat on the grass,
   Not knowing what to say:
   Along came a Cat and by him sat,
   And frightened the Spider away!

3. Mister Cat sat on a mat,
   And looked quite jolly and gay:
   Along came a Dog who was hungry as a hog,
   And frightened the Cat away!

4. Mister Dog sat on a log,
   And he began to bay:
   Along came a Cow,
   The Dog said, "Bow Wow!"
   And ran very quickly away!

5. Mister Cow pranced on the grass,
   Enjoying the summer's day:
   Along came the Farmer
   Took Cow home to calm her,
   Now Miss Muffet could come back to stay:

4. When class knows song, ask for individual volunteers to dramatize each character. Working verse by verse, have class sing and accompany the characters as they move. After each verse, discuss in a positive way the movement of each character. Give many children the opportunity to dramatize each verse.

5. When all characters have been demonstrated by several children, select children to play the part of each character. Decide with the class where they will be until it is their turn to move, and where they will move. (Rearrange furniture to provide space, if necessary.)

6. Have "Miss Muffet" go to her place "on the tuffet." Have class begin rhythmic accompaniment, using a moderate tempo conducive to movement, then have class begin singing.

7. To expand the experience, help class develop an orchestration for the song. An example might be:

8. Give class similar experiences, using other songs. Several songs may be combined to develop a program to give for other classes.

Creating a Rhythmic Dramatization of the Story *Worms, Deer and Bear*, Using Orff Instruments—For Primary Grades

1. Tell children that they are going to act out a story which has to do with a family of worms, a deer, and a bear. Explain that the characters will all move in rhythm to accompaniments played by children, and that you would like to teach the accompaniments before telling them the story. Before teaching each accompaniment, prepare entire class by having them mirror the actions suggested below:

Worms   *Preparation for playing accompaniment for twisting:*

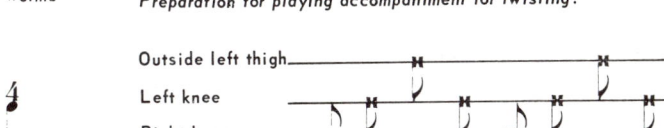

Accompaniment for twisting – soprano xylophone:

Preparation for playing accompaniment for swaying:

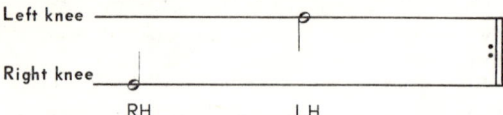

Accompaniment for swaying — soprano metallophone:

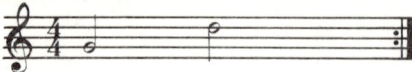

Deer

Preparation for accompaniment for trembling:

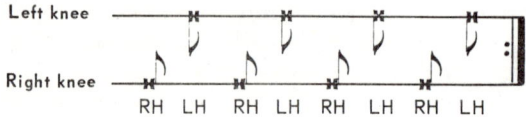

Accompaniment for trembling — soprano glockenspiel:

Preparation for accompaniment for running:

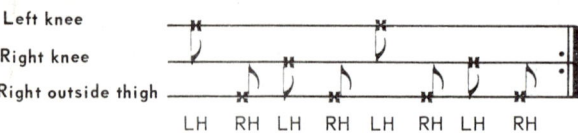

Accompaniment for running — alto xylophone:

Accompaniment for sinking to ground — alto glockenspiel:

Accompaniment for getting up from ground — alto glockenspiel:

Bear

Preparation for playing accompaniment for walking:

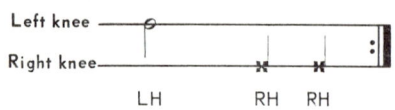

Accompaniment for walking — timpani or bass xylophone:

2. When individual children have been selected and taught to play the accompaniments above, tell class the story as it appears in 7 (below) omitting references to accompaniment and movement in parenthesis. Use as much variation as possible in your voice, to emphasize differences in tempo and dynamics suggested by each of the characters.
3. Discuss the different movements made by each of the characters—what they are and how they are made. (Worms start from a prone position, below the earth, and twist themselves up through the ground to an upright position; they sway on the daffodils. The deer runs; she trembles in fear; she sinks to the ground; she gets up from the ground. The bear walks slowly and heavily, with huge steps.)
4. Give all children ample opportunity to experiment moving in all of these ways, letting children playing the corresponding accompaniments play as the rest of the class moves. Discuss movements made, in a positive way, pointing out children who do well in simulating movement of any one character.
5. Select children to be the family of worms (as many as can fit available space), the deer, and the bear. Decide, with the help of the class, where the worms will twist up through the earth, and from where the deer and the bear will come. If necessary, rearrange the room to provide ample space.
6. Explain that you will tell the story and that the children playing the accompaniments should begin playing when you give them the signal; children acting the parts of the characters should begin moving when they hear their accompaniments. Explain that you will signal when the accompaniment and movement should stop.
7. Tell the story:

"Once upon a time, in a deep, green forest, just below the surface of the earth, a family of worms began twisting its way up through the earth. It was spring, and they wanted to sniff the fresh spring air."

(Signal soprano xylophone to begin playing, and worms to begin twisting. Give children as many measures as is necessary for worms to start from a prone position and twist themselves to an upright position, then signal them to stop.)

"Just as they had poked their heads above the surface of the earth, and had spotted a clump of daffodils to explore, they heard a sound! Something was running toward them from a distant part of the forest."

(Signal alto xylophone to begin playing and deer to begin running. Give deer ample number of measures to do a substantial amount of running before stopping children.)

"Quickly the worms twisted and turned until they had each found a place on a daffodil, well hidden by the foliage."

(Signal soprano xylophone to begin playing accompaniment for twisting, and worms to begin twisting. Stop movement and accompaniment after approximately half a dozen measures.)

"Meanwhile, the running came closer and closer, louder and louder."

(Signal alto xylophone to begin playing and deer to begin running.)

"Finally, they could see what was coming. It was a deer, and it ran and ran until finally it was in full view. Then, quite suddenly, it stopped and turned to look back."

(Signal alto xylophone and deer to stop, soprano metallophone to begin playing, worms to sway on daffodils.)

"In terror, the worms clung to the daffodils, swaying ever so gently back and forth in the wind."

(Signal soprano metallophone and worms to stop, after a few additional measures.)

"They watched and listened! Soon they heard still another sound in the deep woods! It was the sound of slow, heavy steps!"

(Signal timpani, or bass xylophone, to begin playing, bear to begin walking, and after ample movement, both to stop.)

"The deer trembled in fear."

(Signal soprano glockenspiel to begin playing, deer to tremble, both to stop after a measure or two.)

"She ran quickly to a clump of bushes."

(Signal alto xylophone to begin playing, deer to run, both to stop after a few measures.)

"There she sank to the ground, safely out of sight."

(Signal alto glockenspiel to play accompaniment for sinking to the ground.)

"The heavy footsteps came closer and closer, louder and louder."

(Signal timpani or bass xylophone to begin playing, bear to walk. Continue reading, indicating that bear and accompaniment should continue.)

"Soon, into full view of the watching animals, came a huge brown bear! And just as he passed the bushes where the deer was hiding, he stopped! And what do you think he did? He scratched his left ear!"

(Signal bear and timpani or bass xylophone to stop.)

"Now it so happened that this was a *friendly* bear, but the deer didn't know that! And she trembled and trembled behind the bushes."

(Signal soprano glockenspiel to begin playing, and deer to tremble, then for both, after a few measures, to stop.)

"The worms made *very* sure that they were well out of sight as they swayed on their daffodils!"

(Signal soprano metallophone to play, worms to sway, both, after a few measures, to stop.)

"But the bear was simply out enjoying the spring air, and after scratching his *right* ear, he began walking on."

(Signal timpani or bass xylophone to begin playing, bear to walk, and both to continue as you speak.)

"He walked past the deer behind the bushes, past the worms on the daffodils, and finally down the path to the other side of the forest."

(Signal timpani or bass xylophone and bear to get softer and softer, and finally to stop.)

"When he was safely gone, the deer raised herself slowly up on her feet."

(Signal alto glockenspiel to play accompaniment and deer to get up.)

"She looked out from the bushes. When she was sure all was safe, she ran quickly off—in the *opposite* direction of the bear!"

(Signal alto xylophone to begin playing and deer to run, indicating that they should get softer and softer, then stop.)

"The worms decided, too, that they had had quite enough of the outside world for one day, and so they twisted around and around, back down the daffodils, and back into the safe dark earth."

(Signal soprano xylophone to begin playing, worms to twist, and then indicate that they should play softer and softer, then stop.)

8. Discuss the dramatization in positive terms helping children see which motions were especially expressive.
9. Encourage children to explore the use of percussion instruments to add texture, atmosphere, and dramatic effects to the dramatization.
10. On other days, give different children the opportunity to dramatize the story and play the accompaniments.
11. Help children to create another story and rhythmic dramatization, and to create accompaniments for the movement made by the characters.

Creating a Rhythmic Dramatization of the Story *The Three Bears,* Using Orff Instruments—For Primary Grades

1. Tell children that today they are going to act out the story of the three bears. Explain that the characters in the story will be accompanied, when they move, by instruments. Tell them that you would like, first of all, to teach individual children to play the accompaniments assigned to each instrument. Before teaching each accompaniment to a child, prepare the entire class by having them mirror the actions suggested.

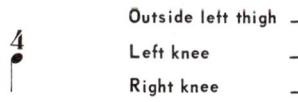

By Lori Kampfer, Camp Ave. School, Union Free School Dist. No. 29, North Merrick, New York.

Little Small Wee Bear

Preparation for playing accompaniment:

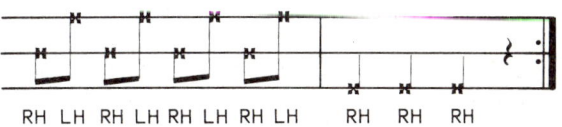

Accompaniment for soprano xylophone, using two mallets:

Middle—Sized Bear

Preparation for playing accompaniment:

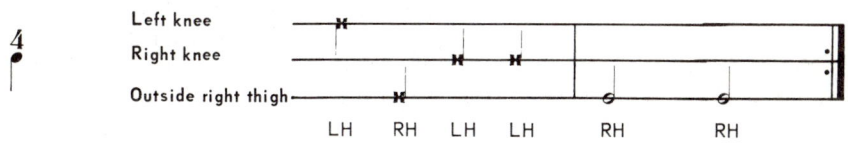

Accompaniment for alto xylophone, using two mallets:

Great Huge Bear

Preparation for playing accompaniment:

Outside left thigh
Left knee
Right knee

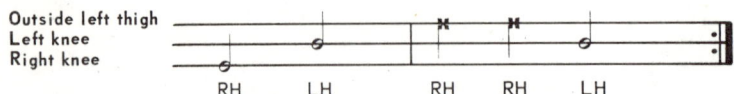

RH   LH   RH   RH   LH

Accompaniment for bass xylophone, using two mallets:

Goldilocks

Accompaniment for tone block:

Accompaniment for falling through the chair:

Alto xylophone — glissando; Cymbal — crash:

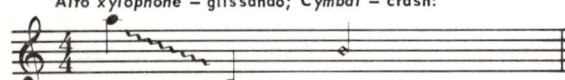

2. Help children explore ways of moving like each of these characters, practicing with the instrumental accompaniments. Little Small Wee Bear might take light, running steps. Middle-Sized Bear might simply walk in moderate steps. Great Huge Bear would probably take slow, long, ponderous steps.

3. Select individual children to play the part of each character and let them practice with the children playing instruments until they perform easily together. Explain that during the telling of the story, when they are signaled to move or play, the accompaniment for each character is to be played only once, except when the character is moving to another spot, at which time the accompaniment should be repeated until character reaches his destination.

4. With the help of the class, decide where in the room should be the home of the three bears, the dining room table with the porridge bowls, the bedroom, the front door of the house, and the woods. (If necessary, rearrange furniture in room to make space.)

Set up instruments and children playing them in a place close to the "bears' house" but far enough away so that they will not interfere with the action.

Before the story begins, have children playing parts of the three bears take their places in the dining room near the porridge bowls and Goldilocks in the woods away from the front door of the house so that the bears will not see her when they leave the house.

Remind all children dramatizing and playing instruments to be prepared to move and play, exactly as practiced, whenever you signal them, and at all other times to improvise actions that are indicated by the story. For example, discuss activities in which bears might be engaged before leaving house. (They could be preparing their porridge.) Make certain children understand what they are to do.

5. Tell story, as follows:

"Once upon a time, there were three bears, who lived together in a house of their own, in the woods. One of them was a Little Small Wee Bear."

(Signal Wee Bear and accompaniment to begin moving and playing.)[1]

---

1. From here on, when the word *Signal* appears, it refers to the character just mentioned, and his instrumental accompaniment, unless otherwise indicated.

"One of them was a Middle-Sized Bear."
(Signal.)

"One of them was a Great Huge Bear."
(Signal.)

"They each had a bowl for their porridge. There was a little bowl for the Little Wee Bear."
(Signal.)

"There was a middle-sized bowl for the Middle-Sized Bear."
(Signal.)

"There was a great bowl for the Great Huge Bear."
(Signal.)

"They each had a chair to sit in. There was a little chair for Little Small Wee Bear."
(Signal.)

"There was a middle-sized chair for the Middle-Sized Bear."
(Signal.)

"There was a great chair for the Great Huge Bear."
(Signal.)

"And they each had a bed to sleep in. There was a little bed for Little Small Wee Bear."
(Signal.)

"There was a middle-sized bed for Middle-Sized Bear."
(Signal.)

"There was a great, huge bed for Great Huge Bear."
(Signal.)

"One day, after they had made the porridge for their breakfast, and poured it into their porridge bowls, they decided to go for a walk in the woods while their porridge was cooling."
(Signal all three bears and their accompaniments to move and play.)

"While they were out walking, a little girl named Goldilocks came to the house."
(Signal.)

"Now Goldilocks had never seen the little house before, and it was such a strange little house that she forgot all the things her mother had told her about being polite, and the first thing she did was to look into the window. Then she peeped into the keyhole, and seeing no one in the house, she lifted the latch. The door was not fastened, since the bears never suspected that anyone would harm them—they were good bears. So Goldilocks opened the door and went in."
(Signal.)

"Now Goldilocks was very hungry, and when she saw the porridge on the table, she forgot all the things her mother would have told her about eating other people's food, and set about helping herself. First she tasted the porridge of the Great Huge Bear."
(Signal instrument.)

"But that was too hot! Next she tasted the porridge of the Middle-Sized Bear."
(Signal instrument.)

"But that was too cold! Finally, she tasted the porridge of the Little Small Wee Bear."
(Signal instrument.)

"And that was just right! So she ate it all up. When she had finished eating, Goldilocks wanted to sit down. First, she tried the chair of the Great Huge Bear."
(Signal instrument.)

"But that was too hard. Next she tried the chair of the Middle-Sized Bear."
(Signal instrument.)

"But that was too soft. Finally, she tried the chair of the Little Small Wee Bear."
(Signal instrument.)

By Michael McLaughlin, Camp Ave. School, Union Free School Dist. No. 29, North Merrick, New York.

By Craig Hansen, Camp Ave. School, Union Free School Dist. No. 29, North Merrick, New York.

"That was just right, so she seated herself in it, and there she sat until the bottom of the chair came out and down she went, plump upon the floor."

(Signal alto xylophone to play glissando and cymbals to crash.)

"Goldilocks began to feel sleepy; so next she went to the bedroom where the three bears slept. First she lay down upon the bed of the Great Huge Bear."

(Signal instrument.)

"But that was too high at the head for her. Next she lay upon the bed of the Middle-Sized Bear."

(Signal instrument.)

"But that was too high at the foot for her. Finally, she lay upon the bed of the Little Small Wee Bear."

(Signal instrument.)

"And that was just right! So she curled herself up and lay there until she fell fast asleep. By this time, the three bears thought their porridge would be cool enough to eat, so they came home for breakfast."

(Signal all three bears and their accompaniments to move and play.)

"First the Great Huge Bear walked over to his porridge."

(Signal.)

" 'Somebody has been at my porridge,' roared the Great Huge Bear when he saw the spoon Goldilocks had left in his bowl. Next the Middle-Sized Bear walked over to her porridge."

(Signal.)

" 'Somebody has been at *my* porridge,' said the Middle-Sized Bear, as she saw the spoon Goldilocks had left in *her* bowl. Finally, the Little Small Wee Bear walked over to his porridge."

(Signal.)

" 'Somebody has been at my porridge, and has eaten it all up,' said the Little Small Wee Bear in his little small wee voice. Now the three bears began to suspect that someone had been in their house, and they began to look around. First the Great Huge Bear went over to his chair."

(Signal.)

" 'Someone has been sitting in my chair,' he roared in his huge voice. Next the Middle-Sized Bear went over to her chair."

(Signal.)

" 'Someone has been sitting in *my* chair,' said the Middle-Sized Bear, in her middle-sized voice. Finally, the Little Small Wee Bear went over to *his* chair."

(Signal.)

" 'Someone has been sitting in my chair, and sat right through the bottom of it,' cried the Little Small Wee Bear, in his little, small, wee voice. Next the three bears went to the bedroom."

(Signal three bears and instruments to walk and play.)

"First the Great Huge Bear went over to his bed."

(Signal.)

" 'Someone's been sleeping in my bed,' roared the Great Huge Bear, in his great huge voice. Next the Middle-Sized Bear went over to her bed."

(Signal.)

" 'Someone's been sleeping in my bed,' said the Middle-Sized Bear, in her middle-sized voice. Finally, the Little Small Wee Bear went over to his bed."

(Signal.)

" 'Someone's been sleeping in my bed,' cried the Little Small Wee Bear, in his little small wee voice, and she's still sleeping there!' Just as the Little Small Wee Bear was speaking, Goldilocks began to wake up. Slowly she opened her eyes. And when she saw the three bears standing in front of the bed, she didn't wait to find out if they were friendly bears—she jumped out of bed."

(Signal.)

"She jumped out of the window, and she ran through the woods, back home to her mother. And she never did find out what nice, friendly bears she had visited!"

By Kathleen Hobbs, Camp Ave. School, Union Free School Dist. No. 29, North Merrick, New York.

6. Discuss story with class. Without being critical of children acting out story, elicit ideas for improving the acting, letting children demonstrate their ideas for change.
7. On other days, let children dramatize the story again, incorporating their new ideas, and letting different children play the parts of the characters and their accompanists.
8. When children know the story well, select children to narrate the story and encourage those who play parts of individual characters to speak their parts.
9. Encourage children to explore the use of percussion instruments to add texture, atmosphere, and dramatic effects to the dramatization.
10. Help children develop story into an assembly program, adding simple costumes and scenery.

Creating a Rhythmic Dramatization of the Story *The Gingerbread Boy* Using Orff Instruments—For Primary or Intermediate Grades

1. Tell children that today they are going to act out the story *The Gingerbread Boy*. Review the story briefly. Explain that the characters in the story will be accompanied, when they move, by instruments, and that you would like to first teach individual children to play the accompaniments assigned to each instrument. Before teaching each accompaniment, prepare the entire class by having them mirror the actions suggested.

Little Old Woman and Little Old Man

Accompaniment for Tone Block:

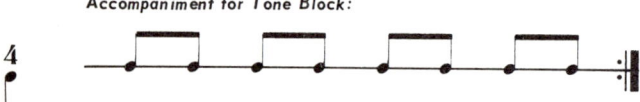

Gingerbread Boy

Preparation for playing accompaniment:

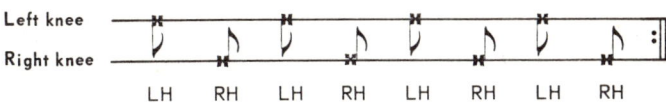

Accompaniment for soprano glockenspiel, using two mallets:

Duck

Preparation for playing accompaniment:

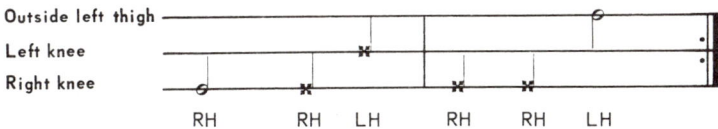

Accompaniment for alto xylophone, using two mallets:

Goose

Preparation for playing accompaniment:

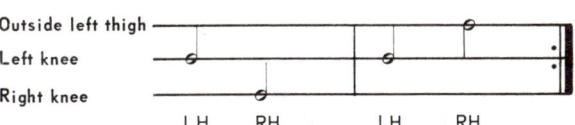

Accompaniment for soprano xylophone, using two mallets:

Cow

Preparation for playing accompaniment:

Note: The accompaniment may be played by one or two children. It is assumed here that one child will play it.

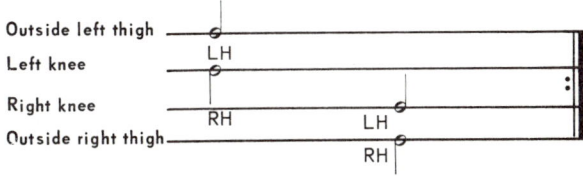

Accompaniment for alto metallophone, using two mallets:

Horse

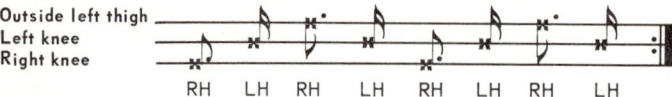

Fox

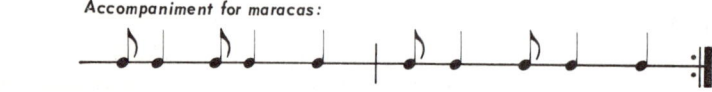

2. Help children explore ways of moving like each of these characters, practicing with the instrumental accompaniments. (The Little Old Woman, Little Old Man, and Gingerbread Boy all run. The Duck and Goose probably would waddle slowly. The Cow would no doubt take long, slow steps. The Horse would gallop, and the Fox lope.)

3. Select individual children to play the part of each character, and let them practice with the children playing instruments until they perform easily together. Let each character practice moving with the Gingerbread Boy (both instrumental accompaniments playing) until they can move and play together. Throughout this practice, remind children that in the story, they will move only for the duration of their melody (two measures). Remind them, further, to move, when they are chasing the Gingerbread Boy, in such a way as not to catch him.[2] Remind the Gingerbread Boy that he is to actually run only when signaled—at other times he should move his legs as though running, but stay in place. (His instrumental accompaniment will not play at these times. The purpose of this is to keep the story from being monotonous by the constant repetition of the Gingerbread Boy's "melody," and also to make dramatization possible in a small space.)

4. With the help of the class, establish where in the room will be: the house of the Little Old Woman and Little Old Man; the Little Old Woman's kitchen; the door of the house out of which the Gingerbread Boy runs; the starting points of the Duck, Goose, Cow, Horse, and Fox. (The animals should be spread about the room with as much space as possible in between so as to give the Gingerbread Boy time to run. If necessary, furniture should be rearranged to provide enough space.)

Set up the instruments and children playing them so that they do not interfere with the action.

Have children selected for characters go to the places assigned to them.

Remind children playing instruments and those playing parts of the characters to be prepared to move and to play, as practiced, when you signal them to do so. At all other times, children dramatizing are to improvise actions indicated by the story.

Make certain children understand what to do.

5. Tell story, as follows:

"Once upon a time, there was a Little Old Woman, and a Little Old Man, and they lived all alone in a little old house. They hadn't any girls or any boys at all. So, one day, the Little Old Woman made a boy out of gingerbread. She made him a chocolate jacket, and put cinnamon seeds on it for buttons. She made his eyes out of fine, fat currants, and his mouth of rose-colored candy. When the Little Old Woman had rolled him out and dressed him up, and pinched his gingerbread shoes in shape, she put him in a pan; then she put the pan in the oven and shut the door; and she thought, 'Now I shall have a little boy of my own.' When it was time for the Gingerbread Boy to be done,

---

2. If children do not know the basic idea of the story, tell them briefly what it is, so that they understand instructions.

she opened the oven door and pulled out the pan. Out jumped the little Gingerbread Boy onto the floor, and away he ran, out of the door and down the street!''

(Signal Gingerbread Boy and his accompanist to run and play.)[3]

"The Little Old Woman and the Little Old Man ran after him as fast as they could."

(Signal.)

"But the Gingerbread Boy just laughed and shouted, 'Run! Run! As fast as you can! You can't catch me—I'm the Gingerbread Boy!' And they couldn't catch him. The little Gingerbread Boy ran on and on."

(Signal.)

"Finally, he came to a Duck walking down the road."

(Signal.)

" 'Stop, little Gingerbread Boy,' said the Duck, 'I want to eat you.' But the Gingerbread Boy just laughed and shouted, 'I have run away from a Little Old Man, I have run away from a Little Old Woman, and I can run away from you, I can!' And off he ran, with the Duck chasing behind."

(Signal Gingerbread Boy and Duck, and their instrumental accompanists, to move and play.)

"And as the Gingerbread Boy ran, he shouted, 'Run! Run! As fast as you can! You can't catch me. I'm the Gingerbread Boy!' And the Duck couldn't catch him. The Gingerbread Boy ran on and on."

(Signal.)

"Finally, he came to a Goose walking down the road."

(Signal.)

" 'Stop, little Gingerbread Boy,' said the Goose. 'I would love to have a bite of you!' But the Gingerbread Boy just laughed and shouted, 'I have run away from the Little Old Man and the Little Old Woman. I have run away from the Duck, and I can run away from you, I can!' And off he ran, with the Goose chasing behind."

(Signal Gingerbread Boy and Goose, and their instrumental accompanists, to move and play.)

"And as the Gingerbread Boy ran, he shouted, 'Run! Run! As fast as you can! You can't catch me, I'm the Gingerbread Boy!' And the Goose couldn't catch him! The little Gingerbread Boy ran on and on."

(Signal.)

"Finally, he came to a Cow walking down the road."

(Signal.)

" 'Stop, little Gingerbread Boy,' said the Cow. You look very delicious—I'd love to have just one bite of you!' But the Gingerbread Boy just laughed and shouted, 'I have run away from the Little Old Man and the Little Old Woman. I have run away from the Duck and the Goose! And I can run away from you, I can!' And off he ran, with the cow chasing behind."

(Signal both Gingerbread Boy and Cow, and their instrumental accompanists, to move and play.)

"And as the Gingerbread Boy ran, he shouted, 'Run! Run! As fast as you can! You can't catch me, I'm the Gingerbread Boy!' And the Cow couldn't catch him. The little Gingerbread Boy ran on and on."

(Signal.)

"Finally, he came to a Horse walking down the road."

(Signal.)

" 'Stop, little Gingerbread Boy,' said the Horse. 'You look as though you'd be a mighty tasty meal! I'd like to *eat* you!' But the Gingerbread Boy just laughed and shouted, 'I have run away

3. From here on, when the word *Signal* appears, it refers to the character just mentioned and his instrumental accompanist, unless other wise indicated. Further, when the Gingerbread Boy has run for the duration of two measures (to accompaniment of Soprano glockenspiel, he should simply run in place (without accompaniment) until the next signal to run.

from the Little Old Man and the Little Old Woman. I have run away from the Duck and the Goose and the Cow. And I can run away from you, I can!' And off he ran, with the Horse chasing behind.''

(Signal both Gingerbread Boy and Horse, and their instrumental accompanists, to move and to play.)

"And as the Gingerbread Boy ran, he shouted, 'Run! Run! As fast as you can! You can't catch me! I'm the Gingerbread Boy!' And the Horse couldn't catch him. The little Gingerbread Boy ran on and on.''

(Signal.)

"And finally, he came to a Fox loping down the road.''

(Signal.)

" 'Stop, little Gingerbread Boy,' said the Fox. 'I'm hungry, and you look very good to eat!' But the Gingerbread Boy just laughed and shouted, 'I have run away from the Little Old Man and the Little Old Woman. I have run away from the Duck and the Goose and the Cow and the Horse! And I can run away from you, I can!' And off he ran, with the Fox chasing behind.''

(Signal both Gingerbread Boy and Fox, and their instrumental accompanists, to move and to play.)

"But the Gingerbread Boy was beginning to get tired. And the Fox had strong legs—and the Gingerbread Boy looked back and saw that he was getting closer and closer. And so, at the very next corner, he turned and ran and ran and ran—until he ran right back to the little old house where the Little Old Woman and the Little Old Man lived—and he ran right in, shutting the door just in time to keep the Fox out! And so the Little Old Woman and the Little Old Man had their little Gingerbread Boy back again! And they all lived happily ever after!''

6. Discuss the dramatization with the class, eliciting ideas for improving. Repeat, using different children to play parts, and incorporating new ideas.
7. When children know the story well, select children to narrate the story, and encourage children who play parts of characters to speak their parts.
8. Encourage children to explore the use of percussion instruments to add texture, atmosphere, and dramatic effects to the dramatization.
9. If desired, this story may be developed into an assembly program, adding simple costumes and scenery.

Creating a Rhythmic Dramatization of the Poem *Work at the Rock,* Using Orff Instruments—For Intermediate or Upper Grades

1. Tell class to join you in the following:

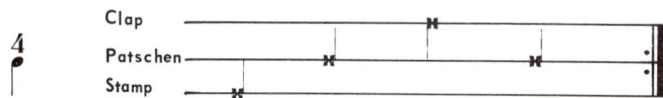

2. Continuing the above, tell class to listen, then to echo you. Do the following, varying the pitch, volume, and tone color of your voice, encouraging class to do the same.

3. When class can echo chant the poem easily, have them chant it through, using the bodily movement employed in the echo chant, varying the pitch, volume, and tone color of their voices:

Chorus: Work at the rock! Work at the rock!
         Drill! Drill! Work at the rock!
Verse 1: Up comes the boss, 'bout ten feet high,
         Raises his arm, points to the sky!
Verse 2: Down swoops an eagle, skims across the ground!
         Keep on working! Don't turn around!
Verse 3: Up blows a wind, swirling 'round and 'round!
         Keep on working! Break that ground!

4. Discuss the voice colors that have been used, helping class decide which ones best interpret the chorus and each of the verses. Let class experiment to decide which sound best. One group decided upon the following:

Chorus: Entire group of girls and boys chant in full volume, using the pitch natural to their own individual voices.
Verse 1: Boys' voices only, starting low, raising in pitch on second line.
Verse 2: A solo boy's voice, starting high and loud, lowering in pitch and dynamics on end of first line, moderate in pitch and volume on second line.
Verse 3: Girls' voices only, starting high and excited on first line, becoming moderate in pitch and dynamics on second line.

5. Select any solo voices decided upon. Using the suggestions of the class, have them chant the rhyme again.
6. Discuss possibilities for a rhythmic dramatization for the chorus and each verse. One class decided upon the following:

Chorus: (and throughout poem) A group of half a dozen boys move their bodies as though chipping at a rock with a pick axe.
Verse 1: One boy (the boss), walking with all the authority of a "boss," struts up to the group and makes the gesture referred to in line 2.
Verse 2: One boy or girl moves as an eagle swooping down from the sky, then back up again.
Verse 3: Half a dozen girls swirl around and around, simulating the wind.

7. Select people to enact the chorus and each of the verses. With help of the class, decide where in the room the action will take place. Have "actors" take places.
8. Have the remainder of the group begin their rhythmic accompaniment (stamp, patschen, clap). After two measures have boys acting out chorus begin. After two additional measures, have entire class begin chanting chorus. Proceed through the poem, without missing a beat, encouraging children acting the verses to enter at the proper times, and the chanters to use the pitch and dynamics decided upon by the class. Let bodily movement (stamp, patschen and clap), and the boys working at the rock continue for two measures after the end of the poem.
9. Discuss the dramatization with class. Practice individual verses, or the chorus, to incorporate any ideas for improving. Let the same group do the dramatization again, as in 8 (above).
10. Select other children to do the rhythmic dramatization, repeating, until all have had the opportunity. Help class, after each repetition, to make their speaking and acting more expressive.
11. To expand on the experience, add the following accompaniments:

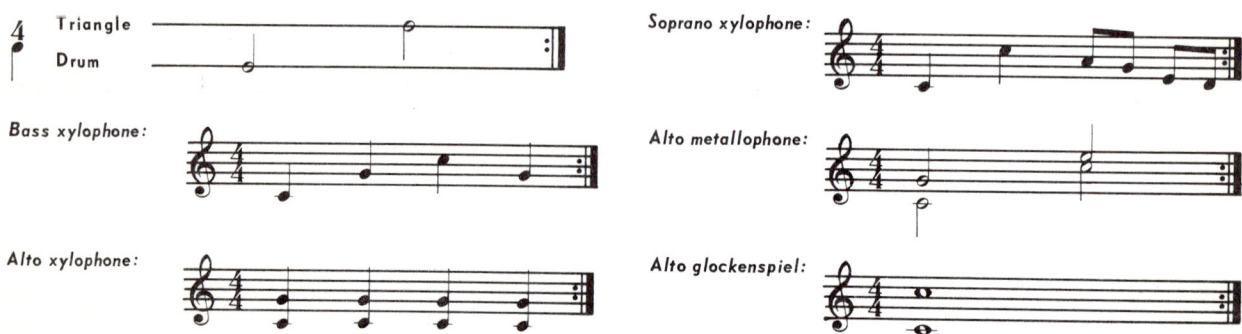

CHAPTER 6

Cultivating Rhythmic Improvisation

Rhythmic improvisation—the ability to create forms from one's rhythmic imagination—is one of the primary goals of all rhythmic experiences. By beginning with experiences in phrase-building in which children clap an answer to the teacher's clapped question, children develop the ability to use clapping in combination with stamping, patschen, and finger-snapping in extended phrases, and eventually to improvise the entire section of a rondo form.

Cultivating Phrase-Building Using Question-and-Answer
Clapping and Chanting—For Primary Grades

(Children should have had much experience associating words to rhythm patterns before this experience.)

1. Tell children that you are going to ask each one of them a question—the same question—and that they are each to give their own private answers. Explain that you will tell them the question, so that they can be thinking of the answer they will give. Tell them that you will ask them what kind of food they like best.
2. Chant and clap the rhythm of the words of the following:

3. Call on a volunteer to answer. (Assume, for convenience, that David answers, "I like ice cream best.")
4. Tell class to chant and clap David's answer, repeating several times:

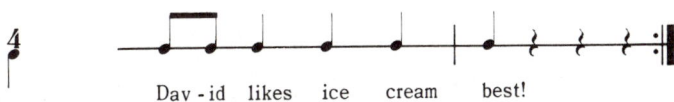

5. Chant and clap the question again (as in 2, above).
6. Call on another volunteer. (Assume Jean answers, "I like lollipops best!")

7. Tell class to chant and clap Jean's answer with you, repeating several times.

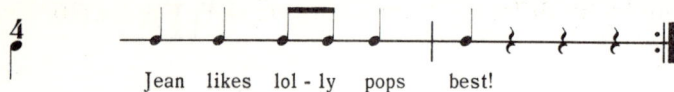

8. When class can clap and chant the answers with a minimum of difficulty, begin adding variations in the bodily movements—stamping, patschen, and finger-snapping, as well as clapping. For example:

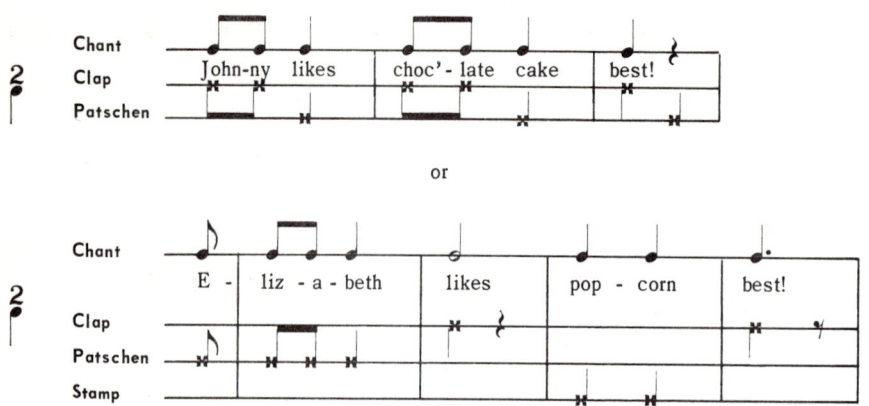

9. When children have had adequate experience in the above to respond quickly and successfully, expand the experience in one or all of the following ways:
   a. Encourage children to play rhythm instruments as they chant their responses.
   b. Encourage children to add bodily movement to their answers. For example:

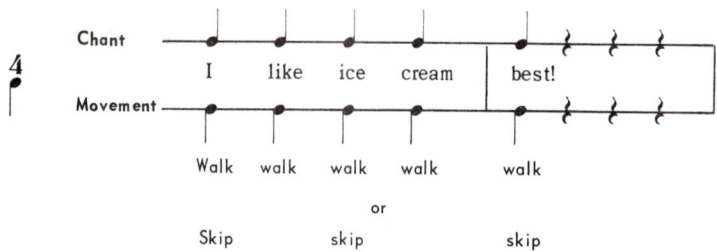

   c. Encourage children to sing their answers, using one of the following patterns:

10. Give children other question-and-answer experiences involving favorite games, their street addresses, and so on. In early stages, always let children know in advance what the question will be so that they can be prepared with an answer.

Cultivating Phrase-Building Using Question-and-Answer Clapping—
For Primary or Intermediate Grades

1. Give children a period of tempo-dynamic or echo clapping as a warm-up.
2. Remind children of the game they played in which you asked them their favorite foods, and they clapped and chanted their answers. Tell them that this time you will ask each one a question through clapping only, and that they are to give their answers by clapping. Indicate which child will be asked the question first, so that he is prepared to clap an answer. Go about the class, giving

as many children as possible different "clapping" questions, letting them clap their answers. Remind children that their answers should be different from your question. The question, and possible answers, are as follows:

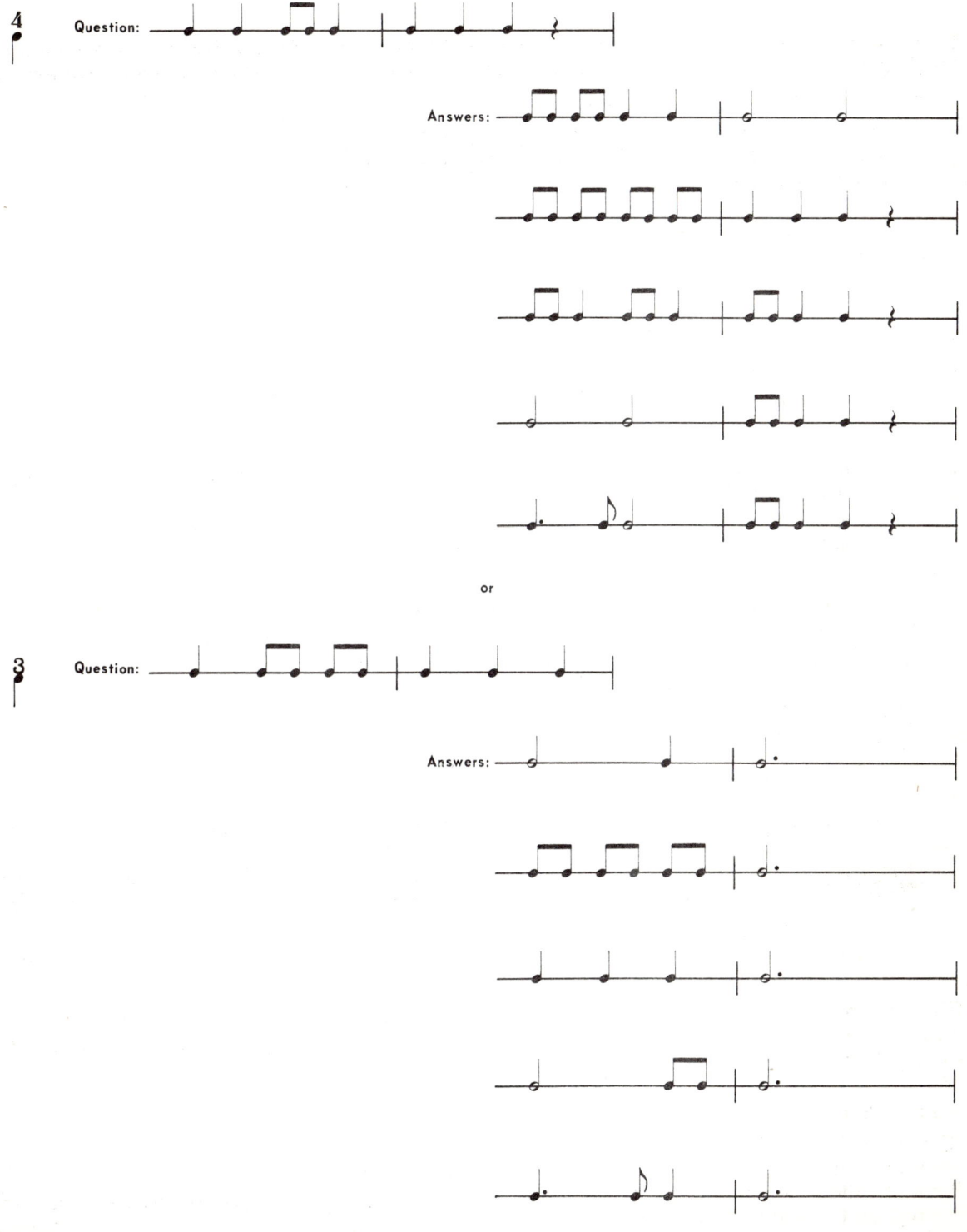

3. On another day, give children experience in question-and-answer clapping and stamping.

Cultivating Phrase-Building Through Question-and-Answer Clapping in Irregular Meter (5s) Using Proverbs—For Upper Grades

1. Give children the following experience in echo clapping and chanting:

2. Divide the class into two groups. Tell group one to clap and chant the first half of each proverb with you. Tell group two to clap and chant the second half of each proverb with you. The following should result:

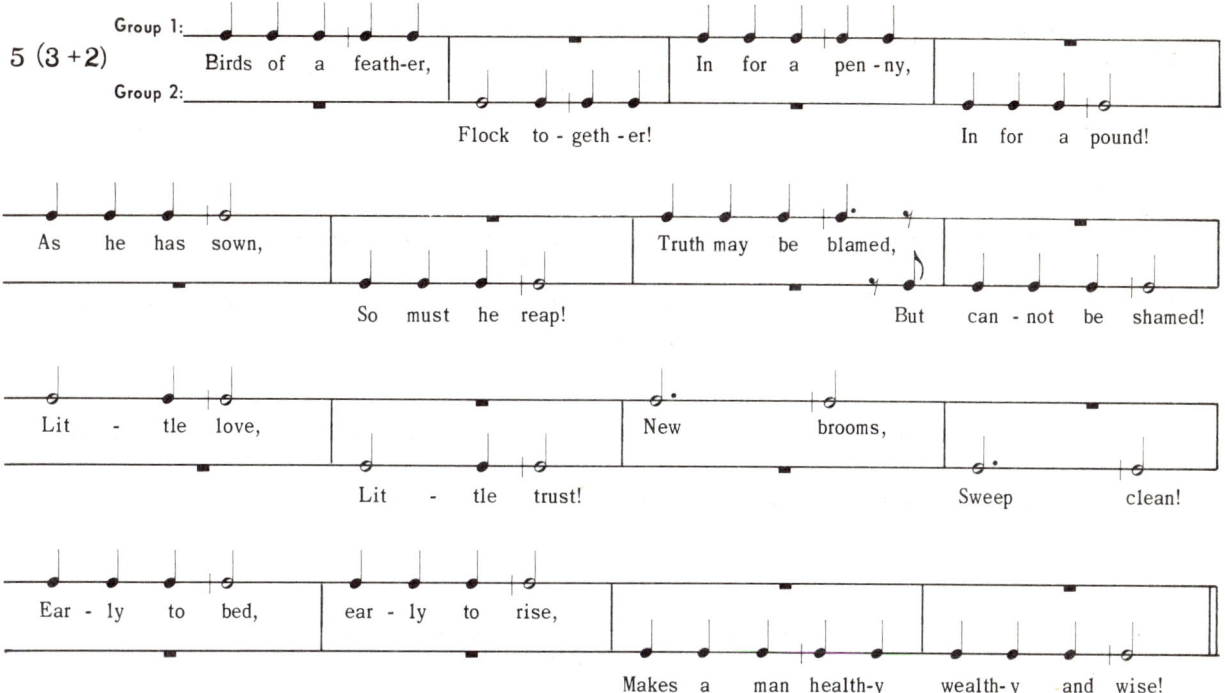

3. Switch groups. Have group two become group one, chanting and clapping first half of each proverb, group two answering.
4. Repeat, letting boys be group one, chanting and clapping first half of proverb, girls answering. Reverse, letting girls be group one, boys group two.
5. When class can chant and clap the proverbs in this manner with relative security, tell class you would like the entire group to be group one, clapping and chanting the first part of each proverb, with individuals clapping and chanting the second half of each proverb alone. Explain that you will all begin together, and that individuals who wish to clap and chant alone should raise their hands to volunteer.
6. Go through the proverbs in this manner, helping class chant and clap first half of each proverb, then calling on a volunteer to finish each proverb. Try to move from one part to the next without missing a beat.
7. Later, perhaps on another day, tell class that you will clap questions in irregular meter, and you would like individuals to answer by clapping. Do the following, or a similar sequence:

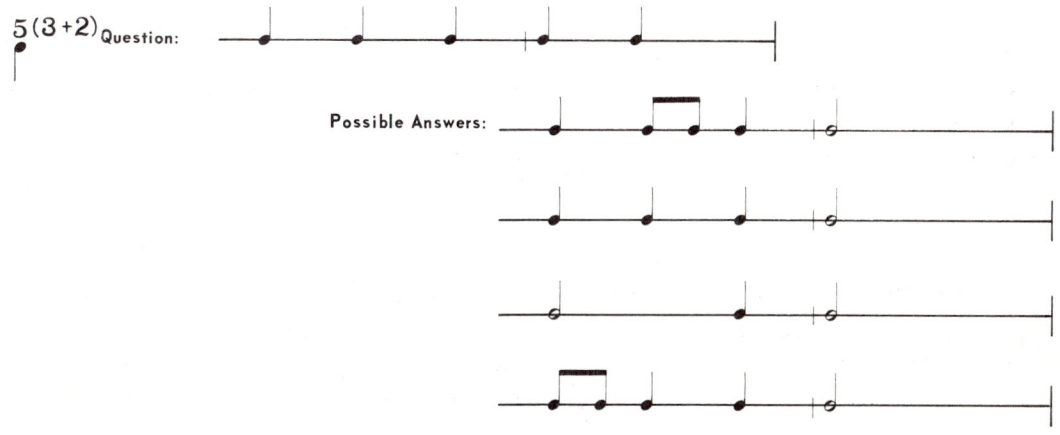

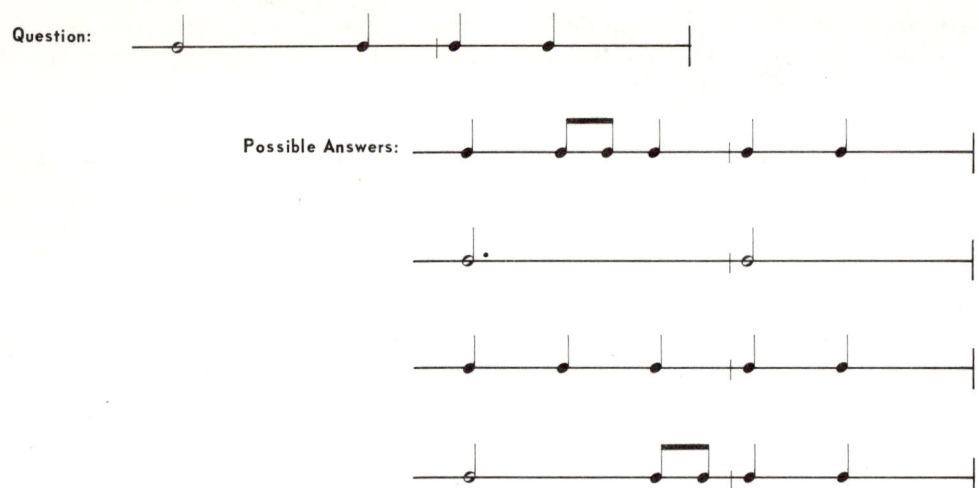

Cultivating Phrase-Building Through Question-and-Answer Patschen, Stamping, Clapping, and Finger-Snapping—For Intermediate Grades

1. Tell children that you are going to ask them a question by means of rhythm—stamping, clapping, snapping fingers, or patschen. Tell them that the first time you ask your question, all will be allowed to answer it at one time, simultaneously, using any of the motions you use, but in a *different* way—a way which seems to answer your question. Tell children to be ready to begin immediately after you finish. Do the following:

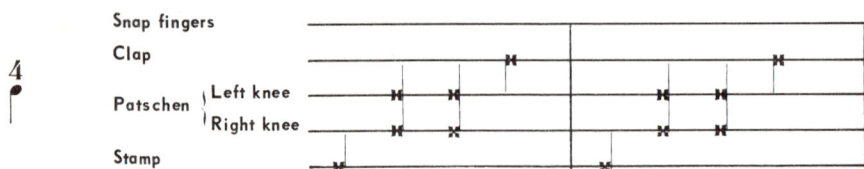

2. Immediately upon finishing the above, without missing a beat, indicate that all are to begin their "answer." Give a motion for them to begin, then keep them in rhythm for the length of their answer (two measures in 4/4 meter) by conducting clearly, but unobtrusively.
3. Ask for volunteers to answer the question alone, selecting, at first, those who seemed to have some degree of success. Select as many children as time allows, indicating the order in which they will answer. Explain that you will ask the question of each volunteer, individually, and that he is to be ready to answer as soon as you finish.
4. Do the pattern in 1 (above) bringing in the first volunteer immediately afterward, without missing a beat, beating time for him so that he keeps a steady tempo for two measures. When he has finished, ask the question again, directing it to the second volunteer. Continue in this way, without missing a beat, until all have been asked the question and all have answered. If any child has difficulty, don't stop, but simply beat out the rhythm for his two measures, then go on to the next person.
5. On another day, let children answer the following "questions" in a similar way:

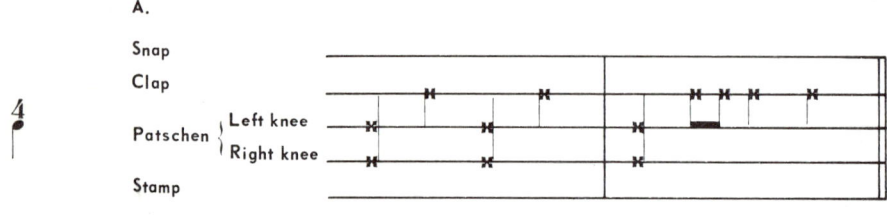

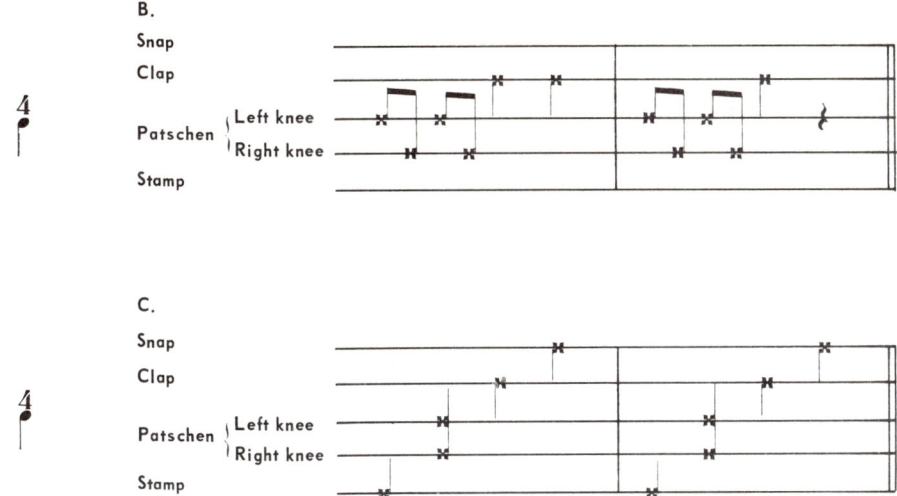

Cultivating Phrase-Building Through Question-and-Answer Patschen, Stamping, Clapping, and Finger-Snapping—For Upper Grades

1. Remind children of past experiences in question-and-answer rhythms. Tell them that today you will ask a question by means of clapping, snapping fingers, stamping, or patschen. Tell them that the first time you ask it, they will all be allowed to answer it at one time, simultaneously, using any of the motions you use, but in a *different* way—a way which seems to answer your question. Tell children to be ready to begin immediately after you finish, and do the following:

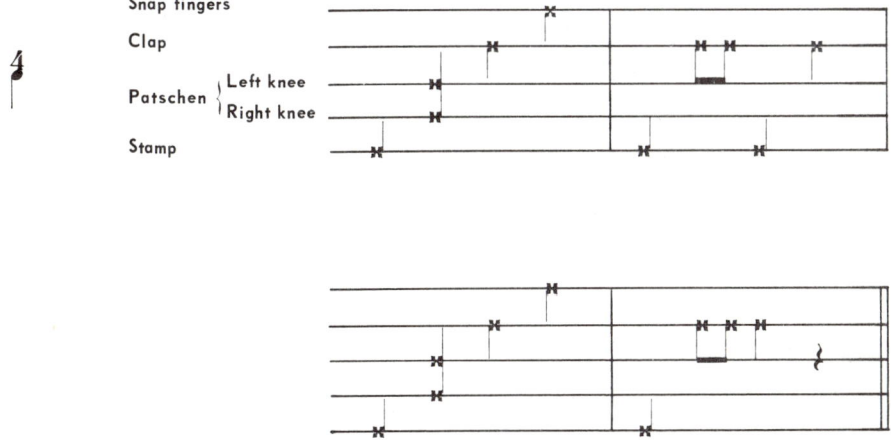

2. Immediately upon finishing the above, without missing a beat, indicate that all are to begin their "answer." Give a signal for them to begin, then keep them in rhythm for the length of their answer (four measures in 4/4 meter) by conducting clearly but unobtrusively.
3. Ask for volunteers to answer the question alone, selecting, at first, those who seemed to have some degree of success. Select as many children as time allows, indicating the order in which they will answer. Explain that you will ask the question to each volunteer, individually, and that he is to be ready to answer as soon as you finish.
4. Do the pattern in 1 (above) bringing in the first volunteer immediately after you finish, without missing a beat and while beating time for him so that he keeps a steady tempo for four measures. When he has finished, ask the question again, directing it at the second volunteer. Continue in this way, without missing a beat, until all have been asked the question, and all have answered. If any child has difficulty, don't stop, but simply beat out the rhythm for his answer, then go on to the next person.

5. On another day, let children answer the following "questions" in a similar way:

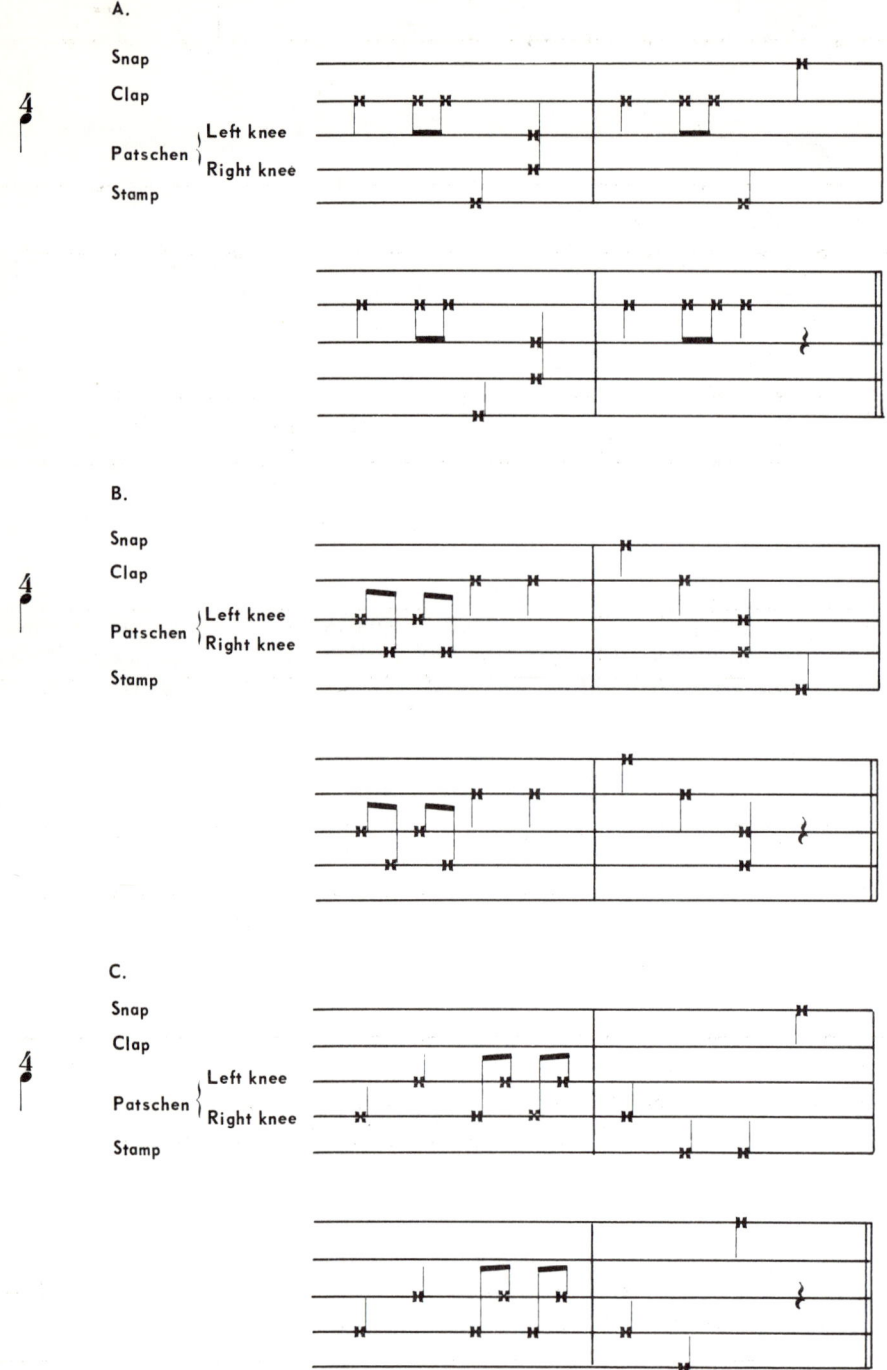

Creating a Rhythmic Rondo Using the Rhyme *Jack Be Nimble*—**For Second Grade**

(Children should have had much experience in question-and-answer clapping before this experience.)

1. Give children a period of tempo-dynamic clapping.
2. Give children the following experience in echo clapping and chanting:

3. When children can clap and chant the entire rhyme easily, explain that today they are going to create a rhythmic rondo using *Jack Be Nimble* as the main theme—or Section A. Explain the rondo form as follows:

Section A—Entire class claps and chants.
Section B—One child improvises an answering phrase (clapped) of the same length as Section A.
Section A—Entire class claps and chants.
Section C—Another child claps an answering phrase.
Section A—Entire class claps and chants.
Section D—Another child claps an answering phrase.
Section A—Entire class claps and chants.

4. Ask for volunteers to clap Sections B, C, and D, stressing the idea that the clapping might show how Jack would sound jumping over a candlestick.
5. Have entire class begin clapping and chanting Section A, *Jack Be Nimble*, making certain that they maintain a steady beat. Bring in each solo, and each Section A, without missing a beat. If children clapping solos have difficulty, don't stop, but let them do the best they can, and help by tapping your foot and/or conducting the rhythm of the entire phrase.
6. On another day, to add variety, do one of the following:

    a. Let children doing improvisation use instruments (drums, triangle, tambourine, tone block) instead of clapping.
    b. Encourage children to create a rhythmic interpretation of A Section, using entire body (jumping, hopping, and so forth).

Creating a Rhythmic Rondo Using the Rhyme *Queen, Queen Caroline*—**For Intermediate Grades**

(Children should have had much experience in question-and-answer clapping before this experience.)

1. Give class the following experience in echo clapping and chanting:

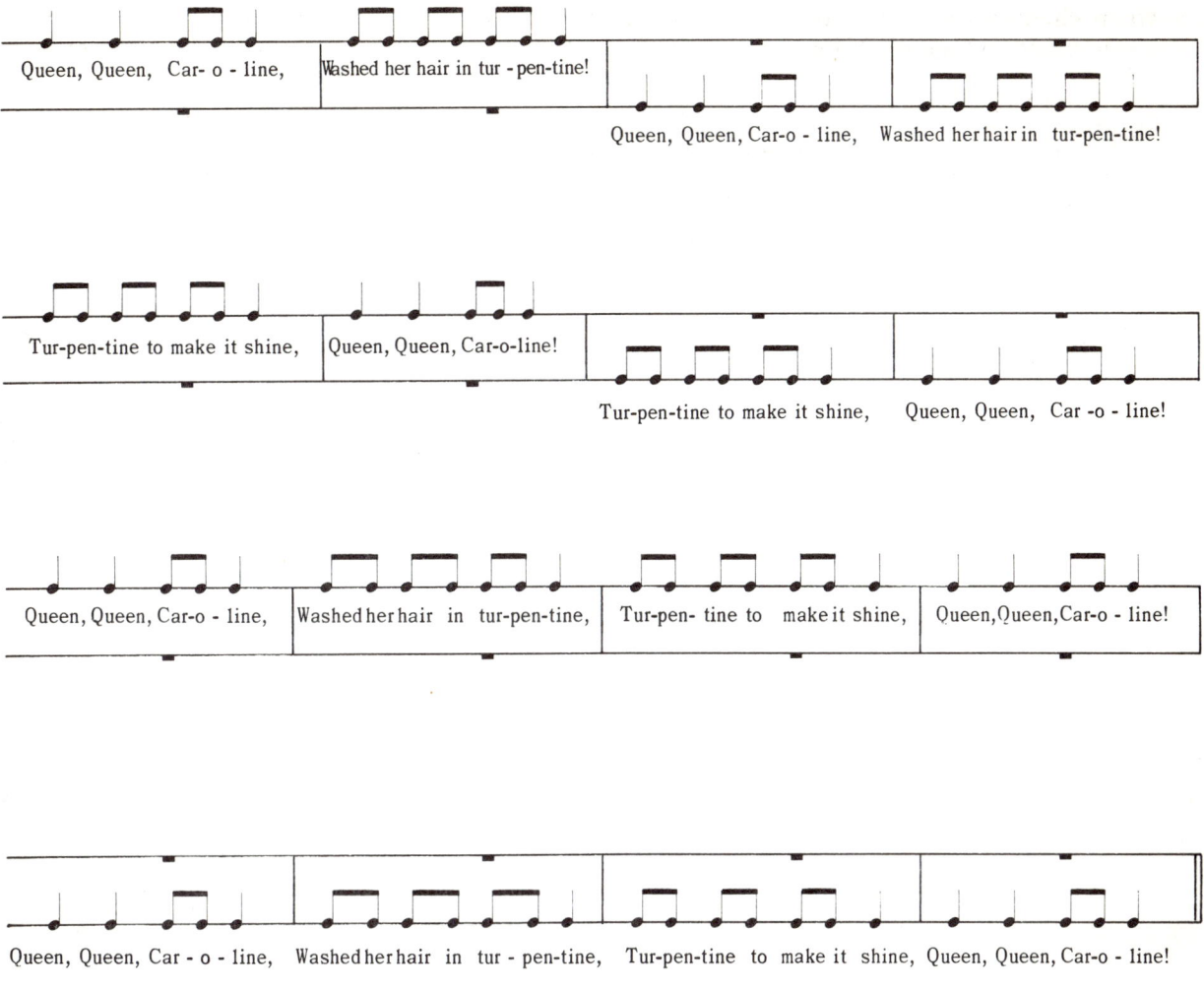

2. When children can clap and chant the entire rhyme easily, tell class that they are going to create a rhythmic rondo, using this rhyme as the Section A, or the theme which recurs. Remind them of other experiences with a rhythmic rondo, and also the structure of the rondo:

Section A—Entire class claps and chants.
Section B—One child improvises (claps) an answering phrase of the same length as Section A.
Section A—Entire class claps and chants.
Section C—Another child improvises an answering phrase.
Section A—Entire class claps and chants.
Section D—Another child improvises an answering phrase.
Section A—Entire class claps and chants.

3. Ask for volunteers to clap Sections B, C, and D, reminding them to clap Section A even when it precedes their solo.
4. Begin class clapping and chanting, making sure they maintain a steady tempo. Bring in each solo, and each Section A, without missing a beat. If children clapping solos have difficulty, don't stop, rather let them continue as best they can, and help by tapping your foot and/or conducting the rhythm of the entire phrase.
5. On another day, do one of the following:
   a. Let the children improvising Sections B, C, and D use percussion instruments (drum, tone blocks, maracas, and so forth) instead of clapping.
   b. Help children create rhythmic interpretation of the Section A.

Creating a Rhythmic Rondo in Irregular Meter (5s) by Rhyming Names of Countries—For Upper Grades

1. Give children the following experience in echo clapping and chanting:

Photo courtesy of C. Bruno & Son, Inc., Melville, New York 11746.

5 (3+2)

Teacher
Students:

Chick - ens   and   geese,   Eat   well   in   Greece!

Chick - ens   and   geese,   Eat   well   in   Greece!

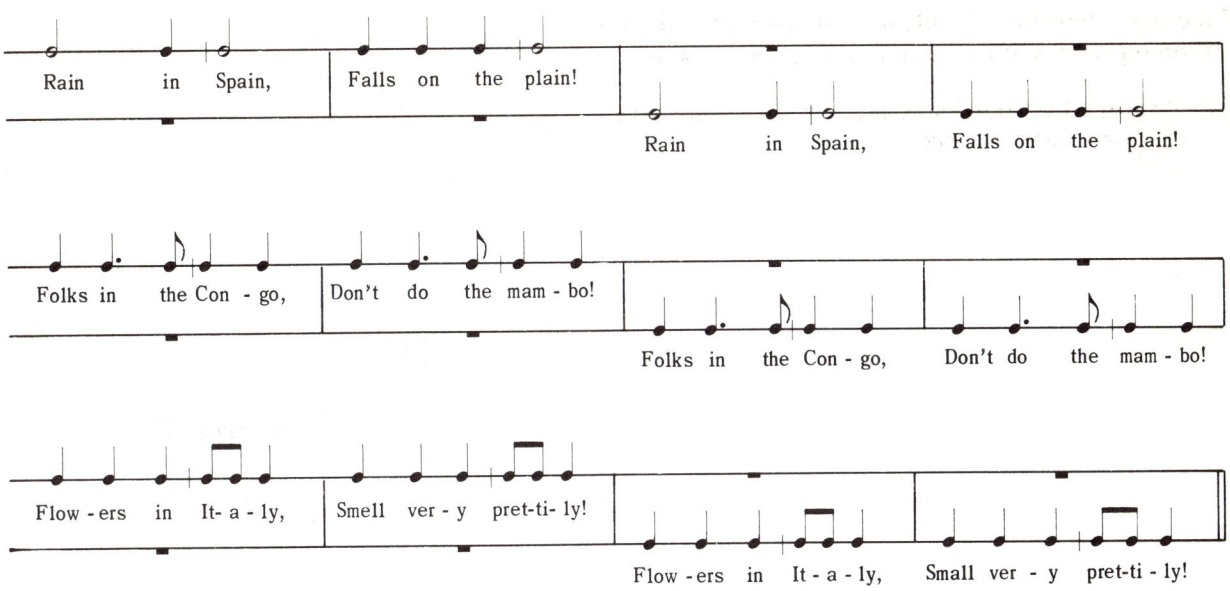

2. Tell children that you would like to see if they can chant and clap the rhyme through without stopping. Help them do the following:

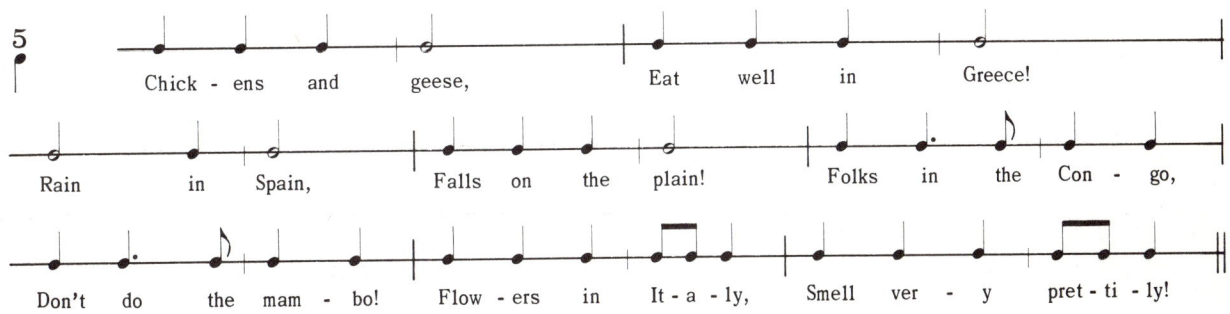

3. When children can clap and chant the entire rhyme easily, explain that today they will create a rhythmic rondo. Remind them that a rhythmic rondo is a type of composition where the main theme (called Section A) alternates with other themes, as follows:

Section A—Entire class claps and chants.
Section B—One child improvises (claps) an answering phrase, of the same length as Section A. (Remind children of previous experiences improvising clapped answers to your clapped questions.)
Section A—Entire class claps and chants.
Section C—One child improvises an answering phrase.
Section A—Entire class claps and chants.
Section D—One child improvises an answering phrase.
Section A—Entire class claps and chants.

4. Tell class that the rhyme they just learned to clap and chant will be Section A. Ask for volunteers to clap Sections B, C, and D.
5. Help entire class clap and chant Section A in a steady tempo. Bring in each solo, and repetitions of Section A without missing a beat. If children clapping solos have difficulty, don't stop, but let them do their best, helping by conducting rhythm of entire phrase.
6. To add variety, on another day, let children doing improvisations use percussion instruments instead of clapping.

Creating a Rhythmic Rondo Using Patschen, Stamping, Clapping, and Finger-Snapping—For Upper Grades

1. Give class a period of tempo-dynamic stamping, patschen, clapping, and finger-snapping.
2. Tell children to watch you, then to echo exactly what you do. Do the following in a moderate tempo. If children have difficulty with any one pattern, repeat.

3. Tell class that the patterns they have been echoing comprise one part of a rhythmic rondo. Tell them you would like to see if they can do this part all the way through without stopping. Give them the signal to begin and help them by leading them in the following:

Teacher and Students:

4. Ask class if they recognize the form of the pattern. (ABA form.)
5. Repeat pattern many times until class can do it easily without you.
6. Tell class that you would like to do a contrasting rhythm pattern as they do the pattern in ABA form just learned. Explain that they will be group one, beginning first, and doing their pattern once through. You will be group two, beginning a measure later and doing an entirely different pattern. Give class signal to begin. After one measure, begin pattern for group two, as below. The following should result:

7. When class can do the pattern for group one easily as you do the pattern for group two, select several children to join you in doing the pattern for group two. Repeat many times, gradually adding children to group two until the groups are evenly divided and can do their patterns easily in combination with one another.

8. Explain that this two-part pattern is Section A of a rhythmic rondo and that Sections B, C, and D will be of equal length (twelve measures, in ABA form, if possible) and will be created by individual children or planned by the group. Remind children of the rondo form:

Section A—Group one and group two performing their patterns simultaneously.

Section B—Individual improvising twelve measures (in ABA form, if possible) or an alternate plan decided upon by the entire group. One possible plan is the following, which may be performed by an individual child or a small group:

Section A—Group one and group two.

Section C—Individual improvising twelve measures (in ABA form, if possible) or an alternate plan decided upon by the entire group. One possible plan is the following, performed simultaneously by two small groups:

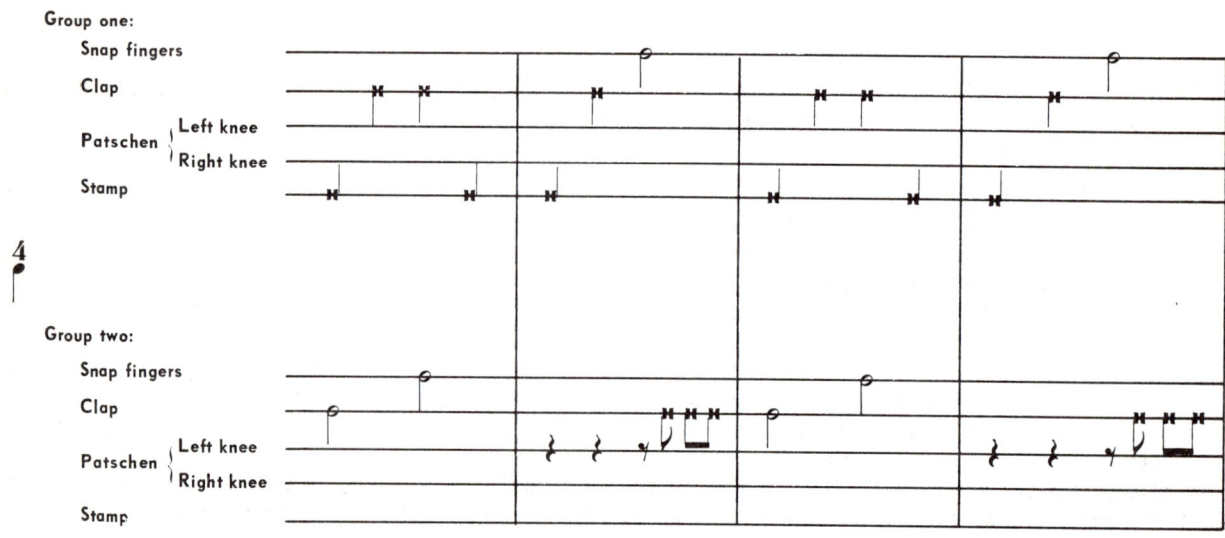

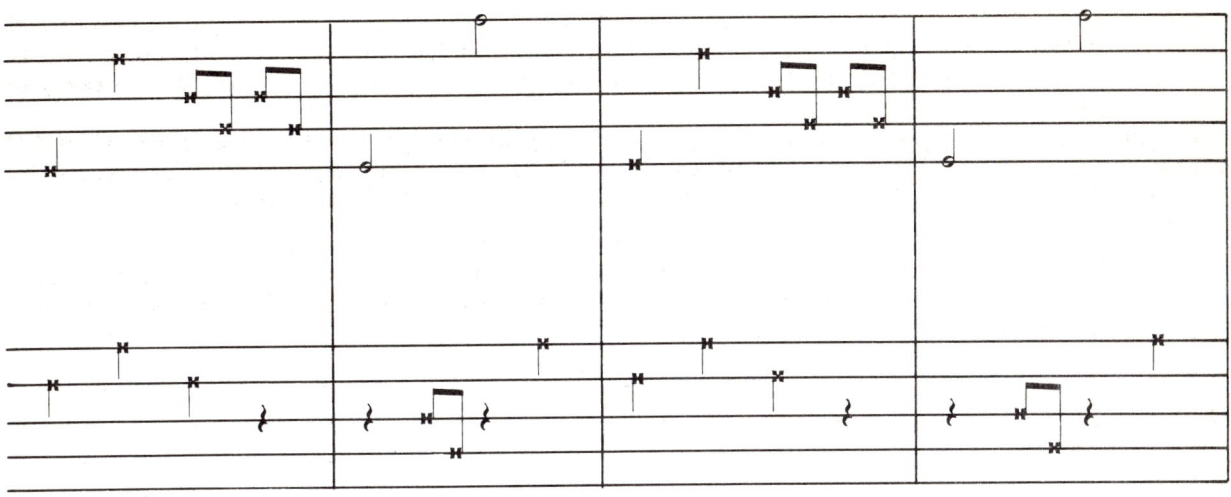

Section A—Group one and group two.
Section D—Individual improvising twelve measures (in ABA form, if possible) or alternative plan decided upon by the entire group.
Section A—Group one and group two.

9. Select volunteers or group to do Section B, C, and D, and remind them to be prepared to do their sections immediately following the preceding Section A, without missing a beat. Signal group one to begin. Bring in group two in measure two. Signal each volunteer or group and group one and two to enter at the appropriate beats, keeping time throughout, unobtrusively. If individual volunteers have difficulty improvising, help them by keeping time and/or doing bodily movement with them.

10. Repeat, letting different children improvise or perform Sections B, C, and D, and switching groups—group one becoming group two, and group two becoming group one.

11. When children performing Section B, C, and D are functioning easily, ask for volunteers to improvise a rhythmic interpretation of these sections. Select three or four children for each section, and encourage them to use their arms, legs, and entire body, moving in such a way that interprets the character of each improvisation, and if possible, reflects the ABA form.

CHAPTER 7

Experiencing Rhythmic Canon

The rhythmic canon presents an exciting challenge to children. Utilizing earlier experiences in rhythm, it demands increased rhythmic independence and rhythmic memory, and gives children enormous satisfaction in its execution.

Creating a Rhythmic Canon with Patschen, Stamping, Clapping, and Finger-Snapping—For Upper Grades

1. Teach the pattern below in the following manner:
   a. Have class echo each measure.
   b. Have class echo first two measures.
   c. Have class echo third measure, then fourth measure.
   d. Have class echo third and fourth measures.
   e. Have class do entire pattern with you.

Note: If difficulty develops in any measure, clarify by having them chant words with you.

2. When class knows pattern well, divide them into four groups. Have them do pattern as a four-part round, each new group beginning a measure apart.

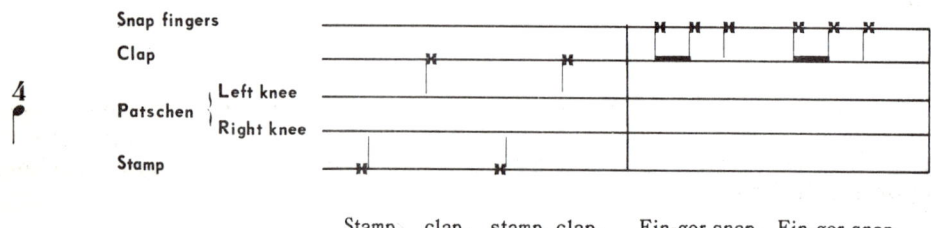

Stamp, clap, stamp, clap, Fin-ger snap, Fin-ger snap,

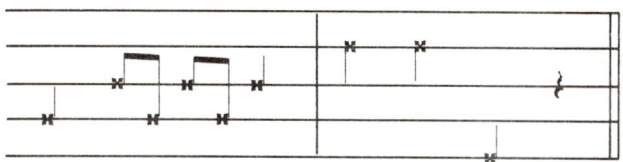

Try pat-ting on your knees, Please do this!

Clapping in Echo Canon, Duple Meter—For Upper Grades

1. Give children a period of tempo-dynamic clapping.
2. Give children an experience with the "Change Game." Explain that you will begin stamping, patschen, clapping, and finger-snapping in a rhythmic pattern and that they are to join you as soon as possible. They are to continue this established pattern, even though you will change your pattern, until you say, "Change," at which point they are to change to the new pattern you have been making, and you, in turn, will begin another pattern. The game continues in this way for as long as you wish.
3. Tell children that you would like to see if they can clap an echo canon. Explain that the echo canon is like a round—one part begins, the other part follows, imitating exactly the first part. Tell children to listen, and upon your signal, to begin clapping, imitating exactly what they heard, as they listen to the new pattern you are clapping. Begin clapping the following sequence in a moderate tempo, signaling children to begin as you clap the first whole note. If children have difficulty, do first eight measures only, saving second eight measures for a later date.

*Children begin quarter notes.

4. To expand upon the experience, notate the canon on the board. Assign some children to clap quarter notes, some to clap eighth notes, some half notes, and some whole notes. Remind them to be silent except when their notes occur. Signal children clapping quarter notes to begin, and help others to come in at appropriate times.

5. To further expand the experience, ask the class to clap the entire canon, all the way through. When they can do so with rhythmic security, select one child to *step* the quarter notes, one to step the eighth notes, one to step the half notes and one to step the whole notes. Start class clapping, letting these children step on their individual notes only.

6. Assign an instrument to each of the notes. For example:

Quarter notes—tone block
Eighth notes—sand blocks
Half notes—finger cymbals
Whole notes—triangle

Select one child to play each instrument. Let these children practice their parts, playing only the note assigned, as class claps the entire canon. When children do this with security, do the entire sequence—children moving to notes, children playing them, and class clapping.

Experiencing Echo Canon Through Patschen, Stamping, Clapping, and Finger-Snapping—For Upper Grades

Photo courtesy of C. Bruno & Son, Inc., Melville, New York 11746.

1. Give children an experience with tempo-dynamic patschen, stamping, clapping, and finger-snapping.

2. Tell children to watch you, then to echo exactly what you do. Do the following in a moderate tempo. If children have difficulty with either pattern, have them echo first two measures of pattern, second two measures, then entire pattern.

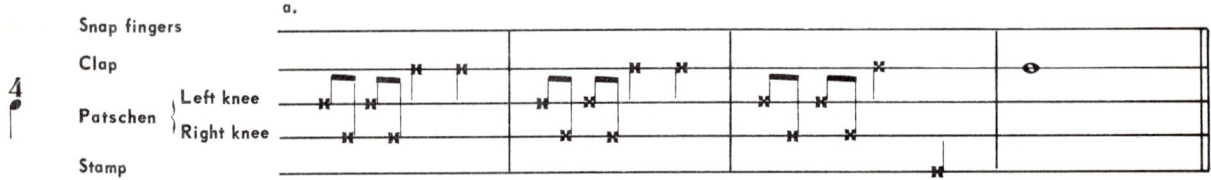

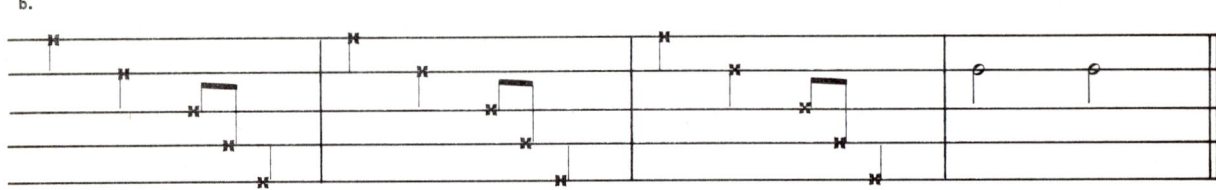

3. Tell class that you would like to see if they can do a rhythmic canon. Remind them that a rhythmic canon is like a round—one part begins, the other part follows imitating exactly the first part. Tell children to listen, and upon your signal, to begin, imitating exactly what they see and hear you do, as they listen to the new pattern you are performing. Begin the following sequence,

in a moderate tempo, signaling children to begin as you clap the whole note in the second measure. If children have difficulty, use a slower tempo.

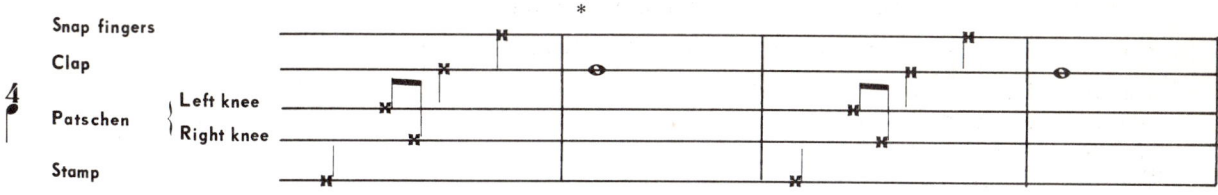

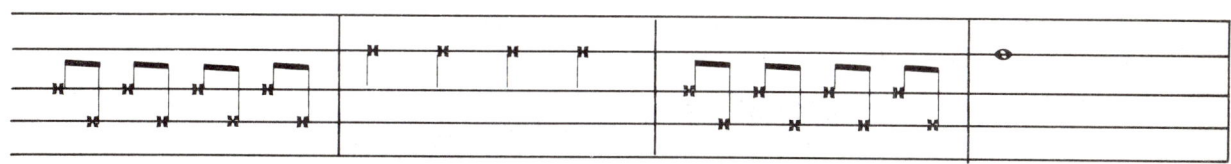

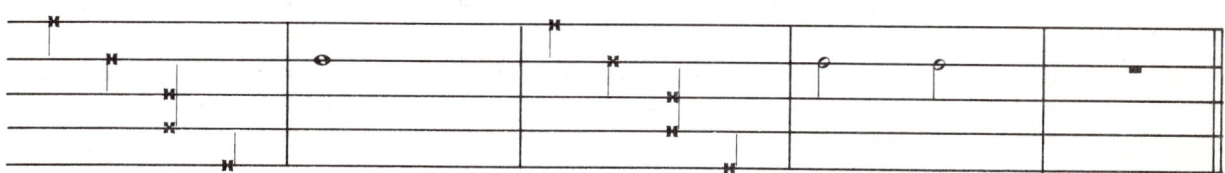

*Children begin on first beat of first measure and continue performing patterns, exactly one measure behind teacher.

4. Divide class into two groups. Let group one join you, group two follow one measure later. Repeat, letting group two join you, group one beginning one measure later.

5. Expand the experience in one of the following ways:

   a. Use the sequence of bodily movement (either in unison or as a canon) as an introduction, interlude, or coda to a song.

   b. Use the sequence of bodily movement as a rhythmic accompaniment to a speech pattern (proverb, poem, original limerick) or a song.

Experiencing Speech Canon in Irregular Meter (5s) Using Names of Automobiles—For Upper Grades

1. Begin a steady accompaniment, as follows, indicating that class should join you:

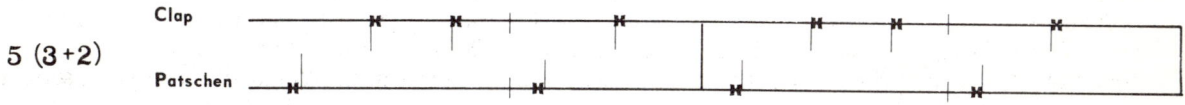

2. Tell class to continue to clap and to do patschen in the pattern above as they listen to you chant, and then echo what they hear. Do the following:

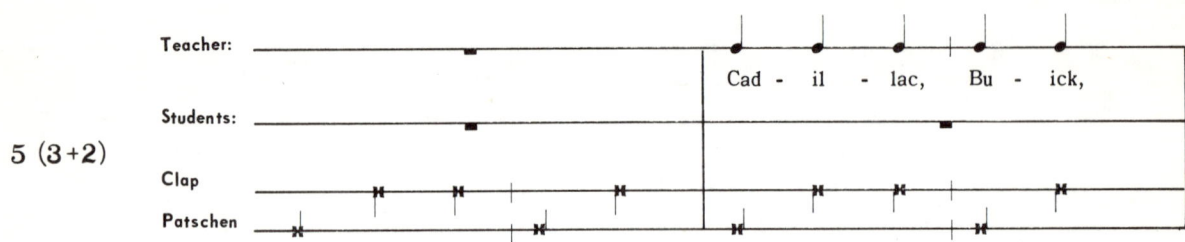

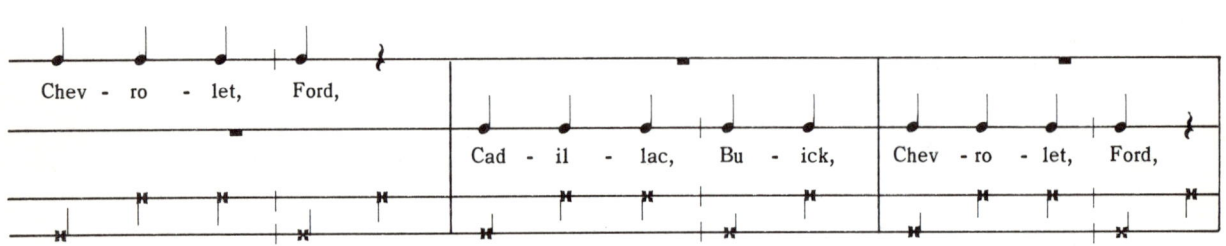

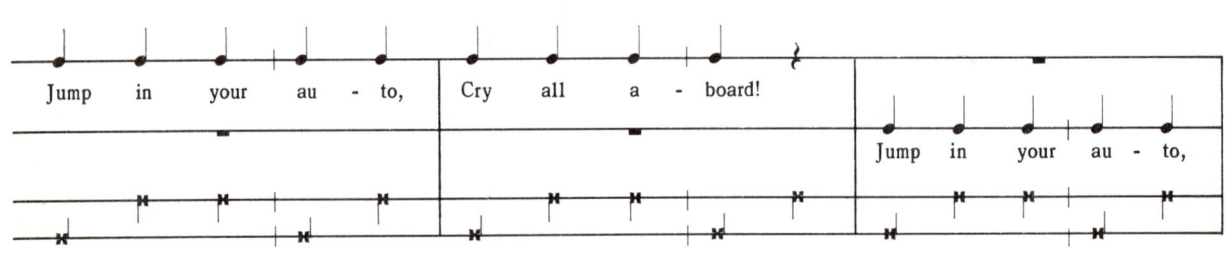

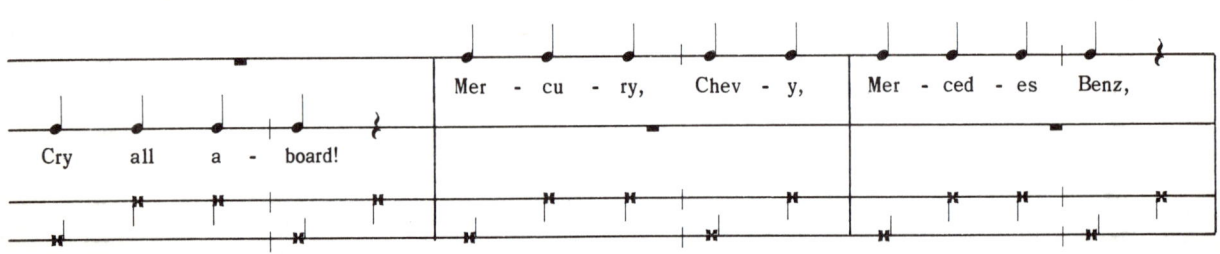

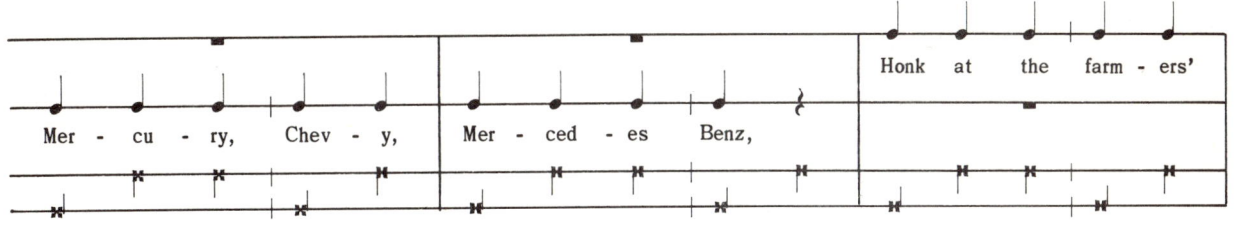

Mer - cu - ry, Chev - y, Mer - ced - es Benz, | Honk at the farm - ers'

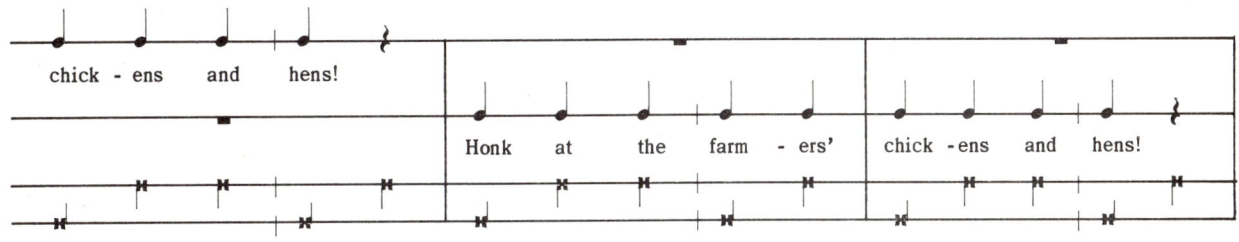

chick - ens and hens! | Honk at the farm - ers' chick - ens and hens!

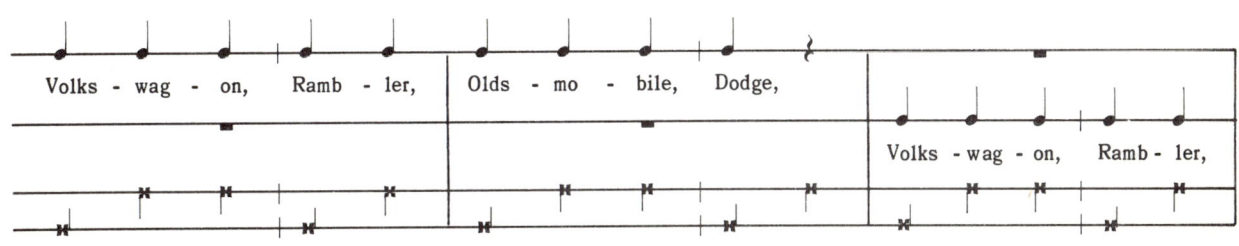

Volks - wag - on, Ramb - ler, Olds - mo - bile, Dodge, | Volks - wag - on, Ramb - ler,

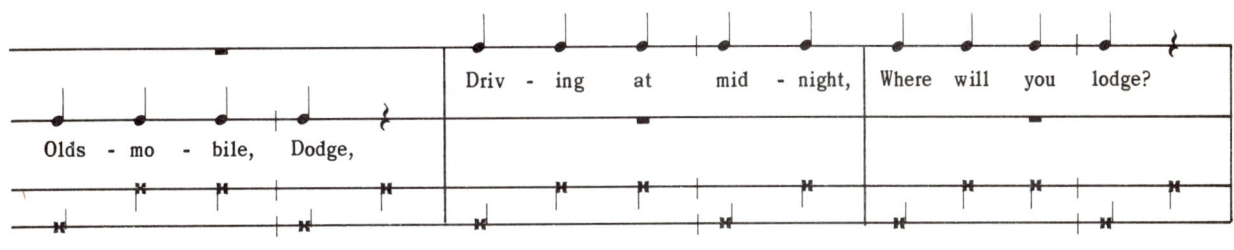

Olds - mo - bile, Dodge, | Driv - ing at mid - night, Where will you lodge?

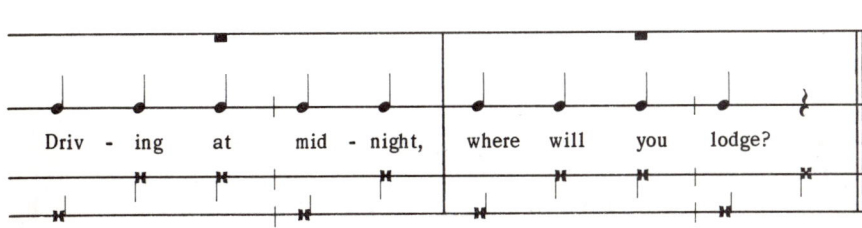

Driv - ing at mid - night, where will you lodge?

3. Tell class that you would like to see if they can do the entire rhyme, all the way through, with the rhythmic accompaniment, allowing one measure of rhythmic accompaniment between each line. Help class chant the following, with rhythmic accompaniment.

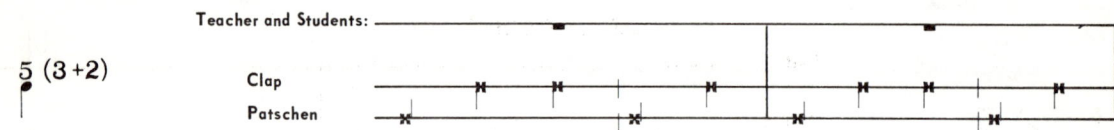

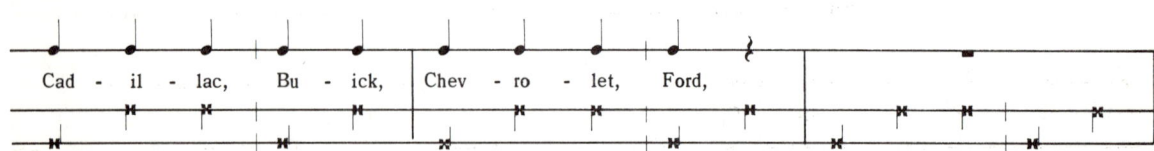

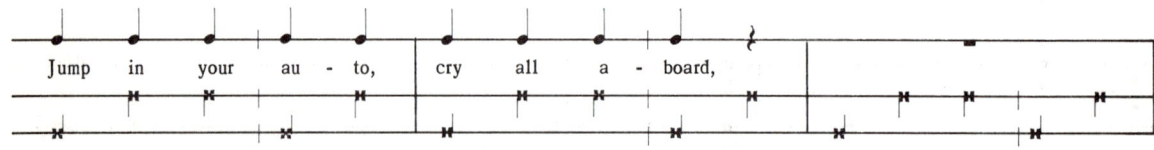

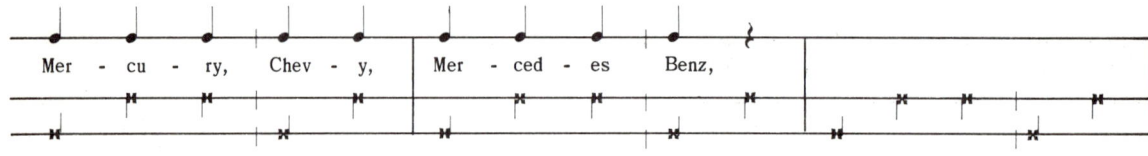

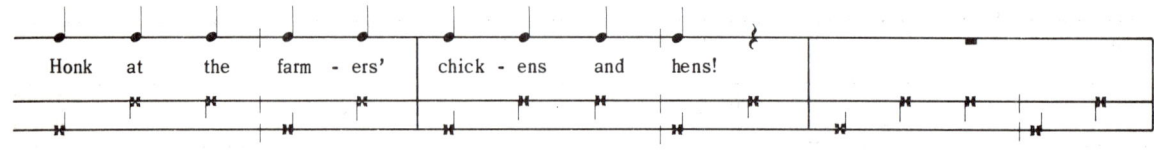

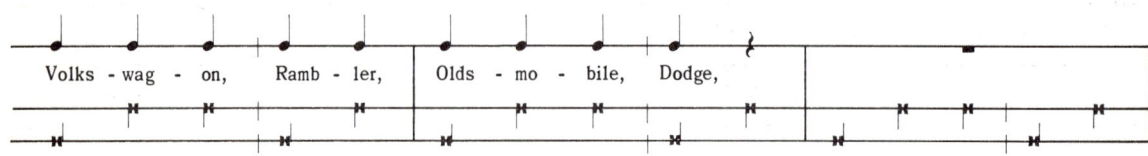

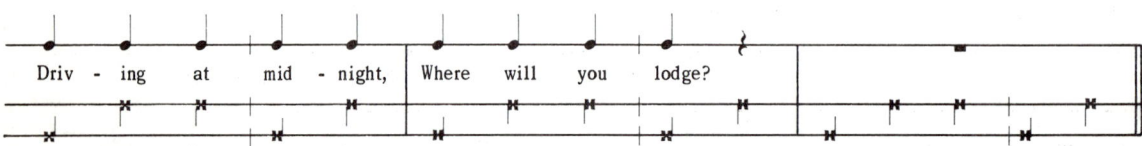

4. Tell class that now you would like to see if they can do this in canon form (in which two parts participate, one following the other). Divide class into two sections. If there is one student able to do so, select him to lead one section; you lead the other. Signal first part to begin. Bring in, and lead the second part, as indicated below:

SPEECH CANON

5. On other days, expand the experience in one or all of the following ways:

a. Help children create a melody for words, using only notes in the pentatonic scale.
b. Help children learn to accompany rhyme, using one or more of the following ostinati:

c. Have children orchestrate rhyme with rhythm instruments:

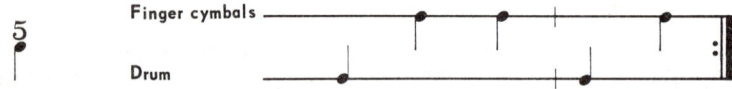

d. Have children accompany rhyme with the following bodily movement:

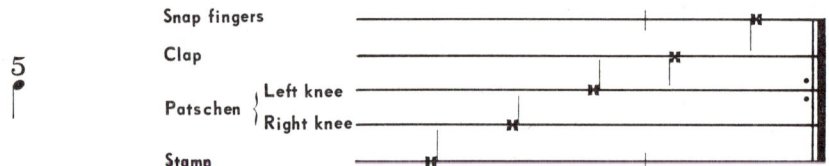

SUGGESTIONS FOR CLASS DISCUSSION OR REPORTS

1. Discuss ways in which nursery rhymes, chants, and jingles can help children develop rhythmic stability as well as a feeling for pulse, meter, and phrase.
2. Discuss the musical value of learning to chant in varying dynamics, pitch levels, and tone colors.
3. Discuss the responses to speech and rhythm—what they are and their value in the musical development of children.
4. Discuss (1) tempo-dynamic clapping and (2) tempo-dynamic patschen, stamping, clapping and finger-snapping; what each is; the value of each in the child's musical development.
5. Discuss (1) echo clapping and (2) echo patschen, stamping, clapping and finger-snapping; what each is; the value of each to the child's musical development; the way in which each can be used at various levels of the child's development.
6. Define melodic ostinato and rhythmic ostinato. Discuss the way each is used in the Orff experience and the value of each in the musical development of the child.
7. Discuss the value of experiences which cultivate phrase-building (question-and-answer experiences) in developing the ability to improvise.
8. Discuss the rhythmic rondo and rhythmic canon, defining each and emphasizing the value of each in developing musicianship.
9. Discuss ways in which bodily movement (using the entire body) can be used meaningfully with speech experiences.
10. Discuss kinds of chants which might appeal to children in upper grades.

11. Discuss ways your technique would differ when helping children in primary, intermediate, and upper grades to create their own chants, or rhythmic dramatizations of chants.
12. Define "mirroring" and give an example of its meaning in the Orff experience.

SUGGESTED ACTIVITIES TO DEVELOP SKILLS AND PRACTICE IN INITIATING MUSICAL EXPERIENCES

1. Lead class in one of the experiences suggested for tempo-dynamic clapping. Discuss the experience with class to determine its value, as well as ways it could be improved.
2. Lead class in one of the experiences suggested for echo clapping. Discuss experience with class to determine its value and ways it could be improved.
3. Select experiences in echo clapping for (1) primary grades, (2) intermediate grades, and (3) upper grades. Lead class in each. Compare how the three differ in meter used, tempo used, length, and complexity.
4. Select experiences in echo patschen, stamping, clapping and finger-snapping for (1) primary grades, (2) intermediate grades, and (3) upper grades. Lead class in each. Compare how the three differ in meter and tempo used, and in length and complexity.
5. Select one of the experiences for primary grades in which melodic and rhythmic ostinati are used to accompany a chant. Present it to class. Discuss the experience to determine its value and the ways it could be improved.
6. Select one of the experiences for intermediate grades in which melodic and rhythmic ostinati are used to accompany a chant. Present it to class. Discuss the experience to determine its value and the ways it could be improved.
7. Select one of the experiences for upper grades in which melodic and rhythmic ostinati are used to accompany a chant. Present it to class. Discuss the experience to determine its value and the ways it can be improved.
8. Study one of the experiences for intermediate grades using patschen, stamping, clapping and finger-snapping to accompany a rhyme (*As He Has Sown* or *Skip to My Lou*). Present it to the class. Discuss the presentation to determine how it could be improved.
9. Study and present to the class the experience using names of children to develop a feeling for accent and meter. (Substitute names of people in your class for the experience.)
10. Study and present to the class one of the experiences in triple meter. Discuss the presentation to determine its value and how it can be improved.
11. Develop your own experience in duple meter using an original chant, your own echo-clapping sequence, and melodic and rhythmic ostinati accompaniments. Make certain you include echo clapping and/or echo patschen, stamping, clapping and finger-snapping as a "warm-up," as well as preparation (through patschen) for each of the melodic ostinati. Present to class. Analyze the experience in terms of its sequential development.
12. Examine and present to class one of the experiences in contrasting meter. Discuss ways to improve the presentation.
13. Examine and present to class one of the experiences in irregular meter. Discuss ways to improve experience as well as its strengths.
14. Develop your own original experience in irregular meter, creating a chant, an original echo-clapping sequence, and melodic and/or rhythmic ostinati accompaniments. Make certain you include echo clapping and/or echo patschen, stamping, clapping and finger-snapping as a "warm-up," as well as preparation (through patschen) for each of the melodic ostinati. Present to class. Discuss ways of improving presentation.
15. Study and present to class the experience creating a rhythmic dramatization of the poem *Work at the Rock*. Discuss the positive aspects of the experience as well as ways to enhance the presentation.
16. Study and present to class one of the stories for rhythmic dramatization (*Worms, Deer and Bear, The Three Bears*, or *The Gingerbread Boy*). Discuss ways to effect a more meaningful experience.
17. Study and present to class one of the experiences cultivating phrase-building through question-and-answer clapping. Discuss to discover ways of improving the experience.
18. Study and present to class one of the experiences of creating a rhythmic rondo or rhythmic canon. Analyze experience for positive aspects as well as ways of obtaining a more effective presentation.

PART II

Melody:
Singing and Playing

Hump - ty Dump - ty   sat on a wall,

The child exploring all the joyful aspects of chanting invariably discovers melody.

The natural rise and fall of his voice as he chants pushes him quite instinctively on to an ever more discriminating expression of the vast range of color, dynamics, and pitches suggested by the words he chants. Inevitably he begins to sing.

It is but a simple step to encourage this natural exploration of melody through singing to include experiences with melody through playing instruments, thus adding the joy of producing new tone colors as well as playing in an ensemble.

In either case, whether it be singing or playing, we want, first of all, to help the child retain the spontaneous enthusiasm he displayed in his experiences with speech and rhythm. We want his exploration of melody to be interesting and challenging.

But we want more. We want to help develop musical understanding. We want to give the child an *inner feeling* for the differences in pitch and rhythm found in melody, the ability to express these differences through singing and playing instruments, and, ultimately, the intellectual understanding of these differences—the ability to perceive them in musical notation.

To accomplish this, it behooves us to follow the natural development of children. The child turning a chant into a song will, for example, when left to his own devices, invariably begin by singing the falling minor third. So it is well that in our initial efforts to encourage his exploration of melody, we begin by giving him two-tone songs using the falling minor third. It follows, too, that we are well advised to progress in a sequential line related to the instincts natural to children, adding to their singing and playing experiences the notes they would add, in the order that they would add them.

Thus, although songs from the major and minor scales are sung throughout, in those situations which are specifically meant to encourage ultimate intellectual understanding of music—musical growth—the sequence of experiences leads first to understanding of and responsiveness to the pentatonic scale. Gradually, as the child's musical comprehension develops, we can help him become responsive to, and have an understanding of, the major scale. With the introduction to the modes, we also develop an understanding of the minor scale.[1]

Throughout, this exploration of new intervals which create the various scales and modes can be made more meaningful by teaching the child the hand signal for each new note, thus adding the visual dimension to the inner feeling for the note and its relationship to other notes, and gradually developing a feeling for the interval relationships that make the various tonalities from which songs are created.

Rhythmically, the child's ability to hear, express, and ultimately to understand differences as they occur in melody is aided enormously by his experiences (previous and simultaneous) with associating rhythm patterns to speech.

Thus, as he claps, stamps, taps knees, snaps fingers, walks, runs, or moves in other ways to those rhythm patterns which are related to speech, an association is created between words, rhythm patterns, and note values. There develops a unique inner feeling for each of these. We can encourage this association by experiences which relate note and movement more directly. Thus, he can learn that a quarter note often suggests walking, an eighth note running, and other notes other movements; and as he moves in these ways, with the direct object of moving like a quarter, eighth, or half note, for example, the association becomes more meaningful.

Gradually, as the child begins to build up sufficient experience in hearing, feeling, and expressing melodic and rhythmic differences, he can be encouraged to relate this "inner information" to the staff—to see the sounds he has made, and to reproduce them in both familiar and unfamiliar patterns, reading from the notation on the staff.[2]

This skill—like that of developing an understanding of the various scales and modes—is a gradual, sequential process which begins in the kindergarten and first grade and continues throughout elementary school, and beyond.

BASIC OBJECTIVES

In all our experiences with melody—be they singing or playing—we want to follow the line of development natural to children as we lead them on to a feeling for, and an intellectual understanding of, all interval and rhythmic relationships found in melody, from the simple to the complex.

Our specific aims and objectives are as follows:

1. To give them the ability to

    a. Feel, as well as reproduce, interval and rhythmic relationships.
    b. Create their own music (improvise).
    c. Understand rhythmic and melodic notation (music reading).

2. To give them the ability to sing

    a. Easily, with a wide vocal range and a pleasing, expressive tone quality.
    b. With good intonation.
    c. Independently (able to sing one part while hearing its relationship to another).
    d. From the musical score, as well as by rote.

3. To give them the ability to play (Orff instruments, including the recorder[3])

    a. Easily, with a good mallet technique.
    b. With a good tone.

---

1. In the case of modes, we are not interested in developing an intellectual understanding among young children. Rather, we want to develop feeling and responsiveness, and the ability to reproduce the expressive qualities inherent in each mode.
2. Rhythmic and melodic notation are introduced in conjunction with two-tone songs and their hand signals, in the first grade.
3. The use of the recorder is discussed in Part 3.

c. While singing or chanting.

d. Independently (able to play one part while hearing its relationship to other parts), with rhythmic stability.

e. With a feeling for ensemble.

INTRODUCING THE ORFF INSTRUMENTS TO CHILDREN

The Orff instruments, described in Appendix I, are sometimes used in a purely instrumental form; most often, however, they are used as an accompaniment to chanting or singing. Because of the new sound colors they add and the ensemble experience they provide, children always respond with great pleasure to them. When their use is accompanied with musical growth, this enthusiasm continues, and it provides a constant impetus to more challenging musical experiences.

Mallet technique is an important factor in the playing of the xylophones, metallophones, and glockenspiels. When properly played, the quality of tone afforded by these instruments adds immeasureably to the musical experience. Mallets should be grasped by the thumb and first and second fingers in a loose fist, with palms down, so that the stem rests under the palms. The index finger should be curved and relaxed (not straight) to avoid cramping the hand and wrist thereby producing a hard tone. To produce a good tone, the child should strike the note in the center with a quick stroke, letting the mallet spring quickly back. In almost all cases, two mallets should be used, alternating hands on each new note.

Other suggestions which help make for successful use of the Orff instruments include the following:

1. In beginning experiences, the teacher should develop her own orchestrations which she teaches the children by rote. In later experiences, when they have developed a musical vocabulary, children can begin to create their own orchestrations.
2. Children should always play and sing from memory (by rote) in beginning experiences, until their "inner ears" are well-developed.
3. The words and music of the chant or song to be accompanied should be so well-mastered that no conscious attention need be given to them when an instrumental accompaniment is introduced.
4. Children should always be prepared for the playing of an instrument. That is, they should have had bodily movement of hands on knees and thighs which corresponds to the movement their hands will make when playing the ostinato pattern on the instrument.
5. The music to be played by the instruments should be kept thin and transparent so that it does not overshadow the chant or song. It should not be continuous, but should be interspersed with changes in tone color, or noninstrumental interludes, to avoid monotony.
6. Children playing instruments should always sing or chant, thus insuring that they keep a steady beat, develop aural independence, and cultivate a feeling for ensemble.
7. When developing an orchestration, it is wise to add one instrument at a time to the chant or song, using that instrument until it is effectively integrated, and until rhythmic and melodic stability is established.
8. Orchestrations are most effective if they provide a contrast to the melody—achieved by playing moving parts when the melody is sustained, sustained parts when the melody moves.
9. It is wise to avoid the temptation of using too many instruments, thus creating a cluttered accompaniment, or making exceeding demands on the skills of children.
10. To create interesting orchestrations in the Orff approach, it is helpful to study the orchestrations already available in the *Orff-Schulwerk* books and in this book, and after some experience using them, to begin experimenting with original orchestrations, always keeping in mind the suggestions above and the level of development of the class.

SEQUENCE OF ACTIVITIES

Listed below is a sequence of activities for melody singing and playing. Although listed separately, singing and playing proceed simultaneously. Generally speaking, by the end of the first grade, children are able to sing songs using all the tones of the pentatonic scale, using hand signals, as well as songs in major and minor, without hand signals.

Understanding of rhythmic and melodic notation is a gradual, sequential process which should progress at the rate of comprehension possible for the child. The sequence suggested below should be taken only as a general guide. Only the teacher can determine at what point a new concept can be successfully introduced and how much experience with each new concept is necessary before proceeding on to another concept. Each class varies in its rate of comprehension.

Singing

Ability to Sing, by Rote, With Hand Signals	Ability to Sing from Melodic and Rhythmic Notation

Grade One

Development of Pentatonic scale:	Two-, three-, four-, and five-tone songs using the following note values:
a. Two-tone songs (sol and mi)	♩
b. Three-tone songs (sol, mi, and la)	♫
c. Simple four-tone songs (sol, mi, la, and do)	𝄽
d. Simple five-tone songs (sol, mi, la, do, and re)	in 4/4 and 3/4 meters

Grade Two

Songs in pentatonic scale.	Five-tone songs using the notation above and adding the following note values:
	𝅗𝅥
	𝅗𝅥.
	half rest ▬

Grades Three and Four

Songs in pentatonic, major, minor, and modes.	Songs in the pentatonic and major scales, beginning exploration of modes, using above notation and adding the following:
Dorian mode (D to D or re to re, no sharps or flats)	
Phrygian mode (E to E or mi to mi, no sharps or flats)	
Lydian mode (F to F or fa to fa, no sharps or flats)	
Mixolydian mode (G to G or sol to sol, no sharps or flats)	
Aeolian mode (A to A or la to la, no sharps or flats)	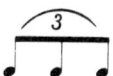

Grades Five and Six

Songs in pentatonic, major, minor, and modes.

Songs in scales and modes, using notation above, in irregular as well as regular meter, and adding patterns similar to the following:

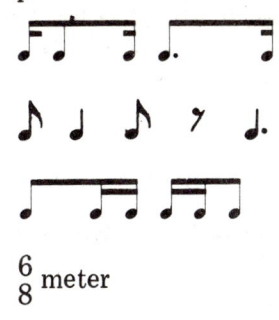

$\frac{6}{8}$ meter

Playing

1. Simple bordun to accompany pentatonic song:

2. Ostinati (moving borduns) to accompany pentatonic songs (K—6, from the simple to the complex, to meet individual abilities and skills).

3. Ostinati to accompany major modes (two-chord songs only).
4. Ostinati to accompany modes and minor scales.

Note: In all experiences throughout this section, and indeed throughout the entire book, the teacher will want to retain and cultivate the joy inherent in the play of children. Two kinds of activities can help: (1) imaginative use of percussion instruments (in any experiences which, by their very nature, suggest use of these instruments) in which children are encouraged to explore the many variations in background texture and dramatic and atmospheric effects made possible through use of these instruments; (2) participation in bodily movement which expresses the mood, atmosphere, or dramatic quality of the song or text as it is felt by the child.

On the following pages will be found suggested experiences for the sequence of activities listed above.

CHAPTER 8

Primary Grades

The foundation for future musical experiences is laid in the primary grades. The child who in the early grades has been encouraged to hear, feel, and express melodic and rhythmic differences in a free and joyful way—at his own pace and in experiences which encourage him to express his own responses—will usually acquire with little difficulty the technical information and skill necessary to move on to the more complex musical activities introduced in later grades.

Two-Tone Song, *Humpty Dumpty,* Using Rhythmic and Melodic Ostinati—For Primary Grades

Photo of Studio 49 alto xylophone courtesy of
Magnamusic-Baton, Inc., St. Louis, Mo. 63130.

1. Give class a period of tempo-dynamic clapping.
2. Give class a period of echo clapping.
3. Tell class to do as you do; then do the following:

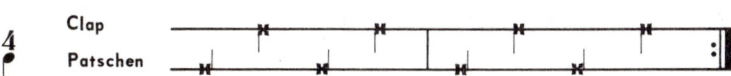

4. Tell class to continue the accompaniment above and to echo whatever you chant. Chant the following, using tone colors and dynamics which reflect the feeling of the text:

5. Ask class to clap and chant the words together, as follows:

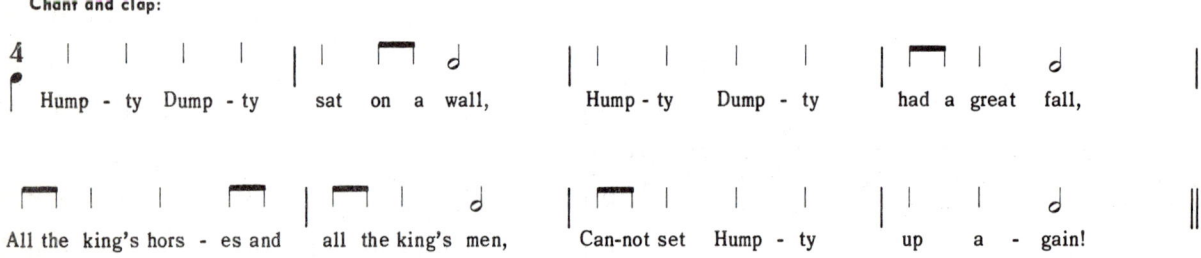

6. Ask class to stamp the rhythm of the words with their feet as they chant.
7. Tell class you would like them to do the patschen-clap accompaniment as they *sing* the rhyme with you. Have them begin the patschen-clap accompaniment. When they are rhythmically stable, begin singing, encouraging them to join you. A melody similar to the following will result:

8. To prepare a child for playing the alto xylophone, tell class to do the following with you:

9. Select a child to play the bordun below on the alto xylophone. Remove the bars adjacent to the notes to be played and remind the child that his hands will move in the same way as practiced above. Show the child how to play the bordun:

Note: In all experiences with instruments with children in the primary grades, remove bars adjacent to notes to be played.

10. Have the class begin the accompaniment. When they are rhythmically stable, have the child playing the alto xylophone begin playing. When all are secure, have class begin singing *Humpty Dumpty*.
11. When class can do the above easily, let them select rhythm instruments to be used as sound effects to be played when the words say "Humpty Dumpty had a great *fall*," "all the King's horses," etc.

Introducing Rhythmic Notation for Quarter and Eighth Notes Through the Two-Tone Song *Engine Number Nine*—**For Primary Grades**

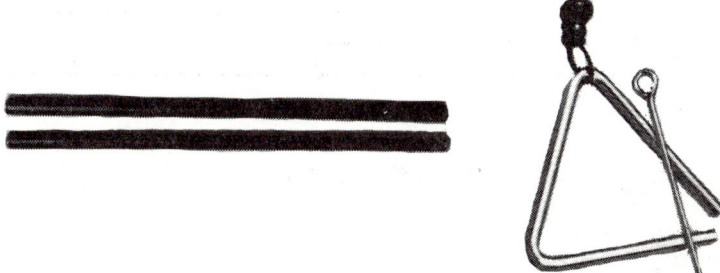

Photo courtesy of C. Bruno & Son, Inc., Melville, New York 11746.

1. Give class a period of tempo-dynamic clapping.
2. Give class a period of echo clapping.
3. Put the following notation on the chalkboard or on a large cardboard:

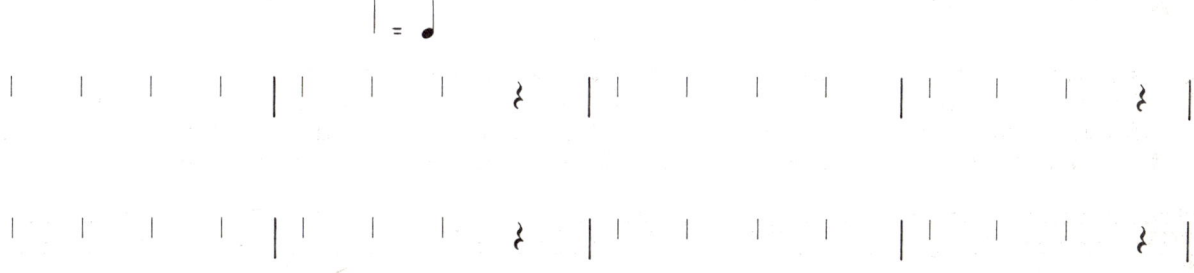

4. Tell class that each straight line represents a quarter note in music and point out the quarter note on the chalkboard. (If class associates a quarter note with walking, remind them of this association.)
5. Point out the rests in the notation and explain that they mean "silence." Tell class you would like to see if they can clap and say "one" each time a line occurs, and "rest" as they throw their hand

out, palms upward, each time a rest occurs.[1] Help them by pointing to the notes in a steady rhythm as they clap and speak.

6. When class can do the above easily, tell them that this is the rhythm for *Engine Number Nine.*

7. Teach them the words to *Engine Number Nine* by chanting them, line by line, as you point to the notation, letting class echo each line.

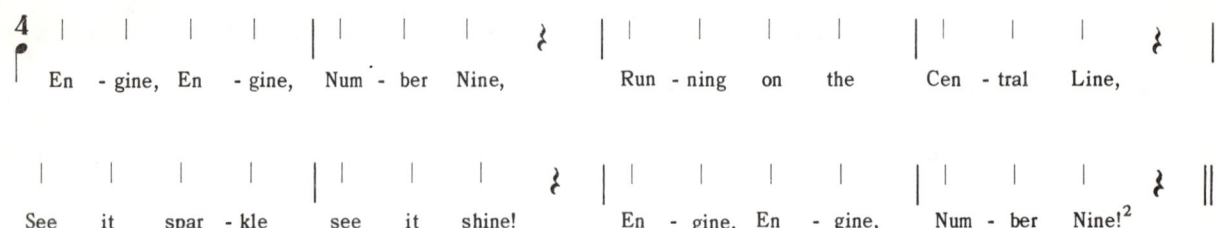

En - gine, En - gine, Num - ber Nine,   Run - ning on the Cen - tral Line,

See it spar - kle see it shine!   En - gine, En - gine, Num - ber Nine![2]

8. To prepare for teaching a bordun accompaniment, ask class to chant, "Chug, chug, chug, chug"; then do the following:

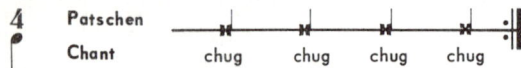

9. Select a small group to say the chant and to move as a train. Select a child to play the "chugs" on sand blocks:

10. Show a child how to play the following:

11. Tell class you would like them to *sing* the chant with you as the alto xylophone plays the ostinato accompaniment and the sand blocks play with chant. Tell them to begin the patschen (as in 8, above). When they are rhythmically secure, tell child playing alto xylophone to begin. After two measures, have child playing sand blocks and group chanting begin. After two measures, begin singing the chant, starting on sol and using only sol and mi (the falling minor third). Encourage class to join you. A melody similar to the following should result:

En - gine, En - gine, Num - ber Nine,   Run - ning on the Cen - tral Line,

See it spar - kle, see it shine!   En - gine, En - gine, Num - ber Nine!

12. To introduce the eighth note, proceed as follows:

    a. Show class the rhythmic notation for two eighth notes (⌐), tell them their names and how they are counted. ("One and.")

---

1. A rest may also be indicated by tapping the fingers of each hand on the corresponding shoulder.
2. Words to *Engine Number Nine* are from *Music for Young Americans,* Book 2, 2nd ed., *Discovering Music,* by Richard C. Berg, Daniel S. Hooley, Lee Kjelson, Eugene W. Troth, Josephine Wolverton and Claudeane Burns, Consultant, © 1966 by American Book Company.

b. Ask them what they look like. (A door, for example.)

c. Put the following notation on the chalkboard:

Chug - uh   chug - uh   chug - uh   chug - uh

d. Teach a child to play the notation on the maracas to simulate the sound of the train going down the track.

e. Ask class if the train is moving faster or slower with these eighth notes than it moved with the quarter notes. (Faster.)

f. Select a small group to chant the "chug-uhs" and move as a train, with the maracas, as rest of class sings the song.

g. To simulate the movement of *two* trains (one fast and one slow), let group chanting, playing, and moving on quarter notes practice with group chanting, playing, and moving on eighth notes until they can do it easily together. Then have class accompany with rhythmic accompaniment, and alto xylophone player with bordun, as the two groups move. When all perform easily, have class sing the song.

13. As an enrichment experience, do the following:

a. Show class the rhythmic notation for the half note and tell them the name: $\left(\,\right)$

b. Ask class how it differs from the quarter note. (The quarter note is colored in; the half note is not.)

c. Explain that the half note is clapped and chanted as follows:

Ding dong

or

One two

Clap Lift
        clasped
        hands
        upward.

d. Have child play half notes on triangle as children play sand blocks on quarter notes and maracas on eighths, with the appropriate chants.

e. When they can do this easily, have rest of class sing the song.

14. As a further enrichment experience, put the notation below on the board. Have children clap and count it. Then let class select one measure to use as a rhythmic ostinato to a song such as *This Old Man* or *Go Tell Aunt Rhody*.

Note: At a later time, after children have had many similar experiences, let them accompany songs using longer and more complex ostinati.

Two-Tone Song, *One, Two, Buckle My Shoe,*
Using Hand Signals—For Primary Grades

SOL   or   5

1. Give class a period of tempo-dynamic clapping.
2. Give class a period of echo clapping.
3. Tell class to do as you do; then do the following:

MI   or   3

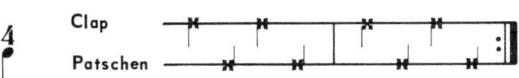

4. When class can do the above easily, tell them to continue, and to echo whatever you chant. Chant the following, enunciating in a way that emphasizes the differences in tone color:

5. Ask class to clap and chant the words together, as follows:

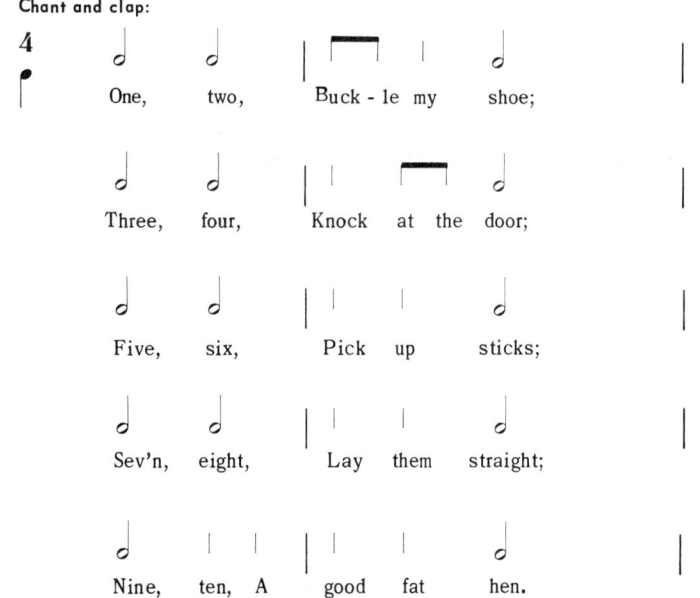

6. Tell class you would like to sing this rhyme as you move your hand in the same way that the melody moves. Tell them to join in when they feel able. Sing the following using the hand signals for sol and mi:

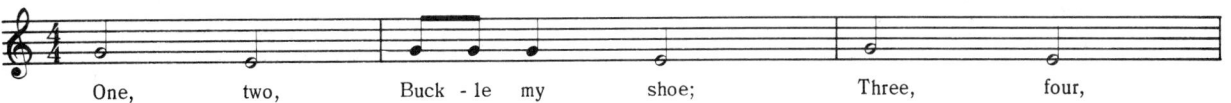

One,   two,   Buck - le my   shoe;   Three,   four,

Knock   at the door;   Five,   six,   Pick   up   sticks;

Sev'n,   eight,   Lay them straight;   Nine,   ten, A   good fat hen.

7. When children can do the above easily using hand signals, expand upon the experience in one or all of the following ways:

   a. Teach them additional verses:

   Eleven, twelve, Dig and delve;
   Thirteen, fourteen, Maids a-courting;
   Fifteen, sixteen, Maids in the kitchen;
   Seventeen, eighteen, Maids a-waiting;
   Nineteen, twenty, My plate's empty.

   b. Teach them to play the following bordun on the alto xylophone:

   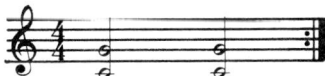

   c. Teach them the following accompaniments using percussion instruments:

   Tone blocks (preferably with high and low sounds):

   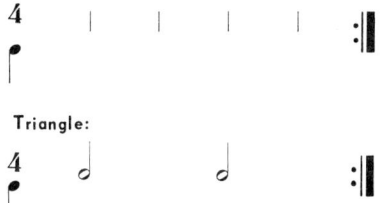

   Triangle:

   d. Help children create a rhythmic interpretation, moving body in different patterns for each phrase.

Two-Tone Song, *Ding Dong Bell,* **Using Rhythmic Notation and Hand Signals—For Primary Grades**

1. Give children a period of tempo-dynamic and echo clapping.

2. Clap the following rhythm pattern for children:

Photo of Studio 49 alto metallophone courtesy of Magnamusic-Baton, Inc., St. Louis, Mo. 63130.

3. Ask them how they would count it. ("one, one, one, rest.")
   Repeat, if necessary, to clarify.
4. Write the pattern on the chalkboard.
5. Ask children to clap and count pattern with you.
6. Clap the following pattern for the children:

7. Ask them how they would count it. ("One and, one and, one, rest.")
8. Put the pattern on the board under the first pattern.
9. Ask children to clap and count pattern with you.
10. Follow the same procedure for each of the following patterns. (Clap it, have children determine how it would be counted, place it on the chalkboard under the preceding pattern, and have children count and clap it.)

   (Count: "one, one and, one, rest.")

   (Count: "one and, one and, one, rest.")

   (Count: "one, one and, one, rest.")

   (Count: "one and, one and, one, rest.")

11. When children have counted and clapped all six patterns individually, have them go through entire sequence, clapping and counting.
12. Tell children this is the rhythm of a rhyme they know, *Ding Dong Bell.* Ask them to say rhyme with you as you point to the rhythmic notation for each line.

Ding, dong, bell,   Pus-sy's in the well!   Who   put her in?

Lit-tle Tom-my Green,   Who   pulled her out?   Lit-tle John-ny Stout.

13. When class can chant and clap the rhyme, tell them you would like to sing it for them. Sing song several times, using hand signals, inviting children to join in as soon as they can.

14. When class can sing the song using hand signals, prepare them for playing the bordun accompaniment by asking them to do the following:

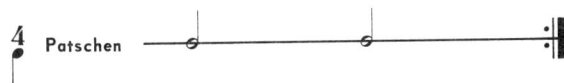

15. Show a child how to play the following bordun on the alto metallophone:

16. Have child playing bordun begin. When he is rhythmically stable, have class begin singing, using hand signals and singing first the syllables and then, after a two-measure interlude by the alto metallophone, the words.
17. Expand the experience in one of the following ways:

    a. Divide class into two groups and have them say chant as a speech canon: group one begins and group two starts when group one begins the words, "Pussy's in the well."
    b. Help class create a rhythmic accompaniment to the song. One possibility is:

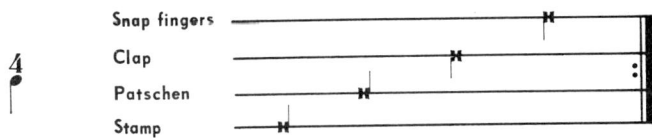

    c. Let them see and follow the notation of the song on the board as they sing.
    d. Teach any or all of the following instrumental accompaniments:[3]

---
3. In this and in all experiences with instruments, when accompaniments are too complex or too difficult, do not hesitate to simplify.

Soprano xylophone:

Soprano or alto glockenspiel:

Porta cello or timpani:

Note: The porta cello can often be used in conjunction with or as a substitute for the timpani or bass xylophone.

Developing Understanding of Musical Notation for the Notes Sol and Mi— For Primary Grades

Note: The following type experience should be extended over as long a period of time as necessary for children to assimilate the basic understandings involved in each step.

1. Put the following on the board:

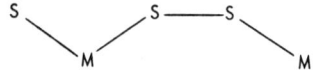

2. Have children sing the syllables above (sol and mi) using hand signals. Repeat many times, pointing to the syllables in a variety of combinations. (S, S, M, M, S, M, M, and so forth.)
3. When children have had adequate experience singing sol and mi in different combinations, write the following on the board:

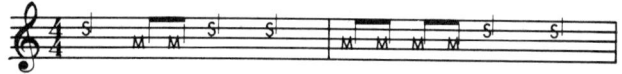

4. Have children clap and count the rhythm.
5. Have children sing the syllables in the correct rhythm, using hand signals.
6. Have individual children notate the above on a staff, as follows:

Note: The teacher will want to be aware of several factors involved in this experience:

(1) Notes may be used instead of S and M.
(2) The meter sign may be omitted or discussed, at the discretion of the teacher.
(3) Technically, there should be a Bb in the key signature. However, in this type of experience, the key signature is deliberately omitted to avoid confusing children.

7. Have children stand. Tell them to step with you in place. Begin stepping quarter notes, and when children are stepping with you, signal them to begin singing the notation in 6 (above) using hand signals.
8. Tell children you would like them to clap a rhythmic accompaniment as they sing the phrase and step the beat. Begin clapping ⌐ | ⌐ | as you step quarter notes. When children are following easily, signal them to sing.

9. Tell children that sol and mi may occur in different places on the staff. Explain that if sol is on a line, mi will be on the line just below. Have children notate the pattern again, this time starting with sol on a line. Repeat several times, letting different children notate, starting with sol in different lines or spaces.
10. On another day, have children make up different patterns using sol and mi, notating on the board, stepping the meter, and clapping a rhythmic ostinato.

Two-Tone Song Based on the Names of Children, Using Rhythmic Notation and Hand Signals—For Primary Grades

1. Give class a period of tempo-dynamic clapping.
2. Give class a period of echo clapping using a child leader.
3. Put the following rhythmic notation on the board:

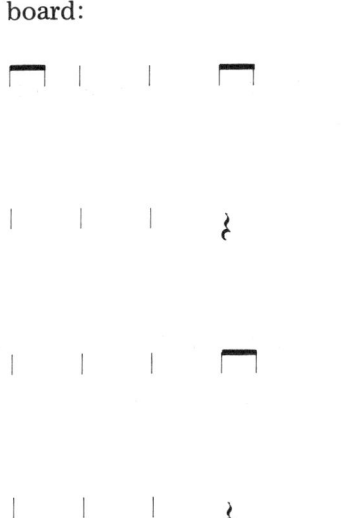

Photo furnished through the courtesy of the Kitching Division of Ludwig Industries.

4. Remind children of the following:
   a. The straight single lines represent quarter notes. (Draw a quarter note on the board: ♩)
   b. The two lines joined at the top represent two eighth notes. (Draw two eighth notes on the board: ♫)
   c. The figure at the end of the second and fourth lines is a rest, and means to take one beat of silence.
5. Ask children to clap and count the lines as you point to them, counting "one" for every quarter note and "one and" for every set of two eighth notes, and saying "rest" for the rests. Point to each line as children clap and count. Repeat several times, changing the sequence of lines until children can clap and count any line easily.

6. Tell children you know a chant that goes with this rhythm pattern. Put the words under the notation, as below. Tell children you will chant as they clap. Chant and clap the following:

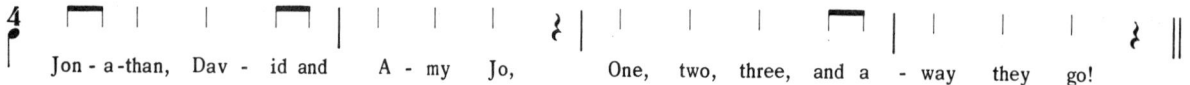

Jon - a -than, Dav - id and A - my Jo, One, two, three, and a - way they go!

7. Ask children to chant and clap the words with you.
8. Write the following on a large cardboard or on the chalkboard:

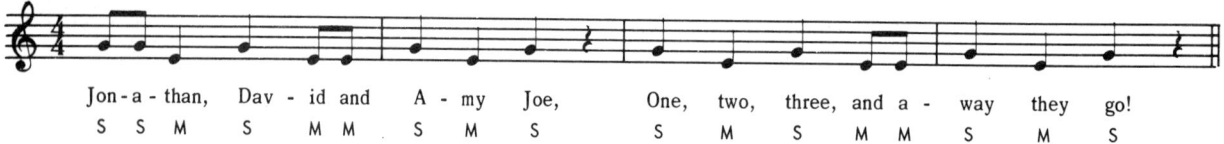

Jon - a - than, Dav - id and A - my Joe, One, two, three, and a - way they go!
S   S   M   S   M   M   S   M   S   S   M   S   M M   S   M   S

9. Tell class you would like to sing a tune that goes with their chant. Pointing to the notes, sing the words. Repeat, asking class to sing with you.
10. Point out the second "verse" (syllables). Ask class to sing the syllables with you as you point to the notes.
11. Show class the hand signals for sol and mi. Ask them to sing song using syllables and hand signals, then words and hand signals.
12. To prepare for playing a bordun accompaniment, tell class to do the following with you:

Patschen

13. Show a child how to play the following on the alto metallophone:

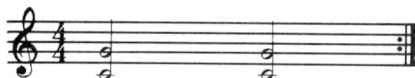

14. Have alto metallophone player begin his accompaniment. When he is rhythmically secure, have class begin singing song using syllables and hand signals. Let alto metallophone player continue playing after the end of the song to supply an interlude of four measures, then have class sing words as metallophone accompanies.
15. To expand the experience, have children do one of the following:

   a. Create another verse to the song, using their own names.
   b. Add additional accompaniments. Some possibilities are:

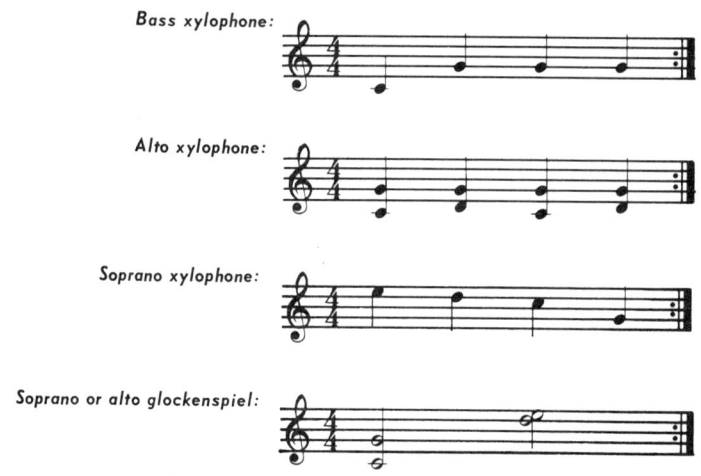

Bass xylophone:

Alto xylophone:

Soprano xylophone:

Soprano or alto glockenspiel:

Note: The ostinati for the alto xylophone and soprano or alto glockenspiel may be played by one or two children.

    c. Help children create rhythm patterns (using entire body) which reflect the rhythmic and melodic characteristics of the song.

Two-Tone Song, *Chocolate Fudge, Peppermint Stick,* **Using Rhythmic Notation and Hand Signals—For Primary Grades**

1. Give class a period of tempo-dynamic clapping.
2. Give class a period of echo clapping.
3. Put the following notation on the board:

4. Ask class what the single lines stand for (quarter notes) and how we count each of them ("one"). Ask them what the lines joined at the top stand for (eighth notes) and how we count them ("one and"). To remind them what quarter and eighth notes look like, draw the following on the board:

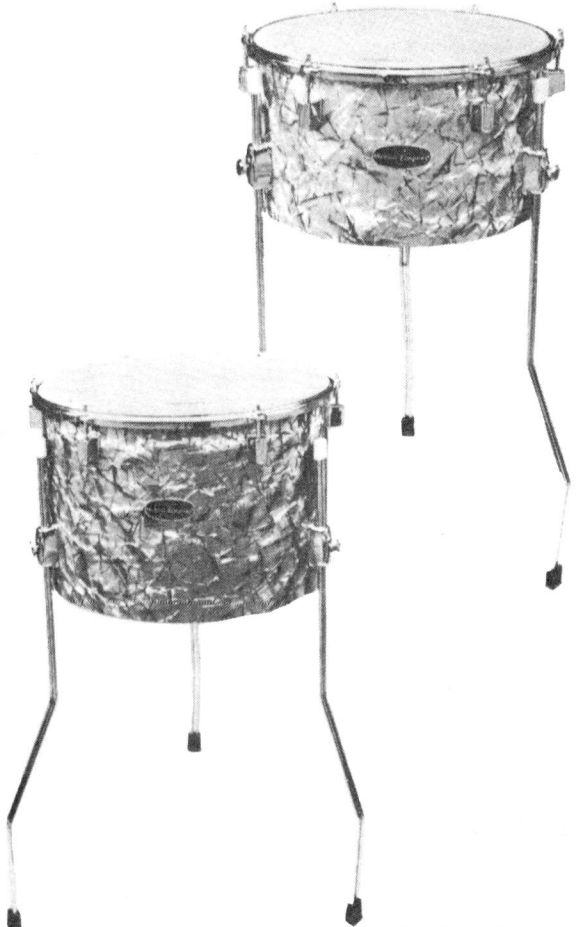

Photo courtesy of C. Bruno & Son, Inc., Melville, New York 11746.

5. Have class clap and count the notation in 3 (above) as you point to it. Go back and forth from one line to the other, repeating one line at times to try to "catch" them until they can count and clap either line easily.
6. Tell class to echo you as you clap and chant. Do the following:

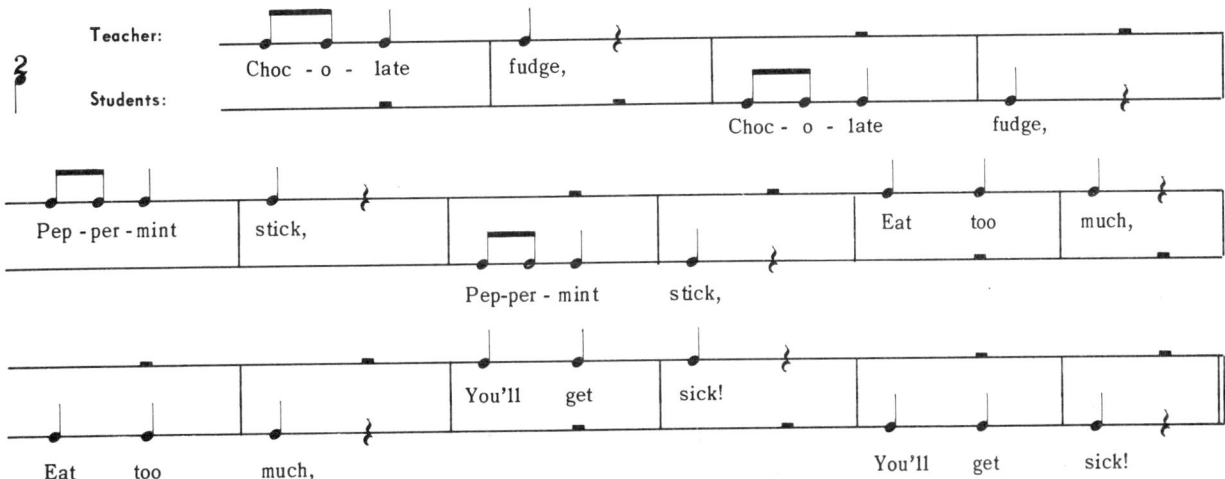

7. Put the notation for the chant on the board, as follows, but omit numbers and words:

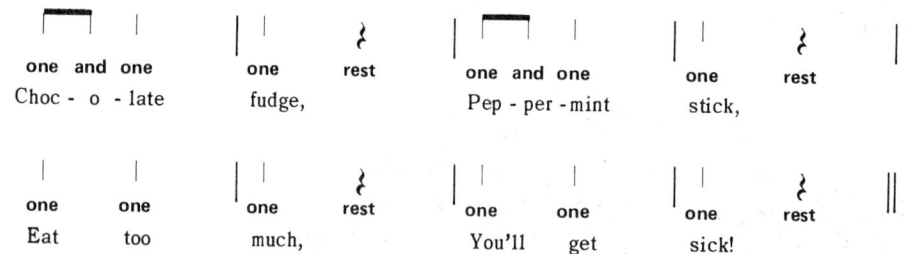

one and one   one   rest   one and one   one   rest
Choc - o - late   fudge,   Pep - per - mint   stick,

one   one   one   rest   one   one   one   rest
Eat   too   much,   You'll   get   sick!

8. Have class clap it, first with counting, then with words until they can do either easily as they clap.
9. Sing the song using the hand signals for sol and mi.

Choc - o - late   fudge,   Pep - per - mint   stick,
S   S   S   M   S   S   S   M

Eat   too   much,   You'll   get   sick.
S   S   M   S   S   M

10. Teach class to sing it as they use hand signals.
11. To prepare class for playing a bordun, have them do the following:

12. Remove bars adjacent to the notes to be played on the alto xylophone and show child how to play the bordun below:

13. Have child playing bordun begin. When he is secure, have class begin singing chant as they use hand signals.
14. Expand the experience in one of the following ways:

   a. Add a second verse created by children to the chant. For example:

   Butterscotch toffee,
   Caramel cream
   Taste so good they
   Make you scream!

   b. Add one of the following accompaniments:

Two-Tone Song, *Wee Willie Winkle,* **Using Rhythmic Notation and Hand Signals—For Primary Grades**

Photo furnished through the courtesy of the Kitching Division of Ludwig Industries.

1. Give children a period of tempo-dynamic clapping.
2. Give children the experience of echo clapping the following patterns. If difficulty develops in clapping any one pattern, repeat until children echo easily.

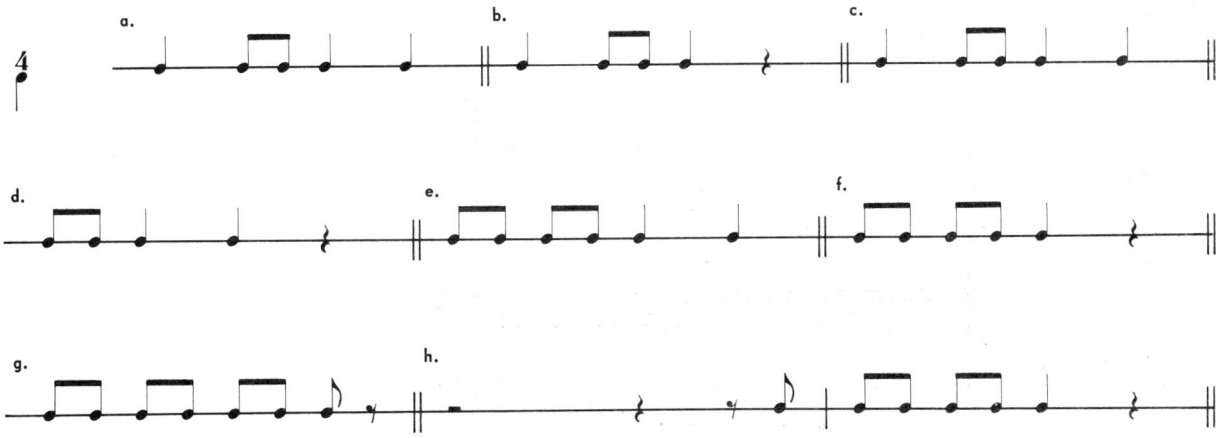

3. Write the following rhythm pattern on the board:

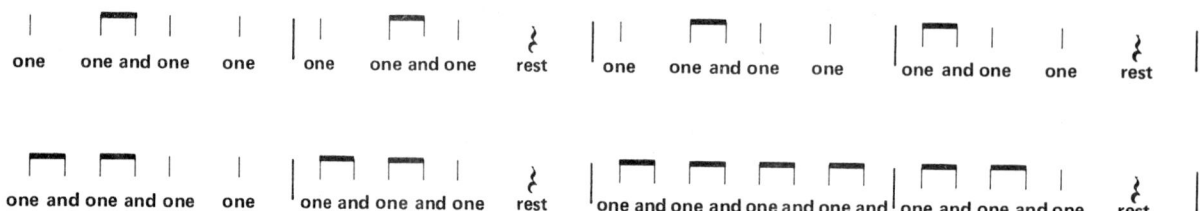

| one | one and one | one | one | one and one | rest | one | one and one | one | one and one | one | rest |

| one and one and one | one | one and one and one | rest | one and one and one and one and | one and one and one | rest |

Note: Do *not* put the counting under the notation on the board.

4. Have children read and clap the notation from the board.
5. Tell children this is the notation for *Wee Willie Winkle.* Pointing to the notation, chant the rhyme. Repeat, asking children to join you.
6. Tell class you would like to sing the rhyme for them. Sing the following using words and hand signals. Repeat, asking class to join you.

S M M S M   S M M S   S M M S M   S S M S
Wee Wil-lie Wink - le runs thru' the town, Up- stairs and down - stairs in his night - gown!

S S M M S M   S S M M S   S S M M S S M M   S S M M S
Rap-ping at the win - dow, Cry-ing thru' the lock, Are the chil-dren in their bed, for now it's 8 o'-clock!

7. Sing rhymes using syllables and hand signals. Repeat, asking class to join you.
8. To prepare for playing a bordun accompaniment, have children do the following with you:

4   Patschen

9. Show a child how to play the following bordun accompaniment on the alto or bass xylophone:

10. To expand the experience, teach children additional accompaniments:

Alto xylophone:

Alto glockenspiel:

Alto metallophone:

Soprano xylophone:

Bass xylophone or porta cello:

11. To further expand the experience, help children create a rhythmic dramatization of the song.

Two-Tone Song, *Barber, Barber, Shave a Pig,* **Using Melodic Notation, Rhythmic Notation, and Hand Signals—For Primary Grades**

1. Give children a period of tempo-dynamic clapping.
2. Give children a period of echo clapping.
3. Tell children you are going to sing a tune, using hand signals, and that you would like them to echo you.[4] using syllables and hand signals, and encouraging children to do the same.

Teacher:

Students:

---

4. In this and in all experiences where children echo sing, remind children to use light, high voices, and to listen carefully so that they blend and sing in tune. When out-of-tune singing occurs, the teacher should by all means call this to the attention of the class without naming specific children.

4. Tell children you would like to show them how the tune looks when it is written down. Write the following on the chalkboard:

5. Explain that this shows us the direction our voices go when we sing the tune. Have children sing the tune with syllables and hand signals as you point to the notes.

6. Tell children that now you would like to fill in the notes so that they not only show the *direction* our voices go, but also how fast or slow they move from one note to another. Fill in the notes, as follows, but do *not* put syllables, numbers, or words under them.

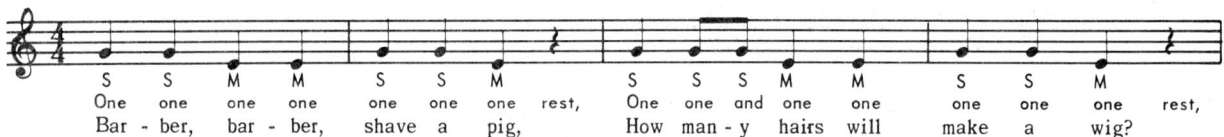

7. Ask children how many different kinds of notes they see (quarter notes and eighth notes). Remind them of their association with each. (A quarter note is often used for walking and an eighth note for running.)

8. Tell children you would like to see if they can *say* the *note values*. (Say "one" each time a quarter note appears and "one and" each time two eighth notes appear.)

9. Pointing to the notes, have children say the second "verse" above (rhythmic counting).

10. Tell children that now you would like to sing the words for them. Pointing to the notes and using hand signals, sing the words to the song *Barber, Barber, Shave a Pig,* encouraging children to do the same. Repeat until children know words, letting various children have turns pointing to the notes as class sings.

11. To prepare children or playing a bordun accompaniment, do the following:

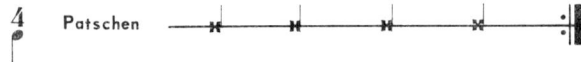

12. Show a child how to play the following on the bass xylophone:

13. Have child playing bass xylophone begin accompaniment. When he is secure, have class begin singing song—first syllables, then rhythmic notation, then words, allowing a two-measure interlude between each.

14. To expand the experience, add the following accompaniments:

15. To further expand the experience, help children create a rhythmic dramatization of the song which reflects the rhythmic characteristics of the words (light, fast).

Two-Tone Song, *Jack Sprat,* Using Melodic Notation, Rhythmic Notation, and Hand Signals—For Primary Grades

Photo furnished through the courtesy of the Kitching Division of Ludwig Industries.

1. Give children a period of tempo-dynamic movement. (Patschen, stamp, clap, snap.)
2. Give children a period of echo movement.

3. Tell children to echo you, and then do the following: sing words, then syllables, using hand signals. Encourage children to do the same.

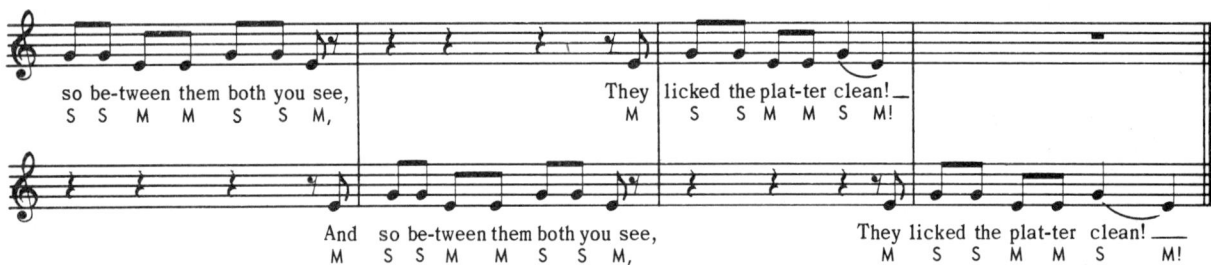

4. Repeat the above as many times as necessary, using a variety of dynamics, until children are thoroughly familiar with words and syllables.
5. Remove all notes but sol and mi (G and E) from the alto glockenspiel.
6. Tell children you would like to see if they can determine how to play the song on the glockenspiel. Let individual children experiment in the following way: Class sings first phrase. Child tries to play it on glockenspiel, with help from rest of class, if necessary.
7. When a child has discovered how to play the first phrase, notate it on the board, melodically only, as follows:

8. Continue working in this way, phrase by phrase, letting different children try to play each phrase on the alto glockenspiel while you notate each phrase as it is worked out, until you have the following on the chalkboard.[5]

9. Tell children that the above shows the *direction* our voices go when we sing *Jack Sprat*. Have them sing the words, then syllables, with hand signals, as you point to the notes.

---

5. In this and in all similar experiences, the teacher may find it more effective to complete the activity on another day.

10. Tell children you would like to fill in the notes to show them the differences in speed with which each note moves—how fast one note follows another in the song. Fill in the notes, as follows, omitting the numbers and words:

11. Tell class you would like to see if they can sing "one" for each quarter note and "one and" for each two eighth notes. Pointing to the notes and using hand signals, sing the rhythmic notation.
12. Have class sing words using hand signals as you point to the notes.
13. To prepare class for an accompanying bordun, have them do the following:

14. Show a child how to play the following on the alto xylophone:

15. Have child playing xylophone begin. When he is secure, have class begin singing, first syllables, then words, allowing a two-measure interlude between verses, and a two-measure coda at the end.
16. To expand the experience, add the following accompaniments:

17. To further expand the experience, help children create a rhythmic dramatization of the song.

Three-Tone Song, *Georgie Porgie,* **Using Melodic Ostinato**
and Hand Signals—For Primary Grades

LA or 6

1. Give class a period of tempo-dynamic movement
   (patschen, stamp, clap, snap).
2. Give class a period of echo movement.
3. Remind children of the hand signals they know for sol and mi by having them echo you as you
   sing the following, using hand signals:

4. Tell children you would like to show them the hand signal for another note. Demonstrate the
   signal for la.
5. Tell children you would like to see if they can echo you as you sing a tune using the new note la.
   Do the following, first with syllables, then with words.

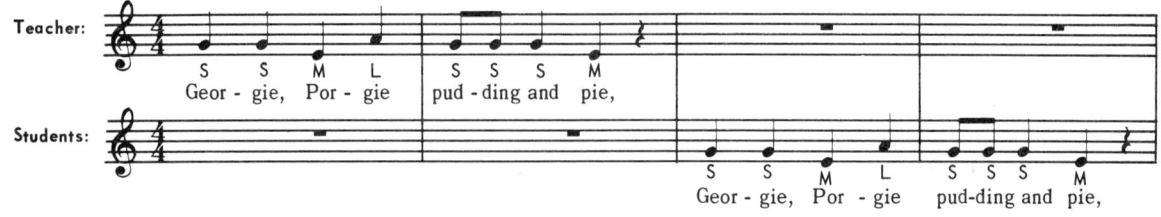

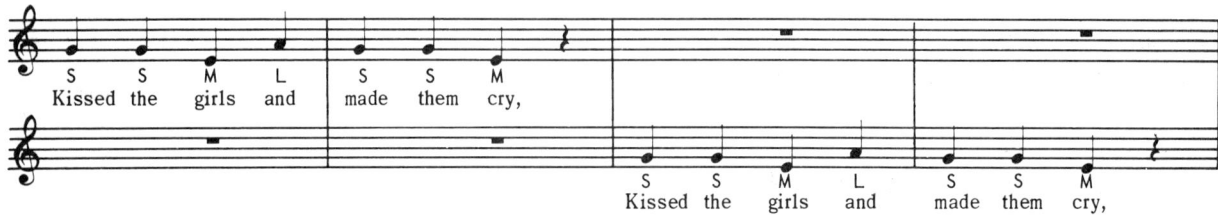

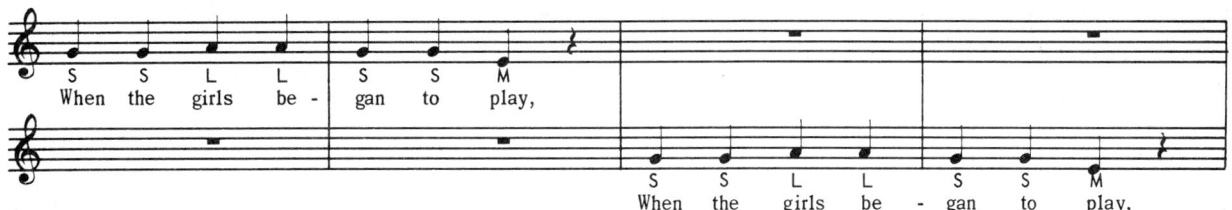

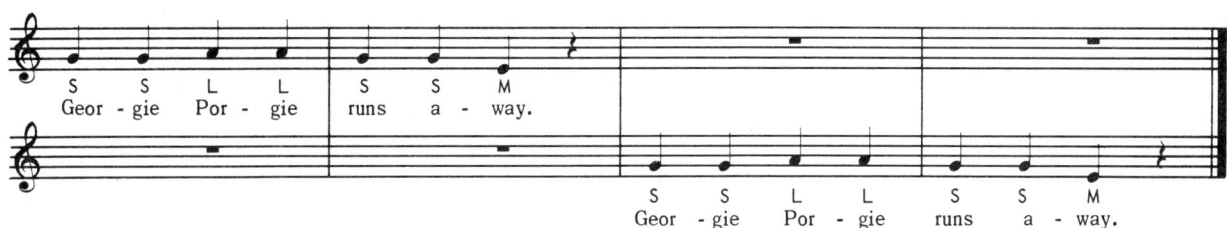

6. Tell children you would like to see if they can sing the song with you. Do the following with hand signals, singing first the syllables and then the words:

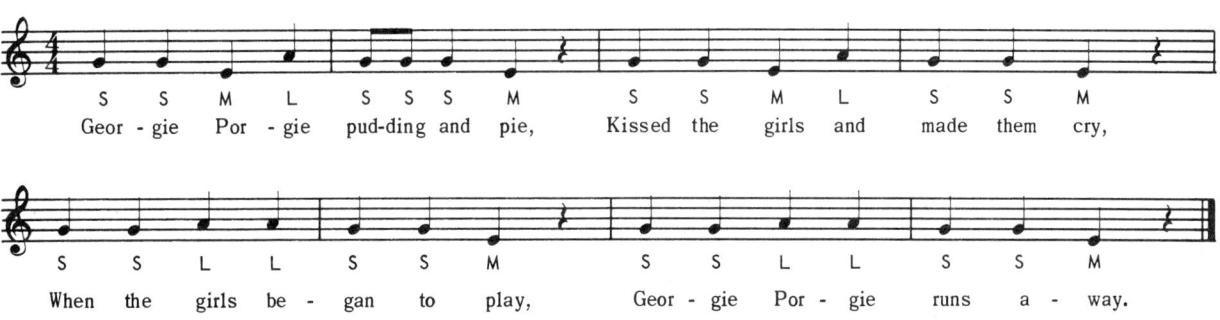

Note: This technic of teaching a song through hand signals is invaluable in developing a visual as well as an aural perception of interval relationships. Further, it can be useful as a tool in developing an understanding of melodic and rhythmic notation by guiding children in notating songs (phrase by phrase) melodically, then rhythmically.

7. Prepare children for doing an ostinato accompaniment by telling them to do as you do; then do the following. (Children will mirror you, doing the opposite.)

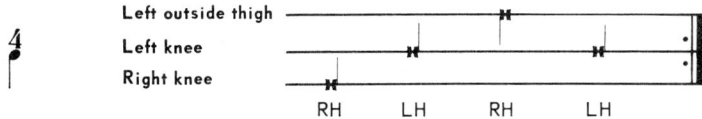

8. Remove all bars except the bars for C, G, and A from the alto xylophone. Show a child how to play the following, using two mallets:

9. Have child playing the ostinato begin playing his part. When he is rhythmically stable, have the class begin singing the syllables, using hand signals. At the end of the song, have alto xylophone continue alone to provide a two-measure interlude. Then have class sing the words, using hand signals. At the end, let child playing alto xylophone continue for a two-measure postlude.

10. To expand on the experience, help children to play the following accompaniments:

Alto metallophone:

Alto glockenspiel:

Timpani or bass xylophone:

Tone block or hand drum:

Soprano xylophone:

Introducing the Half Note Through the Rhyme *Susan, Jimmy,* and Creating a Three-Tone Song—For Primary Grades

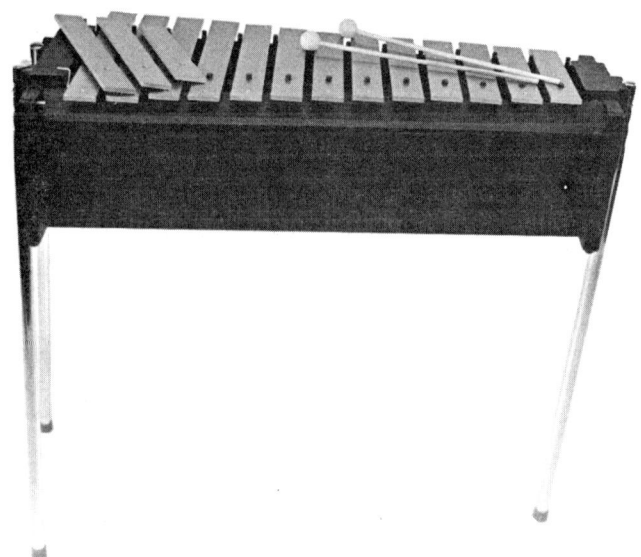

Photo courtesy of Lyons Band Company, Elmhurst, Ill.

1. Give class a period of tempo-dynamic clapping.
2. Give class a period of echo clapping.

3. Notate the following rhyme on the board. (Do *not* put down the number notation.)

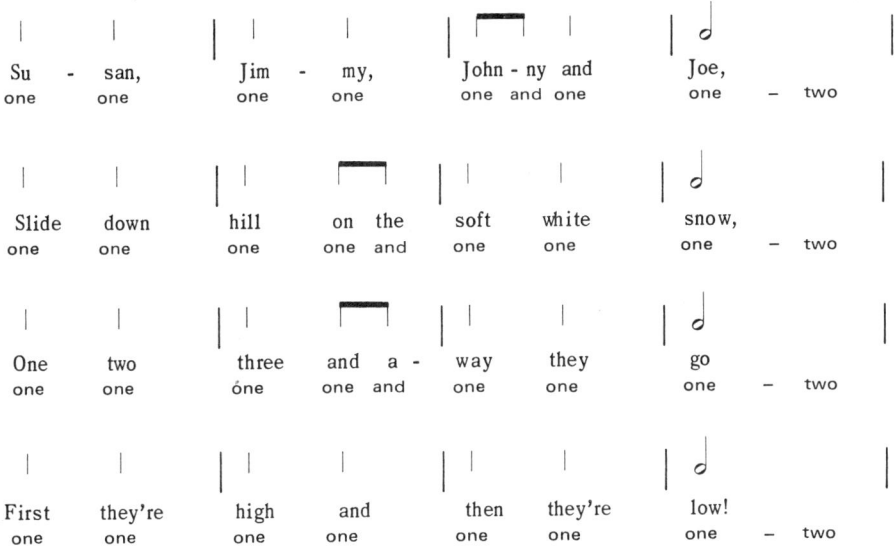

Su - san,	Jim - my,	John - ny and	Joe,	
one one	one one	one and one	one – two	
Slide down	hill on the	soft white	snow,	
one one	one one and	one one	one – two	
One two	three and a -	way they	go	
one one	one one and	one one	one – two	
First they're	high and	then they're	low!	
one one	one one	one one	one – two	

4. Ask children to examine the notes on the board and tell you which note is a new note to them. (The half note, last note in each line.) Discuss the half note, asking children to tell you what it looks like (a golf club, a balloon upside down) and how it differs from the quarter and eighth notes. Remind children that in music *all* notes have a ball either on the bottom or top. Explain that the half note is two counts long and that we count it, "one—two."

5. Ask children to clap and say words of rhyme with you, encouraging them to speak expressively. When they know the words, have them clap and chant the notation.

6. Ask children to sing this rhyme with you. Help them sing it, using hand signals and all three tones they know—sol, mi, and la. One possible melody is the following:

7. To prepare for the instrumental accompaniment, tell children to do as you do, and do the following. (Children will mirror you, doing exactly the opposite.)

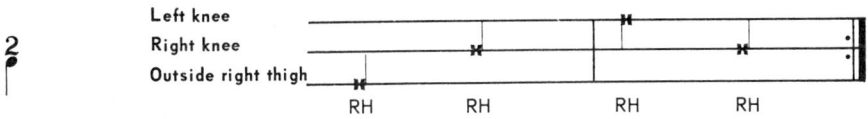

8. When children can do the preceding easily, have them do the following (repeating motions of right hand, but adding left hand).

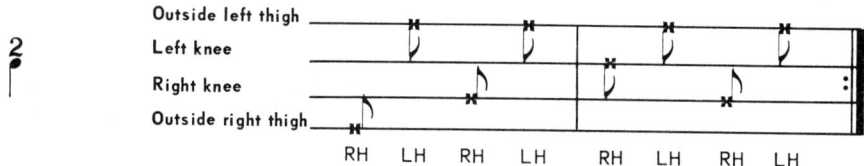

9. Show a child how to play the following on the bass xylophone:

10. Have the bass xylophone player begin. After two measures, have class begin singing the song. Let the bass xylophone continue for two measures after end of song.

11. To expand the experience, prepare children for the following accompaniments and show them how to play them:

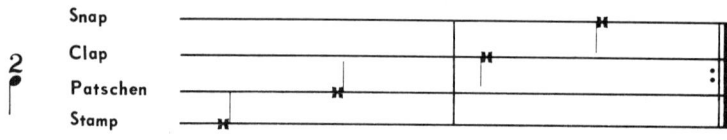

12. To further expand the experience, help children create a rhythmic interpretation which is expressive of the text.

Three-Tone Song, *Humpty Dumpty,* **Using Quarter, Eighth,
and Half Notes—For Primary Grades**

Photo courtesy of C. Bruno & Son, Inc., Melville, New York 11746.

1. Write the following on the board, omitting the words:

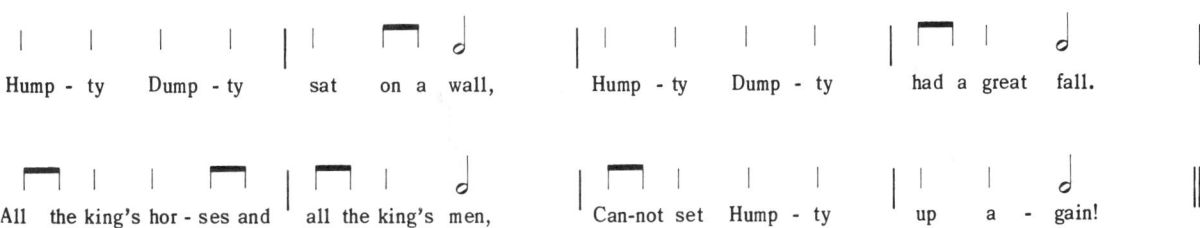

Hump - ty   Dump - ty   sat   on a   wall,   Hump - ty   Dump - ty   had a great   fall.

All   the king's hor - ses and   all the king's   men,   Can-not set   Hump - ty   up   a - gain!

2. Ask for a volunteer to clap the rhythmic notation. When a child can clap the notation correctly, have entire class clap it with him as you point to the notation on the board.
3. Explain that this is the rhythmic notation of a rhyme they all know, Humpty Dumpty.
4. Point to notes on the board as class chants *Humpty Dumpty.*
5. Ask class to step the beat (quarter notes) as they clap and chant the words.
6. Ask a volunteer to play a hand drum in the rhythm stepped (quarter notes). When he can do this easily, ask half the class to chant the following speech ostinato as he plays drum:

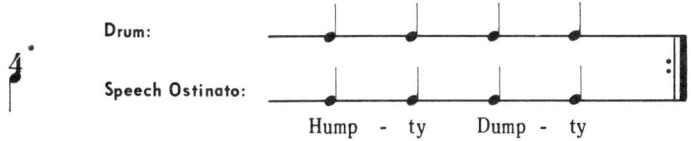

Drum:

Speech Ostinato:

Hump - ty   Dump - ty

7. Ask class to join you in doing the following:

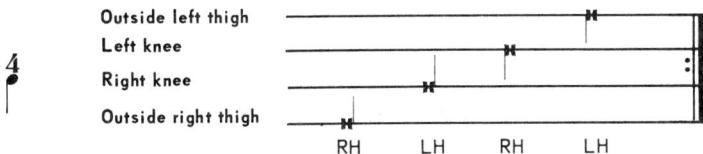

Outside left thigh
Left knee
Right knee
Outside right thigh

RH   LH   RH   LH

8. Show a child how to play the following on the bass xylophone:

9. Tell class you would like them to say the rhyme and chant with the bass xylophone accompaniment as they all do a new rhythm pattern together. Tell them to do as you do; then do the following:

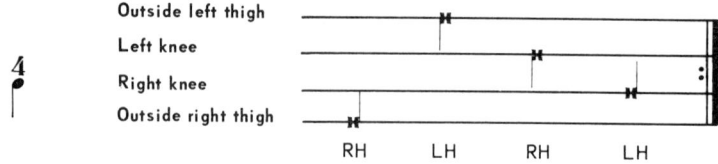

10. When class is doing pattern easily, have them continue, then signal bass xylophone to begin. After two measures, bring in the child playing the hand drum and group doing the chant (6, page 155). After two additional measures, bring in rest of class chanting rhyme.
11. Show a child how to play the ostinato for soprano xylophone:

12. Ask class to do as you do; then do the following:

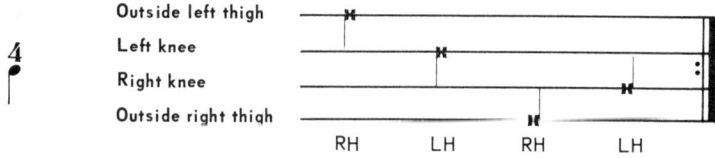

13. When class is doing above easily, have them continue, then signal bass xylophone to begin playing ostinato. After two measures, bring in soprano xylophone. After two more measures, bring in child playing hand drum and group chanting with him. After two additional measures, bring in rest of class chanting rhyme.
14. Show a child how to play a second part for the soprano xylophone:

15. Add this accompaniment to the other ostinati, as two groups say chant and rhyme.
16. Divide class into three groups—group one to say rhyme, group two to chant speech ostinato (6, page 155), and group three to chant the following as a child plays the same rhythm pattern, alternating on a high and low tone block:

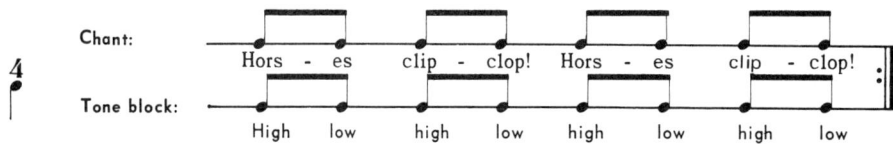

17. Tell class you would like to have them do the entire sequence with a new rhythmic accompaniment. Tell them to do as you do; then do the following, signaling all groups and accompaniments to enter at two-measure intervals:

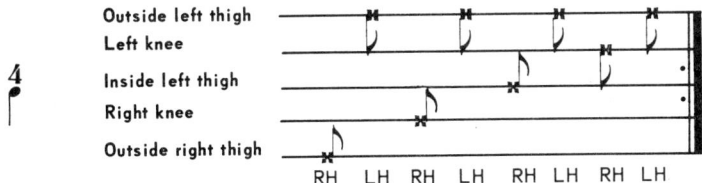

18. Show a child how to play the following on the alto xylophone:

19. Tell class you would like them to chant the following, as a child accompanies, using finger cymbals:

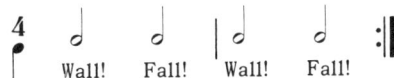

20. Chant the ostinato for them. Select a child to play the finger cymbals and have the entire class chant the ostinato as he accompanies.
21. Divide class into four groups—one group chanting the rhyme; one group chanting the ostinato accompanied by the hand drum (6, page 155), one group chanting with the tone block (16, page 156), and one group chanting with the finger cymbals (19, above).
22. Let the four groups practice doing their parts together.
23. Tell class to do as you do and do the following:

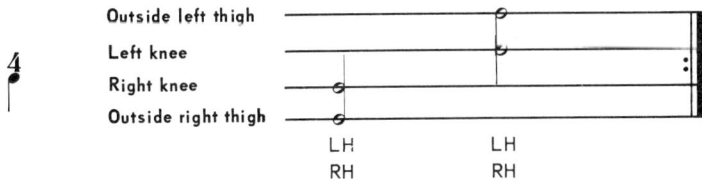

24. Teach a child to play the ostinato for alto metallophone:

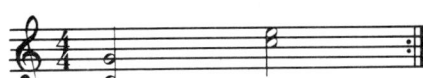

25. Teach a child to play the ostinato for timpani:

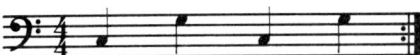

26. Tell class you would like them to chant and play all accompaniments as they *sing* the rhyme. Make certain they understand the order in which each part will enter:

> Bass xylophone
> Soprano xylophone, part one
> Soprano xylophone, part two
> Alto xylophone
> Alto metallophone
> Timpani
> Hand drum
> Tone blocks
> Finger cymbals

27. Tell class you will signal each part to enter at two-measure intervals and when all are established, you will signal class to begin singing. Signal each instrument to begin, and when all are playing together easily, begin singing with class. A melody similar to the following might evolve:

28. As an added experience, teach children the following sequence for chanting:

> "ALL: (loudly)" Humpty Dumpty sat on a wall, Humpty Dumpty had a great fall (sound effect of dish breaking on floor).
> GIRLS: "All the king's horses, clippety-clop, clippety-clop" (castanets on a stick).

> BOYS: "And all the king's men, stamping and tramping, stamping and tramping" (sound of feet).
> ALL: (loudly and slowly) "Couldn't put Humpty together again."
> ONE CHILD: (stepping forward to face the group) "Why not? Was it because he broke his leg?"
> ALL: (emphatically) "No! Didn't you know? Humpty Dumpty was a broken egg."

From *This is Music*, Book 1, by William R. Sur, Adeline McCall, William R. Fisher and Mary R. Tolbert. ©1962 and 1967, by Allyn and Bacon, Inc. Used by permission.

29. When class knows the entire sequence above, have them do it once again, following it immediately with the sequence in 27 (above).

Developing Understanding of Musical Notation for the Notes Sol, Mi, and La—For Primary Grades

Note: The following experience should be extended over as long a period of time as necessary for children to assimilate the basic understanding involved in each step.

1. Put the following on the board:

2. Have children sing the syllables above (sol, mi, and la) using hand signals. Repeat many times, pointing to the syllables in a variety of combinations.

3. When children have had adequate experience singing sol, mi, and la in different combinations, write the following on the board:

4. Have children clap and count the rhythm.
5. Have children sing the syllables in the correct rhythm, using hand signals.
6. Have individual children notate the above on a staff, as follows:

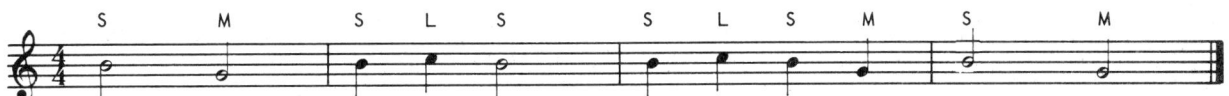

Note: The teacher will want to be aware of several factors involved in this experience:

(1) The meter sign may be omitted or discussed at the discretion of the teacher.
(2) Technically there should be four sharps in the key signature; however, in this type of experience, the key signature is deliberately omitted to avoid confusing children.

7. Tell children you would like to see if they can step the meter as they sing the song. Have them stand. Tell them to step with you in place. Begin stepping quarter notes, and when they are stepping with you, signal them to begin singing the notation in 6 (above), using hand signals.
8. Tell children you would like them to clap a rhythmic accompaniment as they sing the phrase and step the beat. As you step quarter notes, begin clapping the following:

When children are following easily, signal them to sing.
9. Remind children that the notes sol, mi, and la may occur in different places on the staff. Remind them that if sol is in a line, mi will be in the line below, and la will be in the space above. If sol is in a space, mi will be in the space below and la will be in the line above.
10. Have children notate the pattern again, this time starting with sol in a space.
11. Repeat several times, letting different children notate, starting with sol in different lines or spaces.
12. On another day, have children create different patterns using sol, mi, and la, stepping the meter, clapping a rhythmic ostinato, and notating on the board.

Three-Tone Song, *Donkey, Donkey, Old and Gray,*
Using Melodic Notation, Rhythmic Notation, and
Hand Signals—For Primary Grades

1. Give children a period of tempo-dynamic movement using a child leader.
2. Give children a period of echo movement using a child leader.

Photo courtesy of Lyons Band Company, Elmhurst, Ill.

3. Tell children to echo you; then do the following, first with syllables and hand signals, then with words and hand signals, encouraging children to do the same.

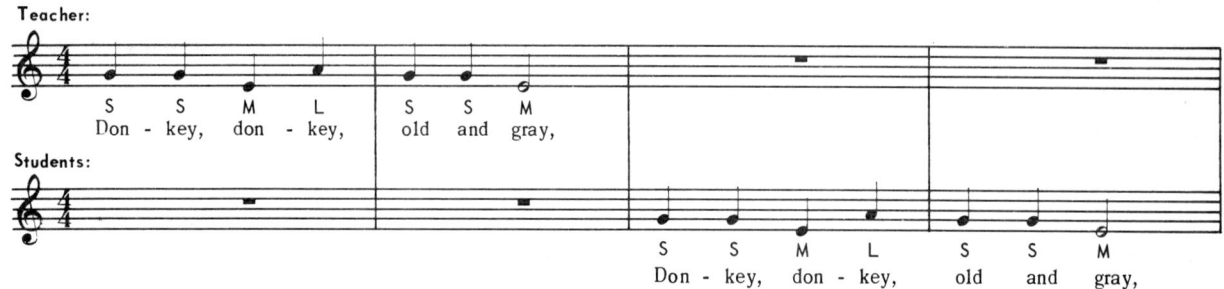

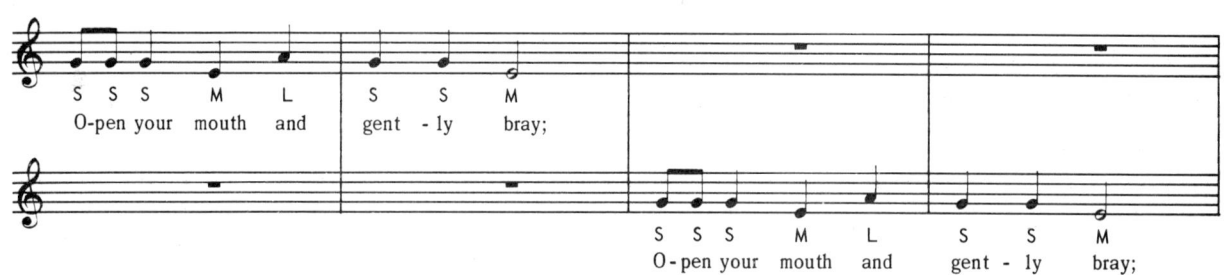

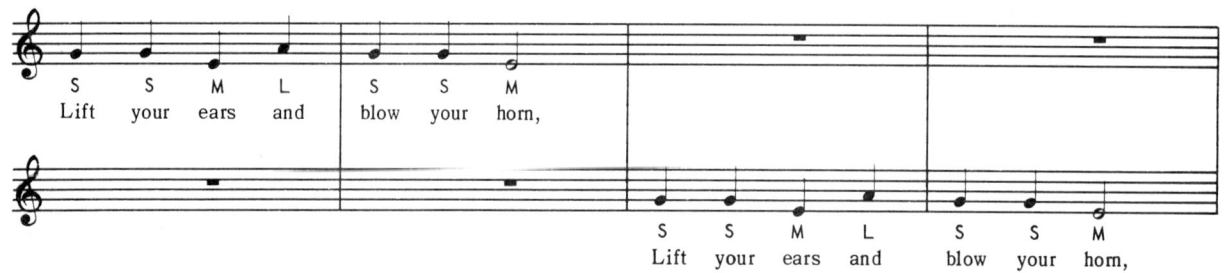

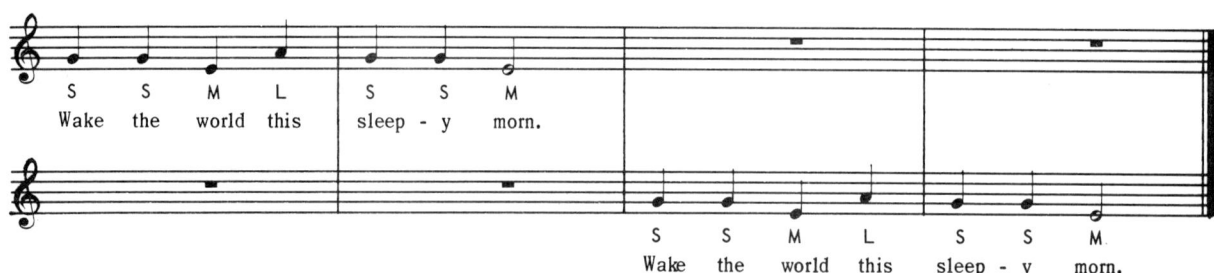

4. When children can echo you successfully, have them sing the song through, first with syllables and hand signals, then with words and hand signals.
5. Tell children you would like to see if they can show the direction the melody moves by writing the notes on the staff on the chalkboard. Draw a staff. Have class sing the first phrase. Ask for a volunteer to draw circles in the lines or spaces to indicate the notes in the first phrase. (Show child

where the first note of the song is—G.) Sing the phrase as many times as necessary, using hand signals to help child get correct notation. Repeat, with each phrase, until the following is on the chalkboard:

Note: Do *not* put the numbers under the notes. These are for teacher's use only.

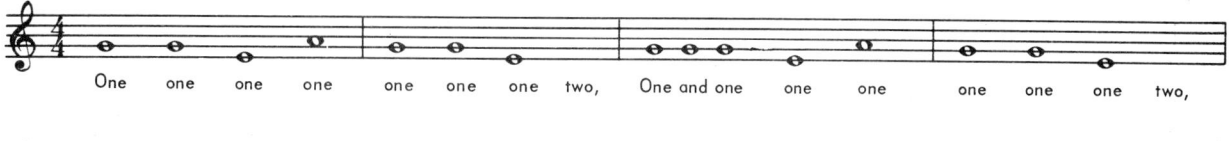

One   one   one   one   one   one   one   two,   One and one   one   one   one   one   one   two,

One   one   one   one   one   one   one   two,   One   one   one   one   one   one   one   two.

6. Tell children you would like to see if they can show how fast or slow the notes move. Have them clap and count the song. (They may sing the numbers, if desired.)
7. When they clap and count song with you successfully, have them clap and count the first phrase (first two measures). Ask them where the long note is (half note counted "one-two"). Have a child point it out on the chalkboard. Remind them that half notes need not be filled in; they simply need a stem. Show child how to draw the stem. Ask children what the other notes in the phrase are (quarters). Clap and count the phrase again, if necessary, to clarify. Show child how to fill in the other notes to make the quarters, and how to add the stem on the right side of each note.
8. Continue working in this way with each phrase until the following is on the chalkboard:

9. Have class sing song, first with syllables, then words, as one child points to the notes. Repeat, letting other children point to the notes.
10. To expand the experience, have children work out the following accompaniments:

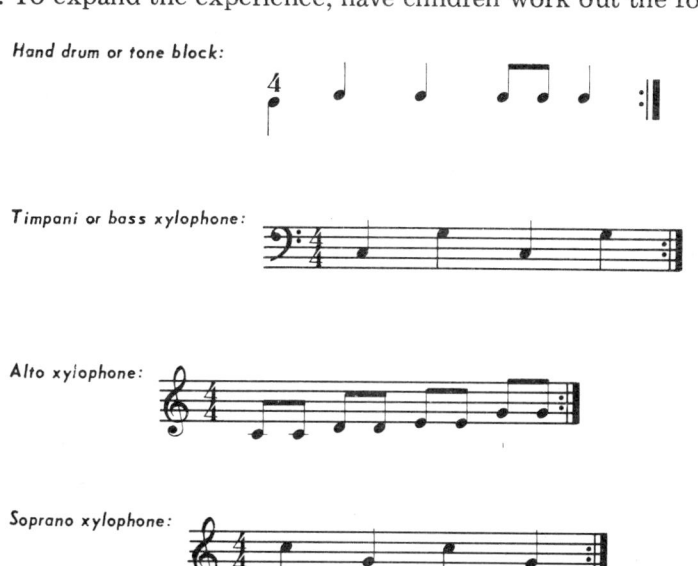

Hand drum or tone block:

Timpani or bass xylophone:

Alto xylophone:

Soprano xylophone:

Alto metallophone:

Alto glockenspiel:

11. To further expand the experience, discuss with children the best way to sing the song so that their voices adequately reflect the text and the mood. That is, should their voices give the feeling of something heavy or light, fast or slow, colorful or subdued, old or young? Have them sing the song using the ideas discussed.

Four-Tone Song, *If All the World Were Apple Pie,*
Using Melodic Ostinati and Hand Signals—
For Primary Grades

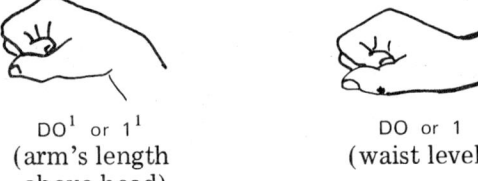

DO¹ or 1¹
(arm's length
above head)

DO or 1
(waist level)

1. As a warm-up and tune-up exercise, ask children to sing and show hand signals with you. Sing, and show hand signals for the following, encouraging children to join you:

2. Have children echo the following, using hand signals:

3. Tell children that you would like to show them the hand signal for a *new* note, then demonstrate the hand signal for do.
4. Tell children you would like to see if they can use this hand signal. Tell them to listen, then to echo you, using hand signals as they sing. Do the following and other similar phrases as children echo you until they can sing and do the hand signals for all notes:

5. Tell children to echo you as you chant a rhyme. Chant the following rhyme, one phrase at a time, as children echo, phrase by phrase, until they know the rhyme:

   If all the world were apple pie,
   And all the sea were ink,
   And all the trees were bread and cheese,
   What should we have to drink?

6. Tell children you would like to sing a song for them while using all the notes they know, with hand signals. Sing the following, first with words, then with syllables. (Repeat several times, inviting children to sing with you, using hand signals.)

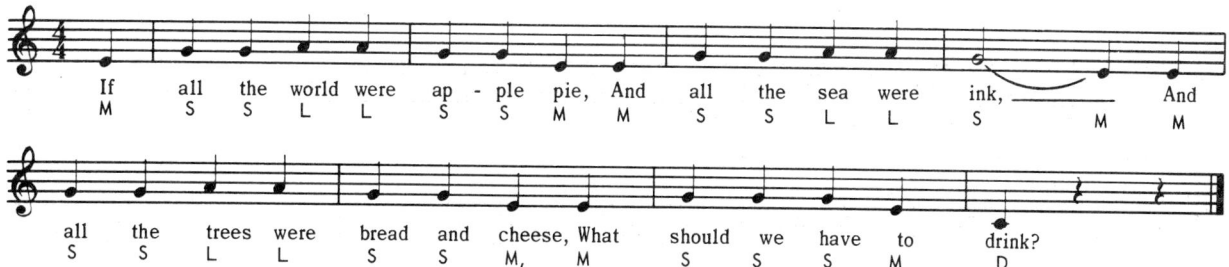

7. Expand on the experience by teaching children to play one or more of the following accompaniments:

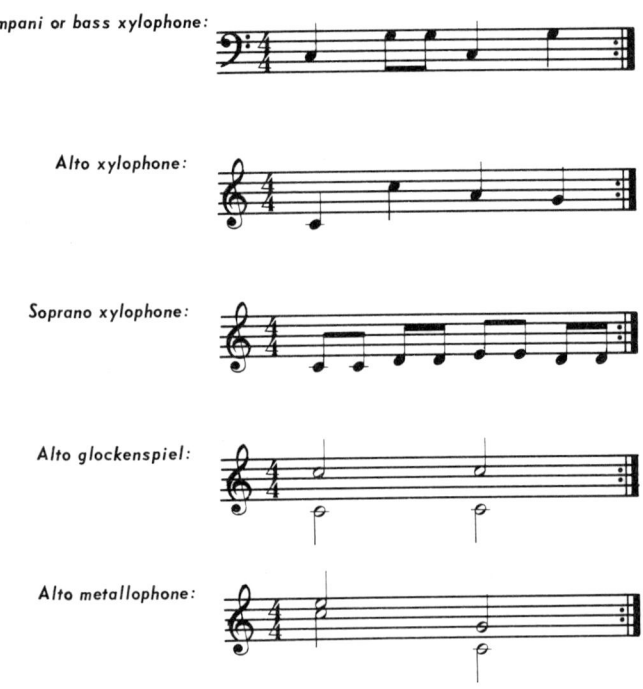

Developing Understanding of Musical Notation for the Notes Sol, Mi, La, and Do—For Primary Grades

Note: The following experience should be extended over as long a period as necessary for children to assimilate the basic understandings involved in each step.

1. Put the following on the board:

        L

 S   S

              M

                  D

2. Have children sing the syllables using hand signals. Repeat many times, pointing to the syllables in a variety of combinations.
3. When children have had adequate experience singing sol, mi, la, and do in different combinations, write the following on the board:

  S   L   S   M   S   M   D   S   D   S   D   S   M   D

4. Have children clap and count the rhythm.
5. Have children sing the syllables, using hand signals in the correct rhythm.
6. Ask individual children to notate the pattern on the staff as follows:

Note: The teacher will want to be aware of several factors involved in this experience:

    (1) The meter sign may be omitted or discussed, at the discretion of the teacher.

    (2) Technically, there should be an F♯ in the key signature. However, in this type of experience, the key signature is deliberately omitted to avoid confusing children.

7. Tell children you would like to see if they can step the meter as they sing the song. Have them stand. Tell them to step with you, in place. Begin stepping quarter notes and when they are stepping with you, signal them to begin singing the notation in 6 (above), using hand signals.

8. Tell children you would like them to clap a rhythmic accompaniment. Ask for volunteers to clap a pattern that might be appropriate. Something similar to the following would be possible:

9. Let class decide which pattern clapped they want to use. Have children stand and begin stepping quarter notes. After two measures, have them begin clapping ostinato. After two additional measures, have them begin singing. Repeat as many times as necessary until they can do this easily.

10. Remind children that the notes sol, mi, la, and do may occur in different places on the staff. Remind them that if sol is in a line, mi will be in the line below, do will be in the line below mi, and la will be in the space above sol. If sol is in a space, mi will be in the space below, do will be in the space below mi, and la will be in the line above sol.

11. Have children notate the pattern again, this time starting with sol in a space.

12. Repeat several times, letting different children notate, starting with sol in different lines or spaces.

13. On other days, have children create different patterns using sol, mi, la, and do, as they step the meter, clap a rhythmic ostinato, and notate the patterns on the board.

Four-Tone Song, *Rosemary Green and Lavender Blue,* Using Melodic and Rhythmic Notation—For Primary Grades

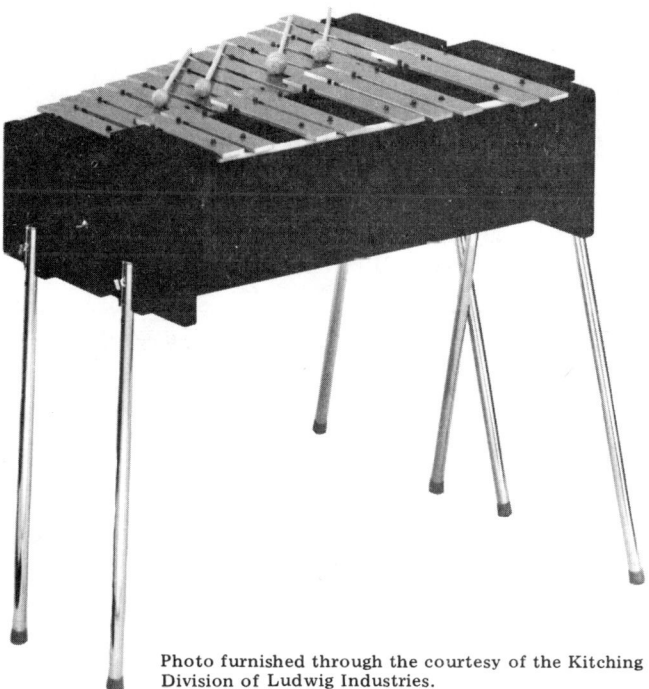

Photo furnished through the courtesy of the Kitching Division of Ludwig Industries.

1. Using the four tones (from the pentatonic scale) they know, give children a period of "echo sing-backs."

2. Give children a period of echo clapping.

3. Tell children to listen, then echo you. Clap and chant the following, enunciating the words in a way that reflects the contrasting tone colors.

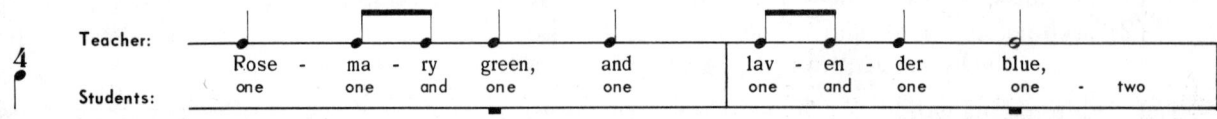

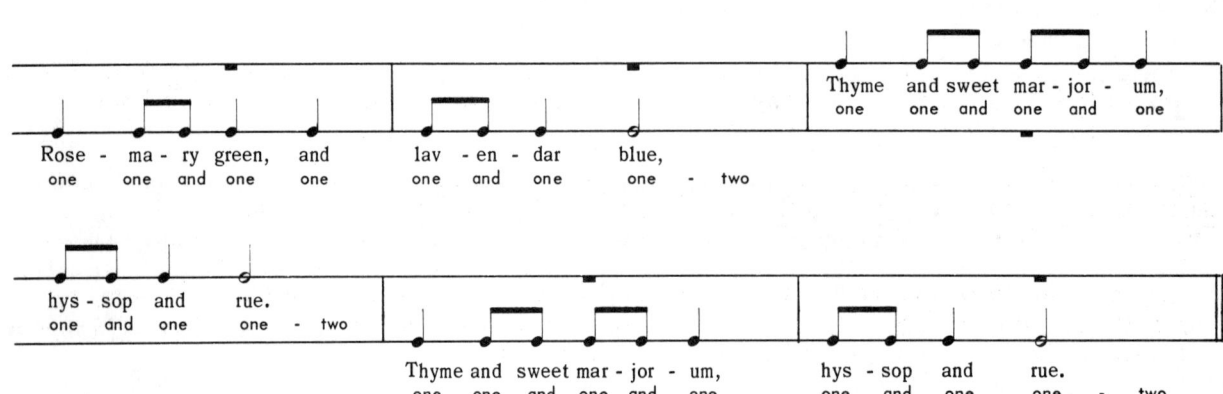

4. When children can clap the rhythm and chant both words and notation, tell them you would like to see if they can help you notate the rhyme on the chalkboard. Clap the first phrase chanting the notation. Ask for a volunteer to write it on the board, help him, and let class help, until the correct notation appears:[6]

5. Repeat, with second phrase, until the following appears on the chalkboard:

6. Tell children you would like to sing the rhyme for them. Tell them to listen, then echo. Sing the following—first the words, then syllables, with hand signals.

6. If children have difficulty notating two measures at a time, have them notate only one measure at a time.

hys - sop and   rue!
S   S   M   D

Thyme   and sweet mar - jor - um,   hys - sop   and   rue!
S   M   L   S   S   M   S   S   M   D

7. When children can echo the above easily, with hand signals, tell them you would like to see if they can write down the song in a way that shows the direction their voices go when they sing it. Working phrase by phrase, help them notate the melody in the following manner:

8. Remind children of the way they notated the *rhythm* of the chant (4 and 5, above). Using that as a guide and, if necessary, clapping and chanting each phrase again, help them fill in the notes so that the rhythm is notated as well as the melodic direction, as follows:

9. Help children learn to play the following accompaniments, preparing them, in each case, with the appropriate hand movements before having them play the instruments. As each accompaniment is learned, let child accompany the class as they sing the song, adding each new accompaniment, one at a time, until all instruments are playing while class sings.

Bass xylophone:

Alto xylophone:

Hand drum or tone block:

Soprano or alto glockenspiel:

Alto metallophone:

Introducing the Triplet Through the Rhyme *Riddle-Me*, and Creating a Four-Tone Song—For Primary or Intermediate Grades

Photo of Studio 49 soprano xylophone courtesy of Magnamusic-Baton, Inc., St. Louis, Mo. 63130.

Note: Introduction to the triplet is not restricted to an experience with a four-tone song. It may be introduced just as effectively with a two- three- or five-tone song.

1. Give class a period of tempo-dynamic clapping.
2. Give class a period of echo clapping.
3. Notate the following on the board. (Do *not* write down the counting.)

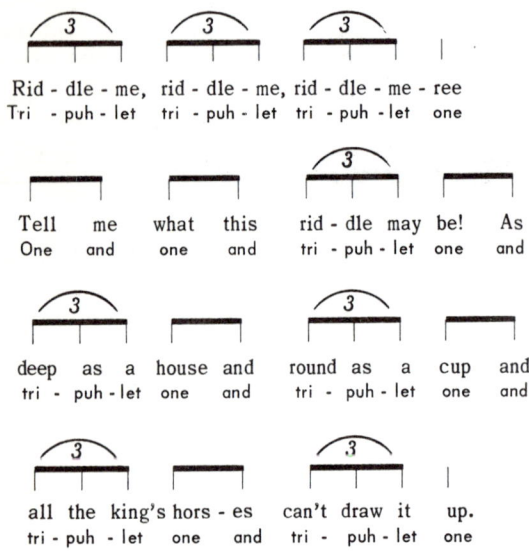

Rid - dle - me, rid - dle - me, rid - dle - me - ree
Tri - puh - let   tri - puh - let   tri - puh - let   one

Tell   me   what   this   rid - dle   may   be!   As
One   and   one   and   tri - puh - let   one   and

deep   as   a   house   and   round   as   a   cup   and
tri - puh - let   one   and   tri - puh - let   one   and

all   the   king's   hors - es   can't   draw   it   up.
tri - puh - let   one   and   tri - puh - let   one

(The answer to the riddle is "a well.")

4. Ask children if they notice anything different about the notes on the board. (The three joined notes—the triplet figures—are new to them.) Have a child point to the triplet. Have entire class count the sets of triplets in the rhyme (eight).
5. Explain that three notes connected in this way are called a triplet (pronounced, for this purpose, "tri-puh-let"). Have children say it and clap it many times.

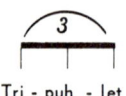

Tri - puh - let

6. Ask children the name of the last note in the first line, above the word "ree," and how it is counted. (It is a quarter note and is counted "one.")
7. Ask children if there are other quarter notes in the rhyme. (Last note in song.)
8. Ask children what the two connected notes at the beginning of the second line are called and how they are counted. (They are eighth notes and are counted "one and.") Ask how many pairs there are in the rhyme and have a child point to each pair. (There are six pairs.)
9. Ask children to clap and say the words with you. When they can do this easily, have them clap and say notation.

10. Ask children to sing this rhyme with you. Help them sing it, using hand signals and all four tones they know: sol, mi, la, and do. The following might result:

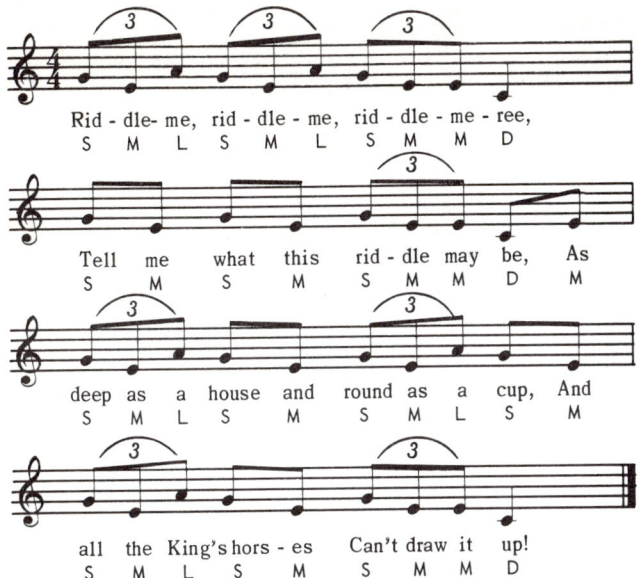

Rid - dle- me, rid - dle - me, rid - dle - me - ree,
S   M   L   S   M   L   S   M   M   D

Tell   me   what   this   rid - dle   may   be,   As
S   M   S   M   S   M   M   D   M

deep   as   a   house   and   round   as   a   cup,   And
S   M   L   S   M   S   M   L   S   M

all   the   King's hors - es   Can't draw it   up!
S   M   L   S   M   S   M   M   D

11. To prepare for an instrumental ostinato, tell children to do as you do; then do the following. (Children will mirror you, doing exactly the opposite.)

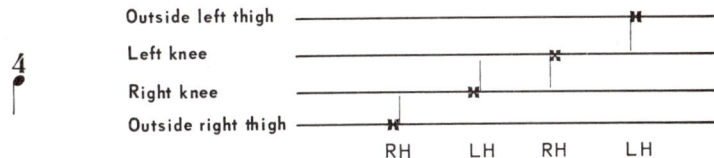

Outside left thigh
Left knee
Right knee
Outside right thigh
RH   LH   RH   LH

12. Show a child how to play the following:

Bass xylophone:

13. Have the bass xylophone play two measures as an introduction; then have class begin song. At end of song, have bass xylophone continue for two measures as a postlude.
14. To expand on the experience, teach children one or more of the following:

Alto xylophone:

Soprano xylophone:

Alto metallophone:

Soprano or alto glockenspiel:

Five-Tone Song, *Engine Number Nine,* **Using Melodic Ostinati, Rhythmic Ostinato, and Hand Signals—For Primary Grades**

RE or 2

1. Give class a period of tempo-dynamic movement (patschen, stamp, clap, snap).
2. Give class a period of echo movement (patschen, stamp, clap, snap).
3. Remind children of the hand signals they already know for sol, mi, la, and do by having them echo you as you sing the following, using hand signals:

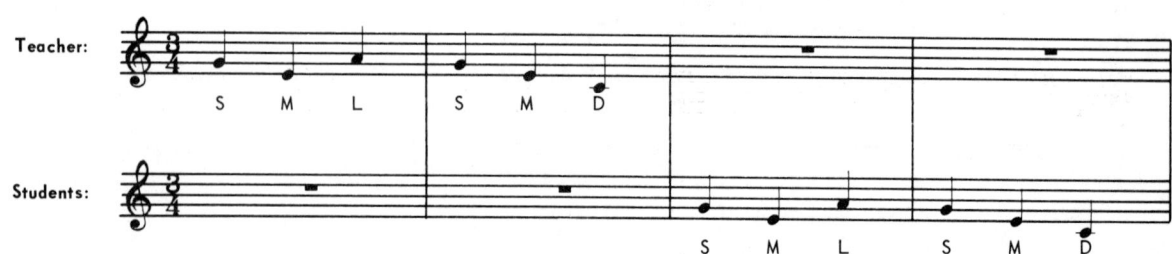

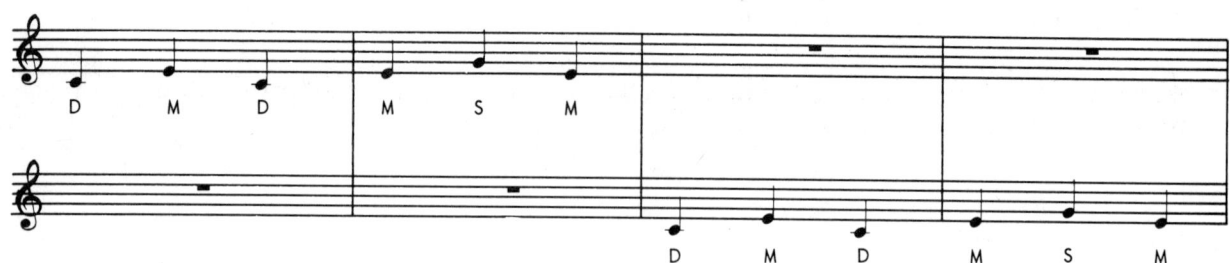

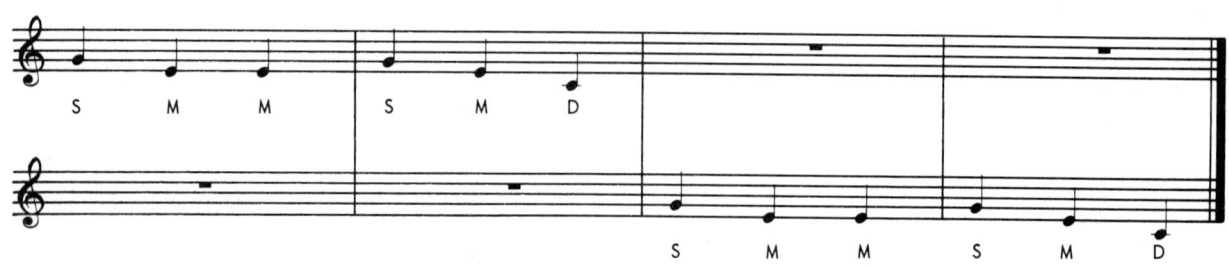

4. Tell children you would like to show them the hand signal for another note. Demonstrate the hand signal for re.

5. Tell children you would like to see if they can echo as you sing a tune using the new note re; then sing the following, first with syllables, then with words:

Engine Number Nine

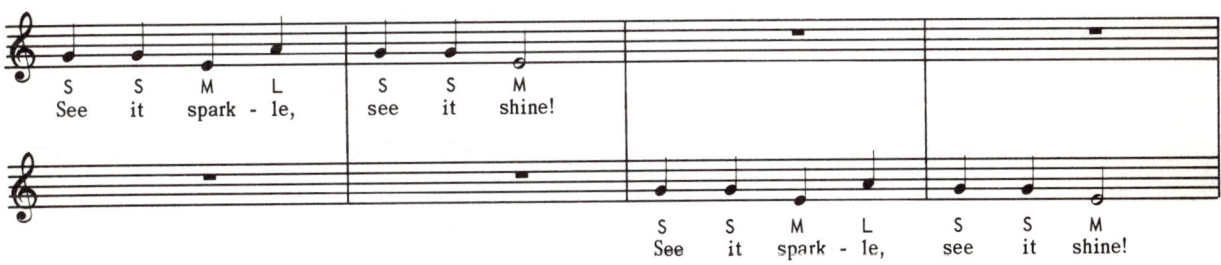

Words to *Engine Number Nine* are from *Music for Young Americans*, Book 2, 2nd Ed., *Discovering Music*, by Richard C. Berg, Daniel S. Hooley, Lee Kjelson, Eugene W. Troth, Josephine Wolverton and Claudeane Burns, Consultant, Copyright 1966 by American Book Company.

6. When children can echo the above successfully, have them sing the song all the way through, first with syllables and hand signals, then with words and hand signals.

7. To prepare children for playing the first ostinato, tell them to do as you do; then do the following. (Children will mirror you, doing just the opposite.)

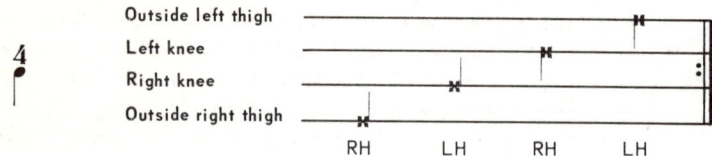

8. When class can do the above in a steady rhythm, begin to say the following in rhythm with the hand movements, indicating that they should join you.

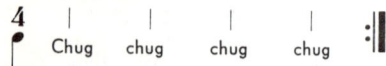

9. When class can say the "chugs" while moving hands across thighs and knees, select one child to play the sand blocks in the same rhythm. Let him practice playing sand blocks as class moves hands and says the "chugs."

10. Select a small group to say the "chugs." Have entire class begin doing hand movements. After two measures, bring in the group saying "chugs" and child playing sand blocks. After two additional measures, have class begin singing the song.

11. Show a child how to play the following ostinato after reminding him that his hands will move exactly as they have been moving. (Remove the F and B bars from the xylophone and give child two mallets, letting him practice alone until he can play it easily.)

12. Tell class you would like them to do a different movement this time. Tell them to do as you do; then do the following:

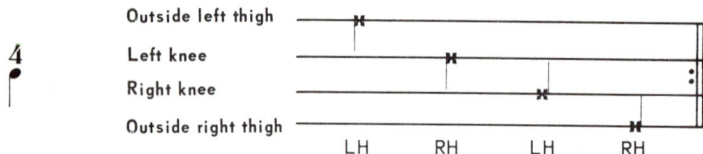

13. When class can do the above easily, have them begin doing it in rhythm. After two measures, bring in the group chanting the "chugs" with the child playing sand blocks. After two additional measures, bring in child playing alto xylophone. After two more measures, have class begin singing the song.

14. When class can do this easily, select a child to play a second ostinato on the alto xylophone and show him how to do the following:

Alto xylophone (second ostinato):

15. Tell class you would like to accompany the song with still a different movement. Tell them to do as you do; then do the following (with class mirroring).

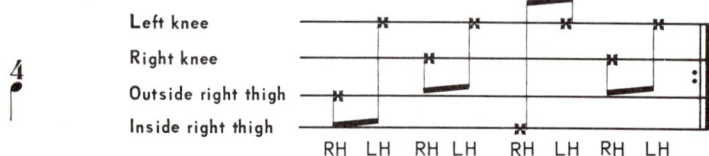

16. When class can do the new movement easily, have them begin doing it in rhythm. After two measures, bring in the group doing the "chugs" with the child playing sand blocks. Two measures later, bring in child playing first ostinato for alto xylophone. Two measures later, bring in child playing second ostinato on alto xylophone. Two measures later, have class begin singing song. At the end of the song, have second ostinato finish two measures after end of song, first ostinato finish four measures after end of song, and sand blocks and group doing "chugs" finish six measures after end of song, as class also stops bodily movement.

17. Show a child how to play the ostinato for soprano xylophone, removing bars adjacent to the notes to be used to facilitate playing:

18. When child can play the ostinato, have him join the accompaniment, bringing in each group as in 16 (above): class doing movement in preparation for next ostinato; group doing "chugs" with sand/block player; first ostinato; second ostinato; third ostinato; and class singing. Let each part perform two measures alone before introducing the next part. End each part, one at a time, as indicated above.

19. On other days add other ostinati, always preparing children by having them move hands across knees and thighs in the direction their hands will move as they play each ostinato.

Note: For rhythmic security, child may sing "Ding! Dong!" softly as he plays.

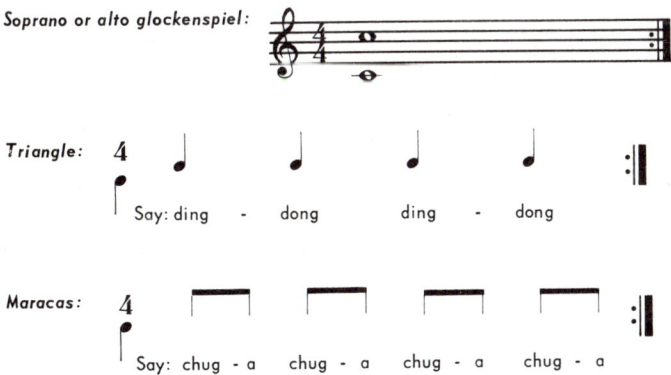

20. To expand on the experience, let children create a rhythmic dramatization of the song.

Five-Tone Song, *Little Drops of Water,* **Using Melodic and Rhythmic Notation—For Primary Grades**

1. Give class a period of tempo-dynamic movement using a child leader.
2. Give class a period of echo movement using a child leader.

3. Tell class you would like to see if they can do just as you do. Tell them to listen and then sing what they hear. Do the following, using hand signals and a voice expressing the quality of the text.

Teacher:

S   S   M   L   S   M
Lit - tle drops of   wat - er,

Students:

S   S   M   L   S   M
Lit - tle drops of   wat - er,

S   S   M   L   S
Lit - tle grains of   sand,

S   S   M   L   S
Lit - tle grains of   sand,

S   S   M   M   S   M
Make the might - y   o - cean,

S   S   M   M   S   M
Make the might - y   o - cean,

S   S   M   R   D
And the pleas - ant land!

S   S   M   R   D
And the pleas - ant land!

4. Tell children you would like to show them how the song they just echoed looks. Put the following on the chalkboard (omitting the numbers beneath the notes):

One one one one   one two, one two,   One one one one   one two, rest rest,

One one one one   one two, one two,   One one one one   one two, rest rest.

5. Remind children that this is a picture which shows the direction our voices go—up or down—as we sing this song. Have children sing song, with syllables, then words, as you point to the notes.
6. Tell children you would like to see if they an help you fill in the notes so that they show not only the direction our voices go, but also how fast or slow. Ask them to clap and count the first two measures with you. Remind them that the notes counted "one" are quarter notes; then complete the first note to show children how they look. Help individual children complete the remaining quarter and half notes. The following should result.

Note: Words have been added to help the teacher; do *not* put them on the chalkboard.

7. Have children sing the song as you point to the notes, using syllables, then numbers, then words.
8. To prepare children for an ostinato accompaniment, ask them to do the following with you:

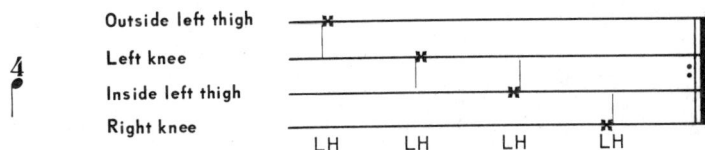

9. When children can do the above easily, add movement for the right hand:

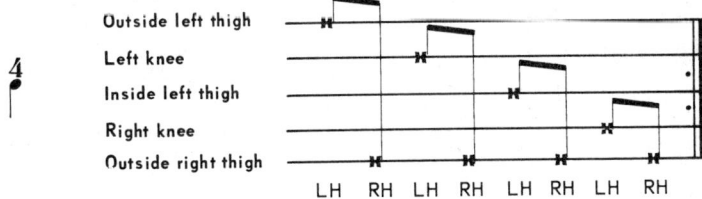

10. Show a child how to play the following on the bass xylophone:

11. Tell class you would like them to sing the song as the bass xylophone accompanies and as they all do another hand movement. Have them begin hand motions which prepare them for playing the ostinato for alto xylophone (see page 176). When they are well-established, have bass xylophone play a two-measure introduction and continue, as class begins singing on third measure. At end of song, have bass xylophone continue for two measures as a postlude.

12. To expand the experience, show children how to play the following accompaniments, and prepare children for them.

Developing Understanding of Musical Notation for the Notes Sol, Mi, La, Do and Re—For Primary Grades

Note: The following experience should be extended over as long a period as necessary for children to assimilate the basic understandings involved in each step.

1. Place the following on the board:

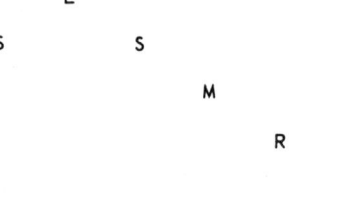

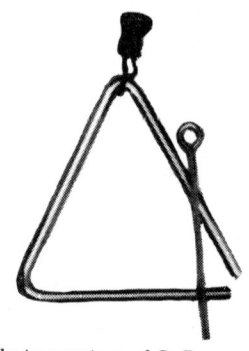

2. Have children sing the notes, using hand signals, as you point to them. Repeat many times, pointing to the notes in a variety of combinations.
3. When children have had adequate experience singing these notes in different combinations, write the following on the board:

4. Have children clap and count the rhythm.

5. Have children sing the syllables in the correct rhythm, using hand signals.
6. Ask individual children to notate the pattern on the staff, as follows:

S   M R D   D   S   L   S   S   L S M R D   R   M   D

Note: The teacher will want to be aware of several factors involved in this experience:

(1) The meter sign may be omitted or discussed at the discretion of the teacher.

(2) Technically, there should be four sharps in the key signature. However, in this type of experience, the key signature is **deliberately** omitted to avoid confusing children.

7. Tell children you would like to see if they can step the meter as they sing the song. Have them stand. Tell them to step with you, in place. Begin stepping quarter notes, and when they are stepping with you, signal them to begin singing the notation in 6 (above), using hand signals.

8. Ask children if they can think of a clapping pattern that would sound appropriate as an accompaniment. Let many children volunteer. Something similar to the following would be appropriate:

9. When class has decided on a suitable clapping pattern, have children stand and begin stepping quarter notes. After two measures, have them begin clapping the ostinato selected. After two additional measures, have them begin singing. When the song is finished, let them continue stepping and clapping for two additional measures.

10. Remind children that the notes sol, mi, la, re, and do occur in different places on the staff. Remind them that if sol is in a line, mi will be in the line below, do will be two lines below sol, la will be in the space above sol, and re will be in the space above do. If sol is in a space, mi will be in the space below, do will be two spaces below sol, la will be in the line above sol, and re will be in the line above do.

11. Have children notate the pattern again, this time starting with sol in a space.

12. Repeat several times, letting different children notate, starting with sol in different lines or spaces.

13. On other days, have children create different patterns in a similar manner, using sol, mi, la, re, and do.

Introducing Fa as a Passing Tone in a Pentatonic Song, *There Was a Crooked Man*—**For Primary or Intermediate Grades**

FA or 4

1. Tell class to do the following with you. Sing *Twinkle Twinkle Little Star* using syllables and hand signals. When you arrive at the first fa, sing it and hold it, with the new hand signal. Then proceed singing the entire song, using hand signals.

2. Give class a period of sing-backs, using fa as a passing tone. For example:

3. Sing the following phrase for children, using syllables and hand signals.

M   S   S   M   L   S   M

4. Ask children to sing it back to you, using syllables and hand signals.
5. Notate it on the board, and have class sing it again, using syllables and hand signals as you point to the notes on the board.
6. Tell class you are going to sing a song that contains this phrase at least once, possibly more than once. Ask them to count the number of times they hear the phrase. Sing the following syllables only, using hand signals.

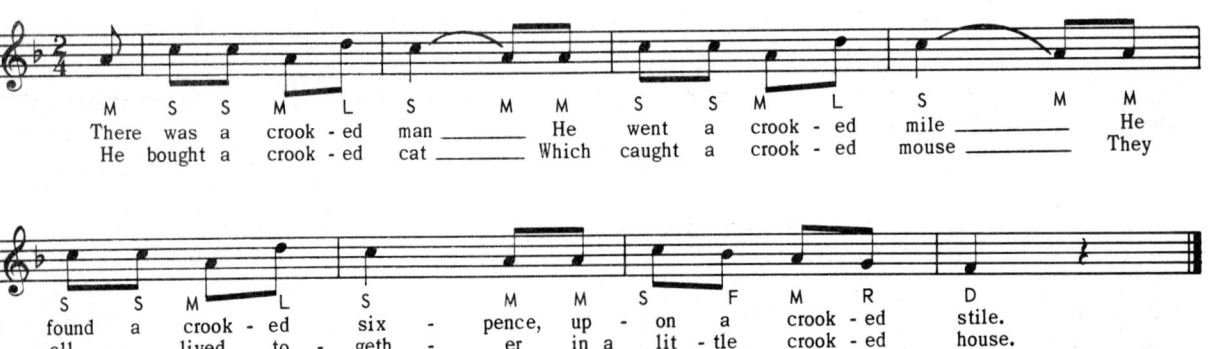

7. Ask class how many times they heard the phrase. (It occurs three times.) Notate the two repetitions on the board. (There should now be on the board all the notes up to and including the note above the word "pence.") Have class sing these three phrases, using syllables and hand signals as you point to the notes.

8. Tell class you would like to see if they can tell you how to notate the last phrase of the song. Sing the final phrase (last two measures, plus last eighth note in third measure from end) using syllables and hand signals. Do it once more, asking class to sing with you.

9. Ask for volunteers to tell you where to put each of the notes in the final phrase until you have completed the song. Have class sing the entire song, using syllables and hand signals.

10. Teach class the following accompaniments:

Note: When the guitar is used, strings must be tuned to notes to be played. In this case, the 6th string, E, should be tuned down to C; the 5th string, A, should be tuned down to F. Furthermore, the guitar may be used in many experiences suggested in this book either as a substitute for, or in conjunction with, the bass xylophone.

11. To expand on the experience, let children create a rhythmic dramatization which reflects the mood and text of the song.

Introducing the Dotted Half Note Through the Rhyme *Hickory, Dickory, Sackory Down,*
and Creating a Five-Tone Song—For Second and Third Grades

1. Give children a period of tempo-dynamic clapping.
2. Give children a period of echo clapping in 3/4 meter.

3. Tell children to echo you as you chant and clap; then do the following, chanting in a way that gives the contrast in tone color suggested by the words.

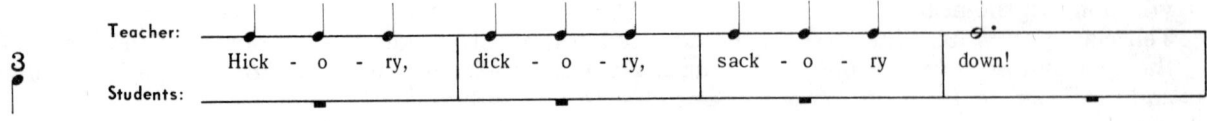

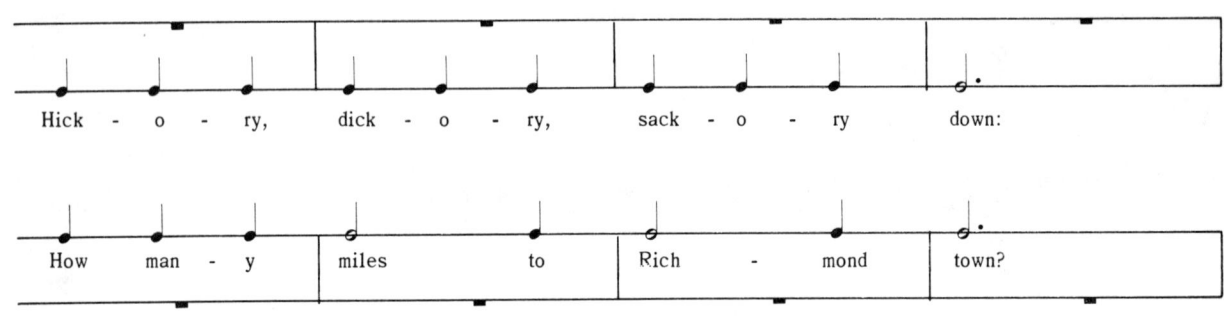

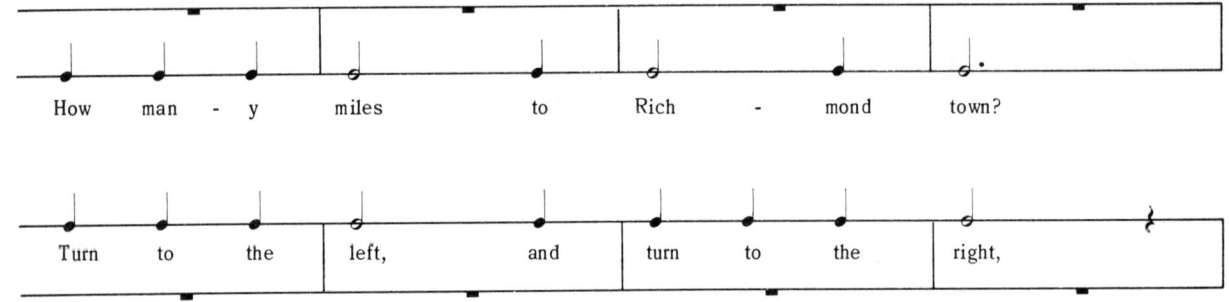

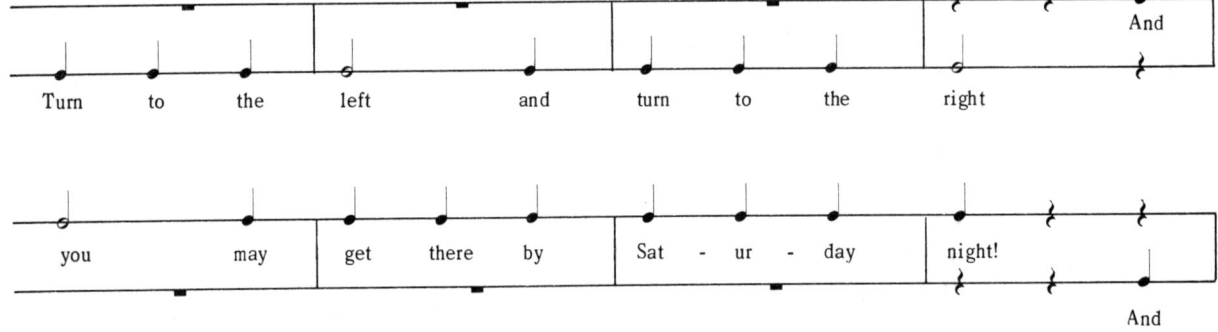

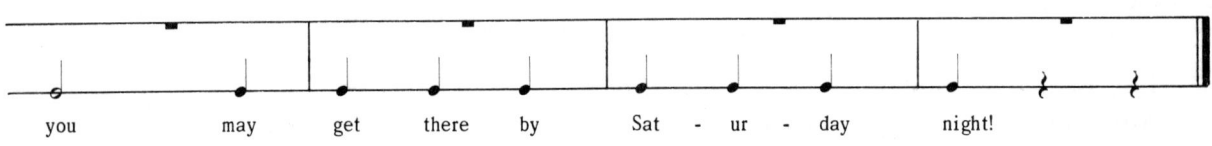

4. Put the following on the chalkboard:

Symbol	Name	Count
♩	quarter note	"one"
♫	two eighth notes	"one and"
♩ (half)	half note	"one two"
triplet (3)	triplet	"tri-puh-let"

5. Explain that these are notes that they know how to notate. Give class a period of echo clapping and counting using these notes.

6. Tell class that today they are going to learn how to notate a new note—the dotted half note—and put it on the board at the end of the list of notes already there:

♩.	dotted half note	"one two three" or "one two dot"

7. Give class a period of echo clapping and counting, using quarter notes, eighth notes, half notes, and dotted half notes similar to 5 (above).

8. Tell class you would like to see if they can notate *Hickory, Dickory, Sackory Down.* Tell them that they will find that some words take the rhythm of the dotted half note. Have class clap and count the first phrase with you. Ask for a volunteer to notate the first phrase, letting class help. Continue in this way, working phrase by phrase, until the entire rhyme is notated rhythmically, as below:

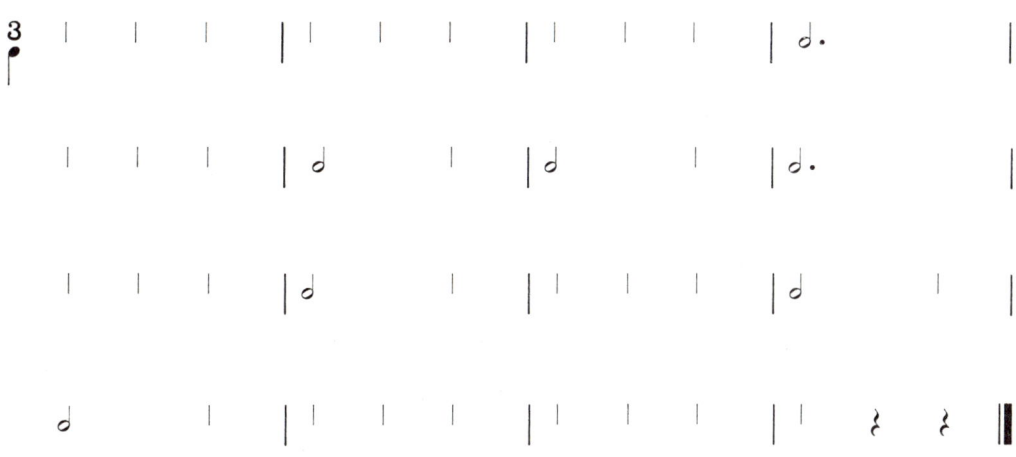

9. Have class clap and count the entire rhyme. If necessary, help them by having them echo you, line by line, as you count and clap.

10. When children can count and clap the entire rhyme, help them turn the rhyme into a pentatonic song, using all five tones. One possible version is the following:

Hick - o - ry, Dick - o - ry, Sack - o - ry down!

How man - y miles to Rich - mond town?

Turn to the left, and turn to the right, And

you may get there by Sat - ur - day night!

11. To enrich the experience, help children create a rhythmic dramatization of the song and teach them to accompany themselves with the following ostinati:

Bass xylophone:

Alto xylophone:

Alto metallophone:

Soprano xylophone:

Timpani:

CHAPTER 9

Intermediate Grades

Children in the intermediate grades take keen satisfaction in their newly acquired skills and perceptions. When activities are structured so that provision is made for individual differences and responses, children of this age are eager to progress to new levels of musical growth and achievement.

Introducing the Dotted Quarter Followed by the Eighth Note Through the Rhyme
Jim and Andy Brown, **and Creating a Five-Tone Song—For Third Grade**

1. Begin clapping and counting quarter notes, having class join you. As they continue clapping and counting the quarter notes, explain that on your signal they are to change to clapping and counting any note value you indicate. Clap and count quarters, eighths, halves, and triplets in any and all combinations, always indicating the change to a new note value on the last beat of a complete measure by saying "change" or giving some similar signal.
2. Divide class into two groups. Assign group one to quarter notes and group two to eighth notes. Tell children that upon your signal, group one will clap what group two is clapping, and group two will clap what group one is clapping. Explain further that you may tell one group to begin clapping a *different* note value, but that whenever you say "change," they are to switch parts. Always begin class clapping quarters and eighths and call for a "change" on the last beat of any measure.
3. Notate the following rhyme on the board, omitting the rhythmic counting:

Jim		and	Joe	and		An	-	dy	Brown		
One	dot	and	one	one		one		one	one	rest	

Took		a	trip	to		New	York	town,		They	
One	dot	and	one	one		one	one	one	rest	and	

Saw		Man	- hat	- tan	and	Brook	-	lyn	too,		They
One	dot	and	one	one	and	one		one	one	rest	and

Then		went	home	to		Kal	- a	- ma	- zoo.		
One	dot	and	one	one		one	and	one	one	rest	

4. Ask children if they notice any new kinds of notes on the board. (The dotted quarter is new—first note in each line.) Tell children that a dotted quarter is most often followed by an eighth note. Have children count the number of dotted quarter notes followed by eighth notes. (Four.)
5. Ask children if they noticed anything else new. (Eighth rests in second and third lines.)
6. Write the following on the board: (Do *not* put the rhythmic counting beneath.)

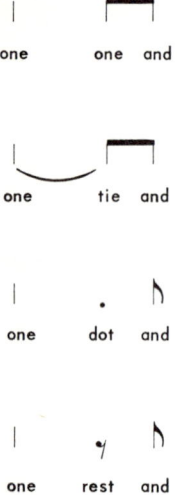

7. Ask children to clap and count first line with you several times.
8. Ask children to examine the second line 6 (above) and ask them what is new. (The "tie.") Explain that the second line is counted "One tie and," clapping on one, swinging the clasped hands to the left on the word "tie," and clapping on the word "and." Demonstrate, and have children join you, repeating several times until they can clap and count it with ease.
9. Have children examine the third line 6 (above) and ask them what is new. (The "dot.") Explain that the dot is similar to the tie. Instead of clapping on the dot, clasped hands are swung to the left on the word "dot." Demonstrate, and have children join you.
10. Ask children to examine the fourth line in 6 (above). Ask them what is new. (The eighth rest.) Explain that the rest is a moment of silence and that instead of throwing the hands to the side, they will throw their hands forward with the palms up and say "rest." Demonstrate and have children join you.
11. Have children go through entire chart in 6 (above) several times until they can clap and count each line easily without hesitation between lines.
12. Have children clap and chant rhyme with you. When they can do this easily, have them clap and chant rhythmic counting. If any difficulty arises, have children echo you, phrase by phrase, as you clap and chant first the words, then rhythmic counting.
13. Help children turn this into a five-tone song either by having the entire group begin singing together or by letting individuals sing each phrase. (When the group has had previous experience with pentatonic songs, they will easily sing the song through without difficulty.) The following is one possible result:

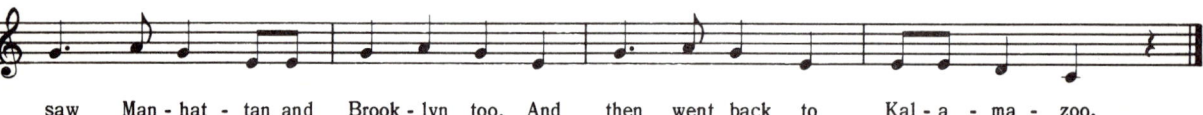

14. To expand the experience, teach children one or more of the following accompaniments:

15. The following songs, found in *New Approaches to Music in the Elementary School,* may be used to further children's understanding of the dotted quarter followed by the eighth note:

   America
   The Little Sandman
   All the Birds Will Soon Be Here
   The Sound of Pipe and Flute and Drum

Introducing Sixteenth Notes Through the Rhyme *Peter Piper Picked a Peck of Pickled Pepper,* **and Creating a Five-Tone Song—For Intermediate Grades**

Photo of Studio 49 bass xylophone courtesy of Magnamusic-Baton, Inc., St. Louis, Mo. 63130.

1. Give children a period of tempo-dynamic movement using a child leader.
2. Give children a period of echo movement using a child leader.

3. Tell children to echo you as you chant and clap the following, first chanting the rhyme, then the number (or rhythmic) notation:

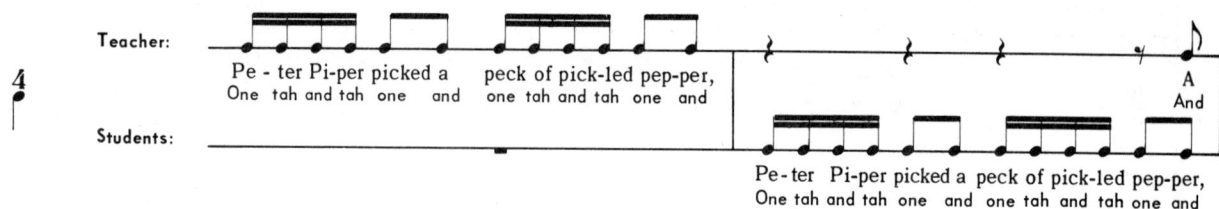

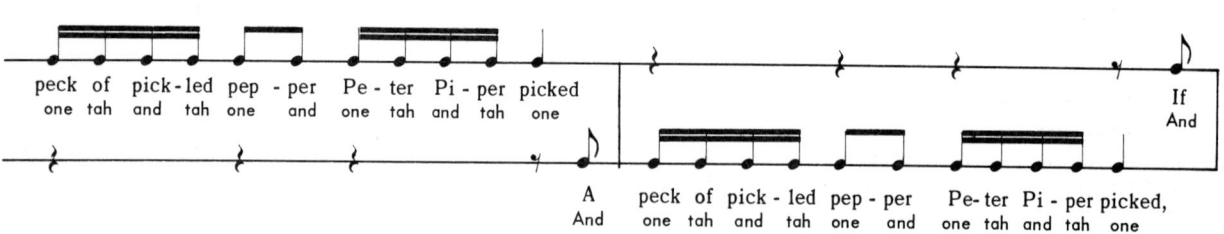

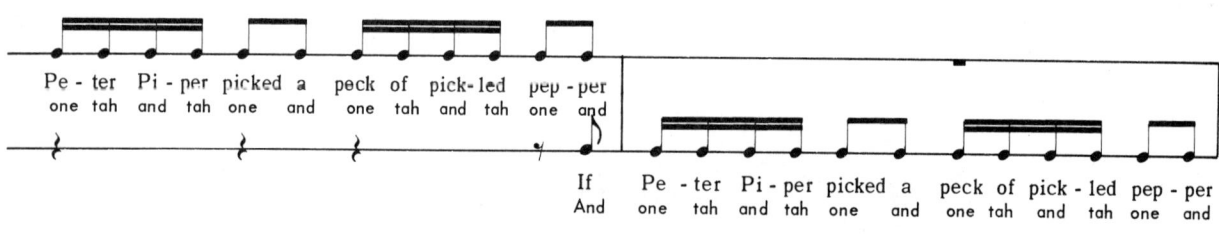

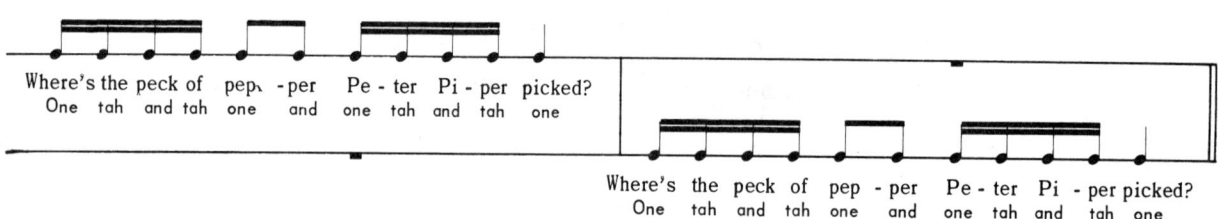

4. Put the following on the chalkboard:

Symbol	Name	Count
♩	quarter note	''one''
♫	two eighth notes	''one and''
♩ (half note)	half note	''one two''
(triplet, bracketed 3)	triplet	''tri-puh-let''
♩.	dotted half note	''one two three'' or ''one two dot''
♩. ♪	dotted quarter and eighth note	''one dot and''
(four sixteenth notes)	four sixteenth notes	''one tah and tah''

5. Ask children which notes they clapped and counted in the rhyme. (Sixteenth notes, eighth notes, and quarter notes.)
6. Ask children which of these notes is new to them. (The sixteenth note.) Explain that it takes four sixteenth notes to equal the value of one quarter note, and demonstrate as follows:

 a. Divide class into two groups, one to clap quarter notes and one to clap sixteenth notes.
 b. Explain that at your signal the group clapping quarter notes is to begin, and when they are secure, you will signal group two to begin clapping sixteenth notes. When you say ''change,'' they are to switch parts, those clapping the sixteenths to clap quarters, those clapping quarters to clap sixteenths. (Both groups should be secure before changing.)
 c. Signal class to begin and give them sufficient experience clapping quarter and sixteenth notes to be certain that they have adequately experienced the feeling of each.

7. Tell children you would like to see if they can help you notate this song rhythmically. Have them clap and count the first phrase with you. Question them as to what notes begin the phrase (sixteenth notes—four of them); which notes come next (two eighth notes), and so on, until you have the following on the chalkboard:

8. Continue working, phrase by phrase, until the entire song is notated rhythmically, as below. (Note rhythmic changes necessitated when rhyme is chanted all the way through.)

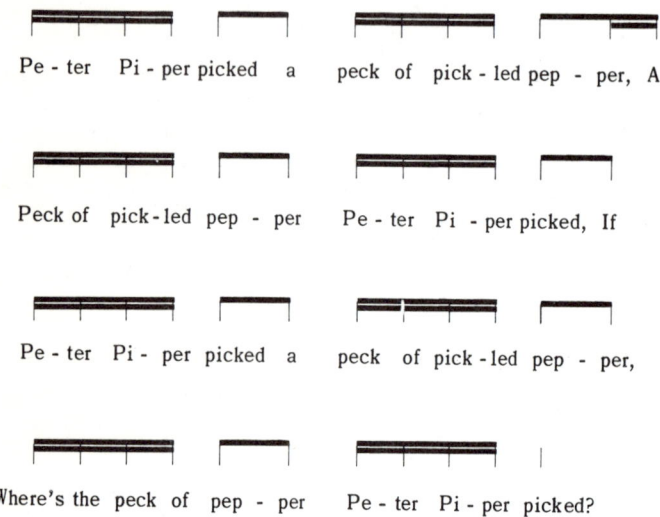

9. Have children clap and chant the rhyme several times, using both words and rhythmic notation, until they can do it easily.
10. Help children turn the rhyme into a five-tone song. One possible version is the following:

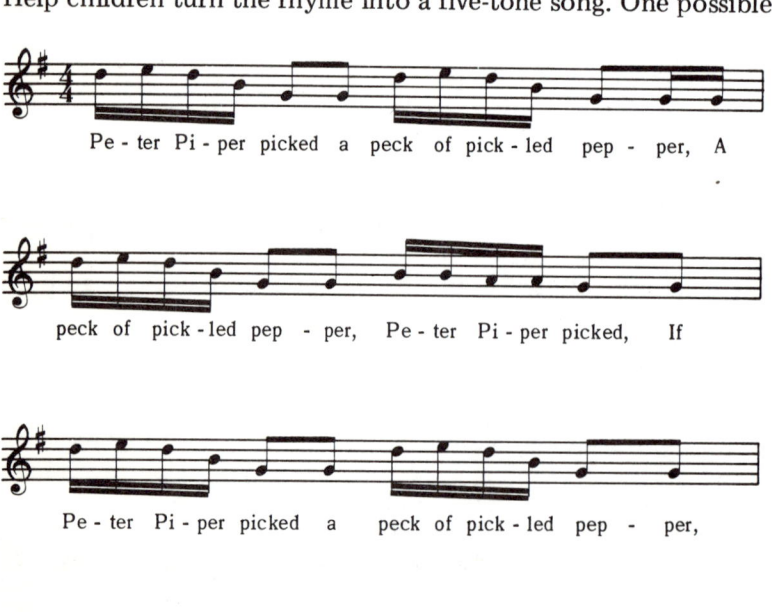

11. To expand the experience, teach children the following ostinato accompaniments, preparing them in each case with bodily movement, as suggested in previous experiences:

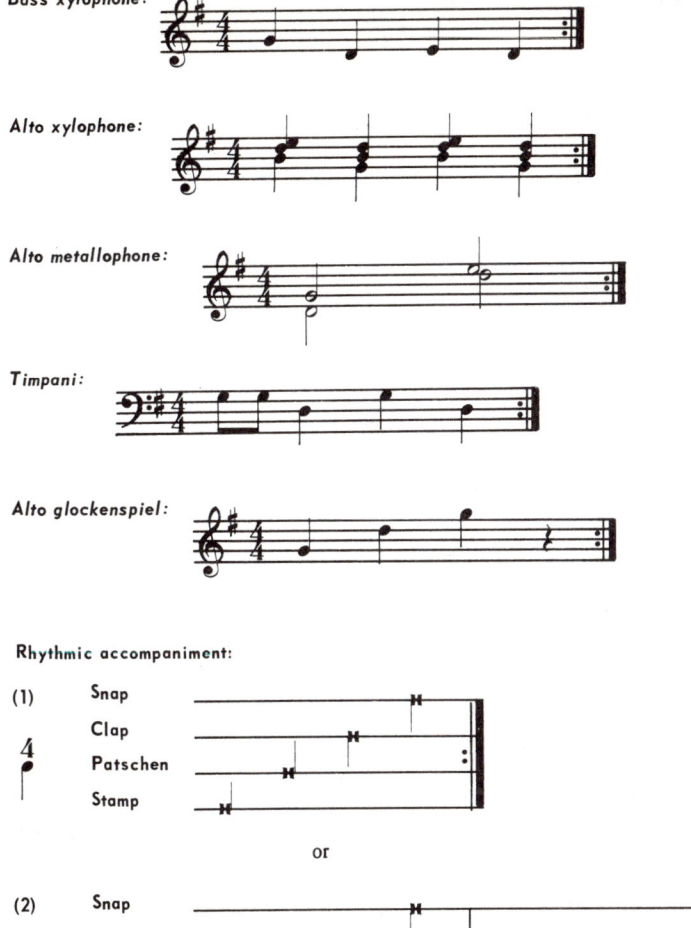

Bass xylophone:

Alto xylophone:

Alto metallophone:

Timpani:

Alto glockenspiel:

Rhythmic accompaniment:

(1)   Snap
      Clap
 4   Patschen
      Stamp

                    or

(2)   Snap
      Clap
 4   Patschen
      Stamp

12. The following songs, found in *New Approaches to Music in the Elementary School* may be used to further children's understanding of patterns using sixteenth notes:

> *A Frog Went A-Courtin'*
> *Love Somebody*
> *Swiss Hiking Song*
> *Old Texas*

Introducing 6/8 Meter Through the Five-Tone Song
Nose, Nose, Jolly Red Nose—For Intermediate Grades

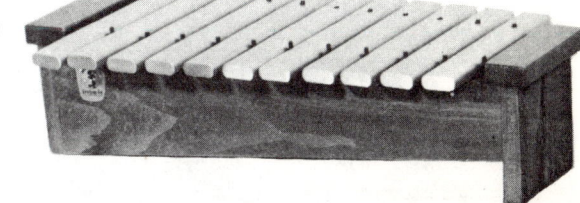

1. Give class a period of echo sing-backs in 6/8 meter, using the five tones of the pentatonic scale.

Photo of Studio 49 soprano metallophone courtesy of Magnamusic-Baton, Inc., St. Louis, Mo. 63130.

2. Put the following on the chalkboard, omitting the words and numbers for rhythmic counting.[1]

3. Ask class if they notice something different at the beginning of the song. (They should notice the numbers 6/8 at the beginning.) Explain that the "6" means that there are six beats in each measure, and that the "8" means that the eighth note gets one count. Ask them how many counts they think a quarter note would get. (Two.)
4. Write the dotted quarter note on the board.
5. Ask children how many dotted quarter notes appear in the song. (Four.) Explain that the quarter note gets two counts and that the dot gets one count; thus, the dotted quarter note gets three counts in 6/8 time.
6. Ask children to help you mark the numbers for the rhythmic counting under the notes, as in 2 (above).
7. Ask class to clap and count the rhythm of the song with you.
8. Tell class you would like to see if they can sing the song, using syllables as indicated under the notes, and hand signals. Give them pitch for sol. Help them sing entire song, using syllables and hand signals.
9. Teach the words of the song by singing it, phrase by phrase, with hand signals, as class echoes.
10. Teach children the following accompaniments:

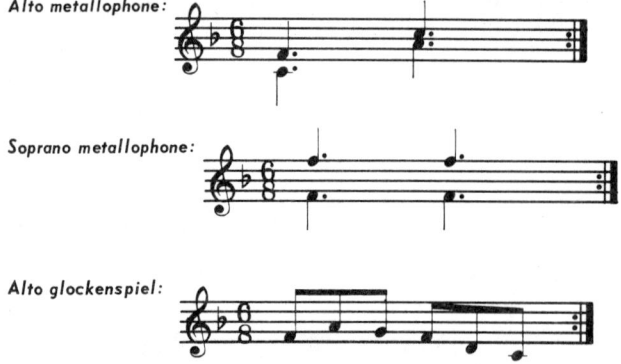

Alto metallophone:

Soprano metallophone:

Alto glockenspiel:

---

1. 6/8 meter poses a unique problem in counting. The easiest solution is probably to explain that the eighth note now becomes the unit for one beat and to have children count in units of six—"one, two, three, four, five, six."

11. To expand the experience, let children practice conducting the song.
12. The following songs, found in *New Approaches to Music in the Elementary School* may be used to further children's understanding of 6/8 time:

> *Looby Loo*
> *Happy Are They*
> *Rig-A-Jig-Jig*
> *When Johnny Comes Marching Home*
> *See-Saw, Margery Daw*
> *Blow the Wind Southerly*

Round-Clapping With the Familiar Song, *Go Tell Aunt Rhodie*—**For Intermediate Grades**

Note: This type of activity can be used with any familiar song, using the rhythm of the song as the second part of the canon. Simply have children begin singing and start clapping canon after one measure of song.

1. Have children sing *Go Tell Aunt Rhodie.*

Go Tell Aunt Rhodie

American Folk Song

1. Go tell Aunt Rho - die, Go tell Aunt Rho - die,

Go tell Aunt Rho - die, The old gray goose is dead.

2. The one she's been saving, The one she's been saving,
   The one she's been saving, To make a feather bed.

3. She died in the mill pond, She died in the mill pond,
   She died in the mill pond, Standing on her head.

4. The goslings are crying, The goslings are crying,
   The goslings are crying, The old gray goose is dead.

5. The gander is weeping, The gander is weeping,
   The gander is weeping, The old gray goose is dead.

2. Use each two measures of song as an echo clap-back, clapping and counting as follows:

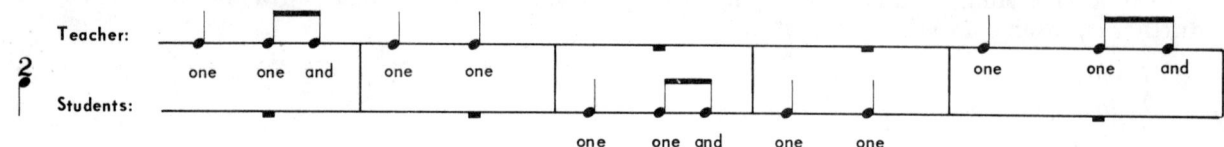

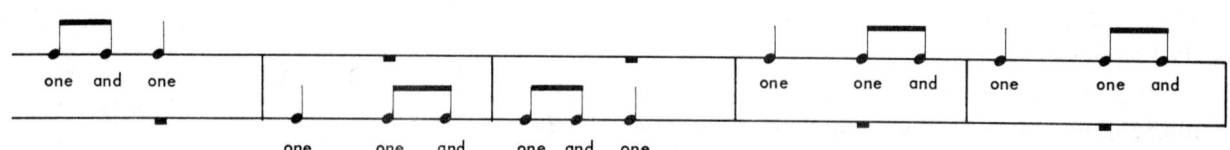

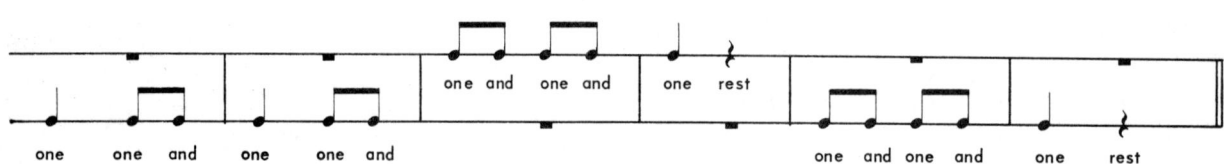

3. Clap and count the first two measures in 2 (above). Have class echo you. Ask for a volunteer to notate these measures on the board. Continue until entire pattern is notated, as below:

4. Have children clap and count pattern several times until they can do it easily, then have them clap pattern without counting.
5. Tell children you would like to see if they can make a canon using the song *Go Tell Aunt Rhodie* as the first part and the clapping pattern in 3 (above), as the second part. Explain that they will begin clapping one measure after the beginning of the song.
6. Signal class to begin singing, and one measure later to begin clapping canon. Help them by singing and clapping with them. Have them repeat canon several times.
7. When children can do the above successfully, erase the notation from the board (3, above) and have children sing and clap canon as a memory training experience.

Cultivating Memory Training Through Rhythmic Clapping—For Intermediate Grades

Note: This type of experience should be given throughout the elementary grades, using all note values, as learned, and in varying degrees of difficulty.

1. Write the following on the board, omitting number notation:

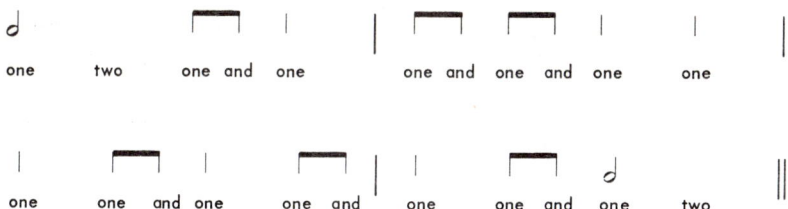

2. Have children clap and count number notation with you several times.
3. Tell children to memorize the rhythm of the first measure because you are going to erase it.
4. Erase first measure. Have children clap and count entire pattern.
5. Tell children to memorize second measure because you are going to erase it.
6. Erase second measure. Have children clap and count entire pattern.
7. Continue in this manner until entire pattern has been erased.
8. Ask for a volunteer to write the notation of the first measure on the board. Let other children notate the other measures, with class helping where necessary.
9. Tell class that this pattern, either in its entirety, or one or two measures, can be used as a clapping ostinato to the song *This Old Man.*
10. Have class select the number of measures they want to use as a clapping ostinato and accompany the song, singing and clapping simultaneously.

This Old Man

1. This old man, he played one, He played nick - nack on my thumb,

Nick - nack pad - da - whack, Give a dog a bone, This old man came roll - ing home.

This old man, he played two, He played nick-nack on my shoe,
Nick-nack paddawhack, Give a dog a bone, This old man came rolling home.

This old man, He played three, He played nick-nack on my knee, etc.

Four—door

Five—hive

Six—sticks

Seven—up to Heaven

Eight—gate

Nine—spine

Ten—hen

**Developing Rhythmic Independence Through Question-and-Answer Clapping
as an Accompaniment to the Song** *Skip to My Lou*—**For Intermediate Grades**

Note: This type of activity should be used throughout the elementary grades, using all note values as
learned, and in varying degrees of difficulty appropriate to the age level.

Skip to My Lou

American Folk Song

Flies in the but-ter-milk, shoo, fly, shoo,   Flies in the but-ter-milk, shoo, fly, shoo,

Flies in the but-ter-milk, shoo, fly, shoo,   Skip to my Lou, my darl - ing.

Chorus

Skip, skip, skip to my Lou,   Skip, skip, skip to my Lou,

Skip, skip, skip to my Lou,   Skip to my Lou, my darl - ing.

2. Little red wagon painted blue, etc.
3. Cat's in the buttermilk, what'll we do?, etc.
4. Lost my partner, What'll I do?, etc.
5. I'll get another one, prettier than you!, etc.
6. Can't get a red bird, blue bird will do, etc.

1. Put the following on the board:

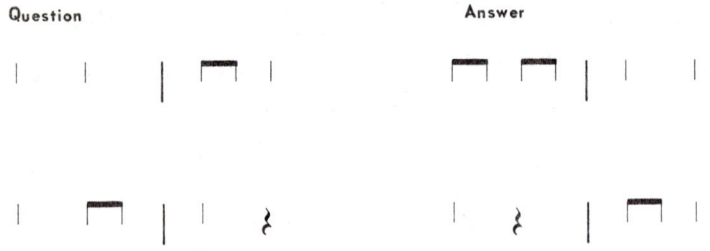

Question

Answer

2. Divide class into two groups. Tell group one to clap the patterns under "question" on the board,
   group two to clap "answers." Explain that after group one claps the first question, group two is to
   clap the answer in the same tempo without missing a beat. After group two claps the answer,
   group one is to immediately clap the second question, without missing a beat, group two to clap
   the second answer in the same tempo without missing a beat.
3. Signal group one to begin and have class clap the two questions and answers.
4. When class can do this through correctly, have them do it several times without stopping.

5. Explain that this sequence may be used as an accompaniment to a familiar song, *Skip to My Lou.* Have class sing a chorus and verse of *Skip to My Lou.*
6. Tell children to be prepared to clap their questions or answers. The first question will begin with the beginning of the song. Signal class to begin singing and group one to begin clapping question. Signal groups to clap at appropriate times, repeating question-and-answer sequence as many times as necessary to complete song.
7. Tell class you would like to see if they can clap their questions and answers without watching the notation. Erase the notation from the board and have class clap and sing from memory.
8. To expand the experience, let individual children experiment with creating their own "questions," clapping them to individuals who have volunteered to answer them.

Two-Part Singing, Using Hand Signals—For Intermediate Grades

Note: This type of experience should be given throughout the intermediate and upper grades in varying degrees of difficulty according to the ability of the children. In initial experiences, rhythm should be kept simple and tempo as slow as necessary. Tempo and rhythm can become more complicated as children gain facility.

1. Tell class you are going to give them an experience in part singing. Explain that they will sing the syllables as indicated by your signals and that part of the class will follow the signals of your right hand as the rest follows the signals of your left hand.
2. Divide class into two groups. Tell group one to follow your right hand and group two to follow your left. Give the pitch for sol.
3. Give hand signals for both groups to begin on the note sol as indicated in the chart below. Proceed slowly with hand signals indicated for group two: mi, sol, la, sol. Then give signals for group one: mi, sol, sol. Give signals slowly enough to allow children to sing with good intonation and help, if necessary, by singing with them. If the part sustaining a note has difficulty maintaining the pitch, signal them to repeat the sustained note on each beat.

```
Group 1   S————S M S S
Group 2   S M S L S————

Group 1   S————S M L S M————
Group 2   S M D M S————L S L

Group 1   M M S L S————
Group 2   S————M D M D D D
```

4. Continue giving similar experiences, gradually increasing the difficulty of intervals sung and rhythms used.

Two-part Singing Using a Melodic Ostinato and Hand-Signaled Melody— For Intermediate and Upper Grades

Note: This type of experience should be used throughout the intermediate and upper grades, varying the ostinato and melody to match the technical facility of the group.

1. Teach entire group the following ostinato by singing it with hand signals as children follow. Repeat several times until they can do it with ease.[2]

2. Divide class into two groups. Tell group one to sing the ostinato just learned and group two to sing the syllables indicated by your hand signals.

---

2. S_1 and L_2 refer to the sol and la below do.

3. Signal group one to begin. After two measures, signal group two to sing the following, guided by your hand signals:

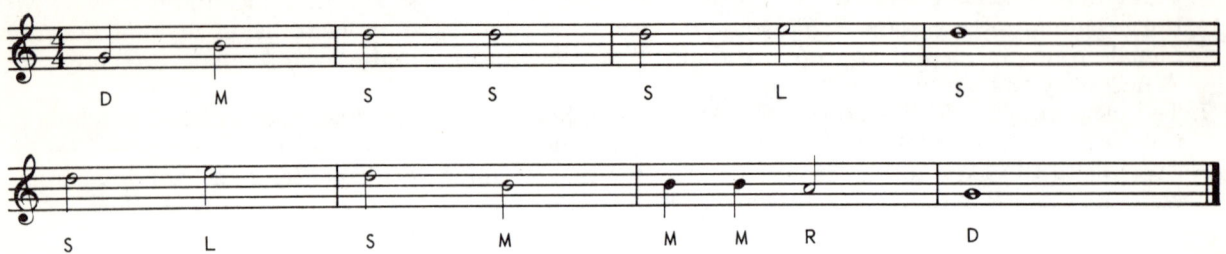

4. On other days, give children other similar experiences using a different ostinato and melody.

Singing In Canon with Hand Signals—For Intermediate and Upper Grades

1. Put the following on the board:

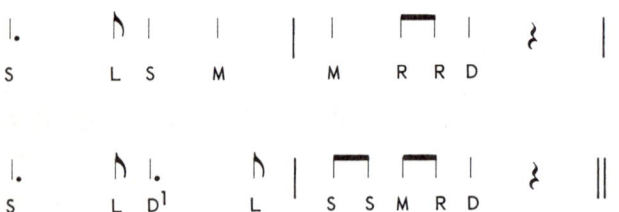

2. Ask class to clap the rhythm of the pattern above with you.
3. Have class sing the pattern in unison, using syllables and hand signals.
4. Tell class you would like to see if they can sing this phrase as a round. Divide class into two groups, explaining that group one will begin and group two will enter one measure later.
5. Signal group one to begin, group two to enter a measure later. Repeat until children can do it easily.
6. Tell class you would like to see if they can step the beat as they sing. Ask them to stand. Begin stepping quarter notes, signaling class to join you. When class is stepping with you, signal group one to begin, and, one measure later, group two to enter.
7. When children can do the above easily, ask what kind of rhythmic ostinato might make a good accompaniment. Let many children volunteer. Something similar to the following would be appropriate:

8. Let class decide which ostinato they like. Signal them to begin stepping quarter notes. Two measures later, signal them to begin clapping ostinato. Two measures later, signal group one to sing. One measure later, signal group two to sing. At end of singing, continue stepping and clapping for two additional measures.

Learning to Sing a Second Part to the Familiar Song *Twinkle, Twinkle, Little Star,* Using Hand Signals—For Intermediate Grades

Note: This type of experience (adding second parts to familiar melodies) should be given throughout the intermediate and upper grades.

Twinkle, Twinkle, Little Star

Twink-le,   twink-le,   lit - tle   star,   How   I   won - der   what   you   are.

Up   a - bove   the   world so   high,   Like   a   dia - mond   in   the   sky,

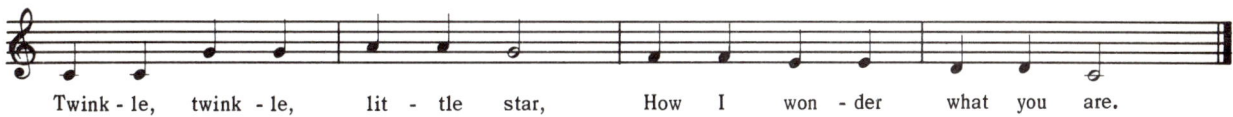

Twink - le,   twink - le,   lit - tle   star,   How   I   won - der   what   you   are.

1. Tell class that you would like to help them sing a second part to a familiar song *Twinkle, Twinkle, Little Star.* Review the song by having class sing it.
2. Tell class that you would like them all to sing the second part, watching and imitating your hand signals and singing the syllables indicated. Give the hand signals and sing the syllables indicated below. When you reach the note ti, have class hold it a bit longer to emphasize the syllable and the hand signal. (Ti will be formally introduced in the next suggested experience.)

D   D   T₁   T₁   D   R   M   L   L   S   L   T   T   D

M   M   R   R   D   D   T₁   M   M   R   R   D   D   T₁

D   D   T₁   T₁   D   R   M   L   L   S   L   T   T   D

3. When class can sing the second part easily, with hand signals, divide children into two groups. Tell group one to sing the melody and group two to sing the notes indicated by your hand signals, as they imitate your hand signals.
4. Signal both groups to begin. Sing with the second part. Keep parts moving slowly and smoothly together.
5. Switch groups, group one singing second part, group two singing melody.
6. On other days, give children similar experiences, learning a second part to a familiar song through use of hand signals.

**Introducing the New Tone Ti, and Its Hand Signal; Learning
an Orchestration to a Song in the Major Mode,**
Ten Little Pirates—**For Intermediate Grades**

TI   or   7

Note: Timpani drums should be tuned to G and D.

1. Put the following on the chalkboard, omitting, for the time
being, the syllable symbols:

Phrase 1

S₁   D   D   T₁   R   D   T₁   D   M   S

Phrase 2

F   R   R   M   M   D   D   R   D   T₁   L₁   S₁

Phrase 3

S₁   D   D   T₁   R   D   T₁   D   M   S

Phrase 4

F   R   R   M   M   D   D   R   S₁   S₁   D

2. Tell class you would like to see if they can count and clap the rhythm of these phrases. Help them as they clap and count.
3. Put the syllable names under the notes. Tell class you are going to sing this song using syllables, and that you would like to see if they can discover any new tones. Sing song, using syllables and hand signals. (Children should discover that ti is new.)
4. Show children hand signal for ti.
5. Tell children that they now know all the notes and hand signals for the major scale. Sing the major scale for them, using syllables and hand signals. Have them sing it with you several times, ascending and descending, using syllables and hand signals.
6. Tell children you are going to sing one of the phrases notated on the board and that you would like to see if they can identify it. Sing one of the phrases with syllables and hand signals. Ask a volunteer to identify it. Have entire class sing it, using syllables and hand signals.
7. Continue in this manner until class can easily identify and sing any phrase using syllables and hand signals. Then have them sing entire song using syllables and hand signals.
8. Tell class you would like to show them how the melody of the song looks on the board. Letting them help as much as possible, put the following on the chalkboard:

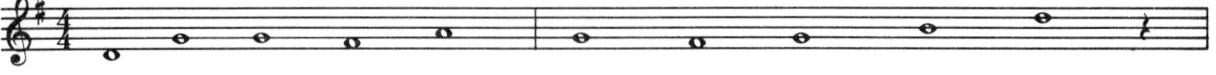

9. Tell class you would like to see if they can help you fill in the notes so that they show how fast or slow they are to be sung. Help class fill in the rhythmic notation until the following appears on the chalkboard. (Do *not* print words under notes. This is for teacher's use only. Letters above should also be omitted. These are the timpani notes which will be worked out by children later.)

Ten Little Pirates

2. Eight little pirates slept until eleven,
   One over slept himself, and then there were seven.
   Seven little pirates cutting up sticks,
   One chopp'd himself in halves, and then there were six!

3. Six little pirates, playing with a hive,
   A bumblebee killed one, and then there were five.
   Five little pirates going in for law,
   One got a chancery and then there were four.

4. Four little pirates going out to sea,
   A red herring swallowed one, and then there were three.
   Three little pirates walking in the zoo,
   A big bear cuddled one, and then there were two!

5. Two little pirates sitting in the sun,
   One got all frizzled up, and then there was one;
   One little pirate living all alone,
   He got married and then there were none!

6. One little pirate, with his little wife,
   Lived all his days a happy little life;
   One little couple dwelling by the shore,
   Soon raised a family of ten pirates more!

10. Have class sing song using syllables and hand signals as you point to the notes.

11. Tell class that the timpani will accompany the song, playing two tones, G and D. Tell them that you would like to see if they can determine where in the song each of these tones will be played. Explain that you will sing the song with them as you play the tone G on the timpani and that they are to raise their hands when they feel that the tone G no longer sounds right. Help class sing first phrase as you play the tone G. If they fail to hear the dissonance on the fourth tone, stop, telling them to listen more carefully. Sing the first phrase again, with class, this time emphasizing the G slightly on the fourth note so that they hear the dissonance. When they do hear it and raise hands, put the letter G over the first note on which it is played and the letter D over the fourth note in the first phrase (9, page 199).

12. Continue working in this manner, phrase by phrase, letting class discover where the notes on the timpani change throughout the song and placing the letter names over the proper notes of the song.

13. Let a child practice playing the timpani part, including a two-measure introduction, as follows:

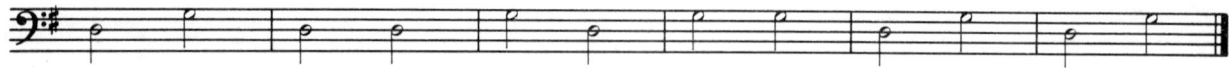

14. Tell class you would like them to hear the first verse of the song accompanied by the timpani. Tell them that you would like them to do as you do as they listen. Begin doing the following as class mirrors you, doing the opposite.

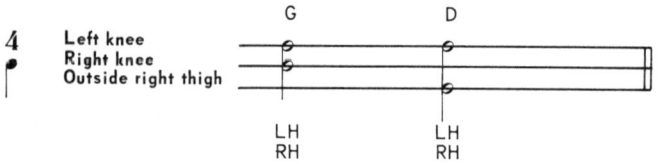

Note: The letters G and D refer to the note markings for timpani, which will also be followed by the alto metallophone player, for whom this preparation is intended, as well as the soprano xylophone player (see 20, page 201).

15. When class can do the above easily, signal the timpani player to begin the introduction. After the two-measure introduction, begin singing the first verse and at the same time doing the hand movement marked G in 14 (above). Change back and forth between the movements for G and D, following the letters marked above the song for the timpani.

16. Show a child how to play the following ostinato, making certain that he understands that he is to play the chord marked G when the note marked for the timpani is G, and the chord marked D when the note marked for timpani is D.

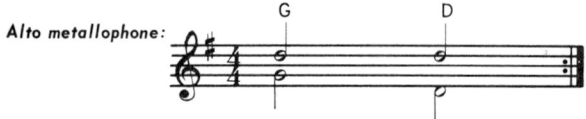

17. Tell class you would like them to hear the second verse accompanied by the timpani, alto metallophone, and a new set of movements. Tell them to do as you do; then do the following:

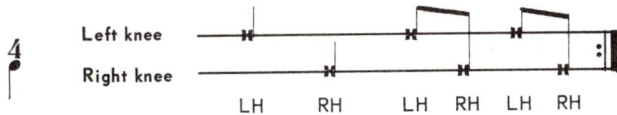

18. When class is doing the above easily, signal timpani player to begin his introduction. After two measures, bring in the alto metallophone player and begin to sing song, continuing to lead the class in the movements above.

19. Show a child how to play the following ostinato:

20. Add the following ostinati, one at a time, with appropriate preparation, as you sing the other verses of the song accompanied by timpani, alto metallophone, and alto xylophone.

21. When class has heard song all the way through, select children to experiment with *pantomiming* the song. Discuss various ways of pantomiming each verse. When children have a general idea of what they will do for each verse, select different children to play the various ostinati and let them practice their parts. Explain that the other instruments, class singing, and children pantomiming the verses will enter after the two-measure introduction by the timpani.

22. Discuss the pantomime, eliciting ideas for improvement. Select other children to pantomime and to play the ostinati; repeat until all children have had the opportunity to participate.

Learning an Orchestration to a Song in the Major Mode, *Three Blind Mice—* **For Intermediate Grades**

1. Tell children you would like to see if they can hear and sing a melody just by seeing the hand signals for it. Tell them that the first note of the melody you will sing begins on mi and that you will sing this for them to get them started on the right note. Sing mi (E in the C major scale).

Photo of Studio 49 timpani courtesy of Magnamusic-Baton, Inc., St. Louis, Mo. 63130.

2. Give them the hand signals for the first phrase:

3. Tell class to sing this phrase, using hand signals. Help them, if necessary, by repeating the hand signals for it and/or by singing it with them using hand signals.
4. Notate phrase on the chalkboard, letting class help you decide where to write the notes on the staff.
5. Continue working in this way until class has seen each phrase described by your hand signals, sung each phrase correctly using hand signals, and helped you notate each phrase on the chalkboard, as follows:

Note: Do not put words *below* or letter names *above* notes. The latter, which are names of notes to be played by the timpani, will be placed later by class.

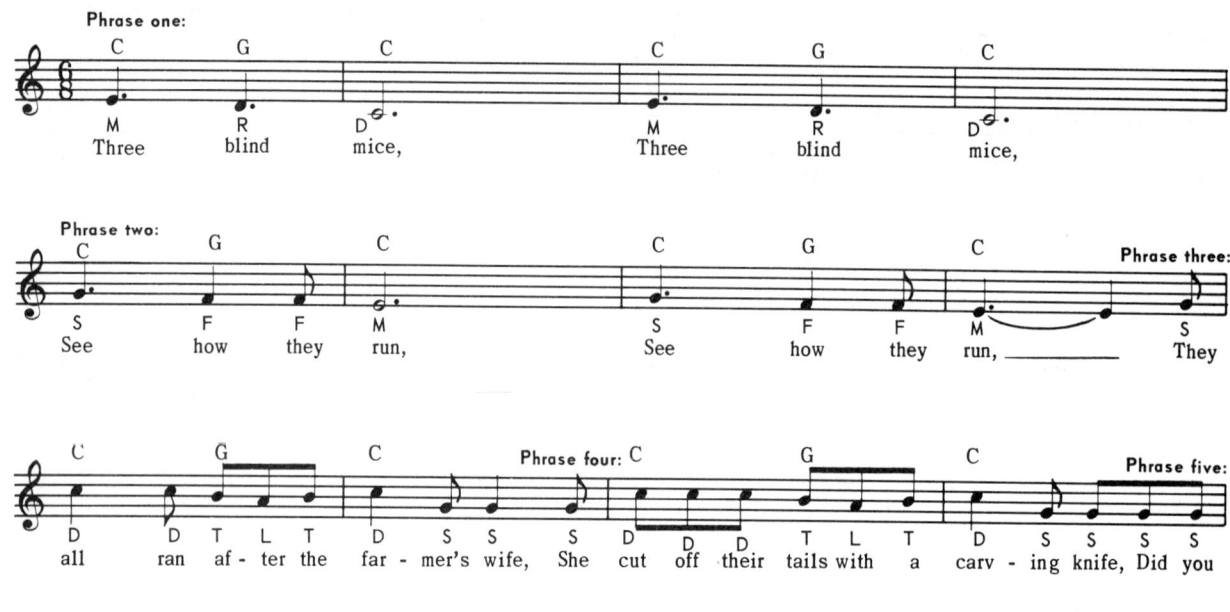

6. Have class sing entire song using syllables and hand signals.
7. Tell class you would like to have them help you decide what two notes, played by the timpani, would best accompany the song, and exactly where they should be played. Explain that you will demonstrate one combination as they sing the first phrase (first four measures).
8. Signal class to begin singing the first phrase, simultaneously beginning the following accompaniment:

9. Ask class if they liked the timpani accompaniment, and if not, what note did not fit. (They will probably be bothered by the second and fifth Cs.) Tell them you will try changing these Cs to the note G.
10. Have them sing the first phrase again, this time accompanying them as follows:

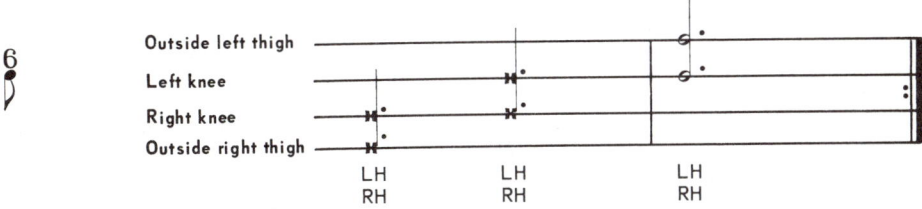

11. Continue experimenting in this way until class decides on an accompaniment they like which also reflects the tonic-dominant relationships in the song. Notate their final decision above the notes of the melody on the chalkboard.
12. Ask class for ideas for a two-measure introduction to be played by the timpani. (Two measures of the accompaniment figure would be acceptable.)
13. Select a child to play the timpani. Let him practice introduction and accompaniment.
14. Tell class you would like to see if they can sing entire song using syllables and hand signals as the timpani accompanies. Signal timpani to begin introduction. After two measures, signal class to begin singing, using syllables and hand signals.
15. To prepare for the ostinato to be played by the soprano or alto glockenspiel, ask class to do the following with you:

16. When class can do the above with rhythmic stability, signal timpani to begin introduction. Two measures later, signal class to begin singing syllables as they continue doing bodily movement.
17. Show a child how to play the following on the soprano or alto glockenspiel:

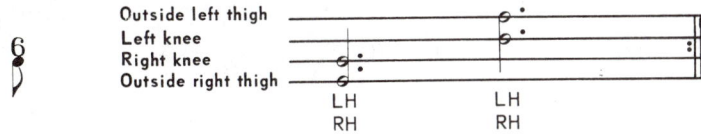

18. Tell class that now you would like them to sing the words to this song which they all know, *Three Blind Mice*, as they are accompanied by the timpani and glockenspiel. Explain that you would like them to do the following with you as they sing and mirror you:

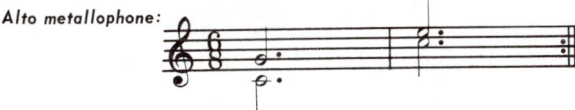

19. When class can do the above with rhythmic stability, signal timpani to begin introduction. Two measures later, signal glockenspiel to begin. Two measures later, signal class to begin singing words as they continue bodily movement above.
20. Show a child how to play the following ostinato:

Alto metallophone:

21. Tell children that this time as they sing you would like them to do a different kind of patschen pattern. Do the following, indicating that class should mirror you.

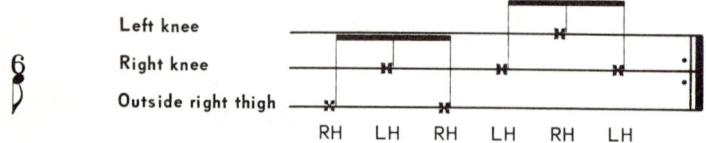

22. When class can do the above easily, have them continue and signal timpani to begin. Bring in the entire ensemble at two-measure intervals in the following order: glockenspiel, alto metallophone, and class singing.

23. Show a child how to play the ostinato:

24. Tell class you would like to have them sing the song with all accompaniments. They will enter, at two-measure intervals, in the following order: timpani, glockenspiel, alto metallophone, alto xylophone, and class singing. Have instruments continue four measures after the end of the song, ending on the first beat of the fifth measure.

25. When class can do the above successfully, divide them into two groups and have them sing song as a round, using the same accompaniment.

26. On another day, to reinforce children's understanding of 6/8 time, have class clap and count the song in a manner similar to the procedure used in *Nose, Nose, Jolly Red Nose.*

Learning an Orchestration to a Song in the Major Mode, *'Twas This Way and That Way—* For Intermediate Grades

Note: Tune timpani to notes G and D.

1. Tell class to do as you do; then do the following:

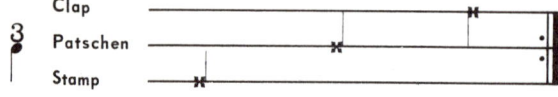

New Era Instruments, made in England by Premier Drum Company, LTD., exclusively distributed in the U.S. by Selmer, Elkhart, Indiana.

2. Continuing to do the above with the children, begin singing the song *'Twas This Way and That Way*.

'Twas This Way and That Way

1. Oh! ___ when I was a farm - er, a farm - er, a farm - er, Oh! ___

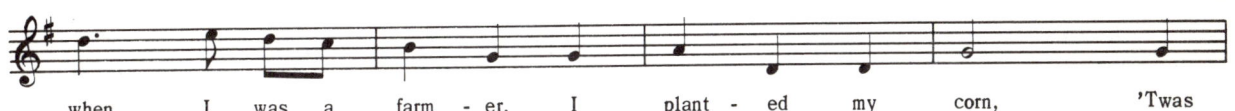

when I was a farm - er, I plant - ed my corn, 'Twas

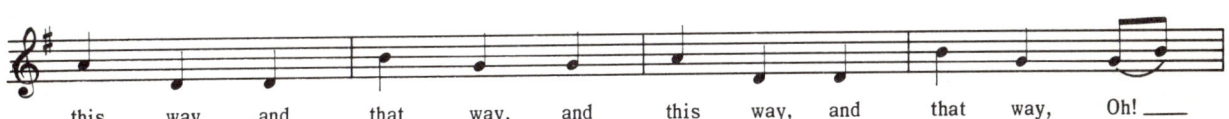

this way and that way, and this way, and that way, Oh! ___

when I was a farm - er, I plant - ed my corn.

2. Oh! when I was a reaper, a reaper, a reaper,
   Oh! when I was a reaper I cut down my grain.
   'Twas this way and that way, and this way and that way.
   Oh! when I was a reaper I cut down my grain.

3. Oh! when I was a miller, a miller, a miller,
   Oh! when I was a miller I ground it to flour.

4. Oh! when I was a baker, I kneaded the bread.

3. Ask for a volunteer to play the timpani. Show him how to play the following, using both mallets, i.e., changing mallets on each note:

4. Tell class that the note being played by the timpani is G. Write the three measures of G on the board, as above. Explain that G begins the introduction and accompaniment of the song and that you would like to see if they can tell you on what word of the song it becomes inappropriate. Tell class you would like them to begin by doing the bodily movement accompaniment (1, page 204) as the timpani player plays the Gs and you sing the song. Explain that they are to raise their hands when they feel the G is no longer correct.

5. Have class begin bodily movement. After two measures, have timpani player begin. After one measure and two beats, begin song. Class should hear dissonance on the word "farmer" when it appears the second time. If they do not, repeat from the beginning, after telling them that they

missed the word and to listen more carefully. On the repeat, emphasize the word "farmer" slightly to underscore the dissonance. When they hear it, explain that the note D fits the measure with the word "farmer." Expand the notation on the board to include the following:

6. Tell class you would like to see if they can hear where the timpani changes back to the note G. Have class begin bodily movement and timpani begin introduction. If they do not hear the need for a change on the third "farmer," stop as before, and tell them to listen as you repeat. When they hear the dissonance, add this measure to the notation on the board. Continue in this way until class has heard all the changes and the following is on the board:

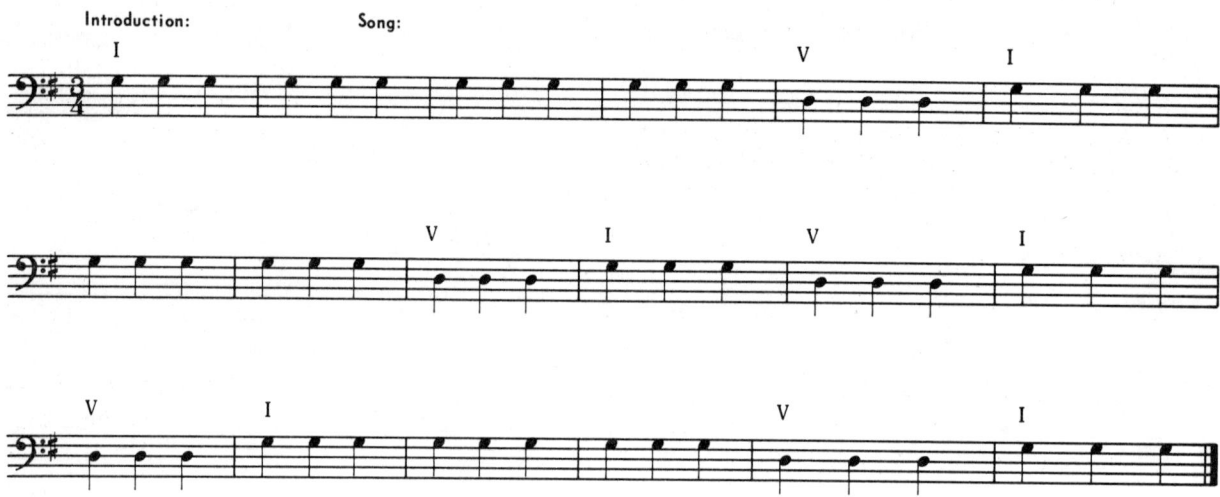

7. Explain that the note G represents the tonic (or I) chord and put it on the board:

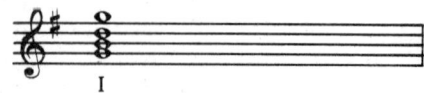

8. Have class sing each of the tones of the tonic chord, using syllables and hand signals.
9. Explain that the note D represents the dominant (or V) chord, and put it on the board:

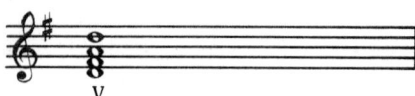

10. Have class sing each of the tones of the chord, using syllables and hand signals.
11. Tell class that on another day you will show them how to play the accompaniment on an autoharp, but that today you would like to show them a different accompaniment. Tell them to do as you do; then do the following, having them mirror you.

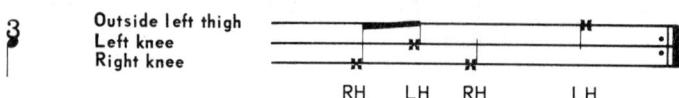

12. Remove notes adjacent to the notes to be played; then show a child how to play the ostinato for alto xylophone, using two mallets, moving hands just as was done in the preparation.

Alto xylophone:

13. Tell children you would like to add the alto xylophone accompaniment to the song and that as you sing the song, you would like them to join you in singing and doing the following rhythmic accompaniment. Do the following and have class mirror you:

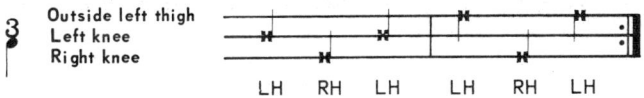

Outside left thigh
Left knee
Right knee

LH   RH   LH   LH   RH   LH

14. When children are doing the above successfully with you, have timpani begin his introduction. After two measures, have alto xylophone begin his ostinato. After one measure and two counts, begin singing, indicating that class should join you.
15. Show a child how to play the ostinato for soprano xylophone:

Soprano xylophone:

Note: Explain that the soprano xylophone player must follow the markings I and V on the notation for timpani on the chalkboard, playing the measure marked I when it occurs and the measure marked V when it appears.

16. Ask for a volunteer to dramatize the first verse. Explain that as you add the soprano xylophone ostinato to the accompaniment, you would like the volunteer to dramatize the verse rhythmically, i.e., trying to keep his bodily movements as much as possible in the rhythm of the song.
17. Have class begin the rhythmic accompaniment learned in 1 (page 204). Have timpani player begin introduction, bringing in alto xylophone and soprano xylophone at two-measure intervals. One measure and two beats after soprano xylophone enters, begin song and dramatization.
18. After appropriate preparation with class, show a child how to play the ostinato for alto metallophone:

19. Discuss the second verse, making sure class knows what a reaper is and getting ideas for how it could be dramatized. Select a volunteer to dramatize second verse. Have class begin rhythmic accompaniment. Bring in instruments two measures apart in this order: timpani, alto xylophone, soprano xylophone, alto metallophone. One measure and two beats after alto metallophone enters, begin song and dramatization.
20. Discuss the other remaining verses to help children form ideas for rhythmic dramatization. Select volunteers to dramatize the verses and do them with the accompaniments as outlined above. Through discussion, help children to be freer in their dramatizations while relating as closely as possible to the rhythm of the song.
21. On another day, teach children to accompany the song on the autoharp.

Learning an Orchestration to a Song in the Minor Mode, *Farewell Good Friends (Shalom Chaverim)*—**For Intermediate Grades**

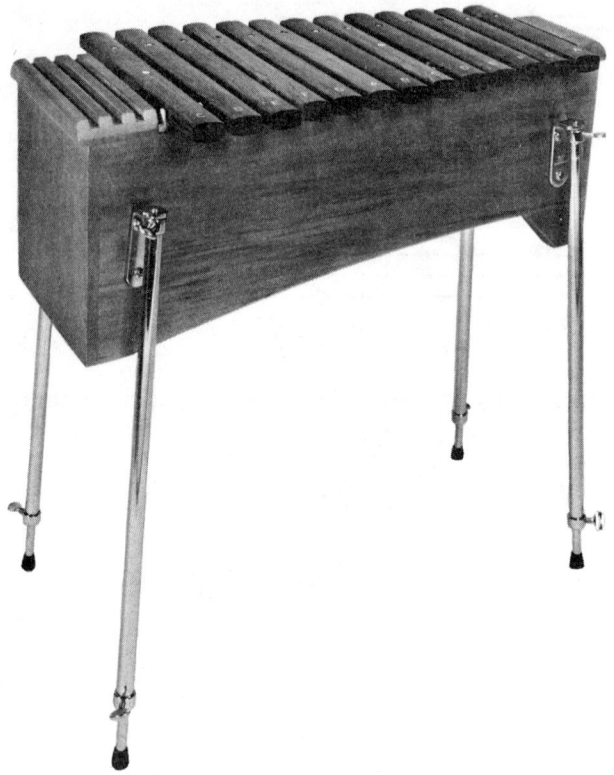

New Era Instruments, made in England by Premier Drum Company, LTD., exclusively distributed in the U.S. by Selmer, Elkhart, Indiana.

1. Put the following on the chalkboard (omitting number notation):

one and one and one   one   one and one and one   rest

one and one and one   one   one and one and one   rest

one   one   one   one and   one   one   one   one and

one   one   one   one and   one   one   one   one and

2. Tell class you will clap two of the lines notated on the board and you would like them to identify the lines. Clap two lines. Have class identify, then clap, chanting notation.

3. Ask if anyone can clap the other two lines. Let individual volunteers try to do so. When clapped correctly, have entire class clap, chanting number notation.
4. Divide class into two groups: one group to clap first two lines, the other group to clap last two lines. Let each group practice alone, this time without chanting notation.
5. Have the two groups clap their lines simultaneously.
6. When two groups can clap their own lines with stability while listening to the other lines being clapped, tell class you would like them to clap their lines as you play a song on the recorder. Tell them you would like each group to clap its lines three times, then stop.
7. Have class begin clapping. After one measure and three counts, begin playing the song on the recorder. Class will continue clapping after you have finished. (When playing the song, use an alto recorder, or if a soprano recorder is used, play the notes B below middle C an octave higher when they occur.)

Farewell, Good Friends (Shalom Chaverim)

From *All Together Sing*, ©1957 and 1962 by Cooperative Recreation Service, Inc. English by A.D.Z. Used by permission.

8. Tell class that this time you would like them to clap their lines and sing along with you using any neutral syllable, such as la. Have class begin clapping. After one measure and three counts, begin playing and signal them to begin singing.
9. Tell class you would like to teach them the words and that you would like them to clap as usual, then to echo whatever you sing. Have class begin clapping their lines. Sing the song phrase by phrase, signaling class to echo you immediately after each phrase, without missing a beat:

   Farewell good friends,
   Farewell good friends,
   Farewell, farewell,
   Till we meet a-gain,
   Till we meet a-gain,
   Farewell, farewell.

10. Tell class you would like them to sing the song through as they do a different rhythmic accompaniment. Tell them to do as you do; then do the following:

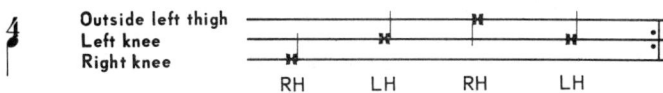

11. When class can do the above with stability, have them sing song all the way through, beginning on the fourth beat (and fourth movement in pattern above).

12. Show a child how to play the ostinato for the alto xylophone, after removing bars adjacent to notes to be played. Remind him that his hands will move just as they did during the last singing of the song.

13. Show a child how to play the part for the timpani:

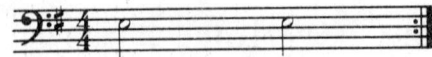

14. Tell class that this time as you sing the song you would like the timpani and alto xylophone to accompany, and that you would like them to do a different rhythmic accompaniment. Tell them to do as you do; then do the following:

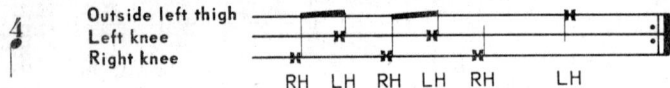

15. When class can do the above easily, have them continue, and signal the timpani and alto xylophone players to enter at two-measure intervals. One measure and three counts after alto xylophone enters, have class begin singing.

16. Substitute the F♯ bar for the F bar. Remove the notes adjacent to the bars to be played, then show a child how to play the ostinato for the soprano xylophone:

17. Tell class you would like to add the soprano xylophone ostinato to the accompaniment, and that you would like them to do a different rhythmic accompaniment. Tell them to do as you do; then do the following:

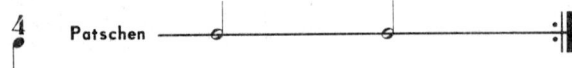

18. When class is doing the above easily, have them continue and bring in the instruments at two-measure intervals in this order: timpani, alto xylophone, and soprano xylophone. One measure and three beats after the soprano xylophone enters, have class begin to sing.

19. Show a child how to play the ostinato for alto metallophone.

20. Continuing in this way, add the ostinati for each of the following instruments to the accompaniment:

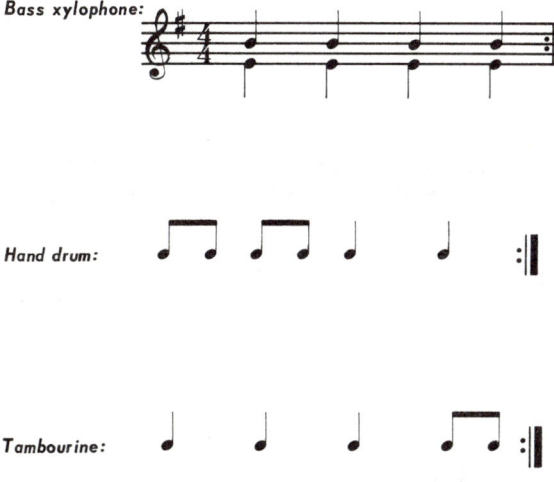

Bass xylophone:

Hand drum:

Tambourine:

21. Expand on the experience in one or all of the following ways:
   a. Help class sing the song as a round, second group beginning when first group sings the second "fare."
   b. Encourage children to create rhythmic improvisations using entire bodies (utilizing space available) as class sings and accompanies.

Learning an Orchestration to a Song in the Minor Mode, *Wayfaring Stranger*— For Intermediate or Upper Grades

1. Give class a period of tempo-dynamic movement (patschen, stamping, clapping, and snapping fingers.)
2. Tell class to do as you do; then do the following slowly, in the tempo you will later use with *Wayfaring Stranger:*

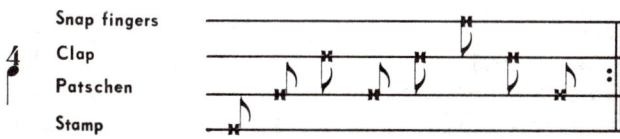

Snap fingers

Clap

Patschen

Stamp

3. When class can do the above easily and in a steady rhythm, tell them to continue as they listen, then to echo you as you sing *Wayfaring Stranger*. Continue the bodily movement as in 2 (page 211) and begin the following:

I'm just a - go - ing o - ver home.

From *This is Music*, Book V, by William R. Sur, Robert E. Nye, William R. Fisher, and Mary R. Tolbert. ©Copyright, 1967 and 1964, by Allyn and Bacon, Inc. Used by permission.

4. Tell class that you would like them to do a different rhythmic accompaniment this time, and, instead of echoing, to sing the song through with you. Tell them to do as you do; then do the following in the tempo of *Wayfaring Stranger*.

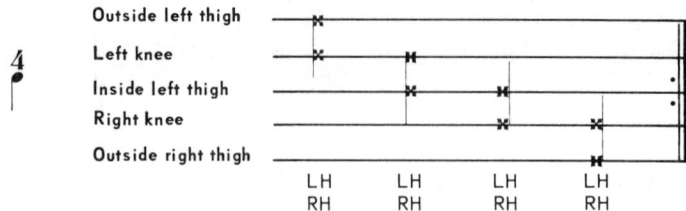

5. When class can do the above easily, in the tempo of *Wayfaring Stranger*, tell them to continue as they sing the song with you. Give them the signal to begin singing, beginning on the last half of the third beat.

6. Show a child how to play the ostinato for the alto xylophone, first removing the E bars and reminding him that his hands will move just as they did in the rhythmic accompaniment in 4 (above).

7. Tell class that this time you would like them to do still a different rhythmic accompaniment as they sing and the alto xylophone plays. Have them do the following with you:

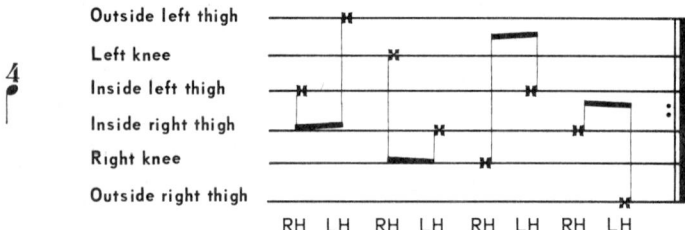

8. When class can do the above, tell them you would like them to try this with the alto xylophone accompaniment as you all sing. Have class begin their rhythmic accompaniment first. After two measures, signal the alto xylophone to begin. After one measure and two and one-half beats, signal class to begin singing.

9. After removing the E bars, substituting the B♭ bar for the B bar, and reminding him that his hands will cross when he plays, just as they did in the preceding rhythmic movement, show a child how to play the soprano xylophone ostinato. Let him practice until he can play it easily.

10. Tell class to do the following rhythmic accompaniment with you:

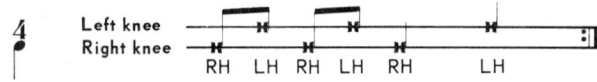

11. When class can do the above easily, tell them you would like to add the soprano xylophone accompaniment to the song. Have them begin rhythmic movement (10, page 214). After two measures, signal the alto xylophone to begin. After two measures, signal the soprano xylophone to begin. After one measure and two and one-half beats, have class begin singing song.

12. Continue in this manner, preparing class for each new ostinato, showing a child how to play each, and adding it to the accompaniment, until the following ostinati have been incorporated into the accompaniment:

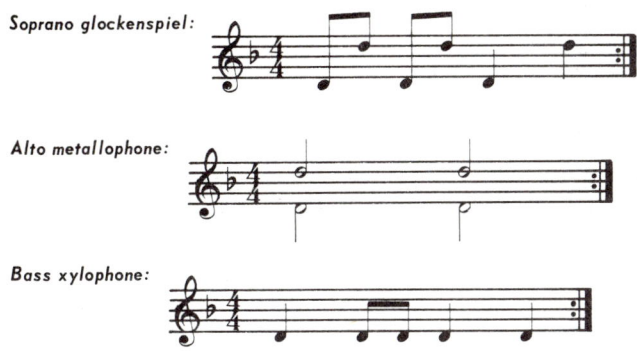

Soprano glockenspiel:

Alto metallophone:

Bass xylophone:

Exploring Syncopation and Learning an Orchestration for a Song in the Minor Mode, *Canoe Song*—For Intermediate Grades

1. Give class a period of echo movement, ending with the following:

2. Tell class to echo you as you sing the following, using first syllables[3], then words, with hand signals.

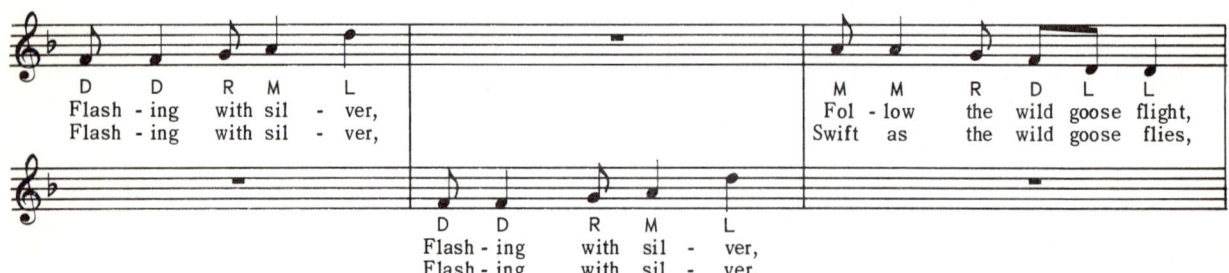

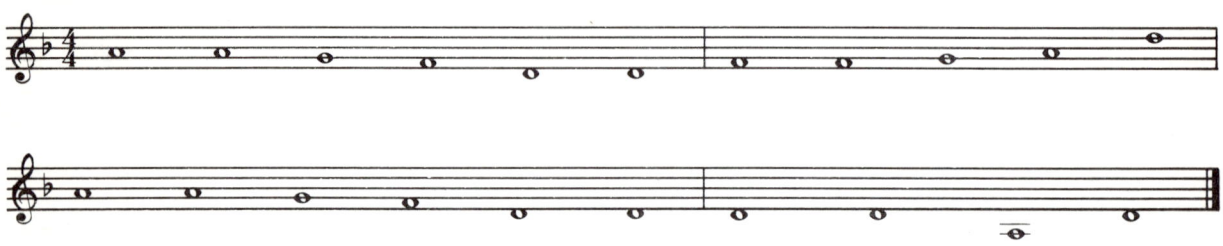

From *All Together Sing* ©1962 by Cooperative Recreation Service, Inc. Used by permission.

3. Tell class you would like to see if they can notate the song on the chalkboard. Sing the first phrase, using syllables and hand signals. Draw a staff on the board. Put the first note (A) on the staff using simply a circle. Ask for volunteers to put the next five notes of the phrase on the staff. If necessary, sing the phrase again, using syllables and hand signals, asking class to echo you. Continue in this manner until the entire song is on the board.

---

3. Note that the syllables used in *Canoe Song* are the same as though the song were written in F Major, F being do. This use of syllables is standard procedure, relating the syllables of the major scale to its relative minor.

4. Tell class you would like to see if they can change the notes to reflect their time values. Clap the rhythm of the first phrase, asking class to echo you. Ask for volunteers to change the notes of the first phrase so that they are rhythmically correct. If trouble develops, do the following:

   a. Write the following on the board:

   b. Tell class to say the words as you point to the notes. Begin chanting first phrase, pointing to the notation on the board and marking the ties where they occur, as follows:

   c. Pointing to the tied notes, explain that the following notation results and write the words under the notes as below:

   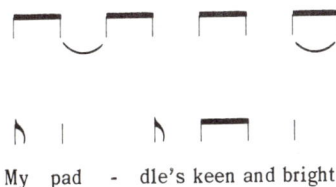

   My pad - dle's keen and bright

   d. Explain to children that when we see a short note followed by a long note, followed by another short note, we call this syncopation, and we say the word rhythm as follows:

   Syn - co - pah

5. Mark the changes in the first phrase on the melodic notation on the board. Continue in a similar manner until the entire song is notated, as below, including the rhythmic counting:

   Syn - co - pah one and one, Syn - co - pah one one,

   Syn - co - pah one and one, Syn - co - pah one - two.

6. Have class clap and sing song, using rhythmic counting.
7. Tell class you would like them to do a rhythmic accompaniment as they sing the words to the song. Ask them to do exactly as you do; then do the following:

   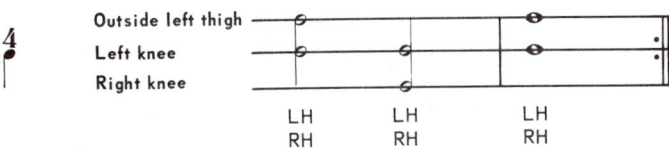

   Outside left thigh
   Left knee
   Right knee

   LH   LH   LH
   RH   RH   RH

8. When class is doing the above easily in the tempo of the song, begin singing the first verse, encouraging them to join you. Sing both verses, helping class continue movement above.
9. Select a child to play the ostinato for the alto metallophone:

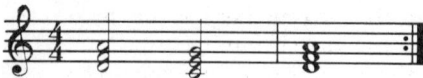

10. Show a child how to play the following on the timpani:

11. Tell class that as they sing the song with the timpani and alto metallophone accompanying, you would like them to accompany with a different patschen. Tell them to do as you do; then do the following:

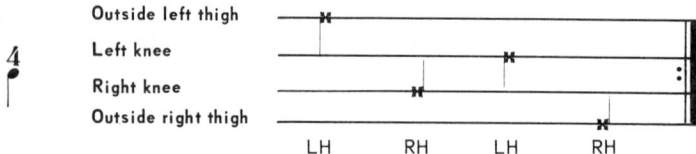

12. When class is doing the above in the tempo of the song, ask timpani to begin. At two measure intervals bring in the alto metallophone, then class singing. At the end of song, have class stop bodily movement two measures after end, alto metallophone stop four measures after end, and timpani six measures after end of song.
13. Show a child how to play the following ostinato:

14. Tell class you would like to have them do a different bodily movement as they sing the song. Tell them to join you as you do the following:

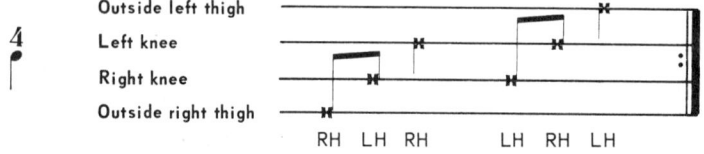

15. When class can do the above in the tempo of the song, have timpani begin to play. At two-measure intervals bring in alto metallophone, soprano (or alto) xylophone, and class singing song.
16. Show a child how to play the ostinato for the alto glockenspiel:

17. Tell class you would like to see if they can sing the song as a round as they add the ostinato for the alto glockenspiel. Divide class into two groups. Tell them you will signal each when to begin singing and that they are to sing the song through twice. Have timpani begin and bring in, at two-measure intervals, the alto metallophone, soprano (or alto) xylophone, the alto glockenspiel, and the first group of singers. One measure later, when the first group begins the second phrase, bring in the second group of singers. At the end of the singing, signal one instrument at a time to stop. For example, the alto glockenspiel might end first, the xylophone two measures later, the metallophone another two measures later, and finally the timpani.

18. To expand on the experience, give children the opportunity to work out a rhythmic improvisation using the entire body, as an accompaniment to the song.

CHAPTER 10

Upper Grades

Having developed a musical vocabulary which includes extensive experience with rhythm and melody, children in the upper grades are usually ready not only to perform, but also to *create* more complex melodic and rhythmic forms.

Reviewing Syncopation in a Pentatonic Song, *Swing Low,*
Sweet Chariot—**For Upper Grades**

1. Give class a period of echo movement, ending with the following pattern:

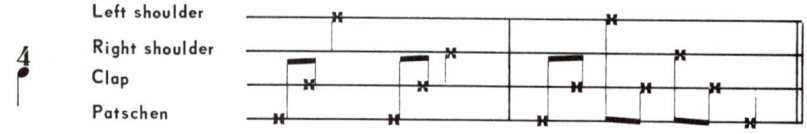

Note: Left hand taps right shoulder, right hand taps left shoulder.

2. Tell class to continue doing this pattern with you as you sing the song. Begin pattern, signaling class to join you. On the last beat of the second measure, begin singing the chorus of the song, encouraging class to join you. Sing the chorus, verse one, and then the chorus.

Swing Low, Sweet Chariot

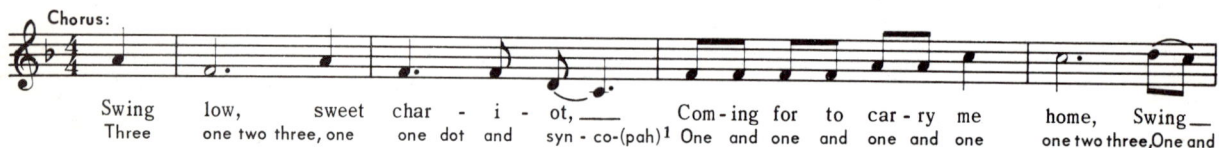

_____

1. When "pah" is in parenthesis, it is not clapped or spoken. It is felt inwardly.

low,   sweet char - i - ot,____   Com - ing for to car - ry me   home!
one two three   one   one dot and syn - co - (pah),   One and one and one and one   one two three.

Verse 1:

I   looked o - ver Jor - dan,   and what did I   see,____
One   syn - co - pah syn - co - pah,   one and one   syn - co - (pah),

Com - ing for to car - ry me   home,   A band____ of an - gels,
One and one and one and one   one two three,   One one and one   one one,

D. C. al Fine

Com - ing af - ter me,____   Com - ing for to car - ry me   home.
One and one and syn - co - (pah),   One and one and one and one   one two three four.

2. If you get there before I do, Tell all my friends I'm coming too.
3. I'm sometimes up and sometimes down, But still my soul feels heavenly bound.

3. Tell class you would like them to see how *Swing Low* looks, notated melodically. Notate song on board, as follows. (If ample time is available, teacher may want to let *class* notate song melodically.)

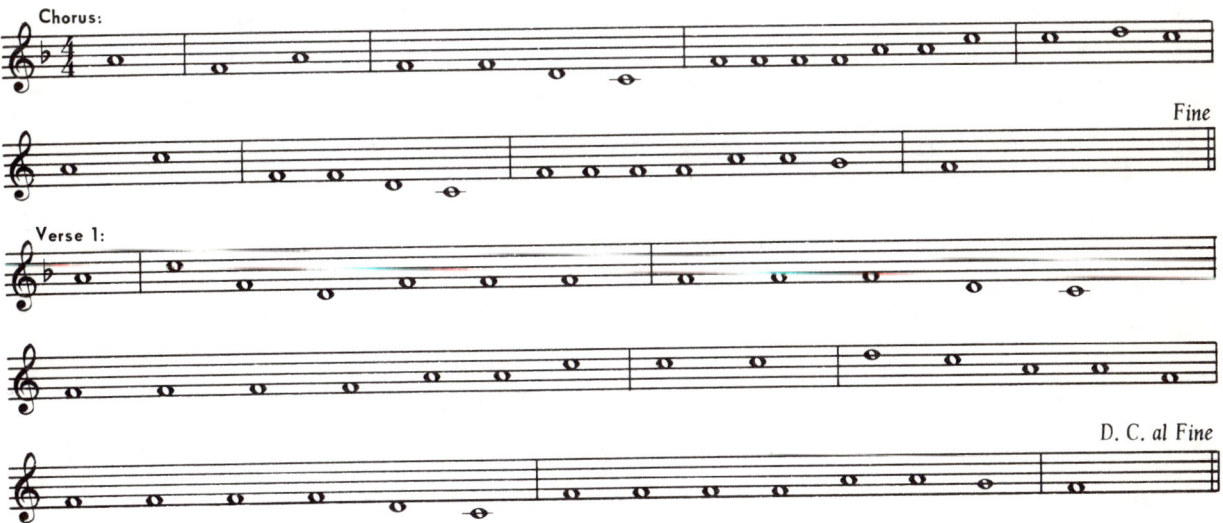

Chorus:

Fine

Verse 1:

D. C. al Fine

4. Tell class you would like to see if they can notate the song rhythmically. Tell them to listen as you chant and clap the first phrase, then echo you. Chant and clap the first phrase, using number notation, then signal class to echo you.
5. Ask for a volunteer to notate the first phrase; help, if necessary. (Child may well have difficulty notating the syncopation in the second measure. If so, take time to review syncopation, referring to the previous experience in this book with *Canoe Song*, on page 217.)
6. Continue in this manner, clapping and chanting the number notation of each phrase, signaling the class to echo you, and selecting a volunteer to fill in the rhythmic notation, until entire song is notated rhythmically.

7. Have class clap and chant number notation of song all the way through.
8. Tell class you would like them to accompany themselves with the rhythmic movement practiced earlier as they sing the entire song. Have them begin the rhythmic movement in 1 (page 220). After one measure and three beats, signal them to begin singing with you on the chorus of *Swing Low*. Guide them in singing the entire song.
9. To expand the experience, do one of the following:

    a. Teach class the ostinato accompaniments for *Swing Low* found in the final experience in this chapter.
    b. Give class the experience combining *Swing Low* and *Sourwood Mountain* at the end of this chapter.
    c. Let individual children sing solos on verses.
    d. Let children create a rhythmic interpretation of the chorus or verses.

Learning an Orchestration and Experiencing Bodily Movement to a Song in the Minor Mode, *Artza Alinu*—For Upper Grades

1. Write the following on the board:

Photo courtesy of C. Bruno & Son, Inc., Melville, New York 11746.

2. Ask a child to clap it.
3. Have entire class clap it. When they are secure, tell them to continue clapping this ostinato as you play the melody of *Artza Alinu* on the recorder.

Artza Alinu

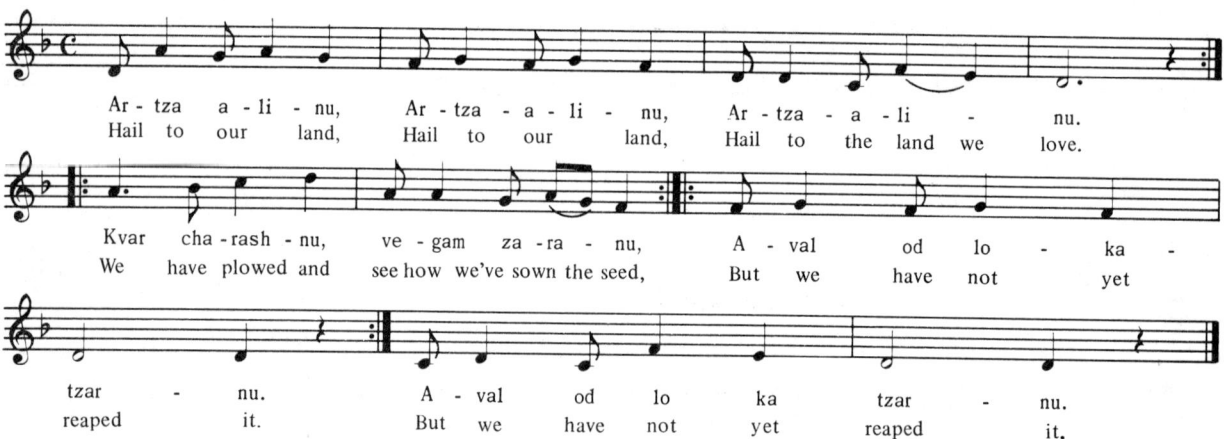

Ar - tza a - li - nu, Ar - tza - a - li - nu, Ar - tza - a - li - nu.
Hail to our land, Hail to our land, Hail to the land we love.

Kvar cha - rash - nu, ve - gam za - ra - nu, A - val od lo - ka -
We have plowed and see how we've sown the seed, But we have not yet

tzar - nu. A - val od lo ka tzar - nu.
reaped it. But we have not yet reaped it.

4. Select a child to play the ostinato pattern on the hand drum as class claps another ostinato for the bass drum:

Bass Drum:

5. Have child playing ostinato for hand drum begin. After several measures, signal class to begin clapping ostinato for bass drum. When all are rhythmically secure, play *Artza Alinu* on the recorder.
6. Select a child to play the bass drum part. Let him practice with child playing hand drum until they play easily together.

7. Tell class to do the following with you:

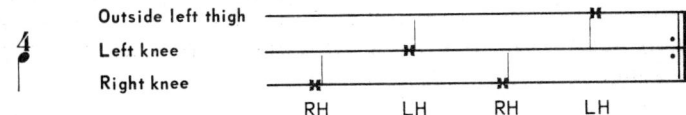

8. When class is doing the patschen easily, tell them to continue without you. Signal person playing hand drum to begin. After two measures, signal person playing bass drum to begin, and after two additional measures, begin playing *Artza Alinu* on the recorder.

9. Show a child how to play the ostinato for the soprano xylophone:

10. To develop the full orchestration for *Artza Alinu*, follow this sequence:

   a. Have class do the preparation for playing the alto xylophone ostinato shown below as you play *Artza Alinu*, accompanied by hand drum, bass drum, and soprano xylophone.

   b. Continue in this way, adding first the alto xylophone (as children prepare for playing the metallophone), then the tambourine and timpani.

Preparation for playing alto xylophone:

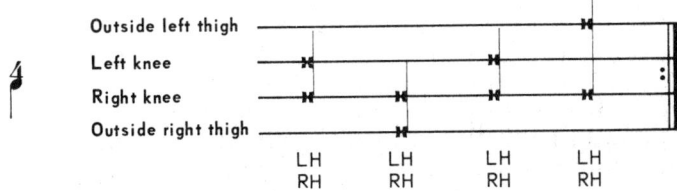

Alto xylophone:

Preparation for playing soprano and/or alto metallophone:

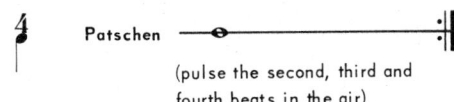

Soprano and/or alto metallophone:

Tambourine:

Timpani:

11. When children have learned the ostinati and can play them together easily, teach class to play the melody on their recorders with you[2] accompanied by the drums, xylophones, and other instruments.

12. Explain that as an introduction the instruments will enter, as was practiced, in the following order at two-measure intervals:

> Hand drum
> Bass drum
> Soprano xylophone
> Alto xylophone
> Metallophone
> Tambourine
> Timpani

13. Signal the instruments to begin playing as outlined above. Two measures after the timpani enters, signal class to begin playing their recorders with you.

14. Tell class that this is an Israeli folk song and you would like them to learn the words. Teach the words by letting class echo each phrase after you sing it.[3]

Pronunciation

Ahr—tza—ah—lee—noo,
Kŏoh—vahr—kal* rahsh noo,
Vŏoh—gahm tza—rah—noo,
Ah—vahl awd lo—kah tzahr—noo

15. Tell class you would like to have them help make an arrangement of the song—singing and playing their recorders, with instrumental accompaniment. One possible arrangement is as follows:

Introduction—instruments enter one at a time at two-measure intervals
Class plays on recorders
Interlude—instruments play two measures alone
Class sings song
Interlude—instruments play two measures alone
Class plays song on recorders
Postlude—instruments play additional measures, dropping out one at a time at two-measure intervals

16. Tell class that you would like to show them a dance step that fits this song. Do the following:

17. Let entire class practice this, standing in place. Then select several people to dance it in a circle as class repeats 15 (above).

Learning an Orchestration and Experiencing Bodily Movement to a Song in the Minor Mode, *Zum Gali Gali*—For Upper Grades

1. Write the following on the board:

---

2. See Part III for techniques for teaching the recorder.
3. In this song, as well as any song using foreign words, the teacher should feel free to use a neutral syllable as la, instead of the original words.
*The K is gutteral, not hard.

2. Ask a child to clap it.
3. Have entire class clap it. When they are secure, tell them to continue clapping the ostinato as you play the melody (top line below) of *Zum Gali Gali* on the recorder.

Zum Gali Gali

1. He-cha-lutz le 'man a-vo-dah; A-vo-dah le 'man he-cha-lutz.
2. A-vo-dah le 'man he-cha-lutz; He-cha-lutz le 'man a-vo-dah.

Zum ga-li ga-li ga-li Zum ga-li, ga-li, Zum ga-li ga-li ga-li Zum ga-li ga-li.

From *All Together Sing* © 1962 by Cooperative Recreation Service, Inc. Used by permission.

Pronunciation

Heh—kah*—lŏotz lŏo mahn ah—vaw—dah
Ah—vaw—dah lŏo mahn hĕh kah*—lŏotz

English Words:

1. Pioneers are working the land,
   Work the land, all brave pioneers.

2. Work for love of land and of life;
   Work the land, all brave pioneers.

4. Select a child to play the ostinato pattern on the hand drum as class claps the ostinato for bass drum:

5. Establish the child playing the hand drum and the class clapping the ostinato for the bass drum. When they are rhythmically secure, begin playing *Zum Gali Gali* again on the recorder.
6. Select a child to play the ostinato for the bass drum. Let him practice with the child playing the hand drum until they play easily together.
7. Tell class to do as you do; then do the following:

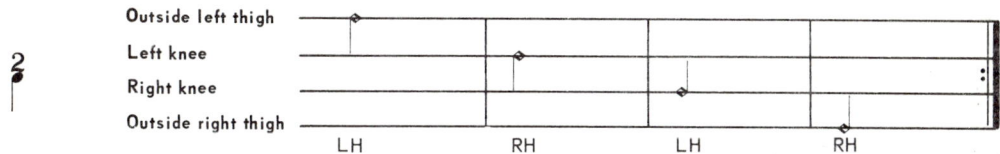

Outside left thigh
Left knee
Right knee
Outside right thigh

LH   RH   LH   RH

8. When class is doing the patschen (7, above) tell them to continue without you in an even tempo, and signal person playing hand drum to begin. After four measures, signal person playing bass drum to begin. After four additional measures, begin playing melody of *Zum Gali Gali* on the recorder.
9. Show a child how to play the part for soprano metallophone:

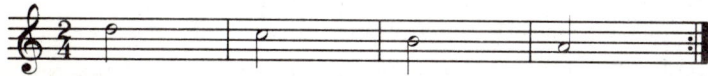

---

*The k is gutteral, not hard.

10. To develop the full orchestration for *Zum Gali Gali,* follow this sequence:

   a. Have class do the preparation for playing the alto xylophone ostinato shown below as you play *Zum Gali Gali* accompanied by hand drum, bass drum, and soprano metallophone.

   b. Continue in this way, adding first the alto xylophone (as children prepare for playing the bass xylophone), then the bass xylophone (as children prepare for playing the alto metallophone), and finally the alto metallophone.

Preparation for playing alto xylophone:

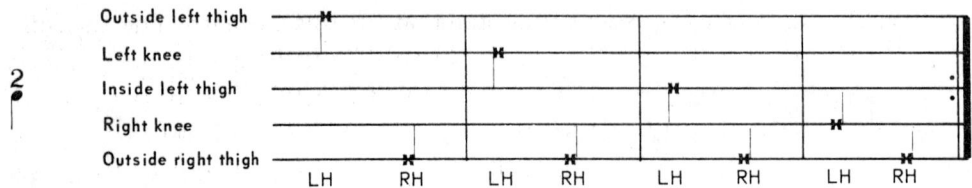

Alto xylophone:

Preparation for playing bass xylophone:

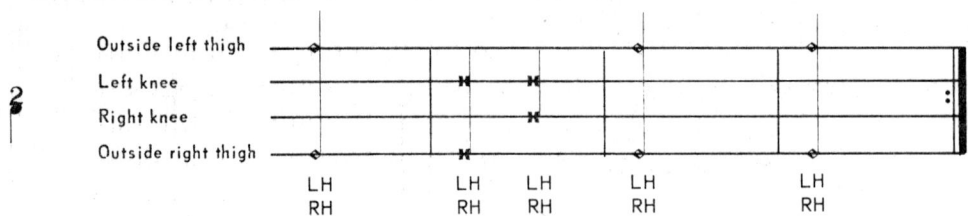

Bass xylophone:

Preparation for alto metallophone:

Alto metallophone:

11. When children have learned to play the ostinati, teach class to play the melody on their recorders as instruments accompany. As an introduction, have instruments follow the same procedure as before, entering one at a time at four-measure intervals.

12. Tell children you would like them to hear this song as it is sung in Israel. Teach them the second-line chant. When they are secure, sing the melody line as a second part.

13. Teach class the words to the verses. Divide class into two groups, one group to sing chant, one to sing melody. Let them do it many times, switching parts, until they can do it easily.

14. Tell class you would like to make an arrangement of this song by singing some verses, playing others on recorders, accompanied by the instruments. Ask children to work out a sequence. One possible sequence is as follows:

Introduction—instruments entering one at a time at four-measure intervals
Class sings song in two parts as instruments accompany
Interlude of four measures (instruments alone)
Class plays melody of song on recorders
Postlude—instruments play four additional measures

15. Tell class that you would like to show them a dance step that fits this piece; then do the following:

16. Let entire class practice this, standing in place. Select several people to dance this step as class repeats 14 (above).
17. To enrich the experience, let children use this dance step as a basis for developing a circle dance, using half a dozen or more dancers.

Learning Orchestrations to Two Pentatonic Songs, Performed Simultaneously,
Swing Low, Sweet Chariot **and** *Sourwood Mountain*—**For Upper Grades**

Note: Remove all the E and B bars from each instrument to be used.

1. Teach the two songs, using hand signals, echo phrasing, or the method most appropriate for your group:

Swing Low, Sweet Chariot

Chorus:

Swing low, sweet char - i - ot,___ Com- ing for to car - ry me home, Swing

Fine

low, sweet char - i - ot,___ Com - ing for to car - ry me home.

Verse 1:

I looked o - ver Jor - dan, And what did I see,___

Com - ing for to car - ry me home? A band of an - gels,

D. C. al Fine

Com - ing af - ter me,___ Com - ing for to car - ry me home.

2. If you get there before I do, Tell all my friends I'm coming too.

3. I'm sometimes up and sometimes down, But still my soul feels heavenly bound.

Sourwood Mountain

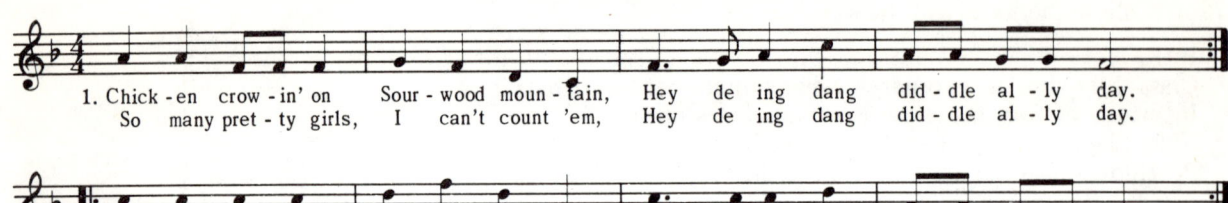

1. Chick-en crow-in' on Sour-wood moun-tain, Hey de ing dang did-dle al - ly day.
So many pret-ty girls, I can't count 'em, Hey de ing dang did-dle al - ly day.

My true love, she lives in Let -cher, Hey de ing dang did-dle al - ly day.
She won't come, and I won't fetch 'er, Hey de ing dang did-dle al - ly day.

2. My true love's a blue-eyed daisy, Hey ...
If I don't get her I'll go crazy, Hey ...
Big dog bark, and little one bite you, Hey ...
Big girl court, and little one slight you, Hey ...

3. My true love lives up the river ...
A few more jumps and I'll be with 'er ...
My true love lives up the holler ...
She won't come and I won't foller ...

From *All Together Sing* ©1962 by Cooperative Recreation Service, Inc. Used by permission.

2. Tell children to do as you do; then do the following, repeating until children can do it easily:

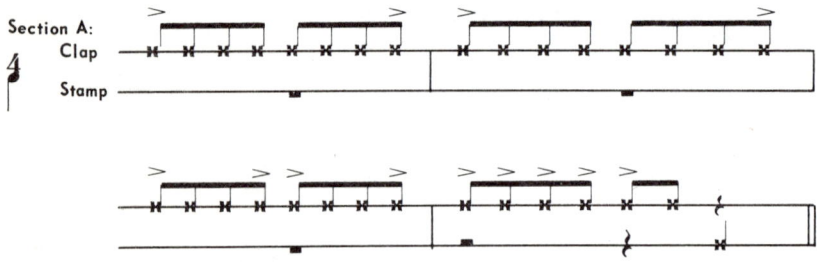

3. When children can do the above easily, tell them to do the following with you, repeating until they can do it easily:

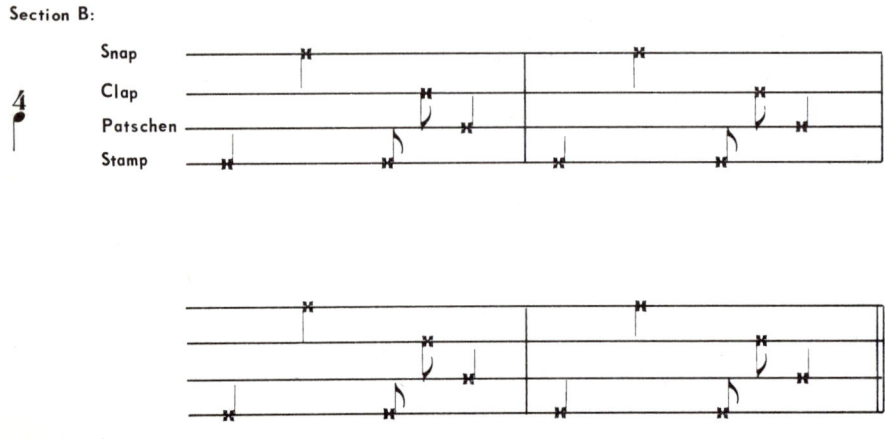

4. When children can do 2 and 3 (page 228), with security, divide them into two groups—group one and group two. Tell them you would like to see if they can do these two patterns in the following manner:

Group one: 4 measures of Section A
                4 measures of Section B
                4 measures of Section A
                4 measures of Section B

                           This will be the introduction

Group two: 4 measures of Section A
                4 measures of Section B
                4 measures of Section B
                4 measures of Section A

Have each group practice alone and then together until they combine easily.

5. To prepare class for playing bass xylophone ostinato, tell them to do as you do; then do the following. (They will mirror you, doing the opposite.) When they have begun to master the pattern, have them sing *Sourwood Mountain* with you as they continue doing pattern.

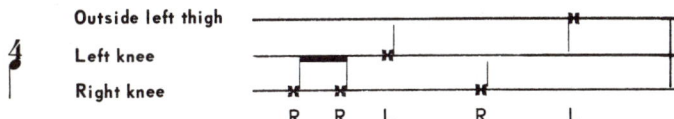

6. Teach a child to play the bass xylophone part and select small group to sing with him, letting them practice together until they have mastered the ostinato.

7. To practice the accompaniment with the song, tell children you would like to combine what they have learned so far, as follows:

Child playing bass xylophone part begins.
After two measures of bass xylophone part alone, group chanting begins.
After two additional measures of xylophone and group chanting, rest of class begins singing *Sourwood Mountain.*

Have them do the above, as outlined.

8. To prepare for the alto xylophone accompaniment, tell class to do the following with you:

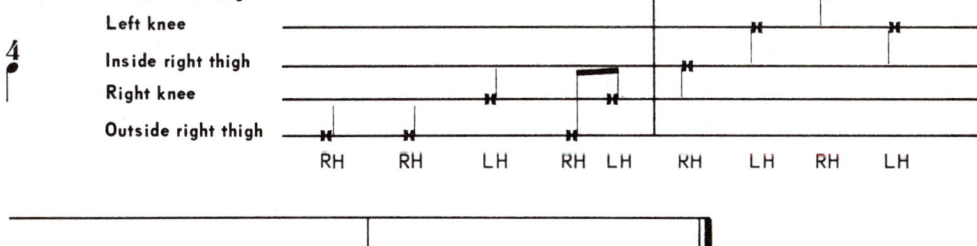

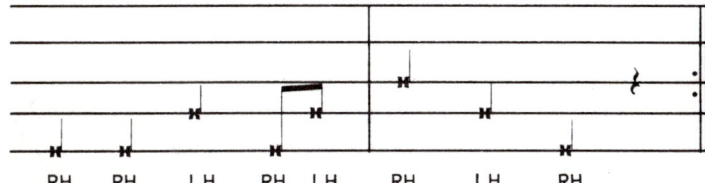

9. When class can do the pattern easily, tell them to continue as you play and sing the alto xylophone part, and to join in singing with you as soon as possible. Have them begin the bodily movement. At the beginning of the first repetition, begin playing and singing (using la or any neutral syllable). Repeat several times, until class is singing the alto xylophone part with you.

10. Show a child how to play the alto xylophone part. Have him practice as class sings with him on a neutral syllable. Select a small group of children to sing the ostinato with him each time he plays.
11. Tell class you would like them to do *Sourwood Mountain* with the two ostinato accompaniments, as follows:

    Bass xylophone begins.
    After two measures, group chanting with bass xylophone begins.
    After two additional measures, alto xylophone begins with singing ostinato.
    After two additional measures, class sings *Sourwood Mountain*.

12. Show one or two children how to play the soprano xylophone part:

13. Repeat 11 (above), adding the soprano xylophone two measures after the alto xylophone part.
14. Show a child how to play the timpani:

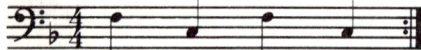

15. Tell class you would like to hear the entire arrangement, including the clapping and bodily movement practiced at the beginning using group one and group two. Explain the sequence as follows:

    Group one and group two begin together (doing Sections A and B as outlined in 4, above) and continue for sixteen measures, then stop.
    Immediately following these sixteen measures, timpani begins.
    After two measures, the bass xylophone begins with chanted ostinato.
    After two measures, the alto xylophone begins with singing ostinato.
    After four measures, the soprano xylophone begins as class sings the song *Sourwood Mountain*.
    After finishing the song, all continue for eight measures, ending on the first beat of the ninth measure.

    This concludes the first section of the experience. The second section may be initiated immediately, or on another day, depending on the available time and the interest of the group.

16. To begin the next part of the experience, prepare class for the alto metallophone part by having them sing the chorus of *Swing Low, Sweet Chariot*, mirroring you as you do the following:

Note: The word "swing" is an upbeat which precedes the first movement of the left hand.

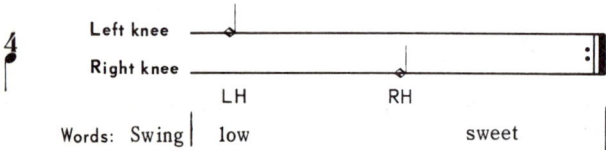

17. Show a child how to play the ostinato:

Alto metallophone:

18. Tell class you would like them to sing the song with the alto metallophone as they do the following rhythmic accompaniment. (This is preparation for the soprano metallophone part. Class will mirror you, doing the opposite.)

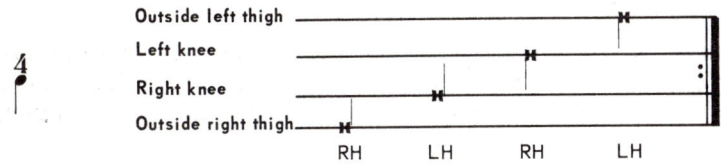

19. Have class begin rhythmic movement above. After two measures, bring in the alto metallophone. After one measure and three beats, have them begin singing *Swing Low, Sweet Chariot.*
20. Show a child how to play the ostinato:

Soprano metallophone:

21. Tell class that as they sing the song again, this time with both soprano and alto metallophone accompaniments, you would like them to do the following (which is preparation for the alto glockenspiel part). Class will mirror you, doing the opposite.

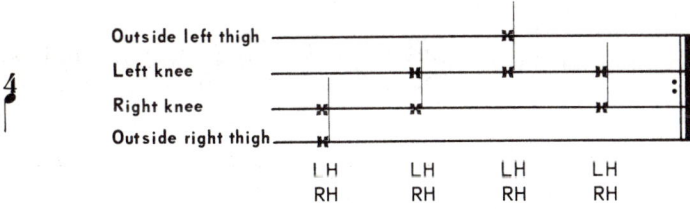

22. Show a child how to play the ostinato:

Alto glockenspiel:

23. Tell class you would like them to sing the song, in the sequence below, adding the alto glockenspiel. Make certain they understand the sequence, then bring in each part as outlined.

The alto metallophone begins.
After two measures, the soprano metallophone begins.
After two additional measures, the alto glockenspiel begins.
After one measure and three beats of alto glockenspiel, in combination with above instruments, class begins singing *Swing Low, Sweet Chariot.*

24. Teach children to play the ostinato for the soprano glockenspiel, using appropriate preparation, letting several children try before selecting one to accompany class.

Soprano glockenspiel:

25. Tell class you would like to combine all the accompaniments learned with *Swing Low.* Explain the sequence as outlined below, then help by bringing in each part in order listed.

The alto metallophone begins.
After two measures, the soprano metallophone begins.
After two additional measures, the alto glockenspiel begins.
After two measures, the soprano glockenspiel begins.
Class begins singing *Swing Low* on the last beat of the fourth measure of the soprano glockenspiel ostinato.
When song is finished, let instruments continue eight full measures, stopping on first beat of ninth measure.

26. Divide children into two groups. Tell them you would like to see if they can do *Swing Low* as a round. Have group one begin, group two beginning on the fourth beat of the first measure as group one sings the word "sweet."

27. When class can do *Swing Low* as a round successfully, have them do it once again, this time adding the instrumental accompaniment, following the sequence outlined in 25, (above).

28. When class can perform both *Sourwood Mountain* and *Swing Low, Sweet Chariot* with their corresponding accompaniments, divide children into two groups—one group to sing each song in the final sequence below—and help them to combine the two experiences in the following manner:

The sequence for Sourwood Mountain *begins first:*

Group one and group two begin bodily movement together (Sections A and B as practiced in 2, 3, and 4 above) for sixteen measures and stop.
Immediately after the sixteen measures, the timpani begins.
After two measures, the bass xylophone begins with chanted ostinato (6, above).
After two measures, the alto xylophone begins with singing ostinato (9, above).
After four measures, the soprano xylophone begins as the rest of class begins singing *Sourwood Mountain.*
After the finish of the song, all instruments continue for eight measures, ending on the first beat of the ninth measure.

The sequence for Swing Low *begins on the first beat of the ninth measure on which* Sourwood Mountain *ended:*

The alto metallophone begins.
After two measures, the soprano metallophone begins.
After two additional measures, the alto glockenspiel begins.
Two measures later, the soprano glockenspiel begins.
Entire class begins singing *Swing Low* on the last beat of the fourth measure of the soprano glockenspiel ostinato.
When song is finished, instruments continue eight full measures, ending on first beat of ninth measure.

The sequence for both songs begins on first beat of ninth measure on which Swing Low *ended:*

Groups one and two do bodily movement (Sections A and B as practiced in 2, 3, and 4, above) for sixteen measures.
On first beat of seventeenth measure, all instruments begin accompaniment for both songs simultaneously for an eight-measure instrumental introduction.
On the last beat of the eighth measure, group one begins singing *Swing Low* in unison (they are to sing only the chorus twice through).
On first beat of ninth measure, group two begins singing *Sourwood Mountain.*

At end of songs, instruments continue for eight measures, stopping on first beat of the ninth measure.

On first beat of ninth measure, groups one and two begin a sixteen-measure postlude of bodily movement as in 2, 3, and 4, pages 228 and 229.

SUGGESTIONS FOR CLASS DISCUSSIONS OR REPORTS

1. Discuss the "inner feeling" for pitch and rhythm—what it is and how it can be developed.
2. Discuss the advantages and disadvantages of starting experiences with melody with the falling minor third, then adding other notes of the pentatonic scale before proceeding to the major, minor, and other modes.
3. Discuss Orff's use of instruments to accompany chanting and singing—how instruments are used, guidelines to be observed in their use and the musical value derived from their use.
4. Discuss the validity of the following suggestions for using instruments:

   a. In beginning experiences, the teacher should develop her own orchestrations, which she teaches children by rote.
   b. Children should always play and sing from memory (by rote) in beginning experiences.
   c. Children should always be prepared for the playing of an instrument through bodily movement which corresponds to the movement their hands will make playing the instrument.
   d. Children playing instruments should always chant or sing.

5. Discuss ways of integrating the sequence of activities suggested for singing and playing in this chapter with other musical activities which each age level should experience (activities such as music listening and bodily movement).
6. Discuss ways of eliciting the creativity of children participating in Orff-Kodaly experiences with singing and playing.

SUGGESTED ACTIVITIES TO DEVELOP SKILLS AND PRACTICE IN INITIATING MUSICAL EXPERIENCES

1. Present to the class one of the experiences in two-tone songs using rhythmic and melodic ostinati and hand signals. Discuss ways of improving.
2. Present the experience for introducing rhythmic notation for quarter and eighth notes. Analyze its strengths and weaknesses.
3. Study and present the experience for developing understanding of the musical notation for the notes sol and mi. Discuss the value of the experience and ways it might be improved.
4. Present one of the experiences for three-tone songs using melodic ostinati and hand signals. Discuss the experience with the class.
5. Present the experience introducing the half note through a rhyme. Discuss the value of this way of introducing the half note.
6. Present to the class the experience using *If All the World Were Apple Pie* and creating a four-tone song. Discuss experience with class.
7. Create alternate ways of presenting the half note, or introducing a four-tone song. Present to class and discuss for positive aspects as well as ways of improvment.
8. Present to the class the experience to develop understanding of the musical notation for the notes sol, mi, la and do. Discuss with the class.
9. Present the experience for introducing the triplet (*Riddle-me*). Discuss with class.
10. Create an alternate experience for introducing the triplet and present to class.
11. Present an experience with round-clapping, patterned after an experience suggested in this chapter. Present to class and discuss.
12. Present an experience using hand signals to develop two-part singing based on suggestions found in this chapter for such an experience. Discuss with class.

PART III

The Recorder

CHAPTER 11

Playing the Recorder

For a child, the opportunity to play an instrument is always exciting. When the instrument is one he can learn to play without too much difficulty, it can become a thoroughly enjoyable experience. When he can *own* the instrument as well, he is generally captivated by it. It becomes his own personalized instrument, one through which he can not only reproduce music already composed, but also make his own music, or improvise.

For these reasons alone, the recorder is of inestimable value as an instrumental experience in the elementary school; children are fascinated by the recorder and are eager to play it. The recorder thus becomes a potential through which it is possible to solidify musical understanding and growth—an instrument through which children can come to understand and read musical notation.

While use of the Orff instruments does bring enormous growth and satisfaction, and is indispensable to expedite the Orff approach, the recorder—which is now sufficiently inexpensive to be available to all children—fills its own significant role in helping to cultivate the child's musical understanding and imagination.

How does one proceed in encouraging children to play the recorder? At what age should they begin? Best results seem to occur when children are introduced to the recorder in the early part of the third grade and are allowed to proceed slowly, with care, playing the instrument extensively by imitation and ear in early experiences. Use of the German

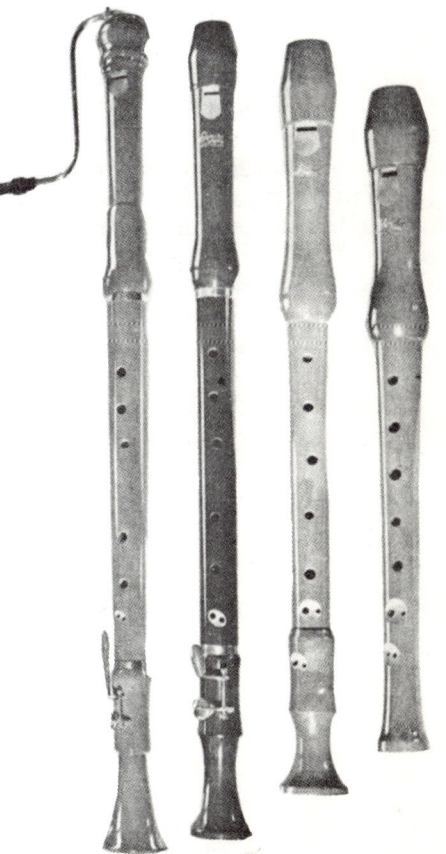

Photo courtesy of C. Bruno & Son, Inc., Melville, New York 11746.

fingering, rather than the English, or Baroque, seems advisable in all situations where large groups of children representing a wide range of ability are included.

No instruction book is necessary. Musical understanding seems to come most quickly when children experience the recorder freely, without a set routine, in conjunction with their other musical experiences. In this way, the recorder does not dominate the music period, but is an integral part of it, providing another means by which the child can consolidate musical learnings and express himself musically.

Basic Objectives

In all experiences with the recorder, the basic aims and objectives include the following:

1. To develop a responsiveness to expressive qualities of the instrument.
2. To learn to produce a good tone.
3. To learn to play expressively.
4. To develop a functional understanding of musical notation.
5. To cultivate the child's musical imagination (ability to improvise in the pentatonic, major and minor scales, and other modes).

SEQUENCE OF ACTIVITIES

Since the creative use of the recorder in conjunction with other musical experiences precludes setting up a strict sequence of activities, the following is suggested only as a general method of proceeding. All experiences suggested should be repeated extensively and in as wide a variety of activities as possible in conjunction with singing, playing ostinati accompaniments (using Orff instruments), bodily movement, and so on.

1. Playbacks (children play by imitating the finger movements of the teacher, patterns in the C scale—from middle C to D, an octave-and-one-tone higher).
2. Identification of the notes B, A, and G on the staff.
3. Playing patterns using the notes B, A, and G from songs.
4. Identification of the note E, just above middle C, on the staff.
5. Playing patterns using notes B, A, G, and E from songs.
6. Identification of the notes C and D (one octave above middle C) on the staff.
7. Playing patterns using notes C and D from songs.
8. Learning, in individual experiences, to identify the new tones D, F ♯, B♭, high E, middle C, low F and high F on the staff, and using these tones in songs.

Introduction to the Recorder: Learning the Notes B, A, and G; Playing an Ostinato Accompaniment to the Song *Old MacDonald*—For Intermediate Grades

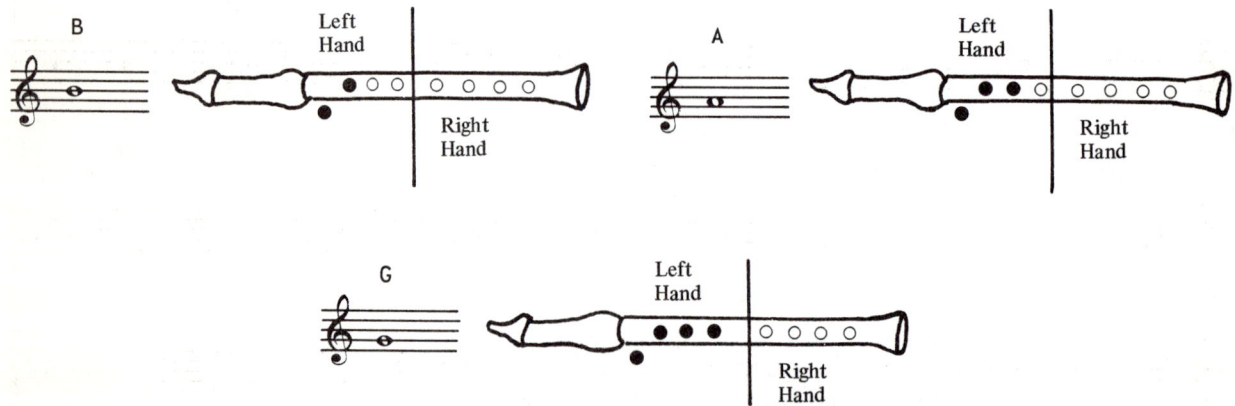

1. Have children take out their recorders and place them on their desks, single hole facing up, mouthpiece farthest from them.
2. Hold up your recorder as though about to play, side with holes toward class, right hand holding the bottom, left hand in position so that the thumb, if pressed down, would cover the hole in the back and the first three fingers would cover the three top holes. Ask class to count the number of holes as you cover each hole. Begin by covering the thumb hole in the back (holding recorder so that children can see you cover it). Then cover each hole in front as children count the seven holes.
3. Tell children to pick up their recorders with the right hand at the bottom and to rest it on their chins with the left hand thumb just over the hole in back and the fingers just above the holes in front. Tell them to *finger* (not blow) the notes you finger. With your recorder resting on your chin, finger B, making certain children see that both the thumb and first holes are covered. Then finger the notes A and G. Repeat several times.

Note: In order to make certain that children hold the recorder in the best possible position, have them cover the next to the bottom hole with the ring finger of the right hand. This will not affect the pitch.

4. Tell children that now you would like to see if they can blow into their recorders. Tell them to put the mouthpiece in their mouths, curved part resting on their chins. Tell them to finger the note B, and when you nod your head, to blow very softly into the recorder using the word "doo."
5. Signal class to blow "doo," hold it several beats, then stop. Undoubtedly there will be difficulties: some children will have blown too hard, and some will not be covering both holes. Show them once again how to finger the notes and, if possible, check to see that each child is covering his holes properly. Remind children to blow very softly and to say "doo."
6. Tell children to echo what you play. Tell them to watch your fingers and to listen, then, when you stop, to play what they saw and heard you play. Repeating any patterns with which children have difficulty and continuing to focus attention on tone quality and intonation, do the following:

7. Tell children you would like them to see what notes they have played. Put the following on the chalkboard:

8. Explain that the first note, B, is written in the third line of the staff. Have children count the lines up from the bottom of the staff. Explain that A is written in the second space. Have children count the spaces from the bottom up. Ask children which line G is written on. Help them by counting up to the second line with them.
9. Explain that the notes B, A, and G make a magic word in music reading. Ask them what they think that word is. (BAG.)
10. Tell children to put recorders on chins. Tell them to finger the notes you point to from the notation on the board and to tell you the name of the note they are fingering. Point to each of the notes above, in all possible combinations.
   (B—A—G—A—A—G—G—B—G—and so forth.)
11. Tell children that now you would like them to *play* the notes you point to. Point to notes in all possible combinations, making tunes by the various combinations.

Note: This type of activity, recorder playbacks (echoing the teacher), followed by playing notation from board as teacher points, should be a part of each recorder experience.

12. Write the following on the board:

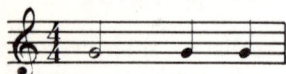

13. Ask a child to identify the notes and to play them. Have entire class play them.
14. Tell class you would like them to play this pattern over and over again as you play a song. Have them begin. When they are firmly established, begin playing *Old MacDonald*. The following should result:

Old MacDonald

Playing the Recorder • 241

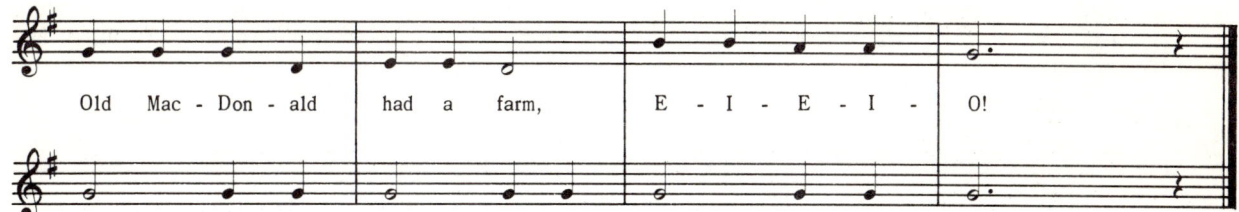

15. Tell class this time you would like some of them to sing the song with you as you play. Divide class into two groups—group one to sing the song, group two to play the recorder ostinato.
16. Have group playing ostinato begin. When they are firmly established, signal class to begin singing as you play the recorder.
17. To expand the experience, do one or all of the following:

   a. As an interlude between verses, have a child play the following on the drum:

   b. Help class create an orchestration for the song using xylophones, metallophones, or glockenspiels.
   c. Help class create a rhythmic accompaniment similar to the following, to be executed by those not playing the recorder ostinato:

   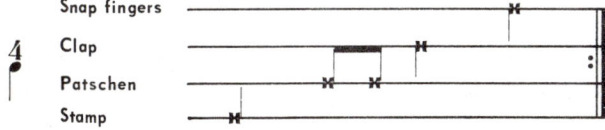

Playing the Notes G and A in the Song *Bridge of Avignon—*
For Intermediate Grades

1. Tell children you would like to see if they remember how to hold and blow their recorders. Tell them to pick up recorders and finger the note B.
2. Check to be certain that children are holding recorders and fingering B properly.
3. Remind children of the best way to produce a good tone: that is, saying "doo" into the recorder and blowing softly. Ask them to blow the note B with you. Help any children who have difficulty producing a good tone.

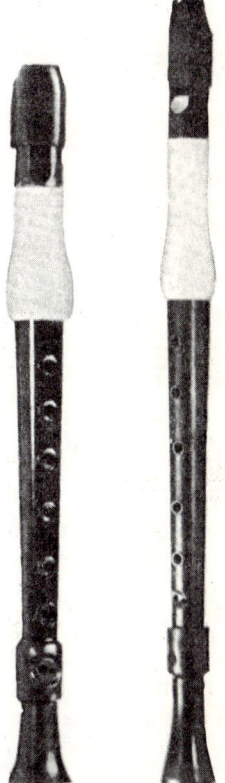

Photo courtesy of C. Bruno & Son, Inc., Melville, New York 11746.

4. Tell children to watch you play, then to echo you, playing the same pattern. Do the following, repeating any pattern that causes difficulty and continuing to focus on good tone quality and intonation.

Teacher:

Students:

5. Put the following on the board:

6. Ask individual children to tell you the name of each note.
7. Remind children of experiences they have had playing the notes you pointed to on the board. Tell them you would like to give them another such experience. Tell them to watch as you point to individual notes and to play each one. Point to the notes below in all possible combinations, interspersing the following phrase at frequent intervals:

8. Put the phrase (7, page 242) on the board. Ask individual children to play it. When several have played it correctly, have entire class play it.
9. Tell children this phrase occurs in a song they know. Tell them you would like to play the song and that you would like them to raise their hands whenever they hear that phrase. Play *The Bridge of Avignon.* Children should raise their hands on the first and third phrases.

The Bridge of Avignon

On the bridge, round and round, Ev - 'ry - one is gai - ly danc - ing,
Sur le pont d'A - vig - non, L'on y dan - se; l'on y dan - se;

On the bridge, round and round, On the Bridge of A - vig - non.
Sur le pont d'A - vig - non, L'on y dan - se tout en rond.

From *Discovering Music Together*, Book 2, Copyright ©1966 by Follett Publishing Company. Used by permission of Follett Educational Corporation.

10. Tell children that this time you would like them to *play* the phrase whenever it occurs as you play the entire song. Remind them that they must be ready to play at the beginning.
11. Tell class to finger the note G and be prepared to begin playing at your signal. Signal them to begin. Play entire song, signaling class to play third phrase at proper time. Repeat, if necessary, until class can join you without difficulty in playing the phrase.
12. To expand the experience, do one of the following:

    a. Teach class the words to the song, then have half of class sing song as the other half plays the first and third phrases on recorder.
    b. Help individual children create a rhythmic interpretation or dance to the song, moving as class plays and sings song as in a (above).
    c. Help class create an orchestration for the song using xylophones, metallophones, and/or glockenspiels.
    d. Help class create a rhythmic accompaniment to the song similar to the following:

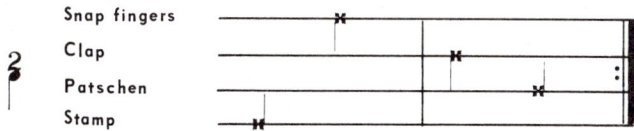

    e. Help class find and play other songs using the notes G and A in a pattern.

Note: A listing of songs from the elementary song series containing tonal groups suitable for recorder can be found in *New Approaches to Music in the Elementary School.*

Playing the Notes B, A, and G in the Song *Ezek'el Saw the Wheel—* **For Intermediate Grades**

Note: Children should know the song *Ezek'el Saw the Wheel*, and it should be available for them to look at.

1. Review the notes B, A, and G by means of echo playbacks. (Children watch you finger and play short, one-measure phrases, then echo, playing the phrases on their recorders.) Stress the importance of good tone quality and playing softly.

2. Write the following on the chalkboard:

Photo courtesy of Lyons Band Company, Elmhurst, Ill.

3. Tell children you would like them to play the notes that you point to. Point to the notes, one at a time, in as many different combinations as possible until children obviously recognize and can play all three notes in any combination. One combination might be:

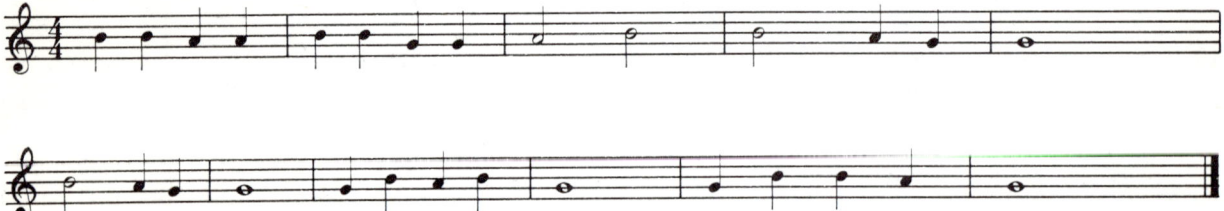

4. Have children look at the song *Ezek'el Saw the Wheel*. Ask them where in the song they find melodic patterns using B, A, and G descending. (On the words "Way up in the middle o' the air" and "Way in the middle o' the air.")

Ezek 'el Saw the Wheel

E - ze - k'el   saw   the   wheel!   'Way   up   in   the

mid - dle   o'   the   air,   E - ze - k'el   saw   the   wheel!

'Way   in   the   mid - dle   o'   the   air,   The   big   wheel   moved   by

Faith, The Lit - tle Wheel moved by the Grace o' God, A

wheel in a wheel 'Way in the mid - dle o' the air.

1. Jes' let me tell you what a hy - po - crite 'll do, _____

'Way in the mid - dle o' the air, He'll talk a - bout me an' he'll

D. S.

talk a - bout you! Way in the mid - dle o' the air. E -

2. Watch out my sister how you walk on the road,
   'Way in the middle o' the air,
   Yo foot might slip an' yo' soul get lost!
   'Way in the middle o' the air.

3. You say the Lord has set you free,
   'Way in the middle o' the air,
   Why don't you let yo' neighbor be!
   'Way in the middle o' the air.

4. Now one of these days 'bout twelve o'clock,
   'Way in the middle o' the air,
   This old world gonna reel and rock,
   'Way in the middle o' the air.

From *Look Away, Fifty-Six Negro Folk Songs.* ©1960 by Cooperative Recreation Service, Inc. Used by permission.

5. Have children practice each of the phrases named (4, page 244) as you point to the notes, repeating until they can play them easily. Then explain that you would like them to sing the song, except for the phrases practiced. On those phrases they are to play their recorders.

6. Tell class to have recorders ready to play on the first phrase. Signal them to begin singing. Point to the notes of each phrase to be played by the recorder and help children to stay together by marking time unobtrusively.

7. Practice any phrases which give difficulty and repeat.

8. To expand on the experience, help children learn to play the following ostinati as an accompaniment, preparing them in each case with bodily movement which corresponds to the direction hands will move in playing the ostinato.

Bass xylophone:

Alto xylophone:
(two children)

Timpani:

Soprano xylophone:
(with wooden mallets)

Alto metallophone:

Playing the Notes B, A, and G in the Song
Hot Cross Buns—**For Intermediate Grades**

1. To encourage children to function as a group, give them a period of tempo-dynamic movement (stamp, patschen, clap, snap).
2. Give children a period of echo playbacks, stressing playing with a good tone quality.
3. Place the following on the chalkboard:

4. Tell children to play the notes you point to. Point to the notes in various combinations, ending with the melody for *Hot Cross Buns.*

Hot Cross Buns

5. Ask children if they recognize the song just played.
6. Tell children to mirror you; then do the following (preparation for playing timpani ostinato).

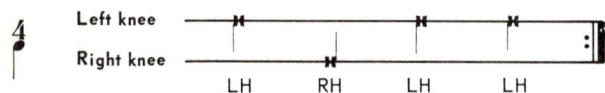

7. Divide class into two groups—one group to play *Hot Cross Buns* as the other group does the bodily movement in 6 (above). Have group doing bodily movement begin, and after two measures, have second group begin playing *Hot Cross Buns.*
8. Show a child how to play the ostinato:

Timpani:

9. Tell children to mirror you as you do the following (preparation for playing the bass xylophone).

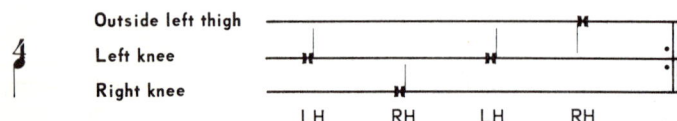

10. Tell class you would like the groups to switch parts this time. The group who played before will do the bodily movement as the other group plays and the timpani accompanies. Have group doing bodily movement (9, page 246) begin. After two measures, bring in the timpani player and after two additional measures, have group playing recorders begin *Hot Cross Buns.*

11. Show a child how to play the ostinato:

Bass xylophone:

12. Have class mirror you and do the following (preparation for playing alto metallophone).

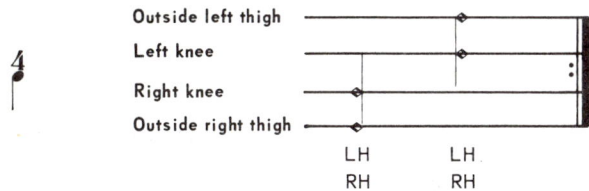

13. When class can do the above easily, switch groups again, this time using bodily movement in 12, (above) and having timpani and bass xylophone accompany.

14. Show a child how to play the following ostinato:

Alto metallophone:
(two mallets)

15. Continue in this way, introducing the additional ostinati for alto xylophone and soprano xylophone, preparing, in each case, by giving bodily movement before adding the ostinato to the orchestration.

Preparation for playing alto xylophone

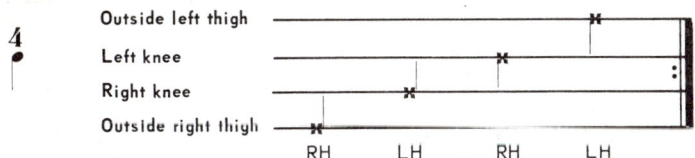

Alto xylophone:

Preparation for playing soprano xylophone:

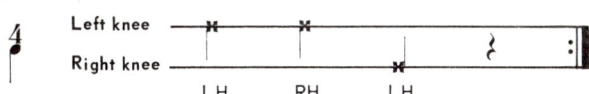

Soprano xylophone:

16. On another day review the song and orchestration of *Hot Cross Buns*, having children notate the song first melodically, then rhythmically, on the chalkboard. (Suggestions for this type of activity have been made in previous chapters.)

Playing the Notes B, A, and G in the Song
Sleep, Baby, Sleep— **For Intermediate Grades**

1. Give children a period of playbacks similar to the
   following, including the note E as much as possible and stressing the importance of listening carefully and producing a good tone. Do not hesitate
   to stop children when tone is bad or to repeat a
   pattern causing difficulty.

Photo furnished through the courtesy of the Kitching
Division of Ludwig Industries.

2. Put the following on the chalkboard, omitting the words for the rhythmic counting:

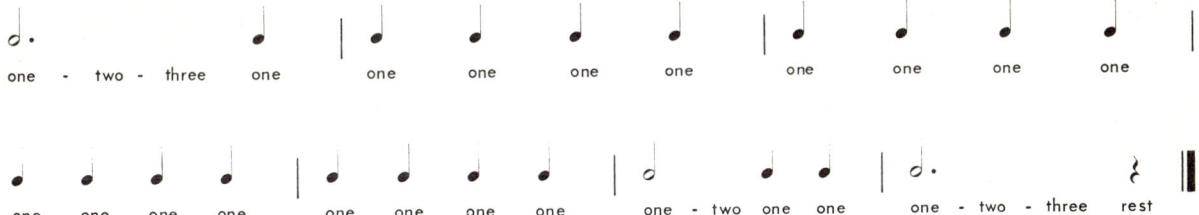

3. Have children clap it and say number notation (rhythmic counting).
4. Assign the quarter notes to one group of children, the half notes to another group, and the dotted half notes to a third group of children. Tell class that all of them should count *all* notes silently, but when the note to which they have been assigned appears, they should clap and count aloud. Have group responsible for half notes begin. Help by bringing in each group as their notes appear. Then have class do pattern *without* your help. Do this several times until they can do it easily.
5. Have entire class clap notation as a group—all clapping all notes, no chanting.
6. Tell class you would like them to do this as a round. Divide class into two groups. Tell group two that they will begin as group one reaches fourth note (first note, second measure). Have group one begin. Bring in group two on fourth note. Help by keeping the beat steady.
7. Repeat, if necessary. Switch groups, group one being second, group two, first.
8. Ask for volunteers to *step* the notation, making the steps match the notation in duration. Let several children show how they would step the first four notes.
9. Select several children to step the notation as class claps and says number notation. Repeat many times, giving other children the opportunity to step the notation.
10. Tell class you would like to teach them the words that go with this notation. Tell them to listen as you clap and chant, then to do exactly the same thing (echo you). Do the following:

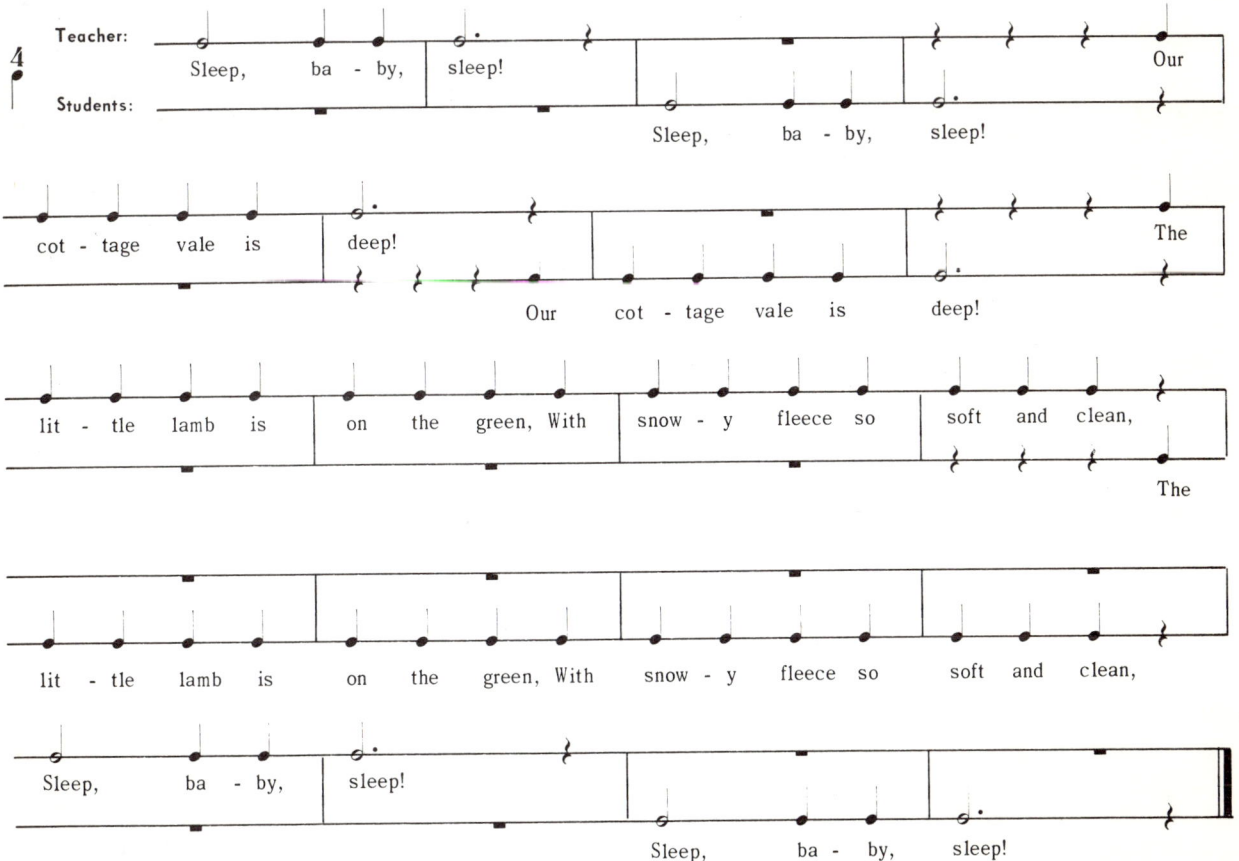

11. Tell children to watch the notation on the board as they *say* the first and last words *only*, thinking all the other words in the proper rhythm. Signal for them to begin. Help by quietly keeping the beat.
12. Write the following on the chalkboard:

13. Ask for a volunteer to play it. Let several try. Have the entire class play it.
14. Tell children you are going to play a song on the recorder and that they are to listen to see exactly how many times they hear the phrase just played. Play the following:

Sleep, Baby, Sleep

(The phrase appears twice in exact form and once in a variation.)

15. Tell children that this time as you play the song they are to raise their hands when the phrase appears. Play song.
16. Tell children to *play* the phrase whenever it appears as you play the entire song. Play song.
17. Tell children that this is part of a song they may know. Tell them what it is, that you will sing the entire song, and that they may join in singing the parts they know. Sing the song several times.
18. Have children *play* the familiar phrase when it appears and *sing* the remainder of the song, as you play entire song on recorder.
19. Tell children the timpani part for the song includes two tones; then write the following on the chalkboard:

Timpani:

20. Tell them that these two notes, exactly as written, are the notes which accompany the first measure of the melody; demonstrate by singing the first measure as you play the two notes on the timpani.
21. Tell class you would like them to tell you what timpani note—G or D—should be played on the next note of the melody (on the word "sleep"). Tell them you will let them hear how it would

sound if you played the note D on the timpani. Begin at the beginning of the song; sing and play the following:

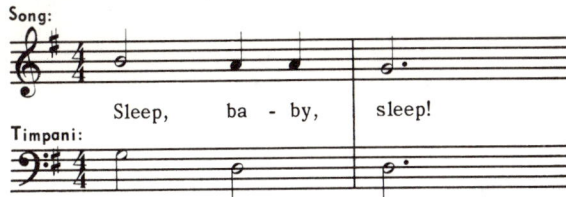

22. Ask children if they liked the sound. (They should not.) Tell them you will now play the note G on the word "sleep." Sing and play the following:

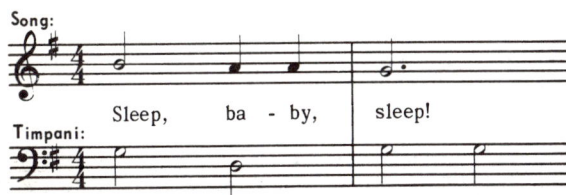

23. Ask children if they liked this better. (They should like it.)
24. Continue working in this way, letting children figure out the part for the timpani. Write each final decision as to notes on the chalkboard until they have the entire accompaniment, which should be similar to the following:

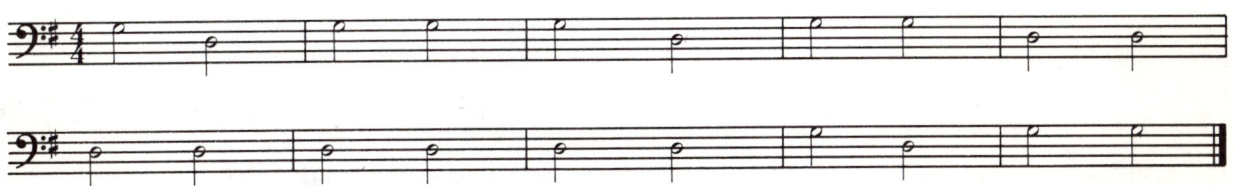

25. Show a child how to play the timpani part, reading it from the board.
26. Have child playing timpani accompany as class sings song, playing recorder on familiar phrase.
27. On another day, review the song, teaching class to play the following ostinati accompaniments (preparing them in each case with bodily movement).

Preparation for playing bass xylophone or alto metallophone:

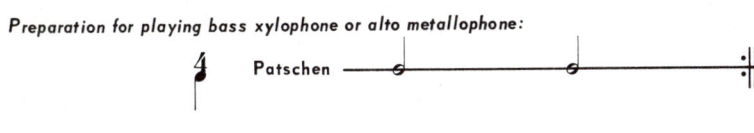

Bass xylophone or alto metallophone:

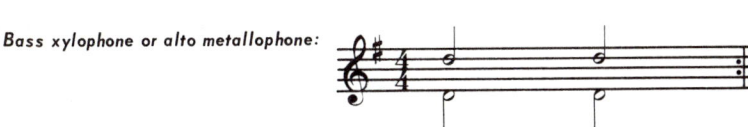

Preparation for playing alto xylophone (to be played on first four measures and last two measures):

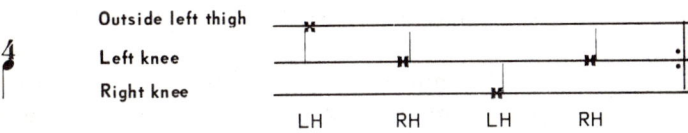

Alto xylophone (to be played on first four measures and last two measures):

Preparation for playing alto xylophone (to be played on measures five through eight):

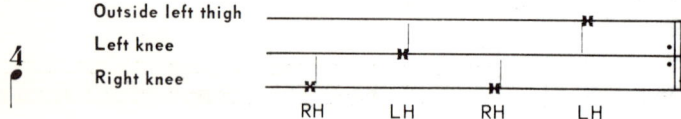

Alto xylophone (to be played on measures five through eight):

Playing the New Note Low E in the Song *Chevy, Buick, Dodge, and Ford*—For Intermediate Grades

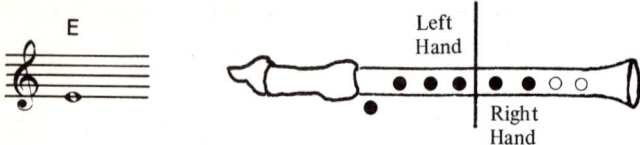

Note: With the ability to play G, A, and E on the recorder, children are now able to play many of the three-tone songs introduced in the preceding chapter which use these notes.

1. As a "warm-up" give children the following experience, singing with hand signals:

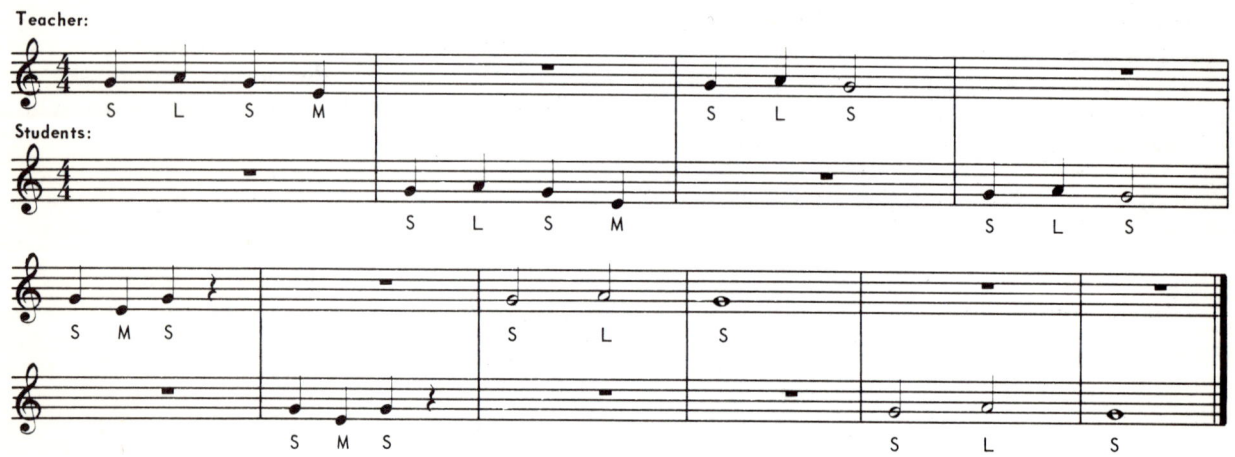

2. Give children a period of playbacks on the recorder, using the above or similar combinations of the notes G, A, and E.
3. Put the following on the chalkboard:

4. Have children identify each of the notes, noting particularly the new note E. Bring the attention of the children to the fact that E is in the first line, G in the second line, and B in the third line, while A is in the second space.
5. Have children rest their recorders on their chins. Tell them to finger and to say the letter names of the notes you point to. Point to the notes in various combinations, leading into the notes from the song below:

Chevy, Buick, Dodge and Ford

6. Tell children to *play* the notes you point to. Point to notes which comprise the melody of the song.
7. When children can play entire song, have them play first phrase again. Then ask for someone to notate it melodically on chalkboard. Continue in this way, working phrase by phrase, until entire song is notated melodically. (Have them use whole notes.)
8. When song is notated melodically, tell children you would like to chant and clap the words to the song, phrase by phrase, as they echo. Chant and clap the first phrase, signaling class to echo you immediately after you finish, without missing a beat. Go on to the second phrase, having class echo you once again, without missing a beat. Continue in this way until class can echo each phrase. (Repeat, if necessary, until class knows words for entire song.)
9. Tell class you would like to see if they can change the notes so that they reflect the correct rhythmic values. Have them clap and chant the first phrase again. Ask for a volunteer (or volunteers) to notate the phrase. Continue in this way until song is in the correct rhythm.
10. Tell class you would like to play the song on the recorder as they sing it. Signal them to begin and accompany them throughout.
11. Tell class you would like *them* to play it on the recorder. Have them play song, repeating it several times, if necessary, until all children can play it.
12. To expand on the experience, help children learn to play the following ostinati:

Improvising in the Phrygian Mode: Learning a Four-Tone Song, *New York and Boston* Using the Notes B, A, G, and E—For Intermediate Grades

1. Remind children of previous experiences in question-and-answer clapping. Remind them that you clap one short phrase and that they answer. Demonstrate, if necessary, by clapping question-and-answer phrases similar to the following:

2. Ask for volunteers to clap answering phrases. Clap the question for each of these children, helping them clap the correct number of answering beats by beating time inconspicuously for them.
3. Tell children that just as they *clapped* an answer to your clapped question, you believe they can *play* an answer to a question you ask on the recorder. Tell them that your question will contain only the notes B, A, and G, and that their answers should contain only these notes. Remind them that they can use any combination of these notes as an answer.
4. Tell them that first you will play the question and that all will play an answer together. Play the question and signal all to play an answer immediately following, without missing a beat. One possible question is the following:

5. Ask for volunteers to play answers alone. Play the question for each volunteer, helping him keep his answer within the eight beats allotted by beating time inconspicuously. Make positive comments whenever possible.
6. Write the following ostinati on the board and teach children to play them:

7. Combine both ostinati in a slow tempo.
8. Put the following on the board:

9. Explain to class that you would like the children playing the ostinati to accompany them as they play the notes you point to on the chalkboard.

10. Have children playing ostinati begin. When they are firmly established, begin pointing to notes on the chalkboard and signal class to begin playing recorders. Point to notes that form a simple melody. One melody could be the following:

New York and Boston

11. Teach class the words of the song by telling them to listen, then to clap and chant what they have heard. The following should result:

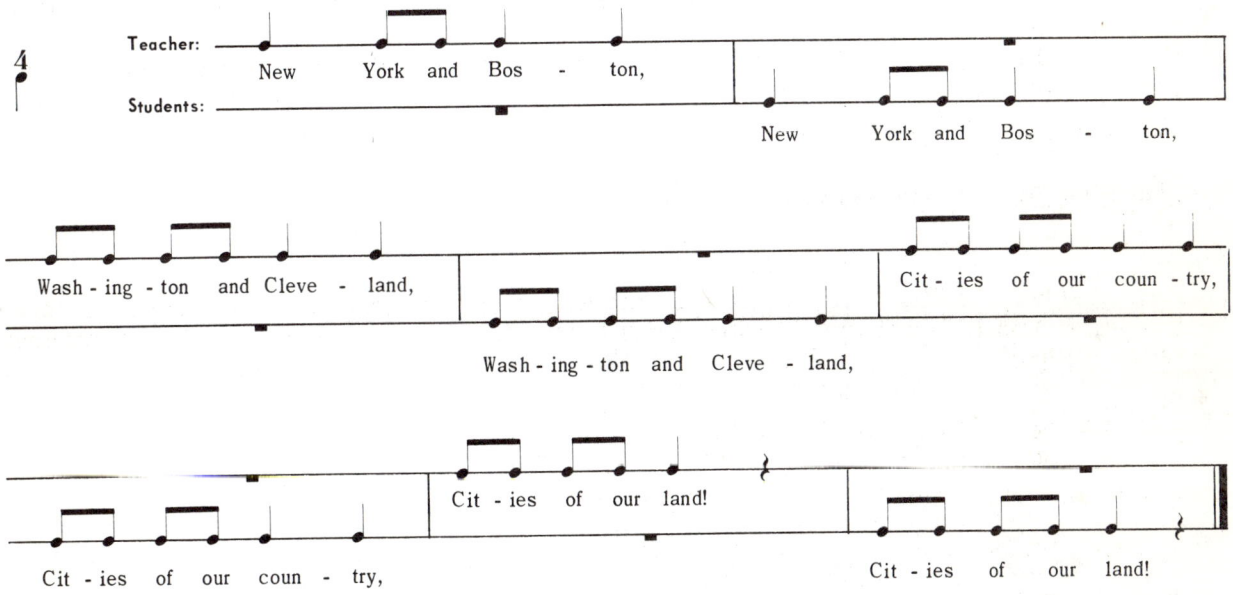

12. Have class chant and clap rhyme. Repeat several times, until they know it well.
13. Tell children that the words they have just chanted are the words to the melody they played earlier. Ask them to pick up their recorders and to listen, then to play what you play. Play each phrase of the song, letting them echo after each phrase.
14. Put a staff on the chalkboard. Ask class to play the first phrase with you once more. Ask for volunteers to notate the phrase melodically. Continue in this way, having class play and individual children notate each phrase until entire song is notated melodically. Go back and help children notate rhythmically by having them clap and chant each phrase, changing the whole notes to correspond to the correct rhythm of the song.
15. When song is notated melodically and rhythmically, have children sing the song using the words they learned in the chant.
16. Tell children you would like to do the following:
    a. Have children playing ostinati play a two-measure introduction and continue.
    b. Have entire class begin singing song on third measure.

c. At end of singing, have ostinati accompaniment play a two-measure interlude and continue.
d. Have entire class play the song on recorders.
e. Have ostinati continue two measures after the end of song as a postlude.
17. As an enrichment, on another day, do one of the following:
a. Ask for volunteers to play interludes (improvising, as in question-and-answer experiences) between singing and playing verses of song.
b. Change the interlude to include the B ostinato only (6, page 254) with the timpani playing the note E only. (Class may decide they prefer this arrangement for verses, rather than interludes— let them decide.)

Learning High C and D and Playing Them in the Song
Love Somebody—**For Intermediate Grades**

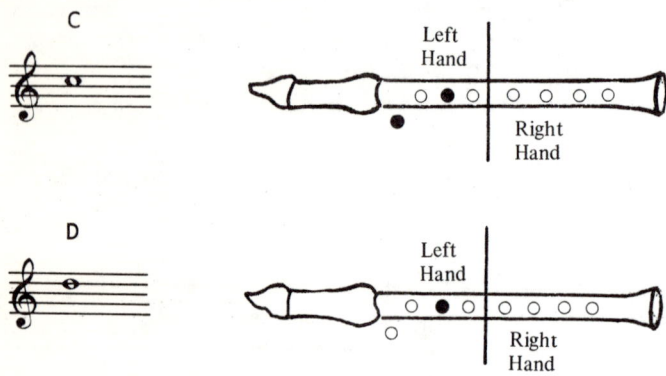

1. Tell class to listen, then to echo you on the recorder. Do the following:

2. Notate the following on the board:

3. Ask class which of these notes are new. Have someone point to them and name them. (High C and high D.)
4. Have class play high C and D once again.

5. Tell class that these two measures are the beginning of a song. Tell them to listen, then to echo you as you play two additional measures of the song. Do the following:

6. Ask if anyone can notate these two measures. Select children to notate them, first melodically, then rhythmically.
7. Tell class to listen, then to echo you for two more measures. Do the following:

8. Ask someone to notate these measures melodically, then rhythmically.
9. Ask class to listen then echo you for the last two measures of the song. Do the following:

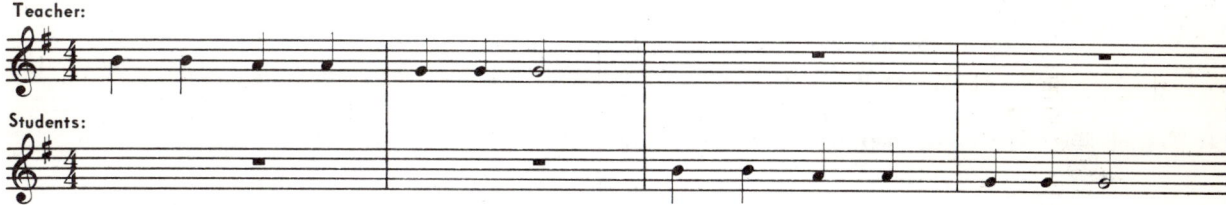

10. Have children notate these two measures, melodically, then rhythmically.
11. Write the words below the song. Then add the chord markings above the staff. All of the following should now be on the board:

Love Somebody

12. Have class sing, then play, the entire song.
13. Tell class you would like to play the timpani part as they sing the song. Play the following as they sing:

14. Ask class if they can guess how you knew which notes to play on the timpani. (The roman numerals over the notes of the song tell you because they indicate the harmony changes. I, of course, tells you to play the root of the I or G chord—G. V tells you to play the root of the V or D chord—D.)
15. Teach a child to play the timpani part.
16. Have entire class sing the song as child plays the timpani and class, simultaneously, does the following:

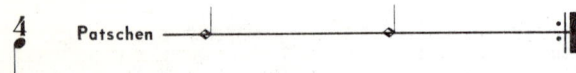

17. Show a child how to play the ostinato:

18. Tell class to do the following:

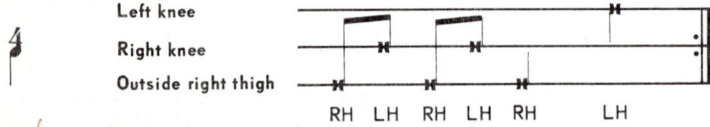

19. When they are doing it easily, indicate that the alto metallophone should begin. After two measures, have class begin singing as child begins timpani part. Have alto metallophone play a two-measure postlude at the end of song, stopping rhythmic movement and timpani at the end of the song.
20. Show someone how to play the ostinato:

21. Tell class you would like them to play the song on the recorder as the soprano xylophone and alto metallophone accompany. Have alto metallophone begin. After two measures, bring in soprano xylophone. After two additional measures, bring in class playing recorders and child playing timpani. Let soprano xylophone continue two measures after song, and alto metallophone four measures, as a postlude.

22. Write the following on the board:

23. Ask class to examine the first two measures. Ask them how many times they are repeated. (Three.)
24. Ask them how the last two measures in the song differ. (The last measure only is different—ending A, D, G.)
25. Teach a child to play the ostinato on the alto xylophone.
26. Tell the alto xylophone player that he will begin playing at the same time as the timpani and recorders. Tell alto metallophone to begin. Two measures later, bring in the soprano xylophone. Two measures later, bring in the alto xylophone, timpani, and recorders.

Playing a Melodic Rondo in the Major Mode—For Intermediate Grades

1. Give children the following experience in echo clapping:

2. Tell children you would like to see if they can clap the entire sequence above with you:

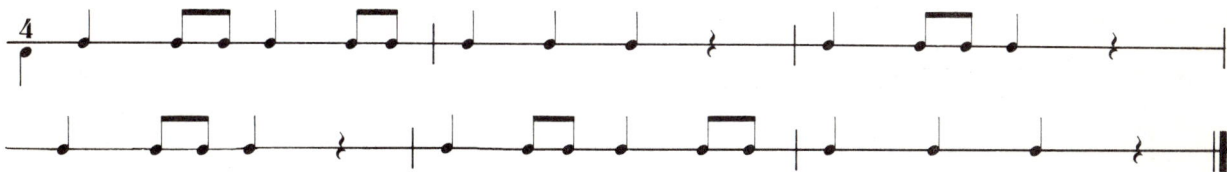

3. When children can do this rhythmic sequence through from memory, tell them you would like to make it the A part of a rhythmic rondo. Remind them of other experiences they have had with rhythmic rondos—the entire group claps the A section and individuals clap the B, C, and D sections. Select volunteers to clap improvisations for the B, C, and D sections. Remind them to be

ready to clap immediately after the completion of the A section and to clap a pattern equal in length to the A section. If desired, the form they will follow may be outlined on the chalkboard:

Section A—All clap
Section B—Child claps an improvisation
Section A—All clap
Section C—Child claps an improvisation
Section A—All clap
Section D—Child claps an improvisation
Section A—All clap

4. Have class begin clapping A section. Bring in each volunteer and class at appropriate times without missing a beat. Beat time inconspicuously to help children improvising.
5. Give children a period of playbacks, similar to the following, using the notes D, C, B, A, and G in all combinations:

6. Ask children if they know the names of the notes they played and notate them on the chalkboard:

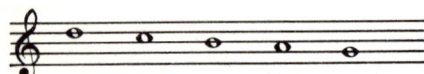

7. Have children identify each of the notes.
8. Tell children to rest their recorders on their chins and to finger the notes as you point to them on the board as they *say* the name of each note.
9. Point to the notes in various combinations.
10. Tell children you would like them to play the notes as you point to them. Once again, point to notes in various combinations.
11. Notate the following on the board (omitting the words for the rhythmic counting).

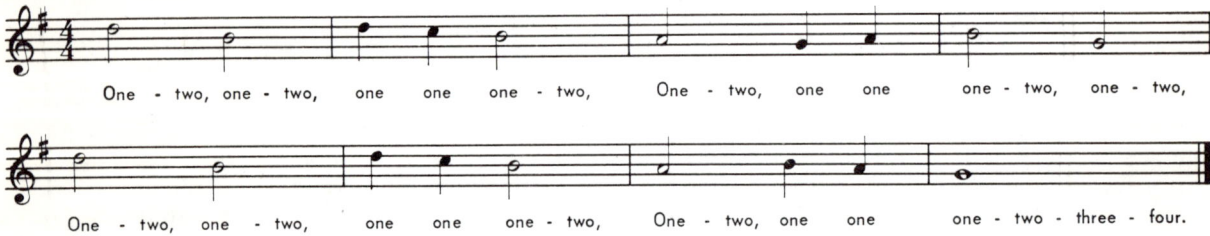

12. Have children clap and count the rhythmic notation of the melody.
13. Have children say the names of the notes.
14. Ask for volunteers to play the melody. Help, if necessary, by pointing to the notes as individuals play.
15. Have entire class play melody. Discuss any problems and repeat until class can play easily.
16. Teach the following ostinati to individual children, preparing class in any case that seems necessary by giving them bodily movement following the same direction they will use in playing the ostinato.[1]

17. Remind class of their experience with the rhythmic rondo. Tell them that now you would like to see if they can do a melodic rondo using the melody just learned (11, page 260) as Section A. Tell them you will need volunteers to play improvisations for Sections B, C, and D.
18. As for volunteers to play Sections B, C and D. Tell children that although they may use any of the notes learned thus far (D, C, B, A or G), they may limit themselves to using the notes B, A, and G, if they so desire.
19. Select volunteers for Sections B, C, and D. Write the sequence to be followed on the chalkboard:

Xylophones play two-measure introduction and A sections.
Timpani and metallophone play two-measure introduction with xylophone and continue playing throughout.[2]
Section A—Everyone plays.
Section B—Individual child improvises.
Section A—Everyone plays.
Section C—Individual child improvises.
Section A—Everyone plays.
Section D—Individual child improvises.
Section A—Everyone plays.
Instruments play two-measure postlude.[3]

Note: In all rondos the instrumental accompaniment for Section A should vary from that of Sections B, C, and D, to provide variety and a variation of tone color.

20. Have instruments begin introduction and signal each section to enter at appropriate times.
21. Make positive comments about children who improvise in such a way that their tunes form a good contrast to Section A.
22. Repeat, on other days, letting different children play the improvisations and ostinati accompaniments.

1. Since this experience is for children who have had extensive prior experience playing ostinati, the teacher may feel it unnecessary to prepare for playing with bodily movement.
2. Timpani and soprano xylophone play first two measures of their parts as an introduction, then go back to the beginning as recorders begin playing Section A.
3. Timpani and soprano xylophone repeat first two measures of their parts for the postlude.

Playing a Melodic Rondo in the Dorian Mode— For Intermediate Grades

1. Teach children the following, preparing in each case with the suggested bodily movement. Let two, then three instruments play together as they learn their parts.

Preparation for playing alto metallophone:

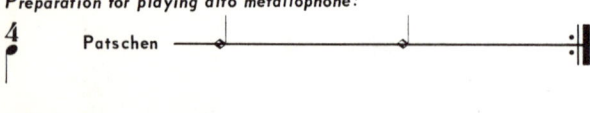

Photo of Studio 49 bass metallophone courtesy of Magnamusic-Baton, Inc., St. Louis, Mo. 63130.

Alto metallophone:

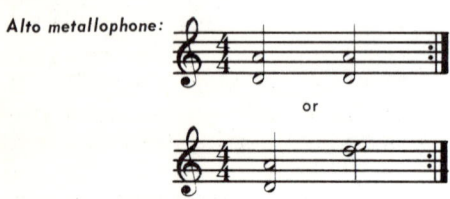

Preparation for playing alto xylophone:

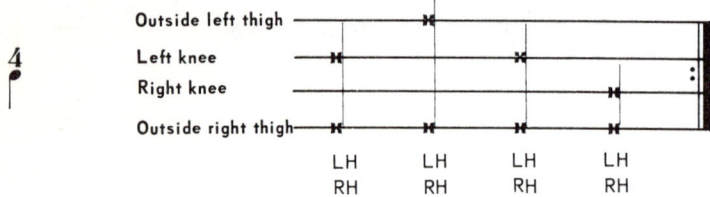

Alto xylophone:

Preparation for playing alto glockenspiel:

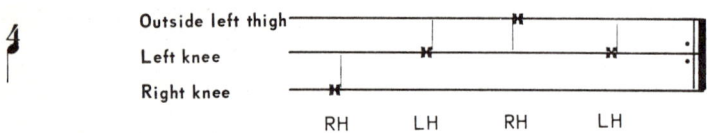

Alto glockenspiel:

2. Tell children you would like to have them listen, then echo whatever you play. Give them a period of echo playbacks using the notes below:

3. Write the notes on the board (as above).

4. Explain that you are going to play a "question" on your recorder using only these notes, and that individual children will be allowed to give an "answer," using only these notes. One possible question, and possible answers follow:

5. Have alto metallophone begin playing. At two-measure intervals bring in xylophone and glockenspiel. After two measures, begin playing your question. At the end of your question, without missing a beat, signal a child to answer. Immediately after his answer, ask a question of another child and let him answer. Continue in this manner, accompaniments playing throughout, until many children have had the opportunity to answer.
6. Write the following Dorian melody on the board. Have them play it, repeating until it is easy for them.

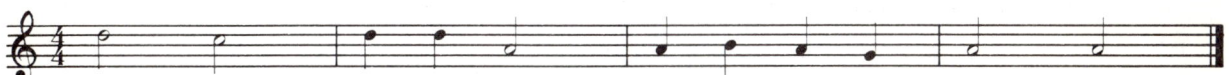

7. Explain that you would like them to play a rondo and that the melody just played will be the A melody which everyone plays. Remind them that in a rondo, A is repeated after every solo so that the form is as follows:

A—All play
B—Solo
A—All play
C—Solo
A—All play
D—Solo
A—All play

Possible B Melody

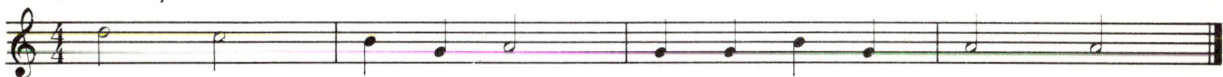

8. Select children to improvise sections B, C, and D.
9. Have instruments begin as before, at two-measure intervals, in this order: alto metallophone, alto xylophone, alto glockenspiel, then A melody played by entire class. At termination of A melody, signal child playing B to begin without missing a beat. Continue in this way until entire rondo has been performed.
10. Repeat, letting other children improvise solos.
11. Give individual children the opportunity to create a rhythmic interpretation of Section A melody, moving each time it occurs.

Learning a New Note, Low D, and Playing It in the Song
Sandy Land—For Intermediate Grades

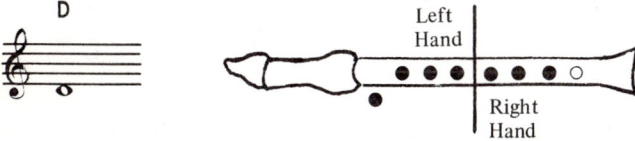

Sandy Land

1. Make my liv-ing in sand-y land, Make my liv-ing in sand-y land,

Make my liv-ing in sand-y land, Lad-ies fare thee well. _____

2. Hie come along my pretty little miss,
Hie come along my pretty little miss,
Hie come along my pretty little miss,
I won't be home 'til Sunday.

3. Raise big taters in sandy land, (three times)
If you can't dig 'em I guess I can.

4. How old are you, my pretty little miss?
How old are you, my pretty little miss?
She answered me with a ha, ha, ha,
"I'll be sixteen next Sunday."

5. One more river I'm bound to cross, (three times)
'Fore I see my honey.

6. Will you marry me, my pretty little miss?
Will you marry me, my pretty little miss?
She answered me with a ha, ha, ha,
"I'll run and ask my mama."

7. Hump back mule I'm bound to ride, (three times)
'Fore I see my honey.

8. Hop come along, my pretty little miss,
Hop come along, my honey,
Hop come along, my pretty little miss,
Marry you next Sunday.

1. Have children follow the score of *Sandy Land* (with chord markings) as you play the part for timpani and sing the first verse.

Timpani:

2. Ask children if they discovered what the numbers I and V_7 mean. (They signify, of course, which chord should be played. In this song, when the I appears, the timpani plays the note G; when the V_7 appears, the timpani plays the note D.)
3. Teach a child to play the timpani part.

4. Have child playing timpani play his part as entire class sings first verse and does the following with you.

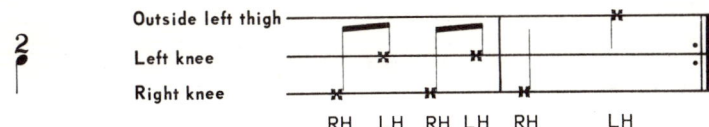

5. Show a child how to play the ostinato:

6. Tell class you would like to add the alto xylophone part to the song as they sing the second verse with you; then do the following:

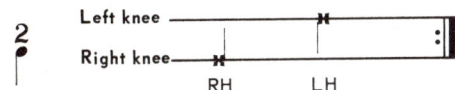

7. Have class begin doing the movements with you. When they are doing them easily, have alto xylophone begin playing ostinato. When alto xylophone player is well-coordinated with class, have timpani begin playing as class sings second verse of *Sandy Land*.

8. Show a child how to play ostinato:

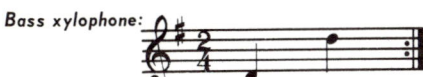

9. Add the bass xylophone part to the accompaniment as class sings verse three while doing the preparation for the alto glockenspiel ostinato. Continue adding ostinati in this way until the following are incorporated into the orchestration:

Preparation for playing alto glockenspiel:

Alto glockenspiel:

Preparation for playing soprano xylophone:

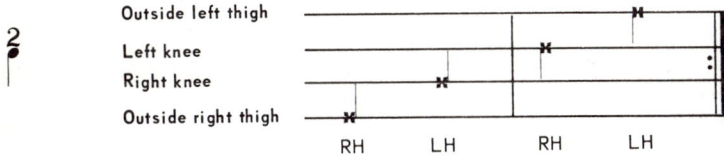

Soprano xylophone:
For I chord sections (Phrases 1, 3 and last measure of song.)

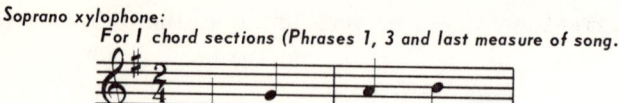

For V7 chord sections (Phrases 2 and 4, except last measure.)

Preparation for playing alto metallophone:

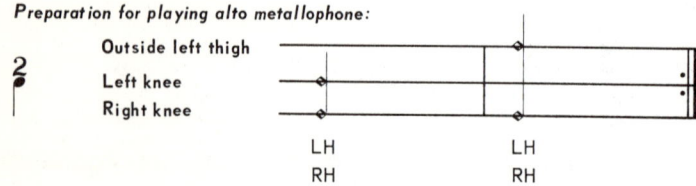

Alto metallophone:
For I chord sections (Phrases 1, 3 and last measure of song.)

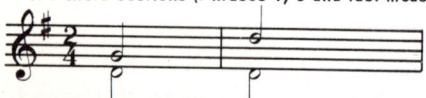

For V7 chord sections (Phrases 2 and 4, except last measure.)

10. Ask class which notes of the song they can play on their recorders. (They can play the last two measures on the words "Ladies, fare thee well.")
11. Ask for a volunteer to play this phrase.
12. Have entire class play this phrase.
13. Have class sing verse, and play last phrase.
14. Give class some playbacks, including the new note low D, the notes G, A, B, C, and high D.
15. Notate the following on the board:

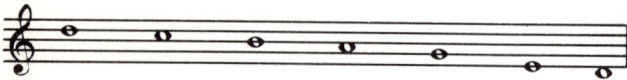

16. Ask class which note they just learned to play (last note, low D) and how it is fingered.
17. Ask for a volunteer to point to each of the notes, to identify them, to finger them on the recorder, and then to play them.
18. Have entire class play each of these notes as you point to them.
19. Ask class to examine the song *Sandy Land* once more to see if there is anything else they can now play with the new knowledge of how to play low D. (They can now play entire song except phrase two.)
20. Have class play phrases one, three, and four, and sing phrase two.
21. Divide class into two groups, one group to play recorders, the other group to sing the song as children accompany by playing the ostinati learned.
22. Have alto xylophone begin first with other instruments entering at two-measure intervals, concluding with song played and sung.

Learning the New Note F♯ and Playing It in the Song
John Brown—**For Intermediate Grades**

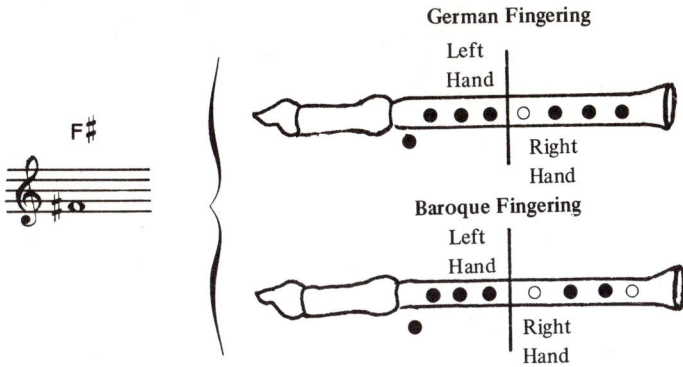

1. Give children a period of playbacks including the notes high D, C, B, A, G, F♯, E, and low D.
2. Notate the following on the chalkboard:

3. Ask children which of the notes is new to them and how they would finger it. (F♯ is new.)
4. Ask for a volunteer to identify each note on the chalkboard, then play these notes.
5. Have entire class put their recorders on their chins. Tell them to finger and give names of each note you point to. Point to the notes in a variety of combinations.
6. Tell class you would like them to play the notes you point to. Point to the notes in many different combinations, ending with the following melody:

John Brown

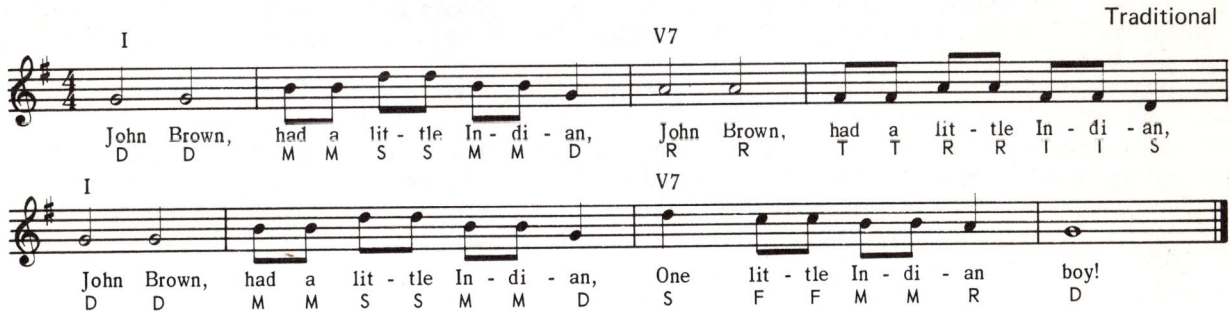

7. Ask class if they recognize the tune they just played. Tell them to sing it with you, using first words and hand signals, then syllables and hand signals.
8. Ask class to help you notate the song on the chalkboard. Tell them that do is G and have a child notate G on a staff on the board. Remind class that if do is on a line, mi will be on the line directly above. If necessary, have class sing phrase with you again, using syllables and hand signals.
9. Select volunteers to notate the first phrase melodically on the chalkboard:

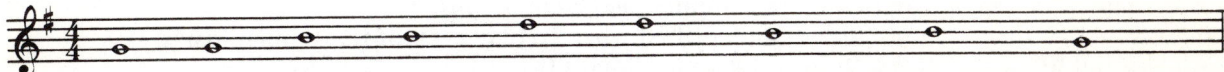

10. Have class sing first two phrases, using syllables and hand signals.

11. Select a volunteer to write the melodic notation for the second phrase on the chalkboard:

12. Continue in this manner until the entire song is notated melodically, as below:

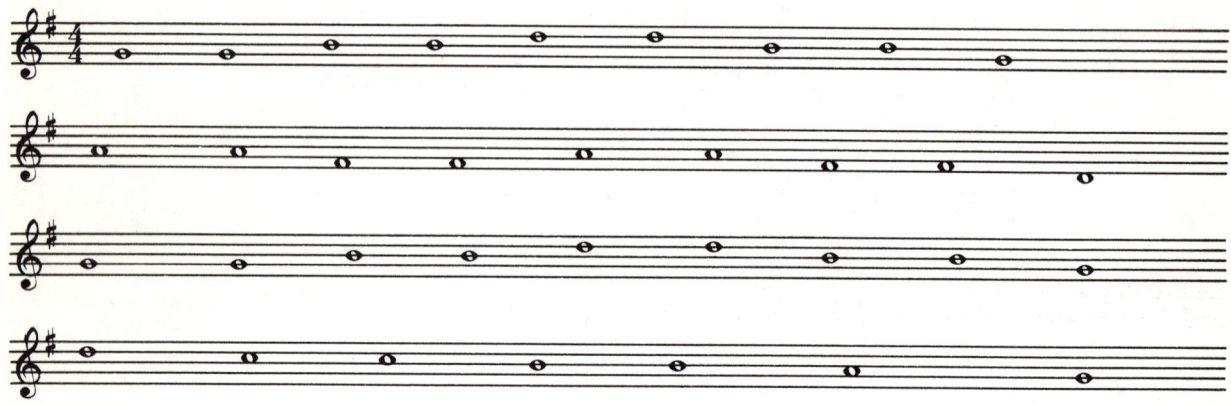

13. Have class clap and chant first phrase:

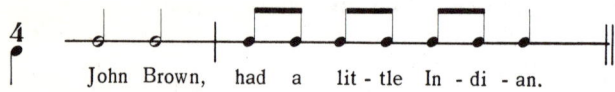

John Brown, had a lit-tle In-di-an.

14. Ask for a volunteer to change the notes on the chalkboard so that they are rhythmically correct. Have class clap and chant phrase again, if necessary, to clarify note values.
15. Continue in this way until entire song is notated rhythmically.
16. Ask for a volunteer to point out where the new note F♯ appears in song.
17. Ask for a volunteer to play the entire phrase which includes F♯ on the recorder.
18. Have entire class play this phrase.
19. Ask for a volunteer to play the first phrase on the recorder. Have entire class play first phrase.
20. Ask class if any other phrase in the song resembles the first phrase. (Third phrase.)
21. Ask for volunteer to play last phrase. Have entire class play last phrase.
22. Ask for a volunteer to play the entire song. Have entire class play entire song.
23. Tell class you would like to see if they can determine where you play each of the timpani parts in the song. Write the two parts you will play on the chalkboard:

Explain that the I and the V_7 are symbols of chords.
24. Tell them you will begin by playing the part marked "I" as they sing the song. When they hear that it does not sound correct, they are to raise their hands.
25. Signal class to begin singing; then begin playing timpani part. They should raise their hands on or shortly after the beginning of the second phrase on the words "John Brown." If they do not, have them stop, tell them to listen more carefully, and begin again.
26. Continue in this way until class has identified when to play each of the timpani parts.
27. Mark the timpani changes on the song above the proper notes (6, page 267).
28. Teach a child to play the timpani part. Have him accompany class as they play the melody on their recorders.

29. Teach each of the following ostinati, adding each to the accompaniment one at a time, and preparing, when necessary, through bodily movement. If an introduction is desired, any part may play their "I" section one or two measures prior to beginning the song.

Learning the New Note B♭ and Playing It in a Question-and Answer Experience—For Intermediate Grades

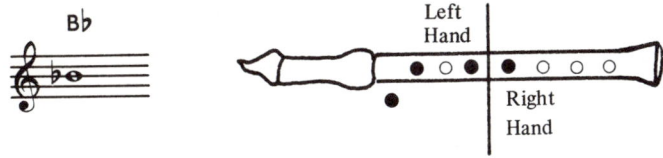

1. Give children a period of echo playbacks using the note B♭.
2. Notate the following on the board:

3. Ask which note is new (B♭). Have someone point to it and teach children how to play it.
4. Tell children to play the notes you point to; then point to the notes on the board in all possible combinations, including different note values.
5. Remind children of previous question-and-answer experiences in which you played a "question" on the recorder and they took turns "answering" it individually on their recorders.
6. Explain that you are going to play a question using these five notes and that you will let individuals answer it on their recorders. Play the same question to several children. Try to lead them directly from the question to the answer without missing a beat. One possible question follows:

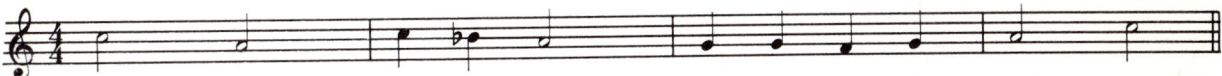

7. Tell children to play the question with you. Have them play it many times until they can play it easily.
8. Tell children you would like them to play a piece in the rondo form. Explain that your question will be the A section, which they will all play, and that individual children will improvise section B, C, and D. Write the following on the board so that they understand the form:

Rondo: A—All play
   B—Solo
   A—All play
   C—Solo
   A—All play
   D—Solo
   A—All play

9. Select children to improvise sections B, C, and D.
10. Have children play the entire rondo without missing a beat between sections.
11. Help children work out an accompaniment for the A section, using percussion instruments. The following are some possible patterns:

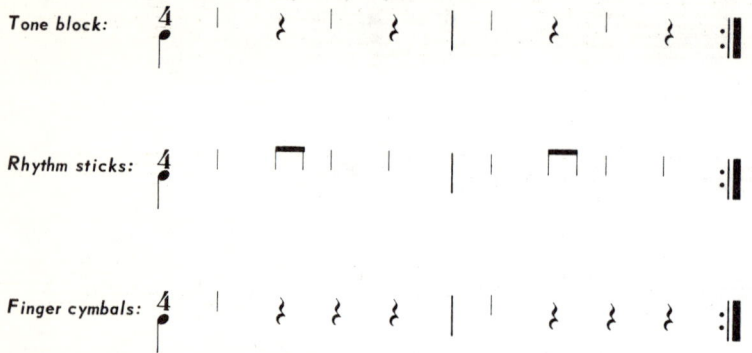

12. Invite individual children to move rhythmically on the A sections, creating a rhythmic interpretation of it. If this is successful, ask different children to move as the soloists improvise the B, C, and D sections.

Learning the New Note High E and Playing It in the Song
Turn the Glasses Over—For Upper Grades

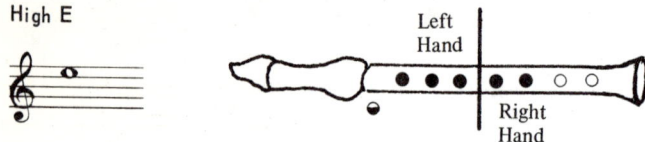

1. Give children a period of playbacks, including the new note high E, and ending with the following sequence which is the melody for the song *Turn the Glasses Over*.

2. Ask for a volunteer to play the new note played in the playbacks (High E). Call attention of class to the fact that it is played just like low E except that the thumb hole is only half-closed (half-holed), and slightly more air pressure must be used.
3. Have entire class play high E.
4. Place it on a staff on the board:

5. Ask if anyone recognized a song in the playbacks. Explain that they were playing sections of a song called *Turn the Glasses Over*, and that you would like them to notate it for you first melodically, then rhythmically.

6. Play the first measure of *Turn the Glasses Over*. Have class echo you. Ask for a volunteer to notate it melodically. Continue in this way, having class echo each measure as you play it on the recorder, then notate the measure melodically, until the following is on the board:

7. Tell class that you will clap each measure of the song and that you would like them to echo you—to clap exactly what they hear. Clap the first measure and have class clap it back. Ask for a volunteer to make the notes on the board correspond to the rhythm just clapped. (If necessary, chant the rhythmic notation as you clap, having class do the same.) Continue working, measure by measure, until the entire song is notated rhythmically, as below. (Do not add words until later.)

Turn the Glasses Over

I've been to Haar - lem,   I've been to Dov - er,   I've trav - eled this   wide

world all o - ver,   O - ver, o - ver,   three times o - ver,

Drink all the so - da pop and   turn the glass -es o - ver.   Sail - ing East.

Sail - ing West.   Sail - ing o - ver the o - cean,   Bet - ter watch out when the

wind be - gins to blow,   Or we'll all fall in - to the o - cean!

8. Teach a child to play the following ostinato:

9. Tell class you would like them to play the song on their recorders while watching the notes on the board as the timpani accompanies.
10. Have the timpani play a two-measure introduction, then signal class to begin playing.
11. Teach children to play the following rhythm patterns on percussion instruments. Let them practice all together with the timpani. When all can play well together, have them accompany the song, with the instruments providing a two-measure introduction and a two-measure postlude.

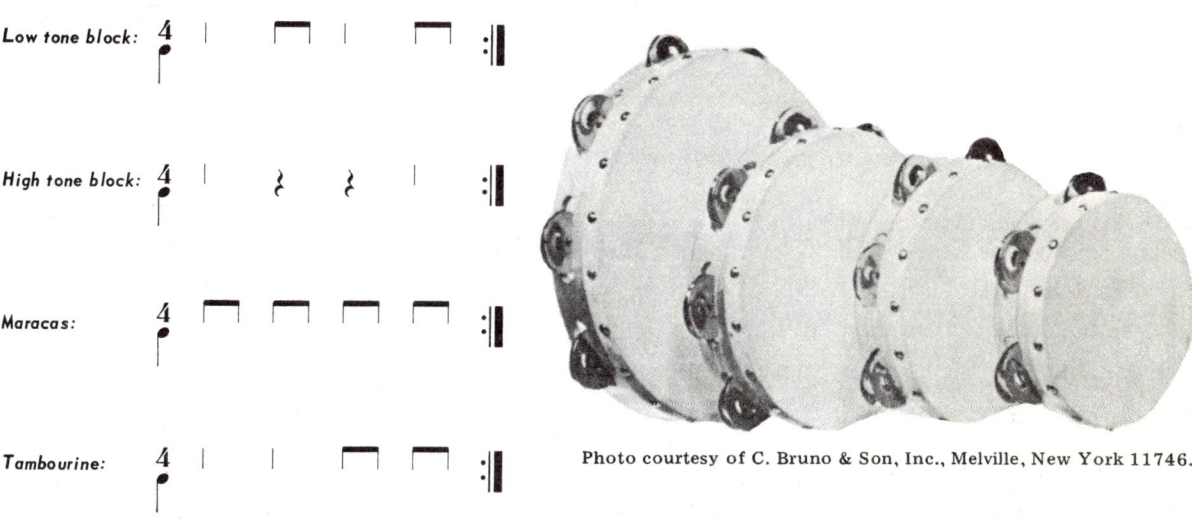

Photo courtesy of C. Bruno & Son, Inc., Melville, New York 11746.

12. On other days, expand the experience by doing one or more of the following:

   a.   Add other ostinati:

Photo furnished through the courtesy of the Kitching Division of Ludwig Industries.

b. Have class sing song, accompanied by percussion and Orff instruments.
c. Have class sing song as a round, accompanied by Orff instruments—second group beginning when first group begins third measure.
d. Have class do the following:

Timpani begins, playing two measures alone.

Percussion instruments enter individually, one measure apart, in this order: low tone block, high tone block, maracas, and tambourine.

Class plays song on recorder.

Four-measure interlude. On first beat of fifth measure, percussion instruments stop, simultaneously alto xylophone enters, followed at two-measure intervals by the bass xylophone, alto metallophone, and alto glockenspiel.

On the third measure after alto glockenspiel enters, first group of round begins singing and class sings song as a round.

When last group ends, instruments continue, playing a four-measure interlude, stopping on first beat of fifth measure.

On first beat of fifth measure of last interlude, percussion instruments enter individually.

When all instruments have entered, class plays song on recorders again.

Percussion instruments give a four-measure postlude, stopping together on the first beat of the fifth measure.

Learning the New Note Middle C and Playing It in the Song
London Bridge—For Intermediate Grades

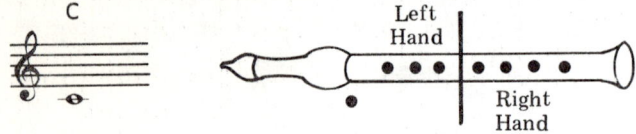

1. Give children a period of playbacks, including all the notes in the C scale. (F, which is introduced in the following experience, should be included.)
2. Place the following on the board:

3. Ask children which of these notes is new. (The third note, middle C.)
4. Teach them to play middle C. (All holes are covered. Children must blow very softly to produce it.)
5. Tell children to play the notes you point to very, very softly. Point to these notes in varying combinations and rhythms until finally you point out the following song:

London Bridge

2. What has this poor prisoner done?
3. Stole my watch and lost my key.
4. Off to prison you must go.

6. Ask children if they recognize the song they just played. Tell them you would like them to help you notate it. Tell them to play the first measure with you once again. Then ask for a volunteer to notate it, melodically, as follows:

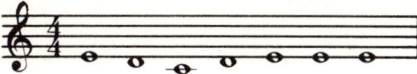

7. Tell class you would like someone to notate the second measure in the same way, *after* the class plays the first and second measures *with you*. Signal class to begin and play the first and second measures together.
8. Ask someone to notate the second measure, letting class help as much as possible.
9. Continue in this way, having class play song from beginning, adding the third measure—notating it—then the fourth measure.
10. Ask class to put down their recorders and to sing the song, clapping the rhythm of the words as they sing.
11. Tell class you will fill in the notes to the first measure so that they are correct rhythmically. Do so.
12. Tell class you would like them to fill in the notes for the next measure after they have sung and clapped the song from the beginning through to the end of the second measure. Have them sing and clap the first two measures, then select someone to add the rhythmic notation to the second measure.
13. Continue in this way until entire song is rhythmically correct.
14. Have class say and clap the rhythm of the notes (as printed under the first verse).
15. Have class perform the song in the following way:

> Sing first verse.
> Play it on the recorder.
> Sing second verse.
> Play it on the recorder.
> Sing third verse.
> Play it on the recorder.
> Sing fourth verse.
> Play it on the recorder.

16. Help class expand the experience in one of the following ways:

   a. Create a rondo using the song as A, letting individual children improvise for B, C, and D sections.
   b. Create an orchestration, playing ostinati on the xylophone, metallophone, and glockenspiel.

Learning the New Note F and Playing It in the Song *Way Down in the Paw Paw Patch*—For Intermediate Grades

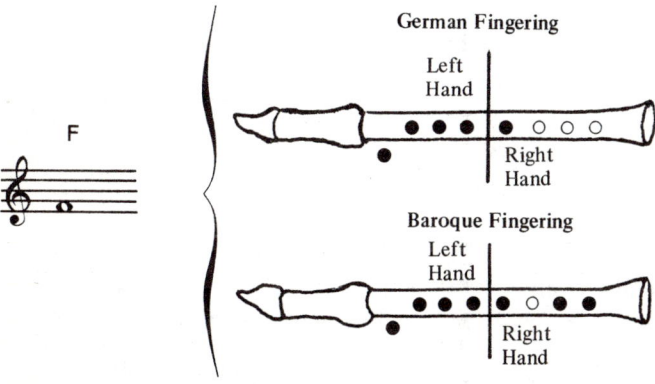

1. Give children a period of echo playbacks using all the notes learned so far and the new note F.

2. Tell children to do the following with you:

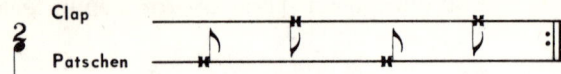

3. When they are well-established rhythmically, tell them to continue as you play a song for them on the recorder. (If necessary, let one child lead the group to keep the rhythm steady.) Play the following:

Way Down in the Paw Paw Patch

2. By and by, we'll go and meet her, etc.

3. Won't that be a happy meeting, etc.

4. Ask class to identify the name of the song.
5. Place the following on the board:

6. Ask children to identify the notes (C and D) and a volunteer to play the measure.
7. Explain that this is an ostinato accompaniment for the song and have entire class play it.
8. Select two or three children with strong rhythmic independence to play it as you play the song *Way Down in the Paw Paw Patch* and rest of class does the patschen-clap accompaniment as in 3 (above).
9. Have class begin rhythmic accompaniment. After two measures, have children playing ostinato begin. After two additional measures, begin playing the song. At end of song indicate that the ostinato should play one additional note, C, and hold it one count as class does rhythmic accompaniment for two additional measures beyond end of song.
10. Ask if anyone thinks he could play the song with you. Select half a dozen to do so. Repeat 9 (above) with these additional children playing with you.
11. Continue in this way, adding children to the melody and to the group playing the ostinato until approximately half are playing the melody, one fourth the ostinato, and one fourth the rhythmic accompaniment.
12. Enrich the experience by doing the following:

   a. Help children notate the song melodically, then rhythmically.
   b. Help children create rhythmic ostinati for percussion instruments to accompany the song. Some possibilities are:

Improvising Above Major and Minor Triads (Tonic and Super Tonic)—For Upper Grades

1. Place the triad F, A, and C on the board, as follows:

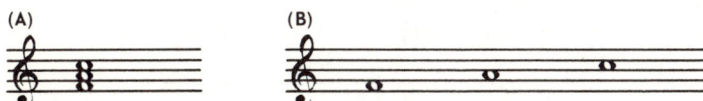

2. Explain to class that the notes they see on the board marked A are called a triad. Explain that a triad is three notes sounding together and that the notes marked B are the notes of this triad as they look separately. Tell class further that the bottom note of the triad is called 1 or root, the next note up is called the 3rd, and the top note is called the 5th.
3. Ask children whether the root of this triad is in a line or space. (Space.) Ask whether the 3rd and the 5th are in lines or spaces. (Spaces.) Point out that whenever the root of a triad is in a space, the 3rd and 5th are in spaces; whenever it is in a line, the 3rd and 5th are in lines.
4. Place a note on the staff. Explain that this is the root of a triad. Have a child add a 3rd and 5th above the root. Repeat several times using different roots.
5. Ask class to examine the F, A, C triad on the board. Ask for a volunteer to make up a melody using these three tones. Let many children try making up melodies. One possible melody is as follows:

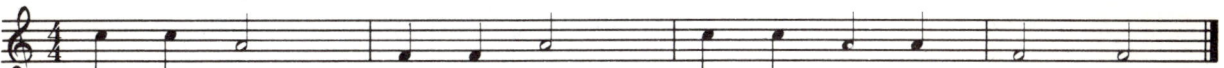

6. Notate, with the help of the children, various melodies children like.
7. Place the passing tones G and B♭ on the staff as follows:

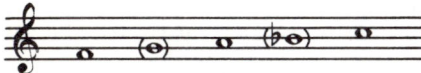

8. Explain that the added note (G and B♭) are passing tones and can be used in passing from one tone of the triad to another.
9. Have individual children experiment creating melodies using all five tones with the notes G and B♭ used as passing tones. One possible example might be:

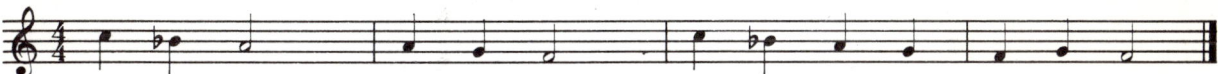

10. Write the triad G, B♭, and D on the board in two ways, as follows:

11. Follow the same procedure (as in 5 to 9, above) for exploring these tones and their passing tones A and C.
12. Place the following on the board and teach a child to play it on the bass or alto metallophone or xylophone:

Alto metallophone or xylophone:

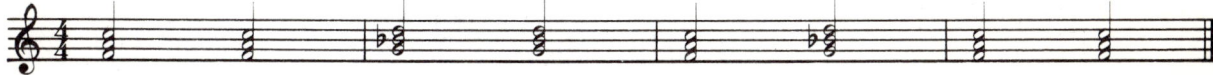

13. Have class examine the part for the alto metallophone or xylophone. Explain that they are going to play a melody over these four measures, playing notes from the F-major triad (F, A, C) where the F triad appears and notes from the G-minor triad (G, B♭ D) where this triad appears.

14. Have a child point out the F triad where it appears.
15. Have a child point out the G-minor triad where it appears.
16. Ask class how many beats they will play in each measure. (Four.)
17. Let individual volunteers improvise melodies above these triads. An example follows:

18. Ask children to examine the passing tones for each of the two triads—F major and G minor. Ask for volunteers to play a melody on the recorder over this arrangement of triads using not only the notes of the triads, but also the passing tones. An example would be the following:

19. As an enrichment experience, have children do one of the following:

   a. Select two melodies (of four measures each) they like which combine well together and make them the A section of an experience with the rondo form.
   b. Help children create rhythmic and melodic ostinati to serve as an orchestration for the above.

Learning the New Note High F and Playing It in the Song *Little Wheel*—For Intermediate or Upper Grades

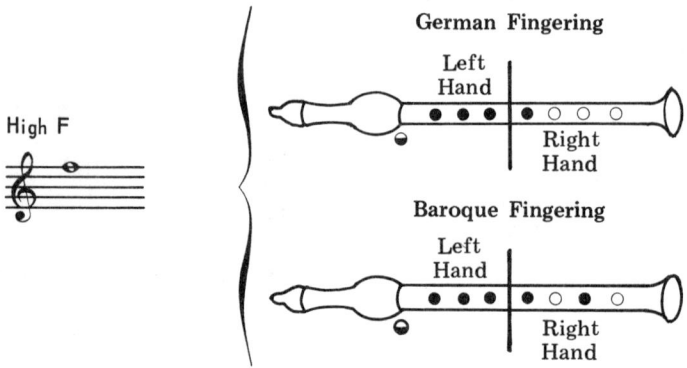

1. Distribute books which include the song *Little Wheel* in the key of F, as follows:

Little Wheel

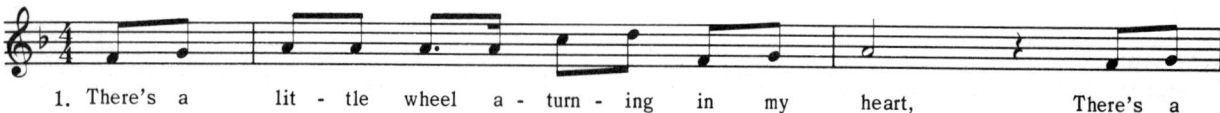

1. There's a   lit - tle   wheel a - turn - ing   in   my   heart,   There's a

lit - tle wheel a - turn-ing in my heart, In my heart, _____ In my

heart, _____ There's a lit - tle wheel a - turn - ing in my heart. _____

2. Oh, I feel so very happy in my heart.

3. Oh, I don't feel no ways tired in my heart.

From *Songs to Keep*, Copyright © 1962 by Cooperative Recreation Service, Inc. Used by permission.

2. Tell class to listen and watch the notes as you play the song, looking especially for any new notes that might appear.
3. Play the song. Ask if they heard any new notes. (One, high F.)
4. Ask someone to tell you where it appears in the song.
5. Show class how to finger F, pointing out in particular that the thumb must be half-holed and that slightly more breath pressure is needed for this note. Ask children to play it. Let them practice many times until they can play it easily.
6. Ask the class to listen as you play the phrase in which the note occurs in the song. Play the following:

7. Ask class to play this phrase with you.
8. Ask class to listen while you play the song, being prepared to play this phrase when it occurs.
9. Play the entire song, signaling class to join you in playing the phrase with the high F.
10. Ask if anyone noticed one phrase which is repeated. (Phrase two is the same as the last phrase.)
11. Ask for a volunteer to play phrase two:

12. Have entire class play phrase two many times until they do it easily.
13. Tell class you would like to play the entire song as they join in playing phrase two, the phrase with the high F, and the last phrase.
14. Ask class how phrase two differs from phrase one. (The last five notes differ.)
15. Ask for a volunteer to play phrase one, then have entire class play it.
16. Clarify the playing of the remaining phrase (just preceding the last phrase), then have class play entire song.
17. Correct any tonal or pitch inaccuracies.
18. Teach children to play the following orchestration:

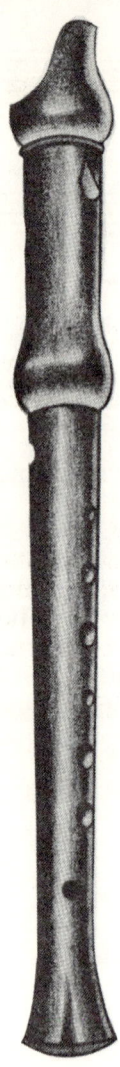

FINGERING CHART for SOPRANO RECORDER
— Two Octaves —

ILLUSTRATED BY RAY KOOS

		Partly closed hole
●		Closed hole
		Thumb pressed into thumb-hole

◐* This fingering is for single holed recorders. If yours is a double holed recorder, cover the hole like this....●○

■ German fingering

19. Tell class you would like to perform *Little Wheel* in the following way:

The alto xylophone, soprano xylophone, and timpani play an introduction, entering one at a time at two-measure intervals.
The class sings verse 1.
The instruments play a two-measure interlude.
The class sings verse 2.
The instruments play a two-measure interlude.
The class sings verse 3.
The instruments play a two-measure interlude.
The class plays the song on the recorder.

20. To enrich the experience, ask children how they could use this song to develop a rondo. (The melody could be played by all, as section A; individual children could improvise to make sections B, C, and D.)

SUGGESTIONS FOR CLASS DISCUSSIONS OR REPORTS

1. Discuss the use of the recorder as an instrumental experience for all children—its musical value as contrasted to other (Orff) instruments and its musical and practical value as contrasted to band or orchestral instruments.
2. Discuss the value of using the recorder freely, in conjunction with other musical experiences, rather than in isolated experiences taught from an instruction book.
3. Discuss the idea that the recorder can help develop a "functional" understanding of musical notation.
4. Discuss ways the recorder can be used to implement experiences in Chapters Two and Three.
5. Discuss the value of playbacks as a recorder teaching technique.
6. Discuss the value of the recorder in helping children learn to improvise.

SUGGESTED ACTIVITIES TO DEVELOP SKILLS AND PRACTICE IN INITIATING MUSICAL EXPERIENCES

1. Learn to play the recorder, and especially the notes B, A, G, E, high C and D, middle C and D, F♯, B♭, high E, and F and low F. Develop a pleasing tone and accurate pitch.
2. Assume your class has never played the recorder. Study and present to them the experience introducing the recorder and the notes B, A, and G. Discuss the ways in which the experience might be improved.
3. Present one of the experiences for the recorder playing the notes B, A, and G in a song (*Bridge of Avignon, Ezek'el Saw the Wheel, Hot Cross Buns,* or *Sleep, Baby, Sleep.*) Analyze the experience with the class, discovering its good and bad points.
4. Present the experience introducing the new note E. Discuss with class.
5. Create an alternate plan to one of the experiences playing the notes B, A, and G in a song. Present to class, and discuss presentation.
6. Present the experience improvising in the phrygian mode and discuss with class.
7. Present one of the experiences playing a melodic rondo (in the major or dorian mode) and discuss with class.
8. Present the experience learning the new note B♭ and playing it in a question and answer experience. Discuss the experience with class in terms of its musical value and ways it might be improved.
9. Select one of the more challenging experiences from the remaining suggestions in the chapter. Present it to class. Discuss ways of improving.
10. Create other experiences for recorder which combine Orff and Kodaly activities. Present to class and discuss ways of improving.

Orff-Designed Instruments

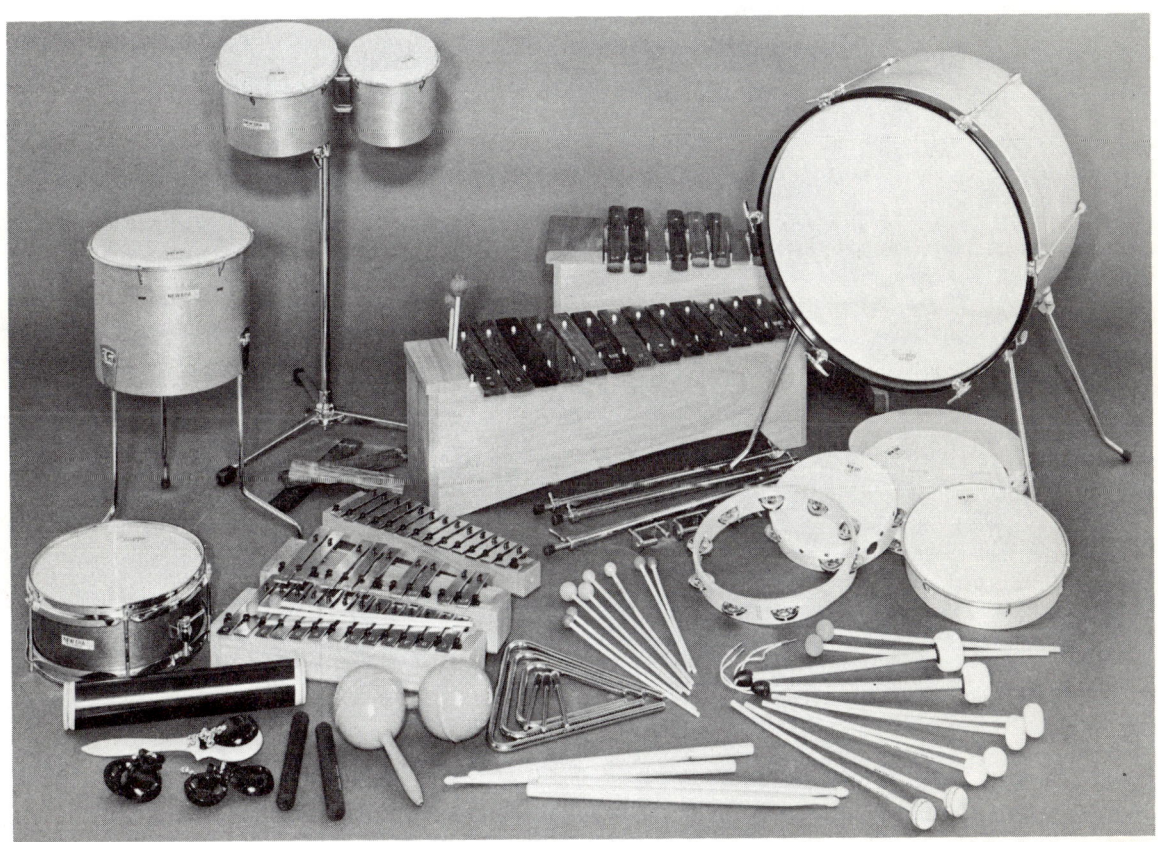

New Era Instruments, made in England by Premier Drum Company, LTD., exclusively distributed in the U.S. by Selmer, Elkhart, Indiana.

The "Orff instruments," so-called because they were designed by Carl Orff to provide children with simple instruments especially suited to them, play a vital part in every aspect of the Orff approach. Giving children an immediate way of creating music, to which all ages respond with great enthusiasm, they also provide a link between the rhythmic and melodic and, in addition, provide contrasts in rhythm and tone color to singing, rhythms, and recorder playing.

Although in the Orff Schulwerk, ample melodic instruments (glockenspiels, metallophones, and xylophones) are available so that each child has one to play, financial limitations in most elementary public schools in this country are such that it is not possible to provide more than one set of these instruments.[1] Most children are thus left with no instrument to play except their bodies (patschen), percussion instruments, or recorders, and must "take turns" on the melodic instruments of the xylophone type. For this reason, and because the recorder is an inexpensive melodic instrument which most children can afford, the authors of this book place special emphasis on this instrument as an instrument for children as well as teachers to play, and as a most important instrument for developing an understanding of musical notation.

ORFF'S GLOCKENSPIELS, METALLOPHONES AND XYLOPHONES

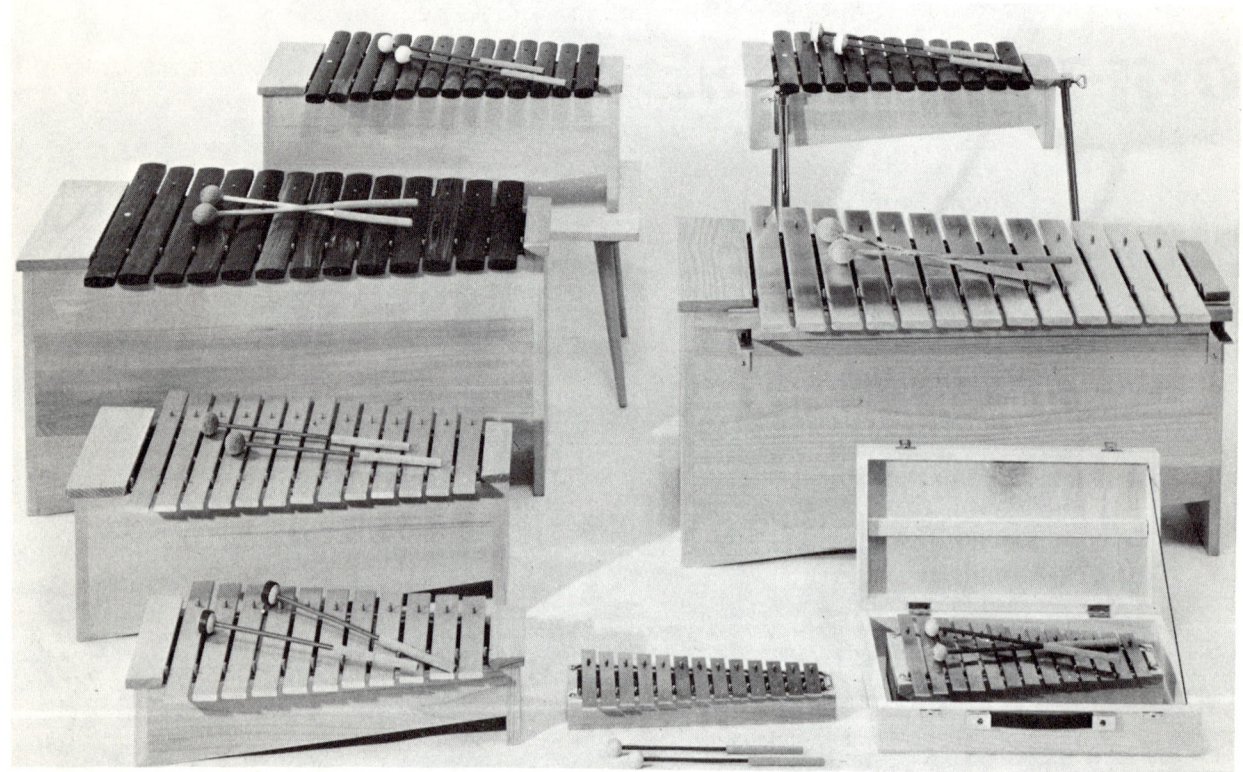

Photo of Studio 49 Orff instruments courtesy Magnamusic-Baton, Inc., St. Louis, Mo. 63130.

Left, top to bottom: Alto xylophone, Bass xylophone, Alto metallophone, Soprano metallophone
Middle, bottom: Soprano glockenspiel
Right, top to bottom: Soprano xylophone, Bass metallophone, Alto glockenspiel

All three of these melodic instruments are available in either diatonic or chromatic form, with the diatonic being preferable for beginning stages. Glockenspiels have metal bars which produce a bright, ringing sound; metallophones also have metal bars, with a more sustained, mellow quality; xylophones have wooden bars which produce a more hollow sound. All bars have the name of the note engraved

---

1. In many cases, it may be necessary for the teacher to build up her Orff instrumentation gradually, as funds are available. In such cases, the authors recommend that instruments be purchased in the following order: alto xylophone, soprano xylophone, alto metallophone, alto glockenspiel, fourteen-and twenty-inch timpani, bass xylophone, soprano metallophone, soprano glockenspiel, and bass metallophone.

on them, and individual bars may be removed to facilitate playing of specific tone patterns. All are tuned in the key of C major, and bars for F sharp and B flat are included. Upon request, bars for C♯, D♯, and G♯ are also available, making it possible to use the instruments in all keys.

Xylophones and metallophones are generally played with felt-headed mallets, glockenspiels are played with wooden-headed mallets.

The range of each is as follows:

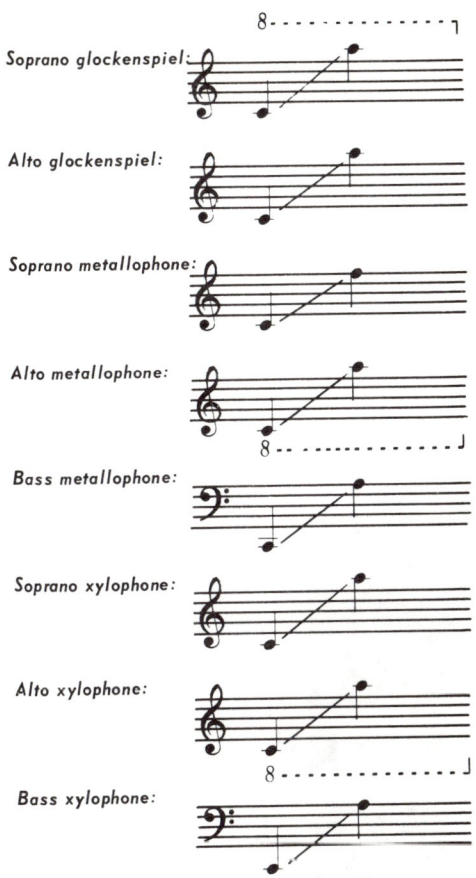

Note: The above are ranges of Studio-49 instruments. The Sonor alto-tenor glockenspiels and xylophones generally have a two-octave range.

RECORDERS

The soprano and alto recorder are most often used in Orff work. The teacher will find the recorder useful as an instrument with which she can improvise as children play ostinati or move rhythmically. As mentioned previously, for those schools which cannot afford the melodic Orff instruments in sufficient quantities to supply all children, it is invaluable as an instrument which most children can afford and learn to play. It produces a pleasant tone which blends well with the child's voice and other melodic and rhythm instruments, and is an instrument through which children can fully explore and develop an understanding of musical notation. The soprano (descant) recorder is advisable as the first recorder experience of children.

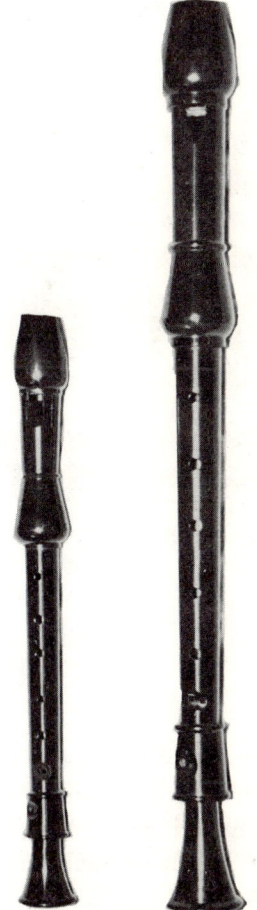

Photo of Schott Recorders courtesy Magnamusic-Baton, Inc., St. Louis, Mo. 63130.

It adapts well to the Orff instruments. The range of each of the instruments is as follows:

STRINGED INSTRUMENTS

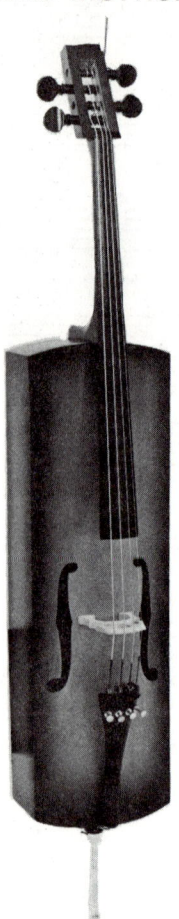

Photo of porta cello
courtesy Magnamusic-
Baton, Inc., St. Louis,
Mo. 63130.

Stringed instruments can play an important role in Orff work, playing simple borduns or ostinati, and adding a basic foundation for other musical instruments. Most commonly used are the guitar, cello, porta cello, and viola da gamba. These instruments can be tuned to the basic bordun—C and G. The strings can be plucked, or when legato effects are desired, a bow may be used.

The normal tuning of each is as follows:

Guitar: E A D G B E
Cello: C G D A
Porta cello: C G D A
Viola da gamba: D G C E A D

PERCUSSION INSTRUMENTS

Photo of Studio 49 Orff instruments courtesy Magnamusic-Baton, Inc., St. Louis, Mo. 63130.

Timpani and Bass Drum

These drums can be tuned to a definite pitch, and are played with soft-headed sticks. The authors recommend the twenty- and fourteen-inch timpani to meet the needs of the average classroom. These two drums are useful in accompanying the C, D, F, and G pentatonic scales.

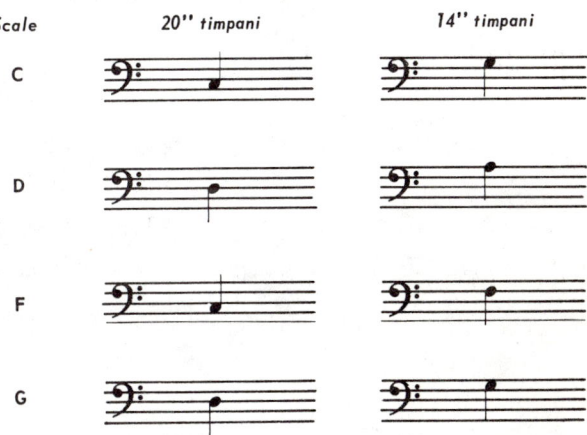

Hand Drum (Tambour) and Tambourine

These are a type of drum with a single drumhead and a circular frame. They may be obtained in sizes from ten to fourteen inches. (Tambours may be obtained as large as twenty inches in diameter.) The tambourine has metal plates, or jingles, attached. Held in the left hand with fingers curled under the shell, both can be played by striking the right hand in the center or on the edges. The tambourine can also be rolled or shaken.

Triangle

A triangular piece of metal, open at one corner, it is held in the left hand by a cord and is struck by a metal beater held in the right hand. The tone varies according to the size, which may range from four to twelve inches.

Woodblock

Although the wood block comes in various sizes and shapes, it is usually about five by three by one and one-fourth inches. It is played by holding it in the left hand, and striking it with a felt-tipped or rubber-headed mallet (in accordance with the tone desired) held by the right hand.

Cymbals

Two large plates of brass which can be obtained in sizes from four to fourteen inches in diameter, cymbals are played by crashing them together as they are moved up and down, or by hitting one of them with a drumstick to create a ringing sound.

Rattles

Maracas are the most commonly known rattle, and are, of course, two gourds which have been dried, scraped out, and filled with seeds, and have been sealed and decorated. Children also enjoy making their own, using boxes which have been filled with beans. Rattles are played by shaking.

Jingle Bells

Small, hollow spheres into which a metal ball has been placed, they are attached to a leather band or stick, and the sound is made by shaking the band or stick.

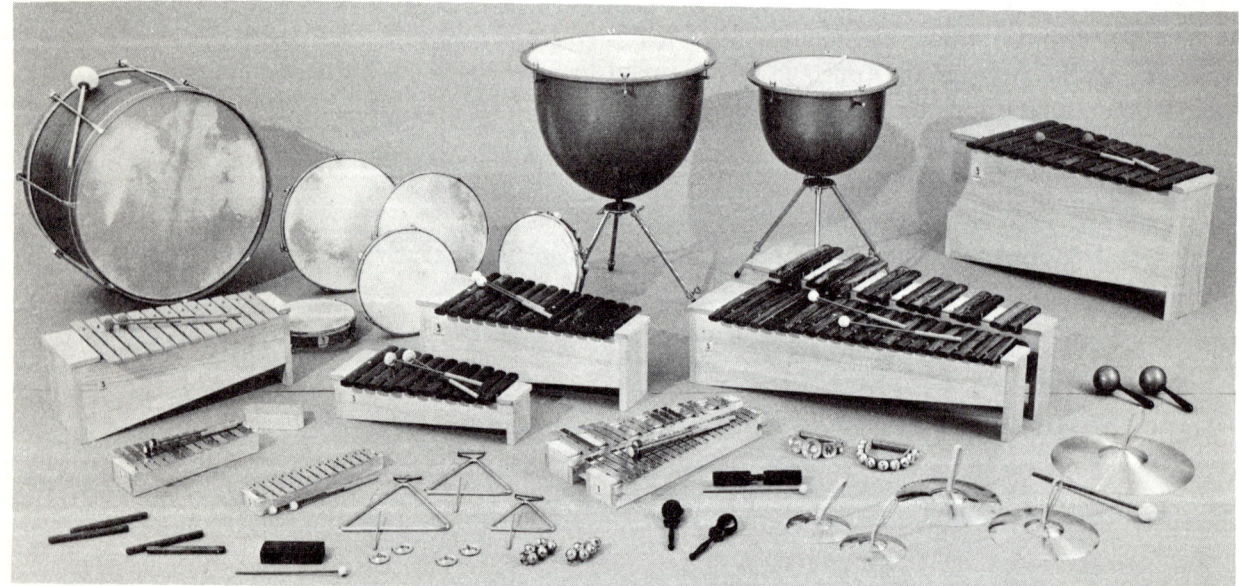

Photo of Studio 49 Orff instruments courtesy Magnamusic-Baton, Inc., St. Louis, Mo. 63130.

A definitive listing of all Orff-Schulwerk instrumentarium can be obtained from the following:

Bruno, C. and Son, Inc., 55 Marcus Dr., Melville, New York 11746 (Sonor).

Kitching Educational Division of Ludwig Industries, 1728 N. Damen Avenue, Chicago, Illinois 60647.

Lyons, Inc., 688 Industrial Dr., Elmhurst, Illinois 60126.

Magnamusic-Baton, Inc., 6390 Delmar Blvd., St. Louis, Mo., 63130 (Studio 49).

Selmer, Division of the Magnavox Co., Box 310, Elkhart, Indiana 46514. (New Era by Premier, distributed in metropolitan New York area by Sam Ash, Inc., Hempstead, New York.)

Nursery Rhymes and Proverbs

NURSERY RHYMES

A diller, a dollar,
A 10 o'clock scholar,
What makes you come so soon?
You used to come at 10 o'clock,
But now you come at noon.

As I was going to St. Ives,
I met a man with seven wives,
Every wife had seven sacks,
Every sack had seven cats,
Every cat had seven kits;
Kits, cats, sacks, and wives,
How many were there going to St. Ives?

Bobby Shaftoe's gone to sea,
Silver buckles on his knee;
He'll come back and marry me,
Pretty Bobby Shaftoe.

Bobby Shaftoe's fat and fair,
Combing down his yellow hair,
He's my love for ever more;
Pretty Bobby Shaftoe.

Bye, baby, bunting,
Daddy's gone a-hunting,
To get a little rabbit skin,
To wrap his baby bunting in.

Cantaloupes! Cantaloupes!
What is the price?
Right for a dollar,
And all very nice!

Come when you're called,
Do as you're bid.
Shut the door after you,
Never be chid.

Eena, deena, dina, duss,
Katla, weena, wina, wuss,
Spit, spot, must be done,
Twiddlum, twaddlum, twenty-one.

Eggs, butter, cheese, bread,
Stick, stock, stone, dead.
Stick him up, stick him down,
Stick him in the old man's crown.

For every evil under the sun,
There is a remedy, or there is none,
If there be one, try and find it,
If there be none, never mind it.

Here we go round the mulberry bush,
The mulberry bush, the mulberry bush,
Here we go round the mulberry bush,
On a cold and frosty morning.
2. This is the way we wash our hands, etc.
3. This is the way we wash our clothes, etc.
4. This is the way we go to school, etc.

Here's Sulky Sue,
What shall we do?
Turn her face to the wall,
Till she comes to.

Hey! diddle, diddle,
The cat and the fiddle,
The cow jumped over the moon;
The little dog laugh'd,
To see such sport,
And the dish ran away with the spoon.

Hickety, Pickety,
My black hen,
She lays eggs,
For gentlemen;
Sometimes nine,
And sometimes ten.
Hickety, Pickety,
My black hen!

Hush-a-bye, baby, on the tree top;
When the wind blows, the cradle will rock;
When the bough breaks, the cradle will fall,
And down will come baby, cradle and all.

I am a gold lock.
I am a gold key.
I am a silver lock.
I am a silver key.
I am a brass lock.
I am a brass key.
I am a lead lock.
I am a lead key.
I am a monk lock.
I am a monkey.

I do not like thee Dr. Fell.
The reason why, I cannot tell;
But this I know, and know full well,
I do not like thee Dr. Fell.

If all the seas were one sea,
What a great sea that would be!
And if all the trees were one tree,
What a great tree that would be!
And if all the axes were one axe,
What a great axe that would be,
And if all the men were one man,
What a great man he would be!
And if the great man took the great axe,
And cut down the great tree,
What a splash, splash that would be!

I'll tell you a story,
About John-a-Nory;
And now my story's begun.
I'll tell you another,
About Jack and his brother,
And now my story is done.

I saw three ships come sailing by,
Come sailing by, come sailing by,
I saw three ships come sailing by,
On New Year's Day in the morning.
2. And what do you think was in them then, etc.?
3. Three pretty girls were in them then, etc.
4. One could whistle and one could sing,
    And one could play on the violin,
    Such joy there was at my wedding,
    On New Year's Day in the morning.

It's raining, it's pouring,
The old man's snoring.

Jack be nimble, Jack be quick,
And Jack jump over the candlestick.

Lady bird, lady bird, fly away home;
Your house is on fire,
Your children are gone.
All but one and her name is Ann,
And she crept under the pudding pan.

Little Bo-Peep has lost her sheep,
And can't tell where to find them;
Leave them alone, and they'll come home,
And bring their tails behind them.
Little Bo-Peep fell fast asleep,
And dreamt she heard them bleating,
But when she awoke she found it a joke,
For they were still a-fleeting.
Then up she took her little crook,
Determined for to find them.
She found them indeed, but it made her heart bleed,
For they'd left their tails behind them.

Little Jack Horner,
Sat in a corner,
Eating a Christmas pie.
He put in his thumb,
And pulled out a plum,
And said, "What a good boy am I."

Little Miss Muffet,
Sat on a tuffet,
Eating her curds and whey!
There came a great spider,
And sat down beside her,
And frightened Miss Muffet away.

Little Robin Red-breast,
Sat upon a rail,
Needle, noddle, went his head,
Wiggle, waggle, went his tail.

Little Tom Tucker,
Sang for his supper;
What shall he eat?
White bread and butter,
How shall he cut it,
Without e'er a knife?
How shall he marry,
Without e'er a wife?

Mary had a little lamb,
With fleece as white as snow;
And everywhere that Mary went,
The lamb was sure to go.
It followed her to school one day,
Which was against the rule,
And made the children laugh and play,
To see a lamb at school.

And so the teacher turned it out,
But still it lingered near,
And waited patiently about,
Till Mary did appear.
"What makes the lamb love Mary so?"
The eager children cry.
"Why Mary loves the lamb, you know!"
The teacher did reply.

Mary, Mary, quite contrary,
How does your garden grow?
With cockle-shells, and silver bells,
And pretty maids all in a row.

Needles and pins, needles and pins,
When a man marries, his trouble begins.

One, two, three, four,
Mary at the cottage door,
Five, six, seven, eight,
Eating cherries off a plate!
O—U—T spells out!

O the grand old Duke of York,
He had ten thousand men;
He marched them up a great high hill,
And he marched them down again!
When they were up, they were up,
And when they were down, they were down,
And when they were neither down nor up,
They were neither up nor down!

Pat-a-cake, pat-a-cake, baker's man!
Make me a cake as fast as you can:
Prick it and stick it, and mark it with B,
And put it in the oven for Baby and me.

Peter, Peter, pumpkin-eater,
Had a wife, and couldn't keep her,
He put her in a pumpkin shell,
And there he kept her very well.

Phoebe rode a nanny goat,
Susy broke her leg,
Father took his wedding coat,
And hung it on a peg.

Pit, pat, well-a-day,
Little Robin flew away;
Where can little Robin be?
Gone into the cherry tree.

Pussy-cat, pussy-cat, where have you been?
I've been to London to visit the Queen!
Pussy-cat, pussy-cat, what did you there?
I frightened a little mouse under her chair.

Ride a cock-horse to Banbury Cross,
To see a fine lady upon a white horse,
With rings on her fingers and bells on her toes,
She shall have music wherever she goes.

Ring-a-ring-a-roses,
A pocket full of posies,
Hush! Hush! Hush! Hush!
We all fell down!

Rock-a-bye, baby, thy cradle is green;
Father's a nobleman, mother's a queen;
And Betty's a lady, and wears a gold ring;
And Johnny's a drummer, and drums for the King.

Rub a dub dub,
Three men in a tub;
And who do you think they be?
The butcher, the baker,
The candlestick-maker;
Turn 'em out, knaves all three.

See saw, Margery Daw,
Johnny shall have a new master,
He shall have but a penny a day,
Because he can't work any faster.

Sing a song of sixpence,
A pocket full of rye;
Four and twenty blackbirds,
Baked in a pie.
When the pie was open'd,
The birds began to sing,
Was not that a dainty dish,
To set before the King?
The King was in his counting-house,
Counting out his money;
The Queen was in the parlour,
Eating bread and honey.
The maid was in the garden,
Hanging out the clothes,
There came a little blackbird,
And snapped off her nose.

Sing, sing, what shall I sing?
The cat's run off with the pudding-bag string!

Do, do, what shall I do?
The cat has bitten it quite in two.

Sneeze on a Monday, sneeze for danger;
Sneeze on a Tuesday, kiss a stranger;
Sneeze on a Wednesday, get a letter.
Sneeze on a Thursday, something better;
Sneeze on a Friday, sneeze for sorrow;
Sneeze on a Saturday, see your sweetheart tomorrow.

Solomon Grundy,
Born on a Monday,
Christened on Tuesday,
Married on Wednesday,
Took ill on Thursday,
Worse on Friday,
Died on Saturday,
Buried on Sunday,
This is the end,
Of Solomon Grundy.

The cock's on the housetop, blowing his horn;
The bull's in the barn a-thrushing the corn;
The maids in the meadows are making of hay;
The ducks in the river are swimming away.

The King of France went up the hill,
With twenty thousand men,
The King of France came down the hill,
And ne'er went up again.

There was an old woman, her name it was Peg;
Her head was of wood, and she wore a cork leg.
The neighbors all pitch'd her into the water,
Her leg was drown'd first,
And her head followed a'ter.

There was an old woman,
Lived under a hill,
And if she's not gone,
She lives there still.

There was an old woman who lived in a shoe;
She had so many children she didn't know what to do;
She gave them some broth without any bread,
And whipped them all soundly, and put them to bed.

This is the way the ladies ride,
   Tri, tre, tre, tree,
   Tri, tre, tre, tree!
This is the way the ladies ride;
   Tri, tre, tre, tree,
   Tri, tre, tre, tree!

This is the way the gentlemen ride;
   Gallop-a-trot, Gallop-a-trot,
This is the way the gentlemen ride,
   Gallop-a-trot, Gallop-a-trot!
This is the way the farmers ride,
   Hobbledy-hog, Hobbledy-hog.
This is the way the farmers ride,
   Hobbledy-hog, hobbledy-hog!

Three blind mice, See how they run!
They all ran after the farmer's wife,
Who cut off their tails with a carving knife,
Did you ever see such a thing in your life,
As three blind mice.

Tom, Tom, the piper's son,
Stole a pig, and away she run!
The pig was eat, and Tom was beat,
And Tom went roaring down the street.

Upon my word and honor,
As I went to Bonner,
I met a pig,
Without a wig,
Upon my word and honor.

Wear you a hat, or wear you a crown,
All that goes up, must surely come down.

PROVERBS

A bird in the hand is worth two in the bush.

A burnt child fears the fire.

A fool's bolt is soon shot.

A king's face should give grace.

A miss is as good as a mile.

A needle's eye is wide enough for two friends;
The whole world is too narrow for two foes.

A penny saved, is a penny got.

Any port in a storm.

A rolling stone gathers no moss.

A stitch in time saves nine.

A quiet tongue makes a wise head.

Be not all sugar, or the world will gulp you down
Nor yet all wormwood, or the world will spit you out.

Better a diamond with a flaw, than a pebble without one.

Better buy than borrow.

Better early than late.

Better happy than wise.

Better sold than bought.

Better the day, better the dead.

Busy as a bee.

Charity begins at home.

Do in hill, as you would do in hall.

Do no good and thou shalt find no evil.

East, west, home is best.

Every man has his price.

Extremes meet.

Forbidden fruit is sweet.

Forewarned, forearmed.

Full bellies make empty skulls.

Gentle is that gentle does.

Good mind, good find.

Good tree brings forth good fruit.

Good words cost naught.

Good workman is known by his chips.

Great oaks from little acorns grow.

Haste makes waste.

He has made his bed, and now he must lie in it.

He who holds the ladder is as guilty as he who mounts the wall.

He who waits for dead men's shoes may go barefoot.

Honesty is the best policy.

Hungry bellies have no ears.

Liars should have good memories.

Like cow, like calf.

Like crow, like egg.

Like father, like son.

Like mother, like daughter.

Little strokes fell great oaks.

Make hay while the sun shines.

Manners make the man.

Man proposes, God disposes.

Many hands make light work.

Many things are lost for want of asking.

Many wells, many buckets.

Measure for measure.

Misfortunes never come single.

Mother's truth keeps constant youth.

Needles and pins, needles and pins,
When a man marries, his trouble begins.

No pains, no gains.

No sweat, no sweet.

One has never so much need of his wit,
As when he has to do with a fool.

One must not look a gift horse in the mouth.

Out of debt, out of danger.

Penny wise and pound foolish.

Right as rain.

Right wrongs no man.

Rolling stone gathers no moss.

Slow help is no help.

The further you go, the further behind.

There is no smoke without fire.

There's many a slip 'twixt the cup and the lip.

The road to Hell is paved with good intentions.

Too far East is West.

When fortune knocks, open the door.

Wide will wear, but tight will tear.

Pentatonic Songs for Singing or Playing on the Recorder

All Night, All Day

1. Day is dy - in' in the west, An - gels watch - in' o - ver me, my Lord. Sleep, my child, and take your rest, An - gels watch - in' o - ver me.
2. Now I lay me down to sleep, An - gels watch - in' o - ver me, my Lord. Pray the Lord my soul to keep, An - gels watch - in' o - ver me.

From *All Together Sing* ©1962 by Cooperative Recreation Service, Inc. Used by permission.

The Bird Song

1. "Hi!" says the black - bird, sit - ting on a chair.
"Once I court-ed a la - dy fair; She proved fick - le and
turned her back, And ev - er since then I've dressed in black."

2. "Hi!" says the blue-jay as she flew,
"If I was a young man I'd have two;
If one proved fickle and chanced far to go,
I'd have a new string to my bow."

3. "Hi!" says the little leather-winged bat,
"I will tell you the reason that,
The reason that I fly in the night,
Is because I lost my heart's delight."

4. "Hi!" says the little mourning dove,
"I'll tell you how to gain her love;
Court her night and court her day,
Never give her time to say 'O nay'."

5. "Hi!" says the woodpecker sitting on a fence,
"Once I courted a handsome wench;
She proved fickle and from me fled,
And ever since then me head's been red."

6. "Hi!" says the swallow, sitting in a barn,
"Courting, I think, is no harm.
I pick my wings and sit up straight
And hope every young man will choose him a mate."

7. "Hi!" says the robin, with a little squirm,
"I wish I had a great big work;
I would fly away into my nest;
I have a wife I think is best."

From *Songs of All Time* ©1957 by Cooperative Recreation Service, Inc. Used by permission.

Barnyard Song

Kentucky Folk Song

1. I had a cat and the cat pleased me. I fed my
cat un-der yon-der tree. Cat goes fid-dle-i -
fee. _____ 2. I had a hen and the hen pleased me. I
fed my hen un-der yon-der tree. Hen goes chim-my chuck,
chim-my chuck, Cat goes fid-dle-i - fee. _____ 3. I
had a duck and the duck pleased me. I fed my
duck un-der yon-der tree. Duck goes quack, quack,
Hen goes chim-my chuck, chim-my chuck, Cat goes fid-dle-i-fee. _____

4. Goose ... swishy-y, swash-y ...   5. Sheep ... baa, baa ...   6. Hog ... grif-fy, gruf-fy ...
7. Cow ... moo, moo ...   8. Horse ... neigh, neigh ...   9. Dog ... bow, wow ...

Repeat all previous lines after each additional stanza.

From *All Together Sing* ©1962 by Cooperative Recreation Service, Inc. Used by permission.

The Boatmen's Dance

Smith

High row, the boat - men, row, float - in' down the riv - er, the

O - hi - o, 1. The boat - men dance, the boat - men sing, the

boat - men are up to ev - 'ry - thing, And when the boat - men gets on shore, He

spends his cash and works for more, O dance, the boat - men dance, O

dance, the boat - men dance, O dance all night, 'til

broad day - light, And go back to the boat in the morn - ing!

Cape Cod Chantey

1. Cape Cod girls they have no combs, Heave a-way, heave a-way, They comb their hair with cod-fish bones, We are bound for Aus-tra-lia. Heave a-way ye bul-ly, bul-ly boys, Heave a-way, heave a-way! Heave a-way and don't ye make a noise, We are bound for Aus-tra-lia.

2. Cape Cod boys they have no sleds,
   Heave away, heave away,
   They slide down hill on cod-fish heads,
   We are bound for Australia, etc.

3. Cape Cod men they have no sails,
   They sail their boats with cod-fish tails,

4. Cape Cod wives they have no pins,
   They pin their gowns with cod-fish fins,

Cotton Needs A-Pickin'

Negro Folk Song

Cot - ton needs a -pick - in' so bad, _____ Cot - ton needs a -pick - in' so bad, _____ Cot -ton needs a pick - in' so bad, __ Gon - na pick all o - ver this field.

We plant -ed this cot -ton in A - pril _____ On the full of the moon. We've had a hot, dry sum - mer, _ That's why it o - pened so soon.

From *Look Away* © 1960 by Cooperative Recreation Service, Inc. Used by permission.

Dogie Song

Cowboy Song

Moderately fast

1. As I was a -walk - in' one morn - ing for pleas - ure, I spied a cow -punch -er all

rid - ing a - long; His hat was throwed back and his spurs was a -jing -ling, And

as he ap -proached he was sing - ing this song: Whoop-ee ti yi yo, git a -

long lit -tle do -gies, It's your mis -for -tune and none of my own, Whoop -ee

ti yi yo, git a -long lit -tle do -gies, You know that Wy -om -ing will be your new home.

2. It's whooping and yelling and driving the dogies, And oh, how I wish you would only go on;
   It's whooping and punching, go on, little dogies, You know that Wyoming will be your new home.

From *A Pocket Full of Songs* © 1961 by Cooperative Recreation Service, Inc. Used by permission.

Farmer in the Dell

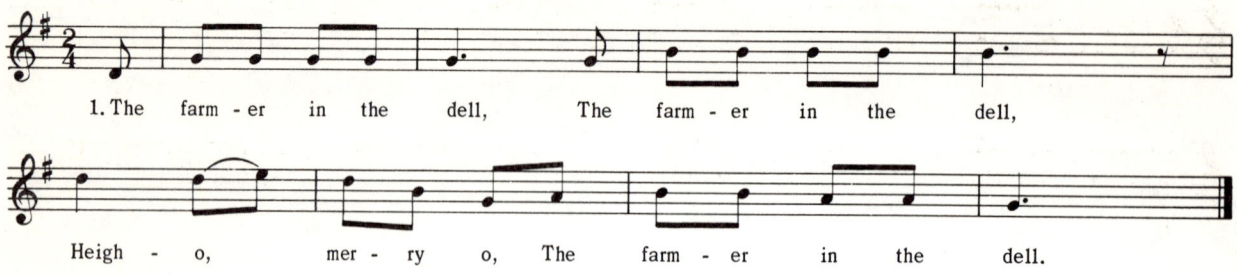

1. The farm-er in the dell, The farm-er in the dell,

Heigh - o, mer - ry o, The farm-er in the dell.

2. The farmer takes a wife, etc.

3. The wife takes a child, etc.

4. The child takes a nurse, etc.

5. The nurse takes a dog, etc.

6. The dog takes a cat, etc.

7. The cat takes a rat, etc.

8. The rat rakes a cheese, etc.

9. The cheese stands alone, etc.

Here Come Four Dukes A Riding

(Boys) Here come four dukes a - rid - ing, a - rid - ing, a - rid - ing, Here

come four dukes a - rid - ing, Tis a ma ras a ma tee.

2. (Girls)   What are you riding here, for?

3. (Boys)   We're riding here to get married.

4. (Girls)   Please take one of us, sir.

5. (Boys)   I think I'll take you, miss.

Itiskit

1. I sent a let - ter to my love, I tho't I put it in my glove, But on the way I dropped it, I dropped it, I dropped it, But on the way I dropped it, And some of you have picked it up, And put it in your pock - et.

2. Itiskit, itaskit, a green and yellow basket,
   I took a letter to my love, And on the way I lost it,
   I lost it, I lost it.

Nobody Knows the Trouble I've Seen

Oh, no - bod - y knows the trou - ble I've seen,
No - bod - y knows but Je - sus, No - bod - y knows the
trou - ble I've seen, Glo - ry Hal - le - lu - jah!

Fine

Some - times I'm up, some - times I'm down; Oh, yes, Lord; Some ;
Al - though you see me going along so, Oh, yes, Lord;

D. C. al Fine

times I'm al - most to the ground, Oh, yes, Lord.
have my tri - als here be - low, Oh, yes, Lord.

Old Brass Wagon

1. Cir-cle to the left, the old brass wag - on, Cir-cle to the left, the old brass wag - on,

Cir-cle to the left, the old brass wag - on, You're the one my darl - ing.

2. Swing, O swing, etc.

3. Promenade home, etc.

Old Dan Tucker

1. Old Dan Tuck - er's still in town, Swing - ing the lad - ies

all a - round, First to the East and then to the West, And

Refrain

then to the one that you love best, ___ Get out of the way of

old Dan Tuck - er! He's too late to get his sup - per,

Sup - per's o - ver, break - fast's cook - ing, Old Dan Tuck - er's out a - look - in'.

2. Old Dan Tucker's a fine old man,
   Washed his face in the frying pan,
   Combed his hair with a wagon wheel,
   And died with a toothache in his heel.

Polly Put the Kettle On

Pol - ly put the ket - tle on, ket - tle on, ket - tle on.

Pol - ly put the ket - tle on, And we'll all have tea.

Rise Up, Oh Flame

Rise up, O flame, _____ By_____ the_____ light glow - ing,

Show to us beau - ty, _____ Vi - sion _____ and joy.

From *Sing A Tune* © 1961 by Cooperative Recreation Service, Inc. Used by permission.

Ol' Texas

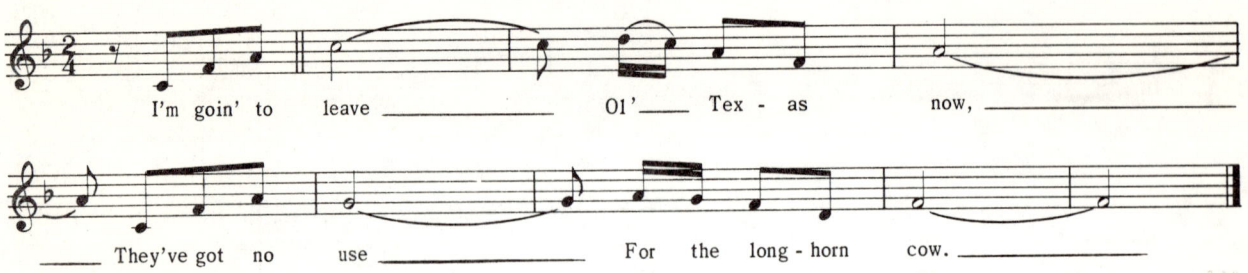

I'm goin' to leave _____ Ol'_____ Tex - as now, _____
_____ They've got no use _____ For the long-horn cow. _____

2. They've plowed and fenced my cattle range, And the people there are all so strange.

3. I'll take my horse, I'll take my rope, And hit the trail upon a lope.

4. Say adois to the Alamo, And turn my head toward Mexico.

From *All Together Sing* © 1962 Cooperative Recreation Service, Inc. Used by permission.

Tideo

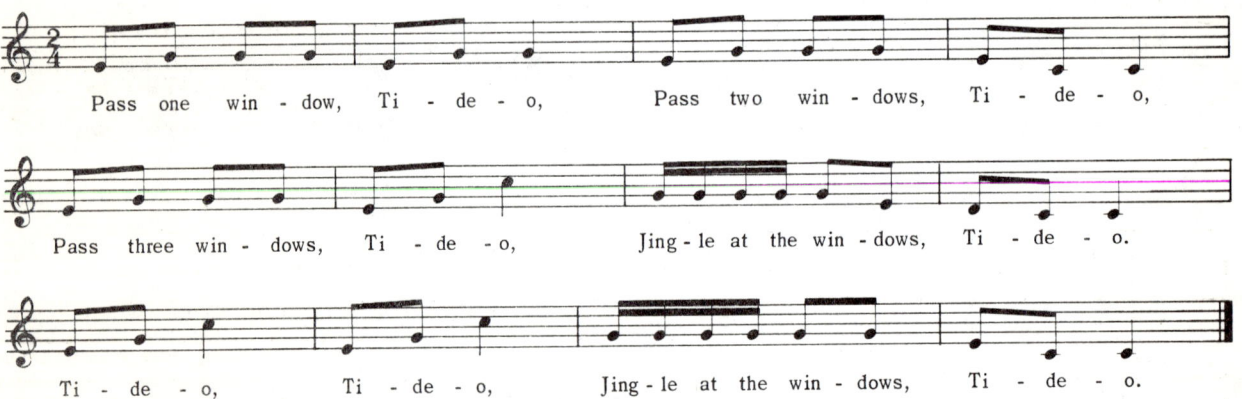

Pass one win - dow, Ti - de - o,   Pass two win - dows, Ti - de - o,
Pass three win - dows, Ti - de - o,   Jing - le at the win - dows, Ti - de - o.
Ti - de - o,   Ti - de - o,   Jing - le at the win - dows, Ti - de - o.

Pentatonic Songs in the Elementary Song Series

Allyn and Bacon—THIS IS MUSIC Series

Kindergarten Book	12-15-20-21-27-40-41-42-48-57-59-65-73-74-80-89-105-111-117-118-154-155
Book 1	13-19-25-26-28-36-46-48-51-55-60-61-63-64-78-80-86-120-146-150
Book 2	6-9-10-16-26-34-36-61-62-82-89-90-93-98-126-128-130
Book 3	11-20-22-24-26-29-30-32-72-80-92-121-134-142
Book 4	6-8-18-20-31-50-94-95-98-99-104-107-111-160
Book 5	11-20-31-32-42-63-80-83-87-92-94-95-99-104-115-124-130-133-140-147-164-166
Book 6	8-22-23-28-42-51-72-73-74-94-97-98-182-187-215

Allyn and Bacon—THIS IS MUSIC FOR TODAY Series

Kindergarten and Nursery	12-21-27-30-37-41-42-45-48-57-59-65-73-74-80-89-104-105-111-113-116
Book 1	12 15-16-26-32-38-40-42-49-50-56-65-67-68-74-89-90-104-115-147-160
Book 2	13-17-53-55-56-57-58-59-60-69-77-97-99-100-104-113-129-144-150-155-162
Book 3	24-27-31-33-104-114-118-122-134-143-152-158-165-177-180
Book 4	34-36-51-114-115-118-119-126-128-129-148-212
Book 5	44-73-109-111-116-135-140-141-156-156-163-172-179-180-198
Book 6	12-20-68-71-80-82-192-195-196-229

American Book Company—MUSIC FOR YOUNG AMERICANS, ABC Series

Kindergarten Book	10-11-14-16-17-20-34-48-51-62-63-64-65-67-70-79-82-90-94-122-124-126-127-128
Book 1	9-11-14-21-70-72-73-75-80-83-92-106-108-130-134
Book 2	18-42-74-125-126-144-146-153-173
Book 3	33-34-37-38-46-50-51-67-79-88-122-156-157
Book 4	19-21-62-77-86-88-90-96-142-178-180
Book 5	4-7-14-67-97-112-114-116-126-137-162
Book 6	19-24-35-38-41-69-76-82-84-85-110-114-142-194-196

American Book Company—MUSIC FOR YOUNG AMERICANS, Second Edition

Meeting Music Book 1	7-9-11-20-21-25-32-40-56-59-63-70-72-73-80-83-88-89-96-98-106-134-145-158-162
Discovering Music Book 2	5-10-18-26-42-74-76-96-121-126-144-146-153-158
Exploring Music Book 3	33-34-37-38-45-46-50-51-81-86-116-119-122-156-184-185-186-187-188-189-190-191
Understanding Music Book 4	19-21-62-86-88-90-96-121-142-178-180
Making Music Book 5	4-7-14-67-97-114-116-126-162
Studying Music Book 6	35-40-60-76-82-110-114-142-170-188-196

American Book Company—NEW DIMENSIONS IN MUSIC Series

Kindergarten Book	7-8 37-48-56-61-69-74-76-81-84-89-90-104-110-129-140-142-146
Book 1 Beginning Music	7-12-60-61-67-76-79-95-133-165
Book 2 Enjoying Music	24-31-40-42-50-53-54-55-91-96-101-134-139-145-163-169-188
Book 3 Expressing Music	10-21-29-32-38-69-70-72-73-74-75-84-98-99-100-116-122-130-143-144-145-154-166-173
Book 4 Investigating Music	27-46-58-78-94-96-103-110-111-138-155
Book 5 Experiencing Music	16-54-98-110-111-130
Book 6 Mastering Music	58-69-84-118-119-128

Follett Publishing Company—DISCOVERING MUSIC TOGETHER Series

Early Childhood Book	12-23-26-27-28-52-54-58-64-66-67-72-75-76-85-92-96-101-102-110-115-118-127-135-136-137-150-155-164
Book 1	9-11-31-41
Book 2	18-47-49-71-84-110-143
Book 3	10-11-45-65-71-84-105-106
Book 4	10-33-46-61-64-67-88-90-91-93-113-130-131-132
Book 5	26-32-34-54-98-107-108-109-113-114
Book 6	11-38-46-48-84-85-86-101-138-139-150

Follett Publishing Company—DISCOVERING MUSIC TOGETHER Series (Rev. 1970)

Children's Edition Book 1	11-12-13-16-17-23-42
Teacher's Edition Book 1	13-14-16-23-35-37-41-45-47-51-66-71-77-83-84-99-101-113
Book 2	17-23-34-37-63-64-65-67-68-69-70-71-72-73-74-75-76-77-78-79-87-90-91-93-132-145
Book 3	7-20-22-23-24-25-26-28-29-30-31-32-33-34-35-36-37-40-59-67-68-69-101-103-120-121-181
Book 4	10-23-24-25-26-27-39-45-51-59-107-110-127-173
Book 5	22-23-24-25-26-27-28-29-30-46-48-63-98-125-126
Book 6	8-22-25-26-27-28-30-31-35-44-81-82-154-155-156

Follett Publishing Company—TOGETHER WE SING Series (Revised Ed.)

Music Around the Clock Book 1	7-27-36-40-51
Music Around the Town Book 2	4-8-21-37-45-73-131
Music Through the Year Book 3	25-32-44-68-83-102-116-128-130
Music Across Our Country Book 4	22-23-31-32-33-36-38-43-46-47-48-84-95-103-121-129-132-133-137-145
Voices of America Book 5	17-44-57-59-73-81-89-143-150-151-157-165
Voices of the World Book 6	32-137-143-145-147-148-152-153-166-181
Together We Sing All Grades Ed.	25-27-32-53-60-69-97-127-129-140-168-175-176-181-216-231-239-240-241-244-250

Ginn and Company—MAGIC OF MUSIC Series

Kindergarten Book	2-56-61-87-92-95-106-136-148
Book 1	4-21-33-34-44-45-95-98-100-103-108-110-138-144-145
Book 2	17-20-30-36-37-38-53-140-154-159-161-163
Book 3	11-15-118-136-155
Book 4	62-64-152-159-160-162-186-189-192-195-196
Book 5	60-61-73
Book 6	56-159

Ginn and Company—OUR SINGING WORLD Series

Book 1	3-5-6-10-11-34-52-57-63-64
Book 2	14-30-39-45-55-56-67-111-124-144-146-147-155
Book 3	12-27-28-58-74-100-105-136-147-149-156-160
Book 4	28-29-30-38-40-49-50-55-64-70-71-79-80-98-124-127-154-155-166-172
Book 5	18-36-50-57-58-63-64-69-84-85-92-112-116-138-141-169-172
Book 6	34-37-46-47-82-89-113-118-163-165

Holt, Rinehart, and Winston—EXPLORING MUSIC Series

Children's Book 1	10-16-22-38
Teacher's Book 1	1-10-42-46-55-59-89-99-101-106-108-115-119-127-129-134-140-141-144-146-147-154
Book 2	4-6-13-30-34-38-39-48-82-95-101-132-141
Book 3	8-22-26-30-33-34-94-95-146
Book 4	4-35-37-58-60-97-98-132-145
Book 5	28-70-71-82-88-140-142-150-188
Book 6	144-155

Holt, Rinehart, and Winston—EXPLORING MUSIC Series (1971 Edition)

Kindergarten Book	8-22-26-44-45-66-74-88-115-130-152
Children's Book 1	1-10-16-22-38
Teacher's Book 1	1-11-21-25-30-36-44-52-58-73-85-90-95-106-121-123-128-131-139-156-158-164-170-186
Book 2	4-6-13-34-38-39-82-95-101-132
Book 3	8-22-26-30-94-95-146
Book 4	8-26-40-44-85-97
Book 5	28-185
Book 6	39-117-118-120-128-148-161

Prentice-Hall, Inc.—GROWING WITH MUSIC Series

Kindergarten Book	9-18-21-40-53-65-85-86-91-112-113-132-136
Children's Book 1	13-35-36-42
Teacher's Book 1	7-21-23-34-40-45-52-56-69-83-86-103-110-117-126-127-130-141
Book 2	19-25-35-47-78-86-87-97-102-117-126-127-138-154
Book 3	6-8-9-16-28-50-75-81-82-91-99-110-112-131-144-163
Book 4	10-25-33-50-100-112-142-148-156
Book 5	14-80-94-96-130-162-178-180
Book 6	7-13-15-38-62-91-102-151-154-203-209

Silver Burdett Company—MAKING MUSIC YOUR OWN Series

Book 1	14-26-28-31-36-44-49-58-69-70-72-97-100-108-134-141
Book 2	6-22-38-39-40-43-46-84-92-94-107-108-109-120-132-138-139-145
Book 3	19-22-33-41-47-50-76-77-132-136-141-158-159
Book 4	8-37-38-39-79-81-98-100-108-123-124-142-147-154-181
Book 5	12-20-22-29-42-99-105-177-196
Book 6	2-20-47-50-108-109-118-121-122-136

Silver Burdett Company—MAKING MUSIC YOUR OWN Series (1971 Edition)

Kindergarten Book	8-13-26-50-68-92-94-127-128-134-152-153-154
Book 1	14-16-33-38-46-51-62-81-96-104-118-134
Book 2	12-28-47-48-51-56-86-106-129-134-145-148
Book 3	15-16-17-18-20-43-44-51-56-80-88-104-116-120
Book 4	11-30-37-42-43-60-93-114-124-137-160-163-164-166-169-174-178-180
Book 5	12-24-26-28-33-103-109-122-177-186-203
Book 6	6-15-25-138-140-143-152-170-184-214

Silver Burdett Company—MUSIC FOR LIVING Series

Music for Early Childhood Kindergarten Book	22-24-30-33-34-58-62-64-65-84-85-86-88-92-99-103
Music Through the Day Book 1	10-13-16-18-22-23-25-28-46-52-55-56-69-73
Music In Our Town Book 2	2-25-47-48-65-72-83-84-98-101-120-121-129
Music Now and Long Ago Book 3	17-25-26-46-51-73-76-87-88-90-100-110-121-126-129-130-134-147
Music Near and Far Book 4	12-17-29-33-44-47-49-87-91-99-104-106-124-140-141-143-165
Music In Our Country Book 5	47-66-78-79-80-89-92-105-143-162-191
Music Around the World Book 6	6-8-37-67-73-106-110-118-133-154-172-176

Summy-Birchard Company—BIRCHARD MUSIC Series

Kindergarten Book	8-17-18-19-21-25-35-43-44-54-57-58-68-88-92-95-96-114-115-139
Book 1	11-14-20-34-35-36-42-56-57-61-62-67-75-77-89-94-95-122-143-147-153-165
Book 2	4-9-20-23-30-32-36-40-44-46-55-59-61-69-71-76-78-89-110
Book 3	3-13-17-24-53-56-68-90-96-98-99-100-104-107-113
Book 4	8-9-10-19-34-37-63-81-84-91-109-113-147-153
Book 5	26-41-52-57-65-66-68-79
Book 6	22-35-70-71-73-86-112-125-126

Glossary of Terms

BORDUN. Two notes, the first and fifth degrees of the scale, played simultaneously in a repeated figure, as an accompaniment to a chant or song.

CHANT. A group of words arranged in a rhythmical and metrical manner for the purpose of recitation.

ECHO CLAPPING. The execution of rhythm patterns through clapping, performed first by a leader, then by a group.

ECHO PATSCHEN, STAMPING, CLAPPING, AND FINGER-SNAPPING. The execution of rhythm patterns through patschen, stamping, clapping, and finger-snapping performed first by a leader, then by a group.

HAND SIGNALS. A set of hand positions using a specific height and shape to represent each of the syllables of the musical scale.

IMPROVISATION. The act of rendering music or bodily movement extemporaneously.

INTERVAL. The distance between two tones inclusive of them.

MIRRORING. An experience in bodily movement (most commonly patschen or patschen in combination with stamping, clapping, and finger-snapping) in which children reflect the movements of the teacher (who is facing them), with the result that children and teacher become reflections of one another.

ORCHESTRATION. The musical accompaniments to a song or chant and the instruments assigned to play each accompaniment.

OSTINATO (plural—ostinati). A repeated musical figure (melodic or rhythmic) played as an accompaniment to a song or chant.

PATSCHEN. The act of patting the right hand on the right knee and the left hand on the left knee simultaneously.

PENTATONIC SCALE. A five-tone scale which omits the fourth and seventh tones of the major scale.

PHRASE-BUILDING. The act of building a feeling for a phrase through question-and-answer-activities.

PLAYBACKS. The execution of a melodic pattern on the recorder, first by a leader, then by a group.

QUESTION-AND-ANSWER PLAYING, CLAPPING, OR PATSCHEN combined with STAMPING, CLAPPING, AND FINGER-SNAPPING. The execution of a phrase which seems to ask a question, through one of the media named, followed by an answering phrase in the same medium.

RHYTHMIC CANON. Rhythmic phrase or phrases executed (through clapping alone or through patschen, stamping, clapping, and finger-snapping) by two or more groups, each group beginning at different intervals, creating an overlapping of groups.

RHYTHMIC COUNTING. A system of counting musical notation in which each note is counted according to its own specific value rather than according to its place in the measure—i.e., a quarter note is always counted "one," a half note is counted "one-two," and so on.

RHYTHMIC RONDO. A musical form with two or more sections alternating with Section A (ABACA or ABACADA), executed through clapping or through a combination of patschen, stamping, clapping, and finger-snapping. The rhythm of Section A is normally executed by a group; that of Sections B, C, and D, by individuals improvising.

SPEECH CANON. A phrase, rhyme, or proverb spoken by two or more groups, each group beginning at different intervals and thus overlapping.

TEMPO-DYNAMIC CLAPPING. The clapping of one note value in different tempi and dynamics by a leader, and, as simultaneously as possible, by a group.

TEMPO-DYNAMIC PATSCHEN, CLAPPING, AND FINGER-SNAPPING. The execution of the aforementioned movements in different tempi and dynamics set by a leader and followed as simultaneously as possible by a group.

Bibliography

BOOKS

Adam, Jeno. *Growing in Music with Movable Do*. Highland Park: Kossuth Foundation, 1971.

Addison, Richard. *Children Make Music*. Edinburgh: Holmes McDougall, Ltd., 1967.

——. *Make Music, A Book of Musical Experiments for Young People*. Edinburgh: Holmes McDougall, Ltd., 1967.

Aronoff, Frances Webber. *Music and Young Children*. New York: Holt, Rinehart & Winston, Inc., 1969.

Darazs, Arpad, and Jay, Stephen. *Sight and Sound* (Students' and Teachers' Manuals). New York: Boosey and Hawkes, Inc., 1965.

Doll, Edna, and Nelson, Mary Jarman. *Rhythms Today*. Morristown: Silver Burdett Company, 1965.

Driver, Ann. *Music and Movement*. New York: Oxford University Press, Inc., 1936.

Eosze, Laszlo. *Zoltan Kodaly, His Life and Works*. Boston: Crescendo Publications, 1962.

Findlay, Elsa. *Rhythm and Movement, Applications of Dalcroze Eurhythmics*. Evanston: Summy-Birchard Co., 1971.

Jaques-Dalcroze, Emile. *Rhythm, Music and Education*. New York: Dalcroze School of Music, Revised Edition, 1967.

Liess, Andreas (translated by Parkin, Adeheid and Herbert). *Carl Orff*. New York: St. Martin's Press, Inc., 1966.

Monsour, Sally; Cohen, Marilyn; and Lindell, Patricia. *Rhythm in Music and Dance for Children*. Belmont: Wadsworth Publishing Co., Inc., 1966.

Nash, Grace C. *Rhythmic Speech Ensembles* (Music with Children Series). Scottsdale: Swartwout Enterprizes, 1966.

——. *Teacher's Manual* (Music with Children Series). Scottsdale: Swartwout Enterprizes, 1967.

——. *Verses and Movement* (Music with Children Series). Scottsdale: Swartwout Enterprizes, 1967.

Raebeck, Lois and Wheeler, Lawrence. *New Approaches to Music in the Elementary School*. Dubuque: Wm. C. Brown Company Publishers, 1969.

Richards, Mary Helen. *Language Arts Through Music, A Trilogy*. Portola Valley: Richards Institute of Music Education and Research, 1971.

——. *The Child in Depth*. Portola Valley: Richards Institute of Music Education and Research, 1969.

——. *Teaching Music Through Songs, Hand Singing, and Inner Hearing*. Palo Alto: Fearon Publishers, Inc., 1966.

———. *Threshold to Music.* San Francisco: Fearon Publishers, Inc., 1964.

———. *Threshold to Music, the Fourth Year.* New York: Harper & Row, Publishers, 1967.

Roesenstrauch, Henrietta. *Percussion, Movement, and the Child.* Far Rockaway: Carl Van Roy Co., 1964.

———. *The Use of Percussion Instruments.* Pittsburgh: Carnegie Institute of Technology, 1960.

Sandor, Frigyes, ed. *Musical Education in Hungary.* London: Barrie and Rickliff, 1966.

Winters, Geoffrey. *An Introduction to Group Music Making.* London: Chappell and Co., Ltd., 1957.

———. *Musical Instruments in the Classroom.* London: Longmans, Green, and Co., Ltd., 1967.

Young, Percy M. *Zoltan Kodaly, A Hungarian Musician.* London: E. Benn, 1964.

CHARTS AND WORKBOOKS

Kukuk, Jack. *Musical Sketchbook 2* (A Workbook for the Second Year of the Threshold to Music Program). Belmont: Fearon Publishers, Inc., 1967.

Lewis, Aden G. *Listen, Look and Sing.* Morristown: Silver Burdett Company, 1971, 1972. (Charts with Teacher's Guides—3 volumes.)

Richards, Mary Helen. *Threshold to Music* (Separate charts for First, Second, Third, Fourth, and Higher Grades). Palo Alto: Fearon Publishers, Inc., 1964 to 1967.

———. *Musical Sketchbook 1* (A Workbook for the First Year of the Threshold to Music Program). Belmont: Fearon Publishers, Inc., 1967.

MUSIC BOOKS

Bachmann, Tibor, and Betz, Russell P. (collected by) *Songs to Read.* Elizabethtown: The Continental Press, 1970.

———. *Reading and Writing Music.* (3 Volumes)—Teachers' and Childrens' Editions, Elizabethtown: The Continental Press, 1969 and 1970.

———. *200 Solfeggios.* Elizabethtown: The Continental Press, 1969.

Bacon, Denise. *Let's Sing Together!* Wellesley Hills: Kodaly Musical Training Institute, Inc., 1971.

Bissell, Keith. *Songs for Schools.* Mainz: B. Schott's Sohne, 1963. Melville, New York: Belwin Mills Publishing Corporation, exclusive distributor for Schott Publications.

Brocklehurst, Brian. *Pentatonic Song Book.* Mainz: B. Schott's Sohne, 1969.

Burakoff, Gerald, and Wheeler, Lawrence. *Music Making in the Elementary School,* (Teachers' and Childrens' editions). New York: Hargail Music Press, 1968.

Carley, Isabel. *A Song Primer.* Indianapolis: Isabel Carley, 1969.

Hall, Doreen (Orff-Schulwerk). *Nursery Rhymes and Songs.* Mainz: B. Schott's Sohne, 1961.

———. (Orff-Schulwerk). *Music for Children.* (5 Volumes), Mainz: B. Schott's Sohne, 1956.

Keetman, Gunild (Orff-Schulwerk). *Rhythmische Ubung.* Mainz: B. Schott's Sohen, 1970.

Kodaly, Zoltan. *Fifteen Two-Part Exercises.* New York: Boosey and Hawkes, Inc., 1952.

———. (Edited by Percy Young). *Fifty Nursery Songs.* London: Boosey and Hawkes, Inc., 1964.

———. (Edited by Percy Young). *333 Elementary Exercises.* New York: Boosey and Hawkes, Inc., 1963.

Marquis, Margaret H. *Songs for All Seasons and Rhymes Without Reasons.* New York: Marks Music Corp., 1968.

Murray, Margaret (Orff-Schulwerk). *Eight English Nursery Songs.* London: Schott & Co., Ltd., 1963.

———. (Orff-Schulwerk). *Music for Children* (5 Volumes). London: Schott & Co., Ltd., 1950.

———. (Orff-Schulwerk). *Wee Willie Winkie.* London: Schott & Co., Ltd., 1965.

Nash, Grace C. *Music with Children* (Series I—Beginners to Advanced; Series II—Kindergarten through Fourth; Series III—Intermediate). LaGrange: Kitching Educational Division of Ludwig Industries, 1971.

Nichols, Elizabeth. *Orff Instrument Source Book* (for *Making Music Your Own* Series, 2 Volumes). Morristown: Silver Burdett Company, 1970.

Richards, Mary Helen. *Pentatonic Songs for Young Children.* New York: Harper & Row, Publishers, 1967.

———. *Songs in Motion.* Palo Alto: Fearon Publishers, Inc., 1965.

Rinderer, Dr. Leo et al., trans. Cykler and Keith. *Music Education.* Park Ridge: Neil A. Kjos Music Co., 1961.

———, et al., trans Cykler and Keith. *Sing a Song to Sight Read.* Park Ridge: Neil A. Kjos Music Co., 1961.

Wheeler, Lawrence. *Ensemble Recorder* (with Orff Instrumentation). Hicksville: Consort Music, Inc., 1970.

Wuytack, Jos. *Lamelou, Canons et Chants.* Paris: Alphonse Luduc et Cie, 1970.

———. *Musica Viva.* Paris: Alphonse Luduc et Cie, 1972.

———, and Aaron, Tossi. *Joy, Play, Sing, Dance.* Paris: Alphonse Luduc et Cie, 1972.

POETRY BOOKS

Arbuthnot, May Hill. *Time for Poetry.* Fair Lawn: Scott, Foresman and Company, 1952.

Cerf, Bennett (collected by). *Riddle-de-dee.* New York: Random House, Inc., 1962.

Emrich, Duncan. *The Nonsense Book.* New York: Four Winds Press, 1970.

Fowke, Edith (collector and editor). *Sally Go Round the Sun.* Garden City: Doubleday & Company, Inc., 1969.

Opie, Iona and Peter. *A Family Book of Nursery Rhymes.* New York: Oxford University Press, Inc., 1964.

———. *The Oxford Nursery Rhyme Book.* London: Oxford University Press, Inc., 1955.

Withers, Carl (compiled by). *A Rocket In My Pocket, the Rhymes and Chants of Young Americans.* New York: Holt, Rinehart, and Winston, Inc., 1948.

RECORDER BOOKS

Burakoff, Gerald. *The Elementary Duet Book for Soprano Recorder.* New York: Hargail Music Press, 1967.

———. *The Elementary Method for Soprano Recorder.* New York: Hargail Music Press, 1967.

Burakoff, Gerald and Sonya. *The Classroom Recorder.* Hicksville: Consort Music, Inc., 1970.

Burakoff, Gerald and Stickland, Willy. *The Duet Recorder Book 1.* Hicksville: Consort Music, Inc., 1970.

Burakoff, Gerald and Wheeler, Lawrence. *Music Making in the Elementary School.* New York: Hargail Music Press, 1968.

Carley, Isabel. *Recorder Improvisation and Technique.* Indianapolis: Isabel Carley, 1970.

d'Auberge, Alfred and Manus, Morton. *It's Recorder Time.* New York: Alfred Music Co., Inc., 1968.

Krainis, Bernard. *The Bernard Krainis Recorder Method.* New York: Galaxy Music Corp., 1962.

Nash, Grace C. *Recorder for Beginners* (Music with Children Series). Scottsdale: Swartwout Enterprises, 1965.

Orr, Hugh. *Basic Recorder Technique* (Volumes 1 and 2 for Alto Recorder; Volumes 1 and 2 for Soprano Recorder). Don Mills: BMI Canada Ltd., 1961.

Salkeld, Robert. *Play the Recorder.* London: Chappell & Co., Ltd., 1956.

Wheeler, Lawrence and Elizabeth. *An Elementary Guide for Learning the Recorder, Playing and Singing with Orff Instrumentation.* Melville: Belwin Mills Publishing Corp. (In preparation, 1972).

Wuytack, Jos. *Polyvitamines ABA.* Paris: Alphonse Luduc et Cie, 1970.

RECORDINGS AND FILMS

Nash, Grace C. *Music with Children* (Four films in classroom setting, each with Instructional Guide-book.) Scottsdale: Swartwout Enterprises.

Orff, Carl, Keetman, Gunild. *Music for Children.* New York: Angel Records Album 3582-B.

——. *Musica Poetica.* Harmonis Mundi Schallplattengesellschaft, Album Nos. 30653, 30654, 30655, and 30656.

Szabo, Helga. *The Kodaly Concept of Music Education.* New York: Boosey & Hawkes, Inc., 1969.

THESIS, REPORTS, AND CURRICULUM GUIDES

Memphis City Schools. *Music Curriculum for Memphis City Schools.* ESEA Title III, 1969.

Ministry of Education, Public Education Department. *Curriculum of Singing and Music Tuition with Instructions.* Budapest: Felsooktatasi Jegyzetellato Vallalat, 1966.

New York State Education Department, University of the State of New York. *Major New Movements in Elementary School Music Education, Suzuki, Kodaly, Orff.* Report on a one-day statewide demonstration workshop, Albany: Bureau of Music Education, 1969.

Orff Institute. *Year-Book 1962.* Mainz: B. Schott's Sohne.

Schneider, Jacques. *Orff Program "Music for Children."* Arlington Heights: The Elk Grove Training and Development Center, 1969.

Soderberg, Janice R. *Development of the Orff-Schulwerk in American Elementary Education.* A Thesis submitted to the faculty of San Francisco State College in partial fulfillment of the requirements for the degree Master of Arts, San Francisco, 1970.

Wampler, Martha M. ed., and others. *Orff-Schulwerk: Design for Creativity*, Bellflower: The Creative Practices Council, Inc., 1968.

Zemke, Sister Lorna. *The Kodaly Music Education Method and Its Application to Primary Grades in the United States.* A Thesis presented to the faculty of the School of Music, University of Southern California, in partial fulfillment of the requirements for the degree Master of Music, Los Angeles, 1968.

SOURCES FOR ORFF INSTRUMENTS

Bruno, C. & Son, Inc., 55 Marcus Dr., Melville, New York 11746 (Sonor).

Kitching Educational Division of Ludwig Industries, 1728 N. Damen Avenue, Chicago, Illinois 60647.

Lyons, Inc., 688 Industrial Dr., Elmhurst, Illinois 60126.

Magnamusic-Baton, Inc., 6390 Delmar Blvd., St. Louis, Mo., 63130 (Studio 49).

Selmer, Division of the Magnavox Co., Box 310, Elkhart, Indiana 46514. (New Era by Premier, distributed in metropolitan New York area by Sam Ash, Inc., Hempstead, New York.)

APPENDIX 7

Alphabetical Index of Rhymes, Proverbs, Songs, and Stories